RESEARCH METHODS FOR SOCIAL WORKERS

SIXTH EDITION

RESEARCH METHODS FOR SOCIAL WORKERS

Bonnie L. Yegidis
Florida Gulf Coast University

Robert W. Weinbach
University of South Carolina

Boston ■ New York ■ San Francisco
Mexico City ■ Montreal ■ Toronto ■ London ■ Madrid ■ Munich ■ Paris
Hong Kong ■ Singapore ■ Tokyo ■ Cape Town ■ Sydney

Senior Series Editor: *Patricia Quinlin*
Editorial Assistant: *Carly Czech*
Marketing Manager: *Wendy Albert*
Production Supervisor: *Patty Bergin*
Editorial-Production Service: *Pine Tree Composition*
Composition Buyer: *Linda Cox*
Electronic Composition: *Pine Tree Composition*
Manufacturing Buyer: *Debbie Rossi*
Cover Administrator: *Kristina Mose-Liban*

For related titles and support materials, visit our online catalog at www.ablongman.com.

Between the time website information is gathered and then published, it is not unusual for some sites to have closed. Also, the transcription of URLs can result in typographical errors. The publisher would appreciate notification where these errors occur so that they may be corrected in subsequent editions.

Library of Congress Cataloging-in-Publication Data

Yegidis, Bonnie L.
  Research methods for social workers / Bonnie L. Yegidis, Robert W.
Weinbach.—6th ed.
      p. cm.
  Includes bibliographical references and index.
  ISBN-13: 978-0-205-58558-8
  ISBN-10: 0-205-58558-2
  1. Social service—Research—Methodology.   I. Weinbach, Robert W.   II.
Title.

  HV11.Y43 2009
  361.3'2072—dc22

                                                    2008001687e

Printed in the United States of America

CONTENTS

PREFACE

Social work practice continues to evolve. Research, now an integral part of practice, is changing along with it. In this edition of *Research Methods for Social Workers,* we have attempted to retain those features that faculty and students told us they liked. At the same time, we have added new material to address the needs of today's students of research and of those conscientious practitioners who aspire to be critical consumers of research reports.

What Can the Reader Expect to Find?

Like the previous editions, this book is designed for a one-semester or one-quarter course on research methods. It is well suited to either undergraduate or foundation-level graduate social work courses. Its content is consistent with both current Council on Social Work Education (CSWE) accreditation standards and curriculum policy guidelines. This book offers a brief conceptual overview of such specialized topics as statistical analysis and evaluation research, and encourages its readers to seek a more in-depth coverage of them.

The book is written for both current and future social work practitioners to assist them in becoming evidence-based practitioners. It presents research as a logical, nonintimidating activity that is inextricably linked to social work practice.

This book contains no unnecessary research terminology or references to obscure, rarely used methods of knowledge building. Necessary terminology is italicized and defined. Students, even those with no prior research background, should find the text interesting and easy to understand. It is written in a crisp, straightforward style and refers to contemporary social work practice on virtually every page. Examples are real—the kind of situations that social workers encounter every day.

Our belief that the knowledge, values, and skills of the social worker are much more of an asset than a liability in conducting research permeates the book. We do not take the approach that research is a "necessary evil" to be grudgingly studied and conducted. It is a logical extension of good practice and absolutely essential to it. Thus, the areas that are given a disproportional amount of attention (relative to other texts) reflect this orientation. For example, tasks such as problem identification and formulation, question selection, and use of existing knowledge receive extensive coverage. Are these not also important tasks in good social work practice intervention? Research design—the rich array of alternatives available to do the job of acquiring knowledge to inform our practice decision making—is also discussed in detail.

Over the years, we have come to believe that to describe research as quantitative or qualitative is, more often than not, to create a false dichotomy. While some research methods are clearly predominantly one type of research or the other, most research studies today have elements of both. Researchers conducting predominantly qualitative research now attempt to quantify their research data to the degree possible; those conducting more quantitative studies often attempt to verify and expand on their findings using qualitative methods. We believe that qualitative and quantitative research methodologies are mutually supportive and of equal importance in knowledge building for our profession. This belief is reflected in every chapter of this book.

Changes in the Sixth Edition

At first glance, it might appear that this edition is much like earlier ones. True, it still has fourteen chapters and even most of the titles and subheadings are the same. However, there are some important updates, revisions, and additions, many in response to the reviewers who shared their thoughtful assessments of the previous edition. Here are some of the more substantive ones:

- We have added expanded content on evidence-based practice in Chapter 1 and diffused it throughout the book. We emphasize the importance of practice ethics, experience, and knowledge of the individual client (as well as research findings) for evidence-based practice.
- We have added a new section on the identification and the use of trustworthy websites for a variety of research tasks, including literature reviews.
- We have added additional discussion of random sampling and random assignment and why they are often not possible in social work research. We have expanded content on purposive sampling and introduced the concept of sampling plans and multistage sampling.
- We have greatly expanded the discussion of validity (of all kinds) in research. The importance of valid measurement of all key constructs, that is, of both dependent and independent variables, is now emphasized.
- We have added content on the importance of qualitative methods in all types of program evaluation.

- The chapter on single-system research (Chapter 14) has undergone a major rewrite in response to current thinking and concerns regarding its assumptions.
- We have added many more examples drawn from contemporary social work practice and eleven new boxes to help in clarifying content presented in narrative form.

There are numerous other additions and deletions. Every chapter contains new material. Older examples have been updated, and some research terminology has been substituted for others to reflect the most current usage.

The chapters are self-contained, but they are designed to be read and discussed in sequence. The For Discussion sections at the end of each chapter emphasize application rather than simply the mastery of key terms or concepts. There are few, if any, right or wrong answers to them. They are designed to promote some active discussion among readers of the book.

Part I (Chapters 1 and 2) places current research within its historical context. It explains what social work research is and how it has evolved. These two chapters stress the links between research and practice, and how each is guided by similar ethics and values. For example, the issue of voluntary informed consent receives expanded coverage in light of power differentials and dual relationships that often exist between researchers and their research participants.

Part II (Chapters 3 through 5) centers on those early research tasks that generally occur before a research design is selected and implemented. It takes the reader through the process of formulating focused questions and/or hypotheses.

Part III (Chapters 6 through 12) looks at the various ways that questions are answered and findings evolve—design issues. Research design is examined from different perspectives. The components of design (sampling, measurement, use of data-collection instruments) and a chapter on analysis of data and knowledge dissemination conclude Part III.

Part IV (Chapters 13 and 14) examines the specific methods used for evaluating practice effectiveness. The general knowledge of research methods discussed in earlier chapters is applied to the important task of evaluating social programs and services.

Acknowledgments

John Clapp, San Diego State University, and Freddie Avant, Stephen F. Austin University, reviewed this edition and recommended changes. We are also indebted to a number of colleagues who critiqued the earlier editions of this book and made many valuable suggestions. They are colleagues Gordon Casebolt, Felix Rivera, Murray Newman, Ram Cnann, Miriam Johnson, James Stafford, Gail Leedy, Stephen M. Marson, Donald S. Pierson, Freddie Avant, John D. Clapp, Sophie Dziegielewski, and Gary Widrick. We greatly appreciate their input and have responded to their helpful suggestions whenever possible. Students who used the previous edition and faculty who adopted it for classroom use also were generous with their comments and suggestions.

Valuable support for our efforts came from Dean Dennis Poole of the University of South Carolina and from administrators and staff at Florida Gulf Coast University. The editors and staff at Allyn and Bacon, especially Pat Quinlin, have been most supportive and helpful.

Bonnie L. Yegidis
Florida Gulf Coast University

Robert W. Weinbach
University of South Carolina

P A R T **I**

RESEARCH AND SOCIAL WORK PRACTICE

1

TOWARD EVIDENCE-BASED PRACTICE

Social workers must make many decisions every day. Good, informed decisions require knowledge.

Where do we get our knowledge? Some of it is acquired through formal education in BSW or MSW programs, or from attending continuing education programs. Or it may come from reading articles in professional journals or textbooks or through on-line searches. It may have come from senior-level practitioners who have been successful social workers for many years. Historically, much of the knowledge derived from these sources has had one characteristic in common—it may *not* have been derived from research! However, this is changing.

The Council on Social Work Education (the organization responsible for the accreditation of bachelors' and masters' programs in social work) recognizes the importance of research content in social work curricula. The Educational Policy and Accreditation Standards (Council on Social Work Education, 2002) specify that research content and skills must be taught in both undergraduate and graduate social work education programs.[1] They are articulated in EPAS 3.9 and 4.6, and form the basis for what we have chosen to include in this book. By teaching students the best ways to conduct research, it is hoped that they will be equipped to acquire the knowledge needed for making good, informed decisions in whatever social system level they may work. However, understanding how research should be conducted has a second benefit—it allows us to critically and knowledgeably evaluate the research methods of others and, thus, to assess the credibility of the findings and recommendations that they generate.

Knowledge of research makes possible a goal that has been widely talked about and advocated. It is evidence-based practice (EBP). EBP has been broadly defined as "the conscientious, explicit, and judicious use of evidence in making decisions."[2] These decisions often relate to the services that we offer, for example, the choice of a method of intervention or the design of a social program. However, EBP is also applicable to other types of decisions that social workers make, for example, selecting the best diagnostic tool for defining a client problem, making management decisions, or making decisions relating to the design of a needs assessment or an outcome evaluation of a social program.

EBP is not just reliance on reports of research studies for decision making, although that is an important feature of it. If that is all that it entailed, it would result in problems. For one thing, it would not take into consideration our own uniqueness as practitioners, who we are, and what we do well and not so well. It would also not factor in professional ethics or professional values, for example, the right of clients to be involved in decision-making that affects them. Thus, EBP entails a careful consideration of: (1) what the best research on the question has suggested; (2) our own practice experience and expertise; and (3) the values and preferences of the clients we serve.

How might this work? Suppose a medical social worker is assigned to work with the parents of a 9-year-old boy who has a diagnosis of acute leukemia. She knows (from medical knowledge acquired through research and the knowledge of his specific situation) that he has a very small probability of surviving more than a few weeks without a bone marrow transplant. She also knows (from the same sources) that the likelihood of a successful transplant is quite small. Her practice experience reminds her that, if the transplant is unsuccessful, his suffering is likely to be worse than if he never had it. She has seen it happen before and it has been very stressful for all concerned. Ethically, she recognizes the need for the child to be involved (to the degree possible) as well as his parents in the decision to have or not have the transplant. She feels an ethical responsibility to inform the parents of how the transplant could result in worse suffering and death for their child. As a caring and concerned social worker, she feels compassion for the child and his parents. That will influence her behavior as well. She cannot and should not make the decision for them, but she also understands that they will look to her for help in making it (and probably seek her advice) and require her support for whatever decision they make. In EBP, how she ultimately presents the options to them (her intervention) will be determined by the combination of all of these factors.

Historical Antecedents

Historically, social workers have not always emphasized the importance of the place of research knowledge for practice decision making as much as have other professionals. In 1979 one writer, a sociologist, shared his perceptions of social work practitioners and their relationship with research. Simpson noted that practitioners tend to shun abstract knowledge and to rely instead on (1) humanitarian impulse, (2) occupational folklore, and (3) common sense. He also observed that most of the knowledge that is used for practice decision making is drawn from the work of researchers in other fields. He went on to describe social work literature as permeated with faddism and lacking an empirical base.[3]

At the same time, leaders in our own profession expressed concern over practitioners' reluctance to rely on scientific research knowledge for practice decision making. During the late 1970s, both the Council on Social Work Education (CSWE) and the National Association of Social Workers (NASW) devoted considerable effort to examining the problem of research utilization. They convened groups of leading practitioners and researchers to study it. They tried to determine, for example, why social work practitioners rarely read reports of research or sought their knowledge in their professional literature, and why they tended to ignore those research findings that reflected unfavorably on their current practice methods. They concluded that responsibility for the gap between practice and research must be shared by both practitioners and researchers, and that both groups must work toward closing the gap.

Practitioners described their distrust of researchers and of much of the knowledge that they generated. They viewed researchers, most of whom historically have been academicians, as people who did not really understand the realities of social work practice. Researchers were perceived as more interested in conducting esoteric research to enhance their careers than in producing knowledge that might inform practice. In addition, they tended to present their research findings in a form that few practitioners could understand and apply to their work.

In response, the researchers in the groups described their frustration with many practitioners' lack of research knowledge and general lack of interest in research. They cited a tendency of practitioners to reject those research findings that did not agree with what they "knew" to be true and to assume falsely that research knowledge was too abstract to be of value to them.

In an effort to resolve some of the tension between practice and research and to increase research utilization, Kirk[4] proposed four objectives for research in social work. They were:

1. *Research findings should be practice relevant.* The goal of research should be to inform practice.
2. *Specific applications to practice should be contained in research reports.* In the past, many researchers neglected this condition, allowing findings to speak for themselves. But the reality is that research findings often speak less than eloquently, if at all, to social work practitioners if the practitioners lack skill in interpreting the findings. Researchers need to describe their findings in simple, straightforward terms.
3. *Research findings should be disseminated effectively.* A practitioner cannot use information that he or she has never seen or heard. Although professional journals continue to be a primary vehicle for knowledge dissemination, they are certainly not the only one. Other ways to share research findings include seminars and workshops, staff newsletters, audio- and videotapes or CD-ROMs of research presentations, and the Internet.
4. *Practitioners should possess both the skill and the incentive to assess and to change their practice behaviors based on research knowledge.* In order to achieve this, social workers must possess a knowledge of scientific concepts and procedures that will allow them to evaluate critically the research methods and findings of others. This implies a capacity to read between the lines in order to determine whether research findings were obtained using those methods that give the researcher's conclusions credibility. Social workers should be able to recognize the difference between sound, ethical research and that which contains findings and recommendations that are suspect because the research was methodologically flawed.

Of course, it was pointed out, the incentive to change our practice based on emerging research knowledge must evolve from several sources. First, practitioners must have the knowledge and understanding of scientific methods required to gain an appreciation of them. If they learn to appreciate the rigor that is built into well-designed research, practitioners are more likely to believe in and to value the findings that are produced. They also will be more likely to distrust the conclusions and recommendations of the researcher whose methods are flawed.

In addition, it was suggested, practitioners will only rely more heavily on research if there is an expectation of reward for this behavior. They are likely to question the value placed on research in their practice settings. For example, they may ask, "Is there more reward for practice based upon research findings or for doing things the way they have always been done? Will there be support for conscientiously evaluating our practice effectiveness, or will it be viewed by others as time that could be better spent in other ways? Will we be encouraged to attend professional conferences where research knowledge is disseminated or to read and discuss professional journal articles with colleagues, or will this be viewed as more time wasted?" The incentive to become practitioners who use research findings for decision making requires support at all levels of human service organizations.

Over the years, the need to bring social work practice and research closer together has produced a wide variety of conceptual models. One was proposed by Scott Briar—he called it "the clinical scientist." If it were practiced, the work of social workers would have many similarities to that of the professionals we have often tried to emulate, physicians. (Earlier, it was the "medical model" in mental health services, and even EBP closely resembles "evidence based medicine" first described in nineteenth-century France) However, Briar's model reflected a realistic understanding that social workers are far less likely to have at their disposal the amount of cause–effect knowledge that may be available to physicians. Clinical scientists, as conceptualized by Briar, would:

- Use with clients the practice methods and techniques that are known empirically to be most effective.
- Continuously and rigorously evaluate their own practice.
- Participate in the discovery, testing, and reporting of more effective ways of helping.
- Use untested, unvalidated practice methods and techniques cautiously and only with adequate control, evaluation, and attention to client rights.
- Communicate the results of evaluations of practice to others.[5]

A little later another author conceptualized the practitioner's relationship with research in a different way. Garvin conceptualized three overlapping research roles that the social work practitioner can play. The roles are (1) consumer of research, (2) creator and disseminator of knowledge, and (3) contributing partner.[6] In performing the first role, the practitioner has a professional obligation to seek, to evaluate, and to use, when appropriate, the research knowledge that is generated by others. The second role implies an obligation to be directly involved in doing research and to share the results of one's own research with others. This role is recognition that there is a wealth of untapped knowledge that exists within the practice milieu which can be systematically collected, organized, and shared for the benefit of other practitioners. The third role, contributing partner, recognizes that not all social workers may have the knowledge or interest necessary to undertake large-scale research projects. But this does not preclude their making contributions to the research efforts of others. Specifically, they can participate in some of the necessary tasks of the research process such as identifying researchable problems or providing data for evaluation of social programs.

As late as 1991, a study revealed that professional journals rarely publish the results of evaluations of practice effectiveness.[7] Perhaps, because the findings of this type of research often lack generalizability (as we shall discuss in later chapters), practitioners were reluctant to submit their findings for publication or review. Or, perhaps for the same reason, there was a built-in bias against publishing the reports of practice evaluations among those who make publication decisions. It was noted that the greatest percentage of published reports of research describe findings from more traditional survey designs.[8]

For many years, our professional literature has been blamed for some of the problems related to research utilization. Writers of letters to the editors of professional journals have regularly complained that articles selected for publication have had little practical value for the practitioner. (Earlier research revealed that a large percentage of the reviewers who help decide whether a paper submitted for publication will be published themselves had little or no record of research and publication.[9]) The arrival in the 1990s of two new professional journals (*Social Work Research* and *Research on Social Work Practice*) may have helped to reverse this pattern. The creation of the Institute for the Advancement of Social Work Research (IASWR) and the Society for Social Work Research (SSWR) was yet another indication that the gap between practice and research was narrowing. The latter hosts a very well attended annual conference in which a wide variety of research findings have been disseminated.

Simpson's indictment of social workers was clearly less accurate than when he wrote it in 1979. But the problem—an antiresearch bias among many social work practitioners and students, and even among some professors—did not seem to have totally disappeared. As recently as 1992, two professors conducted a lively debate on the question: Should undergraduate and graduate social work students be taught to conduct empirically based practice?[10] Would we expect to see such a debate in a major professional journal published within other helping professions, such as medicine or psychology? Would the importance of research knowledge and skills even be debatable? Not likely!

Later in the 1990s, a number of events and developments combined to move us to where we are today—to recognition of the importance of EBP. On a broad level, the demands for accountability that began several decades earlier continued to increase. Funding organizations, the general public, and individual stakeholders increased demands for accountability, specifically for proof that social programs and services demonstrate both their effectiveness and efficiency. More studies were conducted, and their findings (viewed collectively) began to suggest which interventions work and, just as important, which do not.

At about the same time, a dramatic increase in the number of social work doctoral programs occurred. This meant that, at least potentially, more social workers could be educated and trained in advanced social work research methods. They, in turn, could assume teaching roles, replacing researcher educators who, all too frequently, had not received much education in research methods or who had received it in fields such as sociology or behavioral psychology and sometimes struggled to adapt it to the realities of social work practice.

The 1990s also saw important refinements in our understanding of what should constitute the relationship between research and practice and thus moved us closer to our current understanding of EBP. The "scientist-practitioner" model had gained acceptance and had become a major influence on social work education and practice. A central premise of the model is that social work practice should closely resemble scientific research. However, in 1996, an article was published that cast doubt upon the model's value. It was a comprehensive literature review of over thirty books or articles from the previous two decades, many of which had strongly advocated the use of the model. In it, Wakefield and Kirk concluded that "the methods of the scientist-practitioner model are of unproved clinical effectiveness, limited scientific value, questionable practicality, and unknown net benefits."[11] It is important to note that the article was not an indictment of EBP as we know it today. However, it pointed out that social work practitioners have not been (and probably cannot be) simultaneously both practitioners and researchers, regularly conducting research to make their practice more effective. Instead, the authors contended, there has been and should continue to be a division of labor, with researchers continuing to take the major responsibility for determining which practice methods are most effective and with practitioners conscientiously using the findings of research to help in making informed practice decisions—EBP.

The last several years of the twentieth century produced numerous other publications that sought to further refine what was meant by evidence-based practice and how it could be applied in the everyday life of the social work professional. The logical steps involved in becoming an evidence-based practitioner were even identified.[12]

In the twenty-first century, there still remain obstacles and objections to EBP.[13] However, most of the obstacles can be overcome and many of the objections reflect a misunderstanding of EBP. It is not intended to dictate to social workers what decisions they should make, only to get them to use all available data (including their practice expertise, professional values, and their knowledge of individual clients and their values and preferences) in making them. While EBP can result in cost-saving for health insurance providers and other third parties, that is not its purpose—it is to offer services and programs with the greatest potential for success. Besides, what is wrong with cost-cutting, as long as our clients are the ultimate beneficiaries?

Knowledge of what methods of intervention have proven effective (and what have not) has continued to accumulate and, it is important to remember, to undergo change. That is consistent with a key element of the scientific method for accumulating knowledge (discussed later in this chapter)—all knowledge is tentative. Therefore, what we "know" is dynamic. In the 2005 edition of their research methods book, Rubin and Babbie compiled and presented a list of over two pages of examples of interventions that at least one scholarly study found to be successful. In the 2008 edition of the same book, there is no such list.[14] This would seem to be a wise decision by the authors, since some of the "knowledge" chronicled in the 2005 edition may have been updated or even refuted by subsequent research before the book went out of print! What is the message to the social work practitioner? To engage effectively in EBP, we must remain current, that is, to factor the most recent research findings into our decision making. Fortunately, the Internet has made this much easier than it once was. However, not all or even most of the "knowledge" available on the Internet can be considered trustworthy. Today's social worker also needs to know how to evaluate it (discussed in Chapter 4).

The potential for EBP has never been greater. Still, there remains a paucity of research evidence for what are effective interventions for some problems that social workers frequently attempt to address.[15] However, these gaps do not negate the need for social work practitioners to know how research should be conducted, to locate and evaluate critically the research of others, and, when available, to use the findings of researchers as an important component of their practice decision making.

Research and Practice—More Similar Than Different

While there is now a fair consensus that research and practice cannot be totally merged, they are not all *that* different. In fact, many of the attributes that are associated with good practitioners are the same ones that make for a good researcher. Even the tasks of practice and research are quite similar. We mention them here to emphasize the point that research is not some mysterious activity. It entails a logical process not too unlike the steps involved in successful practice intervention.

One earlier (1988) practice model (which was actually a variation of the scientist-practitioner model) was described by Grinnell and Siegel.[16] In it, the authors point out the many ways in which research methods and the social work problem-solving process are alike. The authors note that, in its ideal form, practice problem solving follows a sequence of activities that is virtually identical to the traditional research process. Even the same kind of problems—for example, biased assessment in practice and faulty measurement in research—are likely to be present.

Some authors have drawn an even closer parallel between practice and research, going so far as to equate each step in the research process with one in human service practice. We think that might be pushing the analogy just a little too much, especially since there is considerable variation in research as well as in practice . However, Box 1.1 illustrates some of the parallels that can be drawn when one conceptualizes both research and practice intervention as problem-solving processes.

The various models for research utilization (including more that we have not mentioned) all suggest that research should not be an activity that is foreign to social work practice or that necessarily draws precious resources away from it. On the contrary, social workers who wish to provide the best possible services to their clients can hardly afford not to be evidence-based practitioners. The models underline the fact that a research-oriented and research-involved practitioner is likely to be a better informed and a more effective

BOX 1.1 Research and Practice as Problem-Solving Methods: Related Activities

Research Tasks	Related Practice Tasks
1. Identify needed knowledge.	1. Identify broad problem.
2. Identify focus of the study.	2. Partialize the problem.
3. Specify question(s) for study.	3. Specify problem(s) for intervention.
4. Develop research design.	4. Develop action plan.
5. Collect data.	5. Implement action plan.
6. Organize, analyze, and interpret data.	6. Evaluate, summarize.
7. Disseminate knowledge, identify areas for more research.	7. Terminate intervention, identify other client needs.

and efficient practitioner. In turn, a practice-oriented and practice-informed researcher is likely to produce research findings that will have value and be of benefit to those who deliver services to clients.

Alternative Knowledge Sources

Social workers have always recognized the need for knowledge that would inform their practice with and on behalf of client groups. Often, we have had to rely on less "scientific" sources of information, such as the opinions of supervisors or peers when "stuck" with a particularly difficult client problem or decision. However, these sources have limited utility and can be very misleading.

Is there still a need to use these sources of knowledge? Unfortunately, yes. When research-based knowledge is lacking or is not trustworthy, sometimes we still must turn to them today. However, when we do so, we must use extreme caution.

Logic

Often, we depend on the fact that some things are self-evident and logical. They just "make sense." Unfortunately, logic can lead to beliefs that are just plain wrong in some circumstances. For example, joining a white supremacist group is generally a good indication of the presence of racist or anti-Semitic attitudes. But this logical assumption may break down in the case of an FBI infiltrator or a reporter seeking to understand the group firsthand. Similarly, we cannot depend on the self-evident truth that an individual who attends graduate school values an education, even if most graduate students probably do. He or she may have enrolled to appease a parent, to avoid having to work in the family business, or even to pursue a future partner.

Over-reliance on logic has led to some costly errors among helping professionals. In the 1970s, a program called Scared Straight was promoted as a logical approach to reducing crime. It involved taking young people who had committed minor crimes, such as shoplifting, on a tour of prisons to see what might happen to them if they did not abide by the law. They experienced the booking procedure firsthand and talked with inmates who were serving long sentences. Logically, the experience should have turned the youths into model citizens. But it didn't. Research found that often those who had participated in the program had a higher crime rate than their counterparts who had not been through it![17]

Logic and common sense have produced other costly errors among helping professionals over the years. For example, many communities have implemented the Drug Abuse Resistance Program (DARE) program. Its curriculum, designed to prevent young students from abusing legal and illegal substances, has been taught widely in public schools in the United States. It links local law enforcement agencies with middle school students and teaches students a range of refusal skills that might be put to use when confronted with offers of drugs and alcohol. DARE was initially presumed to be an effective program. However, Van Burgh, Redner, and Moon (1995)[18] conducted a study of over 100 eighth graders that showed that the program was not effective in changing students' knowledge or their skills in refusing drugs and alcohol. Subsequently, other researchers have drawn similar conclusions.[19] Nevertheless, probably because it is so logical and is now so well established, many communities continue to use and support DARE.

Logic (along with the media) would suggest that children who are abused today will become child abusers someday. It makes sense, right? Abuse is humiliating and should leave one angry and wanting to strike back. Besides, if violence is the only parenting behavior one has experienced, why wouldn't an individual treat his or her own children in the same way? Such cause–effect thinking may be logical, but is it really accurate? In fact, research has shown that not all abused children, not even most, become perpetrators of abuse. To date, much more research has been conducted on perpetrators of abuse (and their childhood experiences) than on parents who do not abuse their children. Scientific research eventually may tell us what percentage of people who were abused as children fall into the first category and what percentage fall into the second. Then we can know if an abused child is even any more likely to become an abuser than one who was not abused. Until such knowledge becomes available, we cannot assume that what is logical is necessarily correct.

Tradition

Another dubious source of knowledge is tradition. We may believe something to be true simply because it has never really been challenged, at least not within our culture. This kind of knowledge is particularly dangerous. As social workers, we may confront it on a daily basis. It can take the form of relatively innocuous misconceptions (for example, that all retired military people are good bureaucrats). But it is more likely to result in destructive, negative stereotyping. Traditional beliefs may promote the continued oppression of members of our society. The persistence of erroneous stereotypes, such as that gay men and lesbians choose their sexual orientation and wish to convert others to it, that all older people suffer from intellectual deterioration, or that single-parent families are necessarily dysfunctional, have all helped to foster discrimination against members of these groups.

People have a tendency to hold tenaciously to traditional beliefs, sometimes even in the face of scientific evidence to the contrary. Human beings seem to have a need for some knowledge that represents a universal truth. We crave some areas of certainty in our lives, perhaps because so much of life is uncertain. Unfortunately, once we are convinced that something is correct, occasional selective observations are all that we seem to require to confirm its correctness. This is problematic enough for us in our social transactions, but in our professional roles, tenacious reliance on traditional beliefs can seriously affect our ability to provide competent services. The social work practitioner cannot afford to make practice decisions and to undertake intervention on the basis of traditional beliefs.

Authority

Still another way we sometimes get our "knowledge" is through deference to authority. Social workers employed in medical and psychiatric settings are especially vulnerable to assuming that the physician always has a scientific basis for what, in actuality, may be little more than an opinion. We sometimes mistakenly conclude that "If she said it, it must be true," or "He ought to know, or he wouldn't be where he is today." Unfortunately, people in authority (perhaps, our bosses), just like all of us, are subject to bias, limited experience, and perhaps the need to confuse reality with wishful thinking. Or they may simply be relying on logic or tradition!

Other Problems with Alternative Knowledge Sources

Logic, tradition, and authority can also mislead us in other ways. They can still affect our practice judgment and cause us to waste our time and energies looking for problems that don't exist or to draw erroneous conclusions. Frequently, they promote unhealthy stereotypes and generalizations about people who may become our clients. What are some of them?

Welfare Recipients

Who is a welfare recipient? There never has been any shortage of "knowledge" about welfare recipients in our society. We rarely encounter people who admit that they really do not understand their situation or do not have a solution (often, a punitive one) for it. Families receiving Aid to Families of Dependent Children (AFDC) benefits and, more recently, Temporary Assistance to Needy Families (TANF) have been especially subject to erroneous beliefs. The mother in such families was often described as a "welfare queen." According to this stereotype, she had five or seven children, lived well on the benefit level, had no intention of finding work, and had more children to increase benefits.

How accurate was this "knowledge" of welfare recipients? In 1994 a social work professor published the results of an eight-year study of 3,000 AFDC recipients. Among his findings, the researcher noted the following:

- Most welfare recipients had no more than two children.
- During the previous twenty years, the value of welfare benefit levels had sharply declined when adjusted for inflation.
- States with the highest out-of-wedlock birthrates tended to have the lowest welfare benefit levels.
- Benefits to teenage mothers were lower in the United States than in European nations.[20]

These findings clearly pointed out that AFDC was hardly a good deal in the United States. It would have been totally illogical, for example, for an AFDC mother to become pregnant just to receive a small increase in benefits.

Later research following the welfare reforms of the 1990s seem to confirm some of these findings. According to the Welfare Rights Organizing Coalition,[21] numerous studies have shown that there is no relationship between receiving benefits and increased number of births. Indeed, births to parents receiving TANF are generally fewer than to parents within the general population. It has also been shown that in no state do TANF benefits (including food stamps) lift poor families above the poverty level. Despite the fact that these findings and others argue against the widespread "knowledge" that families receiving public assistance lead an easy life, the stereotype persists among segments of the general public.

People Who Are Homeless

Many people in our society, including some helping professionals, may also feel comfortable with their "knowledge" of homelessness. What are some common beliefs about people who are homeless? They are older men. They are likely to suffer from mental illness and problems with alcohol and other drugs. They are dropouts from mainstream society, prone to violence and public drunkenness. But what does research tell us about homeless people in the United States? There are some similarities to these common stereotypes, but also some important differences. For example, in 2005 data compiled by the U.S. Conference of Mayors[22] revealed that:

- A greater percentage of homeless men have served in the military than the general population.
- Approximately one-third of the homeless were families with children, the fastest growing homeless population.
- About 30 percent of the adult homeless population has an addiction to alcohol or other substances.
- While about 22 percent of the adult homeless population suffers from some severe, chronic mental illness, only a small percentage (5–7 percent) requires institutionalization.

We have offered just two examples of the wide disparity between what is generally believed to be true and what research has revealed. Reliance on knowledge from dubious sources can create problems for the social worker. For example, social workers or other helping professionals who make diagnostic or treatment decisions based on false preconceptions about people who are financially dependent on government assistance or who are homeless would be likely to assume that certain attitudes and problems exist among their clients when they really may not be present at all. They might be misled into misdiagnosis, bad treatment planning, and/or ineffective intervention methods. This is exactly the opposite of what knowledge is supposed to do. It should inform our practice, not mislead it.

Misuse of Research Data

Research studies such as those that we have just cited have the potential to dispel myths and stereotypes derived from less trustworthy sources. But, especially when reported in the popular media, they can also lend credence to them. We would be remiss if we did not point out that one cannot always trust research findings, especially when they are selectively reported for "shock value" or to boost circulation or Neilson ratings. For example, during the 1980s there was great concern about the use of crack cocaine by pregnant women and its long-term health effects on their babies. Logic, common sense, and early research studies suggested that the children can suffer major physical and psychological damage from their mothers' chemical addiction. The newspapers and television picked up on it and frequent stories appeared. And the selective use of research findings only made this "knowledge" more believable. However, a recent meta-analysis[23] (a research method discussed in Chapter 8) of most studies conducted on the topic in the

1980s revealed serious methodological flaws that led to numerous erroneous conclusions about the extent and severity of the potential problem. Later research has shown that most problems among babies of crack-addicted mothers could be attributed to other factors. Unfortunately, the early, flawed studies have been used in at least one state, South Carolina, to assist in the successful prosecution of addicted women for child abuse, thus adding to their problems.

It is also important to note here, however, that even findings from well designed research studies, unless they are presented completely and in an unbiased way, can sometimes be misleading. For example, a Vietnam-era veteran, whose data were widely published in newspapers in 1986,[24] was seeking to present veterans in the best possible light as a way of compensating for the usual media portrayal. Did he perhaps neglect to mention a few facts that might give us a more complete understanding of what he offered? For example, would it be helpful to know that large numbers of Vietnam-era veterans (including one of the authors of this text) "volunteered" for service as he reported, but only because they knew that they would be drafted anyway and were hoping for a better assignment? Or that a high percentage of veterans are college graduates but that many of them only had a college education made possible by benefits from the GI Bill? Or, that a large percentage of those killed were officers (not enlisted men), but they were also pilots? Our message to the reader is this: Even facts derived from sound research can be used to present a biased picture. That is where research ethics (Chapter 2) enter the picture.

The Scientific Alternative

Social work practitioners need many types of knowledge. Given the shortcomings of the other ways of acquiring knowledge we have just discussed, aren't research findings still the best alternative? Yes. Knowledge derived from research, although certainly imperfect and still subject to unethical distortion, is the knowledge most likely to help us do our jobs as social workers effectively. It relies on the use of the scientific method.

The *scientific method* (alternately referred to as "scientific thinking" or simply "science") is a particular way of acquiring knowledge. It is a way of thinking about and investigating assumptions about the world.[25] It differs from *scientific knowledge,* which is really only a collection of facts that were acquired through use of the scientific method. We could theoretically use scientific knowledge even if we did not know how to practice the scientific method. But that would be dangerous. Unless we engage in scientific thinking and understand and use the scientific method, we might have blind faith in scientific knowledge. That would be almost as bad as uncritically depending on logic, tradition, or authority because, as has been suggested, scientific knowledge, when selectively reported, also can be misleading. To correctly use the products of the scientific method (scientific knowledge), we must understand it. That is why we study it.

Certain characteristics of the scientific method set it apart from other ways of acquiring knowledge and, we believe, make it more likely to yield knowledge on which the social worker can depend.

- *Science is empirical. Empirical* is a word that is widely used but not always understood. It means that knowledge derived from scientific methods is based on direct observations of the real world, not on someone's beliefs or theories. Scientific knowledge has undergone a rigorous evaluation and verification process to determine whether what was assumed to be true or what was believed to be true really is true. Because science is empirical, it is not appropriate for validating some phenomenon that cannot be directly observed, such as the existence of God. However, many phenomena that on the surface would seem inappropriate for study through science (for example, how people experienced some event from their perspective) can nevertheless be studied by the imaginative researcher using the scientific method.

- *Science strives for objectivity.* No conscientious and ethical scientist would deliberately introduce biases into research findings. Scientists take deliberate actions to avoid the potential for their own preferences or beliefs to influence the results of research. At the same time, there is recognition that total objectivity may be impossible and that a certain amount of subjectivity is inevitable, and these factors influence findings in all research to a greater or lesser degree. But the scientist attempts to assess how much subjectivity may have played a role and to evaluate its effects in order to arrive at the truth.

- *Science produces provisional knowledge.* As noted earlier, with science, the possibility that the researcher's conclusions may be wrong is always present. Science says, in effect, based on what we know right now, this is what we think to be the case. It leaves open the possibility that subsequent scientific inquiry may lead to modified or even to totally contradictory conclusions. In this way, scientific knowledge is always regarded as tentative. Even the conclusions drawn from statistical tests of inference are based on a premise of "reasonable certainty," usually greater than 95 percent.

- *Science employs a public way of knowing.* In science, it is not enough for a researcher to share findings with other scientists and with the public. It also is expected that the methods used to produce the findings will be made available for critique so that other researchers can try to achieve similar results (called *replication,* in research). In this way, a researcher's findings can be checked, and, once verified, they tend to have greater credibility.

- *Science employs certain rules, procedures, and techniques.* Whereas creativity and innovation are also characteristic of science, there are definitely acceptable and unacceptable ways to conduct scientific research. There are also correct and incorrect sequences in which to perform research tasks, depending on the type of research that is undertaken. Even research that ventures into problem areas where we have very little knowledge attempts to "go by the rules."

Types of Knowledge

If we are to become evidence-based practitioners, at least to the degree possible, we need access to different types of knowledge. They are acquired in different ways using different research methods, a topic we will address in considerable detail in Chapters 6 through 8. While there is a little bit of overlap among them, knowledge tends to come in one of three forms.

Descriptive Knowledge

Descriptive knowledge is knowledge to help us understand. It gives us a reasonably accurate picture of the way things are, or to be more precise, of how they were at the time that the research took place. It does not allow us to go much beyond having a better and more accurate perception of a problem or situation at some point in time, or even what certain individuals perceive to be the situation at the time. Descriptive knowledge is limited, but this is not meant to imply that it is inferior to other types of knowledge. It is not any less valuable or (acquired correctly) any easier to achieve. In fact, descriptive knowledge often requires many months or even years of work and ingenious research methods. For example, research that accurately chronicles the grief reactions of people diagnosed as having HIV infection or what it was like to grow up gay in a conservative community is painstaking work; but it makes a valuable addition to our professional literature. Learning how people experience an event or situation can be of great assistance to social workers who work with people in similar circumstances.

Descriptive knowledge, as we shall discuss in the context of research design in later chapters, may be exactly what the individual social work practitioner needs. It also frequently forms the basis for desirable changes within our society. The accurate description of a problem—for example, the statistical documentation of discriminatory employment practices or identification of the amount of sexual harassment in the workplace—has been the basis both for bringing these problems into public awareness and for subsequent social change. As social workers who advocate for change, we are especially aware of the value of this kind of knowledge.

Predictive Knowledge

Predictive knowledge is knowledge to help us anticipate. It allows us to go a step beyond describing what is or was. It allows us to project into the future and to predict with reasonable accuracy what will be. Predictive knowledge evolves from the accumulation of descriptive knowledge that reveals consistent reoccurring patterns. For example, suppose that several descriptive studies of gay adolescent teenagers reveal that a large percentage of them are victims of bullying. From this, we might evolve the predictive knowledge that a gay teenager, our client, is likely to experience bullying behavior. We can increase the likelihood of success in predicting a problem that he may face when we observe what has tended to happen to others in the past.

Predictive knowledge can tell a social worker what is likely to occur. For example, it can tell a social worker that an untreated abusive partner is likely or unlikely to become violent again, or that a certain psychiatric patient may become disruptive in group treatment. It can help to predict who is "at risk" of experiencing a certain problem and thus who might require careful monitoring and/or intervention. But it stops short of telling a social worker exactly how to intervene to prevent a problem from occurring or to treat one that already exists.

Prescriptive Knowledge

Prescriptive knowledge is knowledge that suggests the method of intervention that is most likely to be effective. In EBP, it is what we would use (along with our experience, client preferences, and so forth) to decide what intervention should be used to address an existing problem or to prevent one that we can predict. Prescriptive knowledge is most frequently based on the findings of carefully designed research studies in which the researcher had considerable control over the ways in which the research was conducted.

When prescriptive knowledge exists, we not only know what is and what probably will be, but we also know what needs to be done to avoid something undesirable or to cause something desirable to occur. In fields such as sociology or anthropology, descriptive knowledge and, to a lesser degree, predictive knowledge are often the end product of research. In EBP, our goal is informed intervention with a high likelihood of success. Thus, we strive to produce prescriptive research knowledge; that is, knowledge that provides guidance for successful intervention. For example, the knowledge that a client with a particular psychiatric diagnosis will benefit from a certain combination of counseling and medication has valuable implications for a social work practitioner. In terms of its value for decision making, it may be even more valuable than the knowledge that her problem occurs in approximately 2 percent of women (descriptive knowledge) or that it will probably result in problems in maintaining employment (predictive knowledge).

Purely prescriptive knowledge is still relatively rare in social work, but it is becoming increasingly available as more and more carefully designed research studies are conducted. The more frequent use of a particular type of research, meta-analysis (described in Chapter 8), also has added more prescriptive knowledge to our professional knowledge base.

It should be emphasized again here that prescriptive knowledge *alone* should not dictate the choice of a method of intervention. That would not be consistent with EBP. There is, of course, no guarantee that you or I will find it to be effective with a given client or a given client group. That is where our own experience, knowledge of ourselves and our client or client group, ethical practice issues, and client wishes and preferences must be factored into the decision as to how best to intervene.

It would also be inaccurate to say that prescriptive knowledge is the *only* type of knowledge that suggests how we might best intervene in a problem situation. Virtually all research findings can have some prescriptive potential. With thought, predictive and even descriptive knowledge can help to inform our practice decision making and thus increase the likelihood of successful intervention. For example, a descriptive study of youth gang activities and the social needs of individuals that they appear to meet might suggest what other activities and programs might provide an attractive alternative to gang membership. Or, the findings of several studies of youth gangs might allow us to predict at what age pressure for membership is most likely to occur. This predictive knowledge can then help us to decide what age an activity or program should "target," and thus how to structure it.

In reality, most research studies generate a variety of knowledge, including some that does not fit cleanly into only one of the three categories. The "knowledge typology" (like most typologies) is not perfect and "clean." However, we included it primarily because it emphasizes the benefits that research can offer to the social work practitioner. It will also prove useful in later chapters when we examine different types of research and, especially, how they differ in purpose.

Basic and Applied Research

A research study is sometimes described as either "basic" or "applied." The labels are assigned based on a study's general goal or purpose, specifically, when and how any knowledge derived from it is intended to be used.

Basic Research

Basic research (sometimes called "pure research") is research that is designed to contribute to our general professional body of knowledge. Social workers conduct basic research, but we also rely heavily on the work of researchers from many other fields to conduct basic research. For example, we benefit from the research of such people as sociologists, anthropologists, economists, and psychologists who help us to understand and predict human behavior. The findings from basic research sometimes are immediately put to use in our practice, but frequently they are not. The knowledge from basic research is often "tucked away," available for us to tap into at some future time for some as yet unknown purpose. We might not use it at all until some new social problem is identified or we conclude that we have misunderstood an old one. Then we might revisit the findings of basic research conducted years or even decades earlier to provide some beginning insight into the problem. For example, some of the basic research conducted in the 1971 Stanford studies of the behaviors of college students when given power over others in a prison setting have been used to help us to better understand the abusive treatment of prisoners in Iraq and Afghanistan by their American guards over thirty years later.[26]

Applied Research

In contrast to basic research, *applied research* is designed to produce knowledge that has immediate (and often narrower) applicability. Its findings are often used for answering some "burning" question or for making some decision that cannot wait, for example, whether an intervention should be terminated or whether a social program should be continued. We identify the potential beneficiaries of applied research before it is conducted and design it in a way that it provides what they need—the data that will help to answer the questions that must be answered.

Applied research is not inherently more valuable or more useful than basic research. Its findings may appear to be more practical and more relevant to successful evidence-based practice. However, we could not be successful evidence-based practitioners without also having access to knowledge acquired through basic research. Sometimes the practice benefits of basic research are quite indirect; we may even be unaware of their contribution to our current practice. As one author has pointed out, "Some research will have impact only over the long haul, shaping theory that in turn informs hypotheses for further study."[27]

The two types of research tend to complement each other. It is probably accurate to say that applied research benefits a relatively small number of individuals immediately, but basic research has the potential to benefit many more people in the long term.

As we might also suspect, not all research falls neatly into one of the two categories (basic or applied). In fact, some basic research studies produce findings that are of immediate use for practice decision making. Conversely, some applied research studies (often along with the findings of other, similar studies) sometimes produce knowledge that represents a major contribution to our professional knowledge base. In addition, some research studies also have elements of both basic and applied research. However, the two terms are still widely used to communicate the broad characteristics of a research study.

Quantitative and Qualitative Research

Another way to broadly categorize research that is based at least partly on its purpose is to describe it as quantitative or qualitative. The categorization is also based on other factors, such as the methods of data collection most frequently used, sources of data, the place of hypotheses, and even the methods of data analysis employed. As we shall see, as in the case of the basic and applied labels, the labels quantitative and qualitative can easily suggest a false dichotomy, since many research studies now often contain elements of both.

Quantitative Research

Quantitative research often has been thought of (erroneously) as being synonymous with the scientific method. It is sometimes even called "empirical research," yet it has no monopoly on either the scientific method or empiricism. It emphasizes the building of knowledge through what is referred to as "logical positivism." It stresses the use of deductive (linear) logic to arrive at conclusions.

It is possible to test hypotheses in studies that entail more quantitative methods because they are characterized by (or attempt to employ) the following:

1. Careful measurement of variables.
2. Relatively large, randomly selected case samples.
3. Control of other variables through random assignment of cases to groups.
4. Standardized data collection methods.
5. Statistical analyses of data.

Quantitative methods are also employed in research that merely seeks to describe some problem or phenomenon. It is used to provide accurate measurement of the distribution of variables and to identify possible relationships between and among them.

The sequence of activities that occurs in quantitative research reflects the *deductive* logic of this approach to knowledge building. In broad terms, this entails:

1. Specification of a theory.
2. Statement of a hypothesis to test the theory.
3. Observation (data collection).
4. Confirmation (or nonconfirmation) of the theory.

This deductive logic is reflected in the sequence of activities that occurs. It is how many of us in years past were taught "the correct way" for research to be conducted. The usual steps in the quantitative process are:

1. *Problem identification.* The problem—that is, the condition or phenomenon that is unsatisfactory—must be clearly understood to the point that it can be specified precisely, along with its magnitude and consequences.

2. *Research question formulation.* After developing a number of broad questions, the answer to any one of which would have potential to partially alleviate the problem (or at least to understand it better), the researcher selects one or more of these questions that will constitute the focus of inquiry for the research.

3. *Literature review.* The state of existing knowledge is assessed and assembled into a logical order to determine what is already known concerning answers to the research questions, or at least to enable the researcher to specify the questions more precisely. The literature review is also used to formulate an appropriate research methodology for the current research.

4. *Construction of hypotheses and/or refinement of research questions.* Based on the literature review and the type of knowledge sought, the researcher formulates hypotheses and/or specific research questions that will provide the focus for research activities that follow.

5. *Design and planning.* A series of decisions are made as to how the research hypotheses are to be tested and/or answers to questions are to be sought. Tasks involved in this activity include the following:

   a. Selecting or formulating operational definitions of key terms.
   b. Specification of what people or objects will be studied.
   c. Development of a method for sampling (if the entire population of people or objects is not to be studied).
   d. Identification and definition of variables to be measured (conceptualization).
   e. Specification of exactly how variables will be measured (operationalization).
   f. Identification and/or development of instruments for measurement (including their pretesting).
   g. Specification and pretesting of methods for data collection.
   h. Specification of methods for analysis of data.

6. *Data collection.* Data are collected according to predetermined methods.

7. *Sorting and analysis of data.* The data are examined, summarized, and analyzed using appropriate statistical methods. If hypotheses have been formulated, tests of statistical significance are used to determine if support for them can be claimed.

8. *Specification of research findings.* Results of data analysis are displayed in tables, graphs, or other standard formats.

9. *Interpretation of research findings.* Results of data analysis are examined in order to draw conclusions relative to the research hypotheses and/or questions. The findings are examined in relation to other knowledge.

10. *Dissemination of research findings.* The researcher uses one or more vehicles to report the methods and findings of the research.

11. *Use of findings by the social worker.* Practitioners who have access to the research report critically evaluate both the findings and the methods that produced them. Based on their assessment of them, they may adapt their practice methods accordingly.

This traditional sequence of events for performing research is described in most research methods texts. However, steps 1 and 11 are not universally included. By including them, we have emphasized our concern for the importance of research utilization by the social work practitioner as an integral part of evidence based practice.

The knowledge generated by quantitative research that is supportive of EBP can take many forms. For example, it can be the findings that provide evidence of a relationship between the incidence of child abuse and substance abuse. Or, it can be the findings of other research that compares the effectiveness of two different approaches to treatment of the problem of child abuse. It can be the results of an evaluation that measures how well a program to treat perpetrators of child abuse achieved its objectives. Or, it can be the product of the social worker's systematic ongoing evaluation of his or her own practice effectiveness with an abusive parent or a treatment group of abusive parents.

For many years, quantitative methods were considered the best (if not the only) way to conduct research. They are still described as such in many high school science classes and in research courses in some other disciplines. Indeed, the principles of quantitative research are ideal for obtaining certain types of knowledge. However, quantitative methods have their limitations. They are not well suited to studying certain phenomena. We cannot always separate knowledge and values; they are hopelessly intertwined in human thought and behavior. For example, quantitative methods can provide reasonably accurate data about the incidence of date rape on college campuses or even what individuals are most at risk. However, it cannot provide much insight into how individuals perceive their experience with it or what it means to them. The limitations of quantitative research, along with the evolution of feminist research (discussed later) have taught us the importance of other, complementary approaches to knowledge building.

Qualitative Research

Qualitative research seeks to understand human experiences from the perspective of those who experience them. (More quantitative methods would emphasize determining what is or what occurred.) It emphasizes words like *subjective, relative,* or *contextual*—words that might have a connotation of failure within quantitative studies. Qualitative research also relies on inductive logic instead of deduction. Often, vast amounts of data are collected, then sorted, and then interpreted.

Data collection often occurs through in-depth interviewing, conducting groups, or by participant observation, (methods discussed in Chapter 8). In-person interviews (an important component of most qualitative studies) generally tend to be less structured and standardized in qualitative research than in quantitative research. Often, what the researcher learns in conducting one interview results in adaptations for the next. Sample representativeness (Chapter 9) often is not a major concern.

In qualitative research, the researcher is really the primary instrument for data collection and analysis. The data are processed as they are received. There is no pretense that the researcher can collect data in an objective, value-free manner. In fact, when interviews are used, the relationships between the researcher and those being interviewed may be openly supportive and even therapeutic at times. When using more qualitative approaches to knowledge building, many of the same activities seen in more quantitative studies still take place. However, they often receive greater or lesser emphasis or may occur in a different sequence. There are two important differences that are especially common. First, hypotheses are unlikely to be formulated prior to data collection and then tested as in quantitative studies. Instead, they may evolve from and be the final product of the research process. Thus, they generally appear late in the report of a qualitative study (if at all), as tentative conclusions drawn from the research study. Second, in qualitative studies, an extensive review of the literature generally does not occur prior to data collection. Vast amounts of data may be collected quite early in the research process. Some will be useful; others may be discarded. During and after data collection, the professional literature is used to either verify or question what the data seem to be suggesting, that is, to help in conceptualizing what is being and has been observed.

The sequence of activities that occurs in qualitative research reflects the *inductive* logic of this approach to knowledge building. In broad terms, this entails:

1. Collection of a wide range of data.
2. Observation of patterns in the data.
3. Formulation of tentative explanations.
4. Development of theories (and sometimes, hypotheses).

Qualitative research also differs more widely in adherence to rules and procedures (than in quantitative research) from study to study, based upon the specific qualitative methodology that is employed. Some studies are quite rigorous and adhere strictly to a specific sequence of activities; others are more flexible. However, below is one fairly common sequence:

1. Problem identification.
2. Research question formulation.
3. Limited literature review.
4. Initial data collection and analysis.
5. Continued data collection and analysis.
6. Data interpretation.
7. Formulation of theories or hypotheses.
8. Dissemination of findings.
9. Use of findings by the social worker.

We are accustomed to seeing the findings of quantitative studies displayed using tables and graphs. Reports also contain the results of statistical testing with conclusions about support or nonsupport for research hypotheses. In reports of qualitative studies, none of these may be present. Findings are more likely to be presented in narrative form or as case scenarios. There may be long descriptions of the researcher's interaction with specific individuals who provided data for the research, including direct quotations from them and speculation by the researcher on what their choice of words may suggest or imply. Increasingly, computer software is being used to perform a content analysis (Chapter 8) of transcripts of interviews to attempt to quantify, for example, the presence of certain emotions as anger, despair, or anxiety. When this occurs, the results of the analysis are also included in the findings.

Our professional literature contains far fewer reports of qualitative studies than it does of quantitative ones (although this trend is not as pronounced as it once was). This may be attributable in part to the form that findings of qualitative studies often take—their "richness" cannot be easily conveyed in an eight- or ten-page article. However, it may also be attributable to the persistence of a "quantitative bias" among the editors and reviewers who make publication decisions—a belief that quantitative research is more methodologically sound and that qualitative research is "less scientific" and, thus, its findings are less credible or less valuable.

Researchers seeking funding for qualitative studies have sometimes encountered this same bias. It is often difficult to convince people who control the awarding of grants and contracts in a foundation or government institute of the merits of a qualitative study. Sometimes, even grant proposal applications contain items that ask what hypotheses will be tested, how control groups will be constituted, and what statistical tests of inference will be used—design features of the more traditional quantitative studies.

In the late twentieth century, the merits of qualitative research were the topic of lively debates among social work researchers. However, it is now generally agreed that both quantitative and qualitative methods are necessary to truly understand many problems or phenomena. For example, how could we really have a complete understanding of an experience such as post-traumatic stress syndrome (PTSD) among returning war veterans if we focused only on, for example, its incidence, the forms that it takes, and what experiences may be associated with it, and did not also explore in different ways such topics as how it is perceived by its victims or how they experience it emotionally?

Neither type of research is inherently superior to the other. Both quantitative and qualitative studies make valuable contributions to our knowledge base and help us to make better decisions as evidence-based practice social workers. Of course, there is good and not-so-good qualitative research, even as there is good and not-so-good quantitative research. Simply running a focus group and writing up a summary of what transpired is not good qualitative research any more than mailing out a hastily constructed survey is good quantitative research. Conducting good qualitative research is not a haphazard process. It requires careful planning and is just as demanding (if not more so) than quantitative studies. For example, the reports of qualitative studies usually tend to be longer than reports of quantitative studies because they are likely to contain in-depth narrative descriptions of interviews with research participants or of the researcher's direct observation of some phenomenon.

The criteria for evaluating the design of a quantitative study have been used for many years and are now universally accepted. There are, as yet, no comparable criteria for qualitative research. However, there are certain questions that are generally appropriate to ask. For example:

1. Were good sources of data identified and used?
2. Were appropriate, productive relationships with research participants established?
3. Did the methods of data collection seem to produce honest and candid responses from research participants?
4. Do the data reflect a diversity of experiences and perceptions?
5. Do the data reflect "richness"?
6. Did the data contribute to existing knowledge about the research problem?
7. Did the research produce credible theories or hypotheses for future research?

The findings of qualitative research and those of quantitative research often complement each other. It is not too surprising, then, that research studies often are "hybrids"—they contain features of both. Qualitative methods may be used to collect and analyze one type of data, while qualitative methods may be used to collect and analyze some other type. Or both methods may be used to attempt to answer the same question so that the results can be compared to help in finding the correct answer. For example, in order to try to gain an accurate perception of the merit, worth, or value of a social program, we might rely on both quantitative data about changes in the social functioning of its clients but also upon in-depth interviews with some of its clients, group meetings with program staff, and so forth.

It is probably more accurate to describe many studies as "predominantly quantitative" or "predominantly qualitative," rather than simply quantitative or qualitative. In the chapters that follow, when references are made to quantitative or qualitative research it should be remembered that "pure" examples of either type of research are now probably more the exception than the rule.

The Current Climate for Social Work Research

The demand for research in the human services has never been greater, largely due to an emphasis on EBP. A high percentage of the research that is conducted by social workers is now some form of mandated evaluation research. Human service organizations contain many excellent potential sources of research data, for example, surveys of and interviews with clients or organization staff, and agency data (such as number and characteristics of clients served) that are routinely collected and compiled. (Recent changes in laws now have made client record data off limits to researchers in many settings.) These data can provide evidence of the effectiveness of services and programs to program managers and administrators, but also to organizations that provide funding for programs and to other stakeholders. However, analysis of program data may also have the potential to identify areas where individuals and programs have not met their responsibilities or have failed to achieve their objectives. Thus, a researcher conducting a mandated program evaluation may receive excellent cooperation and assistance from organizational staff. Or, he or she may encounter resistance and efforts to obstruct research activities that might reveal program deficiencies.

What if we just want to conduct knowledge to contribute to our professional knowledge base? In recent years, competition for funding for human services and emphasis on cost containment have left many administrators a little wary of even "unnecessary" research (that is, research not required by some funding organization). The social worker attempting to conduct it usually can anticipate some resistance on the part of those people who must approve it. Assurances that evaluation is not the purpose of the research may not be enough to gain approval. Most administrators are keenly aware of the evaluative potential of most any type of research, should the findings "fall into the wrong hands." Many human service organizations operate in a task environment that is nonsupportive at best, and sometimes downright hostile to their efforts. Vocal critics, the general public, or even another organization competing for funding might like nothing better than to secure research data that can be construed as critical of the organization.

Is it any wonder that administrators (and board members) are often fearful of research? On the surface, it would seem that they may have more to lose than to gain from it. Still another concern often relates to the protection of client and staff rights, especially their privacy rights. Fears about the possibility of litigation (a major concern of administrators today) are likely to surface when a researcher, even an employee of the organization, asks to collect data from staff or clients. Sometimes, permission to conduct research requires a series of compromises and accommodations that result in research methods that the researcher knows are less than ideal. This is an unfortunate reality. But, if done thoughtfully, these adjustments can be made in a way that will maintain the integrity of the research and its findings. As we shall discuss, no research design is ever perfect, but there are ways to make less-than-perfect research acceptable if we understand and apply the principles of scientific inquiry.

The professionalization of social work over the past few decades also has influenced the ways in which we are able to conduct research. Leaders of organizations such as NASW have worked hard to ensure high-quality services to clients (and to acquire greater public recognition for the contributions that social workers make to society). Professionalization also has been enhanced by the passing of state licensing bills that protect both social workers and their clients. Professionalization has been accompanied by the codification of certain values, ethical standards, and traditions. Overall, these undoubtedly have produced better services and served to protect clients from unqualified or incompetent individuals.

Generally, as we shall see in Chapter 2, professional values are highly consistent with research ethics. On occasion, however, a researcher will (and should) be constrained from using methods and designs that represent sound research but that are unacceptable to social workers and the values that guide their behavior. For example, professional values are likely to argue against such practices as random assignment of clients to two different types of treatment, direct observation of treatment, denial of services in order to see if treatment really makes a difference, or certain forms of deception. If allowed to occur, these practices might produce research findings that are more definitive and possess greater credibility. But of course, research should serve practice; it should never be the other way around. Professional values and ethics must be adhered to, even if the quality of research suffers a little.

Professional values, such as a client's right to services and to confidentiality and the sanctity of a treatment relationship, will and should continue to present impediments to conducting scientific research. The welfare of individual clients cannot be sacrificed in the interest of knowledge building, sometimes even that which has the potential to produce better future services to clients. However, the knowledgeable researcher knows that many apparent conflicts that pit professional values against research imperatives actually result from misunderstandings that can be cleared up. Those that are real can often be resolved through compromise and trade-off. Frequently, an almost-as-good alternative exists and can be employed. The influence of professional values may make research in the social work practice milieu a little more difficult, or it may require special creativity on the part of the researcher. But fortunately, it rarely precludes conducting good research altogether.

Some of the distrust of and resistance to scientific research that social workers have been observed to possess is attributable to their lack of a clear understanding of research. They may be unaware of the ways that it can be conducted so as not to conflict with professional values and ethics. But some of it has a basis in experience. Some of the unethical ways in which research has been conducted and its findings disseminated in the past have contributed to a climate of skepticism. We will describe a few of the more glaring examples of this in Chapter 2.

Sometimes, who we are also presents obstacles to conducting research. Most social workers chose their profession because they wanted to help others. As a group, we are (and should be!) people oriented, placing high priority on the needs of our clients. We sometimes may have difficulty believing that any activity that does not directly and immediately result in better services is worthwhile. Research does not always meet this requirement, as in the case of basic research. However, our concern with helping our clients can also be the driving force that leads us to participate in and to support research. After all, EBP can only occur if research provides the knowledge that we need to help in making informed practice decisions.

Despite some of the obstacles and concerns that we have mentioned, the environment for social work research continues to improve in the twenty-first century. Social workers are becoming more aware that well designed, credible research studies are essential if they are to provide the best possible services to their clients. They are also more aware that sound research is a necessity if we are to demonstrate that our efforts are worth their cost to governments and employers who must make decisions about which services will be supported and who should offer them.[28] Without good research evidence of this, the profession faces the threats of financial cuts and elimination of valuable and needed programs. Other disciplines and professions, which have a longer history of conducting research that demonstrates their effectiveness, could move in to fill roles that social workers historically have filled. Whether out of choice or out of necessity, the market for social work research (especially evaluation research) is now very favorable.

Summary

In this chapter we looked at the history of the relationship between research and social work practice and some of the reasons for it. Many of the steps in the research process are quite similar to those of good practice intervention. Yet, in the past, social workers have tended to rely primarily on such unreliable sources as supervisors' opinions, logic and common sense, tradition, and authority to provide the knowledge they required for making practice decisions. They relied less frequently on the findings of research that employed scientific methods. However, this has gradually changed. We now advocate and acknowledge the value of EBP, with its emphasis on the use of research findings as an important component of practice decision making. We need to understand the best ways to conduct research in order to (1) design and implement our own research and (2) to evaluate critically the research methods and findings of others so that we can make informed practice decisions.

We looked at several broad descriptions of different types of research. Different research methods focus on the production of different types of knowledge (which were classified as descriptive, predictive, and prescriptive). Some studies can be described as basic research, whose primary purpose is to provide broad, generalized knowledge for future use. Other research, which is described as applied research, has as its purpose to provide knowledge for immediate use in decision making. An example would be a program evaluation. The major differences between research that is primarily quantitative and research that is primarily qualitative also were described. They will be discussed in more detail in the chapters that follow.

Finally, we looked at the current environment for social work research, its sources of support and the obstacles it presents. Some of the obstacles result from misunderstandings that can be corrected, but others are likely to continue or even become more prohibitive. They will require researchers to be sensitive and diplomatic, but also to be creative and willing to compromise on occasion.

For Discussion

1. Why is it more realistic to emphasize EBP today than, say, twenty years ago? Why would it be a mistake to rely totally on the findings of research for our practice decision making?
2. Even if he or she never designs and conducts research, why does a social worker need to know the correct ways to conduct it?
3. Why is the scientific alternative a more trustworthy source of knowledge than the other sources discussed in this chapter? Why are the other sources still sometimes better than (and sometimes worse than) no help at all for practice decision making?
4. Do you know of other social work services or programs besides those mentioned that seemed like they should be effective but have not proven to be so? What misleading sources of "knowledge" may have been used to justify them?
5. Why do researchers using the scientific method report both research findings and the methods they used to produce them? Why is it not enough just to report what they found?
6. If research findings include the statement that "24 percent of clients in this group never returned for the second group session," is that descriptive, predictive, or prescriptive knowledge or all three? What if the statement had been, "Clients under age 30 are two times more likely to not return for the second session than clients 30 years or older"?
7. Why are social workers more likely to conduct applied research than basic research? Is there some basic research that could be conducted better by social workers than by people in other fields? What would be some examples?
8. Why do you suppose that many of the advocates for more qualitative research studies have been women rather than men?
9. How are some of the methods employed in qualitative research different from the "right" way that you learned to do research in high school science classes? Why is a mixture of qualitative and quantitative methods often needed to get a comprehensive understanding of a problem or phenomenon?
10. What recent technological developments have helped to support or present obstacles to conducting good social work research?

Endnotes

1. Council on Social Work Education (2002). Educational policy and accreditation standards. Alexandria, VA.
2. Sackett, D. et al. (1997). *Evidence-based medicine: How to practice and teach EMB.* New York: Churchill-Livingstone.
3. Simpson, R. (1979). Understanding the utilization of research and other applied professions. *Sourcebook on research utilization.* New York: Council on Social Work Education, 16–28.

4. Kirk, S. (1979). Understanding research utilization in social work. *Sourcebook on research utilization.* New York: Council on Social Work Education, 12.

5. Briar, S. (1979). Incorporating research into education for clinical practice: Toward a clinical science in social work. *Sourcebook on research utilization.* New York: Council on Social Work Education, 132–133.

6. Garvin, C. (1981). Research-related roles for social workers. In R. Grinnell, Jr. (Ed.), *Social work research and evaluation.* Itasca, IL: F. E. Peacock, 547–552.

7. Fraser, M., Jackson, R., & O'Jack, J. (1991). Social work and science: Many ways of knowing. *Social Work Research and Abstracts, 27,* 5–15.

8. Ibid.

9. Lindsay, D. (1978). The operation of professional journals in social work. *Journal of Social Work and Sociology, 5,* 273–298.

10. Blythe, B., & Witkin, S. (1992). Should undergraduate and graduate social work students be taught to conduct empirically based practice? *Journal of Social Work Education, 28,* 260–269.

11. Wakefield, J., & Kirk, S. (1996). Unscientific thinking about scientific practice. Evaluating the scientist-practitioner model. *Social Work Research, 20* (June), 83–95.

12. Gambrill, E. (1999). Evidence-based practice: An alternative to authority-based practice. *Families in Society, 80,* 341–350; or Cournoyer, B., & Powers, G. (2002). Evidence-based social work: The quiet revolution continues. In A. Roberts & G. Greene, (Eds.), *Social workers' desk reference.* New York: Oxford University Press.

13. Rosen, A. (2003). Evidence-based social work practice: Challenges and promise. *Social Work Research, 27,* Washington, DC: National Association of Social Workers, 197–208.

14. Rubin, A., & Babbie, E. (2005). *Research methods for social work*, 5th ed. Belmont, CA: Brooks/Cole, 7–9 and (2008). *Research methods for social work*, 6th ed. Belmont, CA: Brooks/Cole, 5–6.

15. Ibid, 6.

16. Grinnell, R., Jr., & Siegel, D. (1988). The place of research in social work. In R. Grinnell, Jr. (Ed.), *Social work research and evaluation.* Itasca, IL: F. E. Peacock, 18–21.

17. Finkenhauer, J. (1979). *Evaluation of juvenile awareness projects: Reports 1 and 2.* Newark, NJ: Rutgers School of Criminal Justice.

18. Van Burgh, J., Redner, G., & Moon, C. (1995). A report of project DARE with eighth grade students. www.eduref.org/plweb-cgi/fastweb.

19. Lyman, D., et al. (1999). Project DARE: No effects at 10-year follow-up. *Journal of Consulting and Clinical Psychology, 67,* 590–593.

20. Rank, M. (1994). In *NASW News,* July, 1994. New York: National Association of Social Workers, 6.

21. Welfare Rights Organizing Coalition (2000). Welfare facts and myths. www.wroc.org.

22. The United States Conference of Mayors (2005). A status report on hunger and homelessness in American cities. www.rihomelessness.co.

23. Drug Policy Alliance (2004). Cocaine and pregnancy. www.lindesmith.org/library/research/cocaine.cfm.

24. B. Burkett (1986) as originally reported by J. Wright in the *Dallas Morning News* and later *The State,* Columbia, SC, September 15, 1986, 32.

25. Gambrill, E. (1992). Social work research. Priorities and obstacles. Keynote address, Group for the Advancement of Doctoral Education Conference, University of Pittsburgh, October 1, 1992, 24.

26. Zimbardo, P. (2004) Stanford Prison Experiment. www.prisonexp.org.

27. Proctor, E. (2003). Evidence for practice: Challenges, opportunities, and access. *Social Work Research, 27,* Washington, DC: National Association of Social Workers, 195.

28. O'Neill, J. (2000). Practice-research sync "crucial for survival." *NASW News, 45.* Washington, DC: National Association of Social Workers, 3.

2

ETHICAL ISSUES
IN RESEARCH

In the previous chapter, we described many similarities between research and social work practice. There is at least one other similarity, and a very important one. Both research and practice are shaped by ethical constraints.

In this chapter, we will examine (1) what is meant by research ethics; (2) some well-known research studies whose abuses of research participants contributed to the establishment of current ethical standards to ensure that those individuals who allow us to collect research data from them are protected; (3) contemporary issues such as research with vulnerable people who may volunteer to become research participants and the rights of individuals to participate in research, even if it has the potential to harm them; and (4) the researcher's ethical obligations to others, such as the sponsors of research, other researchers, colleagues, and the general public.

In some areas, research ethical standards have been clearly delineated. However, in others there is often a lack of clear-cut guidelines to assist our decision making. As in our social work practice, ethical dilemmas and constraints are always with us. And that is good, because they cause us to regularly question whether what we are doing is both justifiable and fair to others.

We have chosen to devote an entire chapter to the topic of research ethical issues, because they play such an important part in the design and implementation of research studies. However, our intention is not to simply cover the topic and then dismiss it. Ethical issues impact all aspects of research; they can and do occur anywhere in the research process. Thus, the reader will see reference to ethical issues throughout the later chapters of this book as well.

What Are Ethics?

In both practice and research, ethics sometimes clearly dictate what is forbidden under any circumstances. For example, in social work practice, sexual contact with current and former clients is universally regarded as unethical. Similarly, research that is likely to cause

29

permanent harm to all of its research participants is unethical. More frequently, however, ethics fall into the category of "issues." An issue is debatable—individuals can hold two opposing positions on it, and a good argument can be made for either of them. In practice, an issue might be whether it is unethical to discontinue needed counseling with a client after her medical coverage has been exhausted. In research, an ethical issue might arise over whether deception is necessary to acquire certain types of knowledge, or whether it might actually be harmful to research participants.

The term *ethics,* derived from the Greek word *ethos* (which comes closest to the English word *character*), refers to principles within a society that reflect what the society generally views as right or wrong behavior. Ethics are a little different from laws—they often fall into what is commonly called "the gray area." Thus, we sometimes find ourselves asking the question, "It is not illegal, but is it ethical?" In the context of research, ethical issues generally revolve around three related questions: (1) Who should benefit or suffer from the actions of the researcher? (2) Whose rights should take priority over those of others? and (3) Does the end (increased knowledge) justify the means (the methods used to acquire it and their potential for harm.) In the ideal world, all individuals and groups should benefit from the development of new knowledge. Beneficiaries might include the researcher, those who provide research data, the institution sponsoring the research, the community, and other researchers whose efforts can build on the researcher's findings. But we know that, in the real world, the needs of one group sometimes are met at the expense of another. For example, the methods used by researchers to acquire valuable knowledge can be harmful to a few individuals who provide the data that are needed to acquire it.

Who Provides Data for Our Research?

Most social work research depends on our fellow human beings to provide the data that we need to conduct research. They may be our clients, family members of clients, fellow professionals, or anyone else who can help us to better understand some problem and/or to intervene more effectively in solving it. Whoever they are, they generally have one characteristic in common—they are asked to give much more than they will ever receive from their participation. For this reason and for others, we have an ethical obligation to safeguard their health and well-being.

People who provide data for research purposes are referred to by various terms within the professional literature. Three of the most common are *research subjects, research partners,* and *research participants.* All three refer to the same individuals, but the terms have different connotations. Some people use the most traditional term, *subjects,* because it is universally understood within research circles. Others contend that the term is condescending or dehumanizing and that it is not consistent with the way those who provide data relate to the researcher, especially in studies that use primarily qualitative research methods. They also suggest that it implies that these individuals are somehow subservient, and thus susceptible to exploitation by the researcher. For a combination of these reasons, this term is being used less frequently than it once was.

Those researchers who conduct certain types of qualitative research prefer the term *research partner.* It suggests a different perception of the respective roles of research participants and researcher. They contend that the word *partner* most accurately reflects the relationship between those who provide research data and the researcher. They point out that those who agree to "share so much of themselves" (which often includes very personal information) to assist the researcher in building knowledge are equally as important as the researcher in this endeavor and that the relationship is thus one of equality.

We have chosen to use the third term, participant, throughout this book. This choice is not simply a compromise. *Participant* seems to recognize the importance of those who provide data for research purposes, while also recognizing that their objectives and degree of involvement in knowledge building generally differ from those of the researcher. The term is consistent with both the quantitative and qualitative approaches to acquiring knowledge in social work research. It also conveys the awareness that these individuals are entitled to both respect and attention to their rights. It acknowledges that, while they may sometimes choose to be involved in research that results in their discomfort, they should never be tricked or forced into doing so.

Earlier Abuses of Research Participants

Researchers and those who sponsor or permit their research have an ethical obligation to ensure that research participants are protected from harm. Unfortunately, this is a relatively new idea. Many of the ethical issues that must be addressed by today's researchers simply were nonissues for researchers in the nineteenth and early twentieth centuries. The history of humanity is replete with examples of research that valued knowledge building more than the rights of research participants. It reflects a lack of concern for how research might negatively affect the physical and emotional health of those who provide data for scientific analysis. Research participants often were individuals who were either powerless or defenseless (for example, the poor, minorities, children, the mentally ill, prisoners of war). Others, it was believed, had essentially abdicated their right to protection under the law or under principles of common decency because of their behavior (for example, those incarcerated for a serious crime).

The belated emergence of guidelines for conducting research with human participants occurred during the second half of the twentieth century. It came about because of a gradual recognition that, in a quest for scientific knowledge, the end cannot always justify the means. Our society has come to acknowledge that in some research studies the cost to research participants was not justifiable, no matter how much knowledge was generated.

Some widely publicized research studies are considered "milestones" in the development of today's research ethical standards. They are better known for their contribution to an increased concern for the protection of research participants than for the scientific knowledge that they produced. They employed methods that ranged from those that are now universally condemned to those that still continue to be defended by some people within the scientific community. Many examples of the unethical abuse of human participants could be cited. We have chosen to include a brief description of a few of the better known ones, and noted how each has contributed to one or more standards that are used to protect research participants today.

The Nazi and Japanese Medical Experiments

Following World War II, it was revealed that concentration camps in Europe and prisoner-of-war compounds in Asia had been the scenes of heinous and repugnant medical experiments conducted in the name of science.[1] During the Nuremberg war crime trials in 1945 and 1946, many shocking stories were recounted that detailed how Jews, Gypsies, and other "undesirables" detained in German concentration camps were deliberately exposed to life-threatening diseases in order to study the course of the diseases, and were subjected to unnecessary surgery. Others were exposed to severe cold, were deliberately wounded to study the effects of new antibiotic treatments, or were placed in decompression chambers to study their tolerance for lack of oxygen and other effects of high altitude. Of course, viewed in retrospect, these experiments were little more than sadistic atrocities committed in the name of science.

Prior to the Nuremberg trials, little attention had been paid to the rights of prisoners and other vulnerable groups. All too often, they were regarded as convenient targets for experimentation. The shocking revelations that emerged at Nuremberg set about a process of questioning. People debated the issue of whether incarceration for any reason, even for conviction for illegal activity, can ever justify the nonvoluntary participation of prisoners in medical and other research. A consensus emerged that it cannot. Research participation must be voluntary.

Interestingly, one ethical issue related to the medical experiments conducted on American prisoners in Japanese prison camps did not surface until the 1980s. Access to previously classified documents revealed that American authorities had apparently suppressed information about the experiments after the war, in exchange for access to the medical knowledge acquired through them. As the news of the research became widely disseminated, current medical researchers sought access to data obtained in the prisoner-of-war camps. Newer and broader ethical questions were debated. Should research findings obtained through unethical methods be publicized or made available to other researchers for their use? Can suppression of valuable knowledge that has the potential to save lives be justified on the basis that the researchers' methods cannot be condoned? Who owns the data? Should the survivors of the experiments (who did not participate voluntarily) or the relatives of those who did not survive have the right to decide whether data from the experiments can be released or under what conditions it can be used? Like most research ethical issues, these are difficult questions with no easy answers.

The Tuskegee Public Health Studies

A second group of research studies that addressed some of the same issues took place in the United States. In 1932 the American Public Health Service began its studies of the long-term effects of syphilis on men in the Tuskegee, Alabama, area.[2] Ethical questions relate to whether these men were truly voluntary participants because of their vulnerability (health status, socioeconomic class, and race). But the studies also were influential in the development of today's ethical principle known as "no unnecessary pain and suffering."

The research was conducted on 625 African American males. Most (425) had been diagnosed as having syphilis; the others were followed merely for comparison purposes. In 1937, penicillin was discovered. It soon was shown to be an effective cure for syphilis and became available to the general public several years later. Yet, for purposes of research, participants in the Tuskegee experiment, who were mostly poor and illiterate, were not told about penicillin, and it was not given to them unless they somehow learned about it and requested it. They continued to be given painful regular medical examinations (including spinal taps) to chart the course of their disease. They received only a placebo, an inert substance that had no potential to cure their disease or to alleviate their pain and suffering. In the interim, they experienced the long-term effects of syphilis, including skin disorders, insanity, heart disease, and even death. The study continued until 1957, at which time it was halted following public outcry.

Unlike many of the experiments conducted within Nazi concentration camps during World War II, the Tuskegee experiments probably were not the product of depraved minds. They were methodologically sound from a purely research standpoint. They were designed to gather data that would be accurate and would have the potential to benefit humanity. But perhaps in a more subtle way, those who conducted them now appear no less insensitive in their lack of regard for the protection of research participants than the medical "researchers" of Dachau or Auschwitz. Prior to the availability of penicillin, there may have been a legitimate reason to study syphilis to learn more about the course of an essentially incurable disease. But when the drug became available, there was no logical justification to continue the research, and there was a very good ethical reason to discontinue it immediately. Later, some of the researchers rationalized that the participants were fortunate in that they were given free regular medical examinations and did not have to pay for their burial expenses. Not until 1997 did the U.S. government offer a public apology for their treatment, and they were awarded limited financial compensation for their suffering.

The Milgram Studies of Obedience to Authority

During the 1960s, Stanley Milgram conducted a series of ingeniously designed studies that sought to learn more about the phenomenon of human obedience to authority figures.[3] His research evolved in part from the defenses of Nazi war criminals who contended that they were just following orders and therefore could not be held responsible for their actions. (Similar defenses were subsequently used by American soldiers in Vietnam and by many others in military conflicts in Bosnia and Iraq, where atrocities were committed.) Milgram hoped to learn what ordinary, civilized people are likely to do when ordered by a more powerful individual to do something that they would otherwise never do. He hoped to learn how far they would go in their obedience to authority figures.

The research used adult males as participants. They were told that they would participate in research on learning and they would be assigned a partner for the research. (In fact, the partner was working with the researcher; he was not another research participant.) Through the use of a rigged drawing, the true participants always drew the role of the person assigned to reinforce learning through the administration of what they believed to be painful electric shocks to their research partner. Sitting in a room where they could hear but not see the other individual, the alleged learner who was supposed to be wired to receive the electrical shocks, participants read off pairs of words and asked their partner to match them. When the learner made a mistake, the participant was told to throw a switch placed in front of him to shock the errant learner. The switches were labeled with phrases such as "Extreme-intensity shock" and "Danger—severe shock." As more mistakes were made, the participant was told to throw switches suggesting increasingly severe electrical shocks. As the higher and higher voltage switches were thrown, the learner began to beg for the experiment to end. When the switches continued to be thrown, he began to kick the wall and to scream. Finally, as the highest voltage switches were thrown, the learner became silent, indicating that he might have lapsed into unconsciousness or perhaps died.

Many participants became very emotionally upset by what they were doing and asked and even begged to be allowed to stop. However, most did not stop when ordered to continue. Only a small number of the participants refused to complete the experiment; nearly two-thirds continued to throw the switches as ordered, despite the fact that they had reason to believe that they might be administering disabling, if not fatal, shocks to other human beings.

Of course, as was later explained to the research participants, they only *thought* that they were causing pain to the other individual; no electrical shock was ever administered. They were told that their partners were only "acting" to their throwing the switches. So why did some researchers and even the general public (subsequent to the showing of a made-for-TV movie on the research) object so strenuously to Milgram's methods? How did the Milgram studies come to be almost synonymous with unethical treatment of research participants? For one thing, people questioned whether the physical discomfort and anguish experienced by the research participants could be justified in light of the knowledge acquired through the research (unnecessary pain and suffering). They experienced a great amount of stress. Critics asked if another method could not have been used to get the same results without causing so much duress for the participants. But this question had already been asked about earlier research, for example, the Tuskegee studies.

A second ethical issue raised by the Milgram research was a relatively new one. As a result of it, people began to ask if some research should not take place because its effects on participants could not be undone. Had permanent harm been done to the research participants in the Milgram research? Apparently so. As a result of participating in the research, many of the men tended to view themselves in a different way than they had before. They now knew that, under the right circumstances, they were capable of doing severe physical harm to another person who represented no threat whatsoever to them. As we might anticipate, this was a disturbing revelation. No amount of debriefing to assure them that they had harmed no one while following orders could undo its effects.

The Milgram research helped us to formulate an ethical question: Does the researcher ever have a right to leave research participants in worse physical or emotional condition than that in which they were found? A consensus emerged that such a consequence is not justified if the researcher should have been able to anticipate it. Certainly this had been the case in the Milgram research.

The Laud Humphreys Studies of Homosexual Behavior

Laud Humphreys' studies of homosexual behavior in public restrooms[4] sound quite dated today, but they were an important milestone in the development of ethical standards for the treatment of research participants. They also remain one of the most controversial research efforts in the human science professional literature. They have been defended and touted by some people as innovative, while being denounced by others as simply unethical snooping.

The special focus of Humphreys' research was casual homosexual sex acts between strangers who led otherwise heterosexual lives. He conducted observations of homosexual encounters between men in parks. Humphreys knew that the people he wished to study would be unlikely to agree to let him observe their behavior for research purposes. Even if they did, the data thus obtained would be of questionable value. So he engaged in a series of deceptions. He first gained the confidence of his intended research participants. He frequented the public restrooms and implied through his regular presence that he shared in their activities. He began to assume the role of watch queen, which entailed being a lookout for the police or other potentially threatening people. The payoff for being a watch queen was the opportunity to watch sexual acts being performed—exactly what he needed for his research. But the deception did not end there.

Because he believed that he needed to know more about his research participants, especially about their public lives, Humphreys conducted follow-up interviews. When possible, he recorded the license plate numbers of his participants and obtained their addresses through access to police records. Disguising himself so that he would not be recognized as their watch queen, he interviewed them under the pretense of conducting a survey and obtained additional descriptive data.

Many ethical questions were raised by the Humphreys study. Some of them continue to be debated. Had he violated the participants' right to privacy? Had their participation in the research really been voluntary? They had granted permission for the researcher to watch, but he had misrepresented his real purpose for being there. Was there really any other way that he could have obtained the same knowledge without this elaborate deception? If he had informed the men of his real purpose, would he have been able to acquire accurate knowledge? How much would he have had to tell them about his research in order for them to be true voluntary participants? Some defenders of the research study contend that his deception caused no one any harm. After all, he conscientiously concealed the identities of his participants in his book that described the research.

The way in which Humphreys learned the identities of his participants and conducted his follow-up interviews was especially infuriating to some of his critics. They charged that the men's permission to be interviewed in their homes was not valid because he had been dishonest about the real reasons why he wished to interview them. He misrepresented both the real focus and the scope of his research. He also risked someone making a connection between his survey in their homes and the activities that went on in the public restrooms. Although highly unlikely, a research participant's secret behavior could have come to light as a result of his pursuing them for a follow-up interview at home.

Today's Standards for Protection of Research Participants

Fortunately, today we need not operate in a vacuum in wrestling with ethical issues. As a result of public responses to abuse of research participants in earlier research studies such as those we have just described, there now exists a list of generally agreed-on standards that govern the conduct of research.

In research that uses human beings as participants, ethical standards have been developed. Many organizations now require review and approval of proposed research studies by a team of researchers and other concerned individuals. These groups are labeled an *Institutional Review Board* (IRB), a human subjects review team, ethics committee, or some similar title. The members carefully review proposals for research to ensure that the rights of participants will not be threatened or violated and that protection measures are in place. Until the review team is convinced that this is the case, the research is not allowed to be initiated. They apply several interrelated standards.

Voluntary Informed Consent

We already know what is meant by the word *voluntary*. It refers to "by choice, not because of coercion or intimidation or because of promises of rewards." As we will discuss later in this chapter, it is often difficult to determine if this condition is present. When used in the context of research, *informed* relates to the question: Will the potential participants know what they need to know (at least in general terms) in order to determine if they wish to participate in the research? Prior to agreeing to participate, a person should have a fairly clear idea of what that participation will entail. This is designed to protect participants from unknowingly getting themselves into a situation that they never would have chosen had they been more fully informed from the outset. It also limits the researcher's ability to deceive research participants by grossly misrepresenting the purposes of their research or the nature and limits of the demands that will be made on research participants.

BOX 2.1   Research Participation Request and an Informed Consent Form

Dear Mr. or Ms.,

During October and November of 2008, students from the University of XYZ, School of Social Work, will be conducting a study to learn more about how support groups may be helpful to women who are HIV positive. Specifically, the study will identify the characteristics of these groups that have been found to be most helpful over time, as described by the group facilitators.

You have been selected to participate in this study because you facilitate such a support group in our state. Your participation would require that you complete a brief survey instrument that will be mailed to you, and also participate in a follow-up phone interview with a student researcher. Some biographic and demographic information about you (gender, age, religious affiliation, academic preparation and work experience) will also be gathered. Any data that you provide would only be published or made public in the aggregate form.

BOX 2.1   continued

Participation in this study is completely voluntary. Those who elect to take part in it may discontinue their participation at any time without prejudice, or loss of benefits of any sort.

I hope you will agree to participate in this research. It has the potential to provide valuable knowledge to those in the helping professions who work closely with this population. If you agree to participate, please sign and date two copies of the attached consent form, keeping one copy for your records, and mail the other one back to me in the postage paid envelope. After we receive your signed consent form, you will be contacted by a student to confirm a mailing address where we may send your survey form.

If you have any questions about the study, please contact me at 806-555-1234, or e-mail address: acharles@hotnet.com. Thank you.

Sincerely,

Alfred B. Charles

Professor, School of Social Work
Att.: Informed Consent Form

Informed Consent Form

I agree to participate voluntarily in a study from the University of XYZ, School of Social Work, examining support groups for women who are HIV positive. I understand that my participation in this study involves completing a survey form and participating in a phone interview with a social work research student. I may withdraw my participation in this study at any time without any prejudice or penalties of any sort.

Signature:

Printed Name:

Date:

Consent refers to the fact that there is a clear, generally written, agreement to participate. A consent form, signed by the participant, provides a potential research participant with a description of what to expect. It also provides legal protection for the researcher, who may later need proof that participants willingly took part in the research. This principle is very consistent with the social work practice value of self-determination, which upholds an individual's right to make decisions about matters that affect his or her life and well-being. Box 2.1 is an example of two forms that could be used to acquire the voluntary informed consent of potential research participants. Note that it allows a participant to withdraw from the research at any time if he or she no longer wishes to participate for any reason.

In obtaining voluntary informed consent, special care needs to be taken in obtaining consent from persons who are from groups that are linguistically or culturally different from the majority population. Consent forms should be provided in the research respondent's native language, and clarifying comments and responses to questions about participation in the research should be addressed in the language most familiar to the respondent. This may require using bilingual or native-speaking research assistants to help obtain voluntary informed consent.

Researchers also need to be sensitive to culturally determined patterns of deference to authority, which may cause respondents to feel that they cannot or do not have the right to refuse participation in the study. This may be a relevant issue when the researcher is from a dominant group and the respondent is from a historically less powerful group where there is a shared history. The issue may also exist in cultures that emphasize deference to age or social status, as in some Asian cultures. If a researcher is unfamiliar with the culture of the target population in a cross-cultural research situation, someone familiar with the culture should be consulted regarding issues in obtaining voluntary informed consent and protection of human participants within the specific cultural context.

When cultural differences between researchers and participants exist, people who volunteer to participate in research may also not be doing so voluntarily. A perception of a power differential or an emphasis on deference to people with more social status or educational credentials within the participants' culture may have led participants to believe that they had little choice but to volunteer. Or they may simply not have understood the subtleties of the wording in a consent form that they were asked to sign.

The principle of voluntary informed consent also recognizes that some vulnerable people—for example, very young children or people with a mental disability—may not be able to understand a description of their proposed participation in research and to make an informed decision as to whether they wish to participate. In research that proposes to use people who may be considered incapable of giving voluntary informed consent, another responsible person may serve as an *advocate* to protect them and to decide for them what should be permitted in the interest of scientific knowledge building. A social worker or other helping professional is a logical choice to assume the advocate role.

Children, as they get older, should be allowed a greater role in deciding if they wish to participate in research. This is the ethical principle of *assent,* which also is an important concern in the medical treatment of children.[5] It entails involving older children in decision making to the extent possible, based upon their developing capacity for rational thinking and their need for autonomy. The ultimate decision should result from an interactive process between the researcher, the child or adolescent, and the advocate.

Even when advocates are used, they cannot be expected to make good decisions for others or, in the case of older children, with their assent unless they have adequate descriptions of proposed research methods. Another study that was conducted by researchers from Harvard University and the Massachusetts Institute of Technology from 1946 to

1956 was referred to as the "Fernald Science Club." It was conducted at the Fernald, Massachusetts State School. Dozens of teenage boys with developmental disabilities were fed radioactive food to study its possible effects. Parents had been asked to sign consent forms for their sons to participate in the research. However, the description on the form made no mention of radiation.[6]

No Unnecessary Pain and Suffering

Medical research and many research studies that social workers conduct have the potential to cause pain and suffering. In social work research, the pain is more likely to be emotional than physical, although physical discomfort (symptoms of emotional distress) may occur as well. For example, studies that entail interviewing adult victims of child abuse are likely to require research participants to think about and react to events that they would prefer to repress. This can be very painful (or it may provide a healthy catharsis if the interviewer is sensitive and uses his or her social work skills appropriately).

It is impossible to know all of the potential risks to participants that proposed research poses. By definition, science always works in areas of inquiry where cause–effect knowledge is fragmentary, if not totally absent. However, the realities of science do not absolve the ethical researcher from protecting participants from *unnecessary* risk. Certain questions are appropriate. Can the knowledge be derived in a way that has less potential to cause physical or emotional harm to the participant? Have protections been built into the research design that will minimize the risk of causing pain and suffering? If the research absolutely must cause some physical or emotional discomfort, will its severity and duration be the absolute minimum that is necessary to acquire data?

One study conducted by the University of California at Los Angeles during the 1980s and 1990s illustrates the difficulty of balancing the need for knowledge and the principle of no unnecessary pain and suffering. It also shows how this principle can be related to the principle that we discussed earlier: voluntary informed consent. The researchers were attempting to learn if some people were unnecessarily taking antipsychotic drugs that may produce involuntary tremors. Fifty young patients being treated for schizophrenia had their medication abruptly discontinued. Of these fifty participants, twenty-three experienced severe relapses (including one suicide). Although their parents had signed consent forms for their children, they alleged that they were never told how severe the relapses might be or that it would be safer if the medication were continued.[7]

The UCLA research was designed with good intentions. It sought to acquire knowledge that might help to alleviate a problem experienced by schizophrenic patients—unnecessary medication and its side effects. But in attempting to address the problem, some of the patients were harmed. Many ethical questions can be raised. Did the ends justify the means? Was the pain and suffering experienced by some of the participants in the research (and their families) necessary? Wasn't there another way besides stopping their medication (perhaps by gradually reducing it) to learn if the medication was necessary, while causing the patients less pain and suffering?

An important subissue that relates to pain and suffering is the presence of any negative aftereffects that people might experience from their roles as research participants. (Remember, this was a major issue in the Milgram studies.) A researcher is ethically obligated to leave research participants as they were found, or at least in no worse condition.

In recognition of the fact that virtually all research involving human participants has the potential to harm or change people in some way, human subject review teams generally pay careful attention to a researcher's plans for debriefing and restoration of participants after data have been collected. They may wish to ensure that, for example, counseling or other indicated follow-up will be provided, if needed.

Anonymity/Confidentiality

As social workers, we need not be reminded of the importance of safeguarding the privacy and identity of our clients. The ethical principles of anonymity and confidentiality exist to safeguard research participants from the harm that can come to them if their identities are intentionally or inadvertently associated with any data that are collected. The two terms are used in research much as they are used in other areas of social work practice. The ideal condition under which participants provide data is *anonymity*. When it exists, even the researcher does not know the participants' names and cannot attribute to them any data that were provided. An example of anonymity might be a mailed questionnaire survey that does not use case numbers or other identification on the questionnaire or on the return envelope. The researcher cannot know who returned one and who did not or who said what in their replies. This protects the participants' anonymity, but it can have real logistical disadvantages for researchers. For example, what if researchers wish to send a follow-up questionnaire to those who did not respond or to acquire clarification about some data provided by those who did not respond?

A more realistic and generally acceptable alternative involves protection of confidentiality. Especially when data are collected by in-person interviews, researchers are likely to know and recall who revealed what about themselves. However, under principles of *confidentiality,* the researcher is ethically obligated not to reveal the participants' identities or to in any way let others be able to associate any of the data provided with any one participant. Upholding confidentiality may require careful editing of the data to remove any identifying information before disseminating its findings. This may require that some potentially valuable data cannot be included, unless it can be aggregated along with that of other participants in some way.

The principle of confidentiality often governs how social workers handle data about their clients. As researchers, it seems familiar and natural to also protect participants from harm. However, people outside the academic and practice communities may attempt to get a researcher to compromise the principle. What if, for example, a research report reveals that a participant is guilty of a crime such as fraud or has threatened the well-being of others? Does the public have the right to know the identity of that participant and to take appropriate legal action? It is a good idea to check out relevant laws and statutes when such issues arise or, better yet, before they do.

In the role of researchers, social workers may not enjoy the protection of privileged communication, as this varies from state to state. Research data can and have been subpoenaed and will continue to be subject to public scrutiny. For this reason, some researchers have chosen to destroy the names and other identifiable data from files about their research participants once the data have been coded and case numbers assigned.

For some actions that we may learn about in the process of conducting research (such as child abuse), we may have no options. We have an ethical (and a legal) obligation to notify the proper authorities that transcends the role of researcher. However, the appropriate course of action is not always that clear. Researchers who conduct research on illicit behaviors, such as substance abuse or unsafe sexual practices among adolescents, often face an ethical dilemma.[8] Should they respect the confidentiality of research participants who share knowledge of their behaviors or share it with parents or other helping professionals, since such behaviors are putting the participants "at risk"? What is the researcher's primary responsibility to his or her participants—to protect confidentiality or to protect their health and welfare? Is the risk to participants less important than the knowledge that can be acquired (that can potentially help others in a similar situation) by promising and adhering to promises of confidentiality? Such issues are not easily resolved. Whatever decisions are made, they can leave the researcher feeling a little "uneasy."

Need to Conduct the Research

Although sometimes not mentioned specifically among the criteria by which review panels evaluate a research proposal, there is a fourth ethical concern that should always be considered. Even if the proposed research represents no physical or emotional threat to them, research participants have a right to assume that whatever demands are made on them (for example, their time or other costs) are necessary for the advancement of knowledge. Ethically, research cannot be justified that merely provides a research learning experience for the researcher, that does not promise to significantly advance knowledge, or that might provide knowledge that simply is not worth knowing. Thus, IRBs may question whether some proposed research is justifiable, given the nature of the products that it promises to yield. It may represent an unnecessary imposition on its participants.

Sometimes research may not be approved because it seems designed only to advance some political or economic agenda. The issue of conducting research for purposes other than the advancement of knowledge came to the fore during the late 1980s as a result of the activities of people active in the antivivisection movement. A frequent argument against the use of animals for experimentation by the American cosmetics industry was that research on chimpanzees, rabbits, guinea pigs, dogs, and other laboratory animals was not conducted to learn anything new. Its primary purpose was to provide legal protection for manufacturers against charges that products had not undergone sufficient testing prior to their release in the market.

Is there a danger that social work researchers might conduct unnecessary research for purposes other than the advancement of knowledge? Yes. Even ethical researchers may inadvertently conduct unnecessary research. Perhaps they do not conduct a thorough review of the literature to determine what knowledge is already available. Thus, they repeat the work of others and waste the time and energies of their research participants, as well as their own.

Research may also be conducted for purely educational purposes, that is, to give social workers supervised practice in conducting research. This can occur within colleges and universities, and even within human service organizations. Deriving new knowledge may not be a high priority—the same research questions may be studied year after year, and nothing productive is ever done with the data thus acquired.

What is wrong with this practice? Learning to conduct research by actually designing and implementing it can be a very effective way to become a good researcher. However, conducting research over and over on research questions whose answers are already available is ethically questionable, even if it does not represent a major imposition for research participants. It is a waste of scarce research resources and, what's more, it does not "model" good research. With a little extra effort, new questions (those begging answers) can always be found.

Concern over the ethics of unnecessary research is recognition that scientific inquiry involving human participants almost always represents an unequal trade. It offers less to participants in the research than it takes from them. This "bad deal" can be justified only if some greater good can come out of the research, specifically, the advancement of knowledge that can help others.

Contemporary Issues Related to Research "Volunteers"

By the latter part of the twentieth century, the standards for ethical protection of research participants had been developed. They have changed little since then. However, ethical issues are still with us and always will be. One important question centers on the standard of "voluntary informed consent." Some people choose to become research participants, even if the research might result in some discomfort or suffering. Yet, we know that there is something about their situation in that, "if conditions were different," they probably would choose not to participate. Ethically, can they be considered "volunteers"?

What are some of the situations that cause us to question whether it is ethical to allow some people to participate in research, even when they wish to do it? Perhaps they have little to lose (they may have a terminal illness and wish to make some contribution to knowledge before they die). Or some people find themselves in a situation (they may be homeless and/or struggling financially) where even small rewards for research participation (a few dollars, a meal, or the opportunity to get out of the heat or the cold) can provide a strong incentive to become research participants. Similarly, prisoners within correctional settings may volunteer to participate in research studies. However, we must ask, would they agree to be research participants if they were not incarcerated? Can we be absolutely certain that they are not being coerced by something or someone, or influenced by some implied promise of reward, such as more privileges or time off their sentences? How can we know if they are agreeing to do something that they would not do under other circumstances? And, what if they are? Is it not their right to do so?

There is a similar ethical issue in research that involves new or experimental drugs or other interventions. For example, efforts to find a cure for or to delay the course of AIDS or other serious illnesses such as cancer, Parkinson's syndrome or Alzheimer's disease have resulted in the experimental use of many unproven drugs. Some of them have painful and even potentially lethal side effects. Yet many people have willingly agreed to become research participants in medical research designed to test the efficacy of various medications and treatment regimens. Their "willing" participation, perhaps as a result of desperation or an inability to afford more proven medication (the cost is usually borne by the researchers), has caused us to ask a number of questions. Would they undergo the risks and discomfort if they had any alternative? Are researchers who conduct the research taking unfair advantage of their unfortunate situations? Or are they merely trying to make something good happen? Similarly, people who have been convicted of the crime of pedophilia have agreed to undergo aversive therapy to attempt to cure a problem that many currently regard as incurable. Has their desperation (and, perhaps some pressure from prison authorities) caused them to undergo the considerable physical discomfort that they would otherwise have not selected? Probably. Is that necessarily unethical?

There are many other groups that are vulnerable to their unethical use as research participants. Their rights must be protected. However, that entails a difficult balancing act between (1) their right to not be exploited as a result of their vulnerability, and (2) their right to participate in research that may be of benefit to them. Sieber[9] has listed different categories of people who are vulnerable. They include:

People who lack resources or autonomy.
People who are stigmatized by society.
People who are in a weakened position, perhaps in an institutional setting.
People who cannot speak for themselves and their best interests.
People whose illegal activities might become known to law enforcement authorities.
People associated with research participants who may be damaged by data revealed by the participants.

Medical research provides some of the clearest and most dramatic examples of ethical issues relating to the vulnerability of research participants who might "volunteer" to become research participants. However, these issues are just as prevalent in social work research. Naturally, most of our research focuses on people and the problems that they experience. While these problems are not always life-threatening, they can be serious obstacles to life quality. People (often current or prospective clients) may "volunteer" to participate in a study of some new method of intervention or one designed to evaluate the merit or value of some social program. Perhaps (to complicate matters further), the intervention being tested is offered at no cost to them, while the "usual" intervention is only offered for a fee. Is the research exploiting their vulnerability, and thus unethical? This is not an easy question to answer.

Is it ever ethical to use our own clients or former clients as research participants? Or what about a colleague's clients, where the colleague serves as what researchers refer to as a *broker,* a person who asks if they would be willing to participate in our research? Either group may readily agree to volunteer to participate in our research. Or, what about the use of potential research participants who are not our clients but who share a problem or condition with us who we may have met through a support group or in even a social situation? Would any of these individuals be considered volunteers in the purest sense of the word? We might ask: Would they agree to serve as research participants if a previous relationship between us and them did not already exist? Can we be certain that obligation, gratitude, or even fear of offending us is not influencing their decision?

What we have just described can be referred to as *dual-role relationships.* They are especially difficult for social work researchers seeking to conduct research in an ethical way. When researchers have a preexisting relationship with potential participants, it is sometimes very difficult to know if their agreement to provide research data makes them volunteer participants in the strictest sense and, if it doesn't, whether research can still be conducted without a violation of research ethics.

The presence of a dual-role relationship has often prevented good research from being conducted. However, IRB boards have sometimes approved some research studies despite the presence of a dual role relationship. Why? This occurs most frequently when access to data would not have been possible had there not been a preexisting relationship with the participants. Anyone else attempting the same research would have had much greater difficulty in establishing trust and may not have been able to get potential participants even to agree to participate. For example, one social work researcher was allowed to conduct in-depth interviews with parents who had lost an adult child to AIDS to better understand how different people cope with such a loss. She had gotten to know her research participants while providing social work services to their sons or daughters.[10] Another researcher interviewed children whose parent had suffered a massive traumatic head injury and had survived, but at a much lower level of functioning. She had experienced the problem in her own family and was able to locate her participants because she was a member of an organization that consisted of persons in similar circumstances.[11]

Were the research participants in these two studies truly "voluntary"? Probably not. The IRB board members who approved them also acknowledged that the interviews with participants were likely to be stressful for them. However, no one was likely to be seriously harmed. In fact, the researchers later concluded, it was probably psychologically beneficial to the participants to express some of their feelings about their losses to a caring professional who they already trusted. The fact that the potential benefits of the research for others in similar situations probably outweighed any discomfort to participants was another factor in the decision by IRB members to allow the studies to be conducted.

When dual-role relationships exist, certain special precautions are required to protect research participants. Special effort must be made to assure potential participants that they will suffer no loss or disadvantage (including the respect of the researcher) if they decide not to participate. The preexisting relationship should also not be damaged in any way. A third, neutral person (not the researcher) should be provided to offer counseling, if needed, and to help at any time in deciding whether or not it is in the potential participant's best interest to continue participation. Finally, if feasible, participation should be anonymous, so the researcher cannot know exactly who participated and who did not. Of course, in studies where the researchers themselves must gather data using in-person interviews with participants who they already know in another relationship (such as the two examples previously described), anonymous participation is impossible.

There is still another issue related to voluntary informed consent that social workers sometimes encounter when they attempt to conduct research. Because of the nature of our work and the trust often placed in us by clients, we may have access to very sensitive or private data not readily available to outside researchers. Clients often tend to become quite candid in what they say and do around social workers because they trust that the social worker is concerned primarily with helping them to solve their problems. Thus they tell us much about themselves.

Should data (in the form of case records) which were gathered for the purpose of providing assistance to clients ethically be used for another purpose for which they never were intended—research? Do clients and patients really give voluntary consent to be research participants? Sometimes, but not usually. Recent federal legislation, the 1996 Hospital Insurance Portability and Accountability Act (HIPAA), has made access to medical records data difficult, if not impossible, to use for research in many medical and psychiatric settings. However, in some settings, such as teaching hospitals, patients can still agree from the outset that data collected relative to their treatment can be used for research and teaching purposes. Even in other settings, records data sometimes are still used for research if clients or patients agree to their use. However, is this really voluntary informed consent, since it could be argued that consent may be granted under some duress? Undoubtedly, some participants want to provide information that might help others with the same problem. However, others may fear that not agreeing to participate may antagonize their social worker and thus affect their treatment

Other Contemporary Issues Relating to Protection of Research Participants

The social work researcher is perhaps less likely than researchers in some other disciplines to participate in research that will result in irreparable psychological damage to participants. We are sensitized to recognize the ways in which life experiences can negatively affect people's self-esteem or their ability to function. For example, we would not participate in or condone research that would involve telling our clients that we think they should get out of a healthy marriage in order to study their emotional responses, or lying to medical patients by telling them they had a fatal disease in order to observe what changes they might make in their lives. We know the potentially negative consequences of any behavior designed to alter how we think of ourselves or of others. Our training in human sensitivity combined with our professional values, precludes most research that could negatively and permanently alter the self-concept or mental or emotional health of our clients or others. However, does that mean that all research designs that entail deception of any kind are unethical? Not necessarily.

In some instances, deception may be necessary to study behavior or emotional responses that would be easily influenced if (1) a complete understanding of the intent of the researcher were known, and (2) the deception is a relatively harmless one. But unnecessary deception can be an unnecessary and dangerous shortcut. It sometimes has been used when other, less potentially harmful methods such as simulations or certain other methods would have been equally effective. Before we even consider using deception, the ethical researcher would ask: Is deception absolutely the only way that I can get the knowledge that I need? And if so, what will I do to be certain that I will not leave my research participants in worse physical or emotional condition than when the research began?

Another old ethical dilemma is still with us, and probably always will be. It is most often discussed in relation to recent medical research, but is equally relevant for many forms of social work research. It relates to whether it is ever ethical to deny some research participants access to an intervention method that may prove helpful for them. For example, what is the best way to examine the effectiveness of one of the many experimental drugs being developed for the treatment of persons who are HIV positive or have other serious or life-threatening illnesses? Or, how do we learn most definitively if a social program is really effective? Traditionally, the most rigorous research designs have used a control group (Chapter 6), a group of people that is identified as having some problem but who are merely followed and not offered the intervention. In medical research, members of the control group might instead be given a placebo (such as a sugar pill), but they would not know whether they were receiving the experimental drug. The use of a control group may be methodologically sound, but is it ethically defensible? Either method might generate more precise and more definitive findings than another research design that would simply provide the intervention to all participants and then monitor the course of their illness. But what about the people in the control groups? What if the intervention is subsequently found to be effective? Their quality of life might have been higher or their lives even saved if they had received the intervention that they were denied. While as we shall see (Chapter 6), there are alternatives that are "almost as good" as designs that use a true control group, researchers would prefer to use one that has the potential to provide the best answers.

The notorious Tuskegee experiments are sometimes still mentioned in criticisms of other research, especially in those studies that rely on research participants that we described earlier in this chapter as "vulnerable." For example, research in Third World countries has attempted to determine if infected mothers in a control group who were given a placebo or low dosages of drugs known to be effective for delaying the onset of HIV symptoms (which often are very expensive) had a comparable or higher rate of passing the disease on to their babies than those given the full dosage of the drug. Critics have questioned whether such research, like the Tuskegee experiments, is unethical and exploitive of participants, in part because it would not be permitted among less vulnerable people.[12] Similar ethical issues would (and should) be discussed if social workers were to, for example, deny services or provide reduced services to control groups of research participants drawn from some of the vulnerable populations that we serve.

The pressure to find a way to prevent serious chronic illnesses or to find a cure for them has spotlighted other common research ethical issues that are relevant to social work research as well. One of these might be described as "the right to be a research participant." For example, what about society's responsibility to people who are denied access to experimental drugs that might save their lives or at least delay the onset of symptoms for diseases like Alzheimer's? They are not available to many who might benefit from them because they have not yet been cleared for use in the United States by the Food and Drug Administration. Most likely, some of these drugs remain in a warehouse awaiting further research into their possible negative side effects. Should the usual seven- to ten-year testing process be waived based on the urgency of the situation? Similarly, how many studies of a program designed to prevent adolescents from experimenting with methamphetamines should we require before we include the program as part of our "best practices" and seek funding for its widespread use? If one well designed program evaluation concludes that it is highly effective, should that be enough for us to factor the results into our decision making (EBP)? Do we need two such studies? More? These issues, like all ethical issues, are not easily resolved.

Other Ethical Obligations of Researchers

The ethical positions adopted by the National Association of Social Workers provide guidelines for both professional practice and research. They limit one's behavior with clients and with research participants. In its Code of Ethics,[13] it is evident that the unethical use of human participants for knowledge building is never condoned. However, the Code of Ethics and our professional literature suggest that the researcher has ethical obligations not only to the participants but also to the sponsors of research, other researchers, colleagues, and the general public. Most obligations relate to broad issues, such as the scientific integrity of researchers, the requirement that they adhere to certain standards in conducting research, and that they honestly report and interpret findings.

What do these position statements tell us about the general characteristics of ethical researchers? For one thing, they recognize the potential of research findings to influence the work and lives of others, and they recognize the seriousness of scientific inquiry. They are aware that any research finding, no matter how unexpected or contrary to what they believe to be true, is potentially valuable and that any misrepresentation of what they learned is potentially dangerous because, in an era of EBP, we rely more heavily than ever on research findings for our decision making. Thus, they honestly report null findings[14] (findings that, for example, demonstrate the ineffectiveness of a social program or the failure of some other type of intervention) along with those that find support for beliefs of intervention effectiveness. They place truth above the personal gain that can be attained through the manipulation of data to achieve desired results.

Ethical researchers function with neutrality and, to the degree possible, objectivity. They strive to keep an open mind in order to let empirical knowledge, not their own preferences, form the basis for any conclusions drawn from their research. When this is not totally possible (as it generally isn't), they candidly describe the amount and types of bias that they may have introduced.

Ethical researchers resist outside influences, such as political or economic pressures that might influence either the results of the research or its dissemination. Although they give proper credit to funding organizations that provided support for their research, they do not allow these organizations to distort or suppress their findings.

Ethical researchers do not have too strong a personal investment in their findings. They are aware of the tentative nature of scientific knowledge and remain open to reinterpretation and even contradiction of them. They do not claim to have more definitive answers to research questions than are justifiable based on their findings. They value confrontation and debate with their fellow researchers. They take responsibility for their research methods and findings, and they welcome legitimate critique.

Ethical researchers never attempt to take credit for work that they did not perform and always share the credit for collaborative efforts. They openly acknowledge the support and contributions of others to their research. They insist that appropriate credit be given to students and/or research assistants and consultants who contributed to the research effort. They will not allow their own names to appear as coresearchers on efforts where their own contributions were only minimal or as the primary researcher when others did most of the work.

While recognizing the importance of building knowledge to promote better client services, ethical social work researchers resist any use of research that appears to represent a breach of professional ethics. Their activities are shaped by both research ethical standards and by their professional ethics as social workers. They are social workers first, then researchers. When using clients as research participants, they acknowledge that their clients' best interests must take precedence over knowledge building. They will not allow confidentiality to be violated without permission, even if it requires them to suppress potentially valuable findings. They discontinue any research if it begins to threaten their participants' welfare.

Ethical researchers are also concerned about the ways that research findings are disseminated and used; they want the findings of research to help rather than to degrade or contribute to the harassment of those whom they serve as professionals. They will attempt to halt the use of their research data by others when it is taken out of context to embarrass others, to support erroneous stereotypes, or to otherwise create or contribute to a false public impression about them. They may insist that their findings be presented only in their entirety. Or they may seek to discredit interpretations of their research findings that they perceive to be most self-serving or that otherwise misrepresent them.

Much of what we have been describing falls under the heading of research integrity. It was discussed at a symposium devoted to the responsible conduct of research at CSWE's annual program meeting in Chicago in 2006. Subsequently, a subgroup of those in attendance began to meet to develop a statement which would continue and summarize the discussions. The members, with support from CSWE, produced a document, the National Statement on Research Integrity in Social Work,[15] that is an excellent reference for social workers who wish to meet their ethical responsibilities to all parties likely to be impacted by their research efforts. Excerpts are included in Box 2.2.

BOX 2.2   Excerpts from the CSWE National Statement on Research Integrity in Social Work

---

To ensure the responsible conduct of research, social work researchers need to: (1) work to protect the people and communities whom they study; (2) ethically and effectively participate in mentoring relationships that are crucial to scientific activity; (3) manage apparent and implicit conflicts of interest and commitment; (4) collaborate ethically with researchers from other professions and disciplines; (5) ensure that research data issues are managed properly; (6) employ responsible publication and authorship practices; (7) responsibly conduct and contribute to the peer-review process; and (8) understand and prevent research misconduct (ORI, 2006). In the sections below we discuss each of these areas of concern and briefly discuss particular issues facing social work researchers.

1. Human Subjects and Communities

Social work researchers must strive not to harm the people or communities that they are studying. Research protocols should first ensure the protection of study participants, including consideration for the Basic Ethical Principles described in the Belmont Report. *Respect for persons* "incorporates at least two ethical convictions: first, that individuals should be treated as autonomous agents, and second, that persons with diminished autonomy are entitled to protection" (p. 4). *Beneficence* assures that persons are "treated in an ethical manner not only by respecting their decisions and protecting them from harm, but also by making efforts to secure their well-being" (pp. 4–5). *Justice* requires that the "selection of research subjects needs to be scrutinized in order to determine whether some classes (e.g., patients receiving government assistance, vulnerable racial and ethnic minorities, and institutionalized persons) are being systematically selected simply because of their easy availability, their compromised position, or their manipulability, rather than for reasons directly related to the problem being studied" (p. 6) (National Commission for the Protection of Human Subjects of Biomedical and Behavioral Research, 1979).

BOX 2.2   continued

Research involving vulnerable populations needs to assure that risk of harm is minimized and benefits from the research are equitably distributed. While designing protocols to protect vulnerable people and communities can be extremely challenging, total or arbitrary exclusion of vulnerable populations from research is detrimental to the people the profession serves and can sometimes constitute research misconduct. Social work research in developing countries poses additional and specialized ethical problems in human protection that deserve special consideration. Rather than avoiding these difficulties, researchers should work with their colleagues and the appropriate Institutional Review Boards (IRBs) to develop ways to ethically include vulnerable populations in research. Participation in research should be predicated on the potential participant's understanding of the project, including obtaining informed consent. Finally, social work researchers should keep in mind that students involved as research participants are to be afforded the same protections as any other population.

Before beginning any research investigation, researchers should receive all necessary approval from the organizational regulatory bodies. The organizational regulatory bodies, such as the researcher's Institutional Review Board, will provide another layer of protection for the participants and communities in research, by ensuring that pertinent laws and guidelines have been met by the protocol and that the research is ethical. Researchers should consult with colleagues and the Office of Research Integrity/IRB staffs in their institutions and universities if they have questions regarding regulatory bodies.

2. Mentor/Trainee Responsibility

Social work researchers have a responsibility to mentor trainees in a manner that enhances the professional development of the latter and advances the general progress of the profession. Mentoring junior researchers and trainees in social work research serves to instill the mentee with the ethics, techniques, and community of the profession (Vasgird & Hyman-Browne, n.d.). Social work's commitment to advancing the careers of traditionally underrepresented and marginalized groups indicates a special commitment to mentoring trainees who often experience isolation and exaggerated expectations in academic and research settings. Senior researchers and mentors have a special responsibility to act ethically toward junior researchers and trainees by avoiding implicit and explicit exploitation. Mentoring relationships are complex; collaborative agreements that are developed early in the working relationship and that clearly delineate the rights and responsibilities of all parties can be very helpful in ensuring fair and just outcomes.

3. Conflicts of Interest and Commitment

Social work researchers are encouraged to develop relationships with public and private institutions. However, social work researchers should scrutinize their research endeavors and seek to avoid and eliminate any improper conflicts of interest that might result from their activities. These can involve tangible conflicts, such as untoward financial gain, but may also involve other and intangible forms of improper personal enhancement or advancement. Despite institutional pressures to attract high levels of external funding and to lead multiple projects, social work researchers should judiciously commit only to those projects and positions which they can reasonably undertake. The number and complexity of contemporary researchers' roles make this a challenging domain of responsible conduct.

(*continued*)

BOX 2.2   continued

4. Collaborative Science

Contemporary social work research is rarely an individual enterprise. Multidisciplinary and community-based research are often required, especially for significant research investigations. Social work researchers should engage in collaborative enterprises with other professions and disciplines to advance scientific knowledge. These efforts will require special attention and sensitivity to the ethos and cultures of those research partners. Social work researchers also should seek to clarify, and in many cases commit to a written agreement, issues pertaining to data ownership, authorship, project roles, and financial management.

As the growth of translational science continues, social work researchers will increasingly collaborate with communities. It is important that researchers work hard to understand and reasonably respond to local needs and expectations as research projects are designed, implemented, and published. This is especially challenging as social work researchers often collaborate with community members who come from very different backgrounds and have goals that are divergent from the researchers.

5. Data Acquisition, Management, Sharing, and Ownership

The rapid development of exciting technologies for data acquisition, analysis, and sharing create complex ethical challenges for social work researchers. Researchers need to consult and understand the regulations and obligations involved as they conduct research. The federal government and most other sponsors stipulate what these obligations shall be when a researcher is awarded a grant or contract. Universities also have policies and regulations in this domain which create obligations for researchers who are, in effect, agents of these academic institutions. The best strategy is to discuss the particular approaches the researcher will take with sponsors and their academic colleagues early in the life of the research project. It is important that the entire research team understands these issues as well, as they often intersect with more mundane personnel issues, for example, changing jobs or moving to a new institution.

6. Publication Practices and Responsible Authorship

An important part of social work research is the reporting of study results. Publication of research findings should include appropriate attribution of authorship. Authors and co-authors should be determined on the basis of the type and amount of work completed. There can be controversy over who should be included as an author, especially since being identified as an author or first author on a publication can have implications for tenure, funding, and other professional opportunities; beginning discussions of authorship earlier in the research process can reduce confusion. Many universities, departments, peer-reviewed journals, and professional organizations have specific policies outlining the criteria for who qualifies as an "author" for a publication (Eisner, Vasgird, & Hyman-Browne, n.d.).

Social work researchers must never fabricate data or publish data that are known to be fabricated or otherwise compromised in nature or engage in plagiarism. All ideas and phrasing not originating with the author or co-author should be appropriately acknowledged in publication of results. Researchers should respect ethical obligations, regulations, and laws pertaining to intellectual property, copyright, and patents. Complex developments in technologies and regulations regarding data acquisition, management, sharing, and ownership demand special consideration. The emergent quality of these areas requires social work researchers to regularly study pertinent issues, problems, and solutions as they develop.

BOX 2.2   continued

7. Peer Review

Peer review is critical for the advancement of science. Journals and federal- and private-granting organizations are reliant upon reviewers to ensure the quality of their publications and awards. Social work researchers should participate in the peer-review process in a fair, constructive, and rigorous manner. Additionally, peer-review processes should be timely and protect the confidentiality of all participants. Social work researchers should identify all potential conflicts of interest and also strive to subordinate their personal preferences and biases to the higher purposes of advancing the profession, scientific activity, and the public welfare.

8. Research Misconduct

Consequences for engaging in research misconduct are varied but may include ineligibility for future grants, termination of positions, monetary penalties, or other penalties. Findings of research misconduct result in negative publicity for the researcher/research team and for the university. If the university is also implicated in misconduct (e.g., chronic nonresponsiveness of the IRB) sanctions may include the withdrawal of federal authorizations and funding for selected or for all federally-sponsored research. It is also important to note that local or state jurisdictions might impose criminal or civil penalties if such investigations reveal criminal misconduct or tortious behavior. Loss of personal integrity, moral authority, and community trust transcend the particular events associated with misconduct cases by destroying the relationships enjoyed by researchers and the wider community for years. In sum, research misconduct can be extraordinarily costly to all persons and organizations concerned. Consequences extend beyond issues of liability and damage to reputation, to include damage to: (1) relationships with the participating communities; (2) individuals involved in the work; and (3) professional integrity.

Undetected research misconduct can have even graver consequences, including the dissemination of practice technologies, programs, and social policies that have relied on unfounded or distorted scientific work. The result might be the waste of limited social resources, loss of life, or reduced personal well-being for clients and significant harm to the public welfare. Therefore, social work researchers have an obligation to work hard to prevent research misconduct, to report such misconduct when it occurs, and to support colleagues who attempt to do both despite the personal and professional risks involved.

Source: Reprinted with permission from the Council on Social Work Education © 2007. National Statement on Research Integrity in Social Work.

Summary

In this chapter, we examined some of the major ethical issues that social workers address when they conduct research. Past research has helped to produce current ethical standards that are designed as general guidelines to protect the physical and psychological well-being of human research participants. However, as we discussed, there are many situations where even highly ethical researchers and members of IRBs must struggle with their specific meaning and their application.

We also briefly mentioned some of the other major ethical responsibilities that researchers have toward the sponsors of research, other researchers, colleagues, and the general public. They are designed to ensure that, in the process of knowledge building, researchers respect the needs of others who may stand to benefit or lose from their activities.

For Discussion

1. What are ethical issues? How do they differ from laws or rules?
2. Does it matter whether we use the term "research subjects," "research participants," or "research partners" in describing people who provide information about themselves for social work research?
3. What conditions make it difficult to determine if people are truly voluntary research participants? When might it still be justifiable to allow them to participate in social work research?
4. How did the Tuskegee Public Health studies exploit vulnerable people? What current research ethical standard did they violate?
5. What are some examples of research that might help us to learn whether a method of social work intervention is effective but would be considered unethical?
6. What was the most unethical thing that the Milgram studies did to their research participants? Why would simply asking participants what they would do in hypothetical situations probably not have produced the same findings?
7. Why would subsequent research on homosexual behavior make the Humpreys' studies unnecessary today? Was the research justifiable at the time? What current research ethical standard did he violate?
8. Can research that meets the standard of "voluntary informed consent" ever employ deception? How?
9. Undergraduate psychology courses sometimes require that students participate in their professor's research in order to receive credit for the course. Is this ethical? Under what conditions could it be?
10. The findings of research can be used to benefit humanity. How can they also be used to cause harm to others? What can an ethical researcher do to prevent this?

Endnotes

1. Annas, G. (1992). *The Nazi doctors and the Nuremberg Code: Human rights in human experimentation.* New York: Oxford University Press.
2. Jones, J. H. (1982). *Bad blood: The Tuskegee syphilis experiment.* New York: Free Press.
3. Milgram, S. (1963). Behavioral study of obedience. *Journal of Abnormal and Social Psychology, 67,* 371–378.
4. Humphreys, L. (1970). *Tearoom trade: Impersonal sex in public places.* Chicago: Aldine Press.
5. See, for example, Committee on Bioethics (February 1995). Informed consent, Parental permission, and assent in pediatric practice. *Pediatrics, xcv, 2,* 314–317.
6. Associated Press Report (1997, September 18). Experts blast AIDS studies that endanger poor subjects. *The State,* A15.

7. Health and Medicine (1994, March 11). UCLA didn't ask schizophrenic patients' consent for experiment. *New York Times,* B-9–B-10.

8. Delva, J. (2007). The Human Subjects Review Process: A Subjective View. *Social Work, LII, 2,* 101–102.

9. Sieber, J. E. (1992). *Planning ethically responsible research.* Newbury Park, CA: Sage Publications, 147.

10. Taylor, L. (1998). Parents Who Lost an Adult Child to AIDS. *Abenteuer forschung,* A. Godenzi, editor, University of Freiburg, Switzerland: 189–258.

11. Pryce, N. (1995). A heuristic study using an evolutionary perspective of the experience of adolescents adapting to the head injury of a parent. Unpublished dissertation, Columbia, SC: University of South Carolina.

12. Associated Press Report (1993, December 17). Retarded boys given radioactive food in study. *New York Times,* B-16.

13. National Association of Social Workers (1999). Code of Ethics. Washington, D.C.: NASW Press.

14. See, e.g., Pittfalls and Pratfalls: Null and Negative Findings in Evaluating Interventions, C. Hudson & R. Parker (Eds.). *New Directions for Evaluation, 110,* Summer 2006.

15. Council on Social Work Education (2007). National Statement on Research Integrity in Social Work. Alexandria, VA: CSWE Publications.

PART II

THE PLANNING STAGES

3

RESEARCH PROBLEMS
AND QUESTIONS

Research should begin with the identification of a research problem and then move on to selecting research questions that relate to that problem. While this may seem self-evident, we are sometimes tempted to begin conducting research with insufficient articulation of the problem or of the research questions that emanate from it.

In their discussion of research problem selection in social work research, Rubin and Babbie note that "the impetus for selecting a topic should come from decisions that confront social service agencies or the information needed to solve practical problems in social welfare. . . . A study is more likely to have value for the social work field (and to be considered social work research) . . . if the topic is selected because it addresses information needed to guide policy, planning, or practice decisions in social welfare."[1]

Other authors define a research problem as "an intellectual stimulus calling for an answer in the form of a scientific inquiry."[2] Still another author describes research problems as "situations that are characterized by doubt and ignorance and that represent felt difficulties. There is something in the situation that is unknown, and there is a reason for wanting to reduce this doubtfulness."[3] Definitions (and those within other texts) differ slightly, but they also have a considerable amount in common. For one thing, they suggest that a research problem ought to be stated as a declarative, descriptive statement of a condition—never as a question.

What makes all research problems similar, yet different from other kinds of problems? How are social work research problems different from personal problems, social problems, or even research problems in general? A social work research problem is a specific type of problem. It is an undesirable condition attributable (at least in part) to the nonexistence of some potentially useful knowledge. Not only is this knowledge gap felt by social workers, but there is a desire to fill it. For example, for some social work practitioners, a research problem may be the absence of knowledge that is needed in order to know how to effectively influence some pending legislation. Or, for a social work manager, it may be the absence of evidence that a social program is effective that makes the decision about whether or not to continue it more difficult. For the social work educator or trainer, it may be the absence of knowledge that could indicate which methods are most effective for inculcating certain values, or teaching certain skills that students need. Note that the preceding examples describe problems that are felt by individuals, but are not caused by their own deficiencies. The knowledge that they require does not exist. It has not yet been generated.

Why We Begin with Research Problems

When designing and conducting research, it is important to not get ahead of ourselves. In both qualitative and quantitative research, there is a certain logical sequence of events; in both types, articulating a clear problem statement must precede all other tasks. To, for example, begin with a research hypothesis (Chapter 5), begin with a design for conducting the research (Chapters 6–8), begin knowing what data collection instrument (Chapter 11) will be used, or begin with a plan for statistical analysis of data (Chapter 12) is to ask for trouble later. We would inevitably waste time and energy trying to fit a research problem to the hypothesis, the research design, the data collection instrument, or the statistical analysis instead of (correctly) allowing the research problem to help to influence all subsequent decisions about how the research should be conducted. Thus, the research problem that is ultimately selected and specified should set the stage for and heavily influence all later steps in the research process. It should never be the other way around, that is, all or part of a research methodology should not be developed and then a problem specified that is appropriate for it. A properly conducted project is an integrated whole from start to finish.[4] The start should always be research problem identification and specification, with all subsequent activities flowing from and clearly relating to the problem that is selected.

Identifying and then specifying research problems might seem like research tasks that can be easily and quickly accomplished. Unfortunately, this is not always the case. Often we know of research problems that we would like to study, but have difficulty articulating them in a researchable form. This is true primarily because problems, by their very nature, seem to be perceived in different ways by different people. If there were perfect consensus on exactly what they are, why they exist, and what should be done about them, most problems would have ceased to exist a long time ago!

Identifying Potential Research Problems

For the social work practitioner, the identification and specification of a problem is the first stage of intervention. Thus, beginning the research process with a problem would seem to be a pretty natural thing for us to do. However, in social work research, a problem is a little different. It is not a problem of our client or some client system such as a group, organization or community (as it is in other areas of social work practice). A research problem is *our* problem, a problem that *we* experience in our professional practice, specifically a knowledge gap that leaves us unsure about how best to intervene to address a problem of a client or a client system. We sometimes find ourselves thinking, "If only I knew if . . ." or "I wish I had more knowledge about . . ." If the missing knowledge existed, we believe that we would be able to intervene more effectively and with greater likelihood of success. For example:

- A social work therapist might think, "If only I knew how others have experienced this loss and what it meant to them."
- A family counselor might think, "If only I knew if it would promote or decrease candid discussion of the family's problems if I were to include the mother's boyfriend in treatment sessions."
- A social worker running a support group might think, "If only I knew if providing name tags for members will result in better group participation."
- A social work administrator might think, "If only I knew if my staff would appreciate my reviewing some of their correspondence before it goes out or whether they would resent it as 'micro-managing.'"
- A social worker engaged in community organization might think, "If only I knew whether it would be better for me to personally chair a 'get-out the vote' campaign or to attempt to encourage leadership from within the community."

Often, research problems are identified through interaction with others. Sometimes clients tell us about some phenomenon or behavior that is relatively new (at least to us) or that has not been studied for various reasons. It may be something we need to understand better if we are to intervene effectively with certain client groups. For example, as norms and practices continually change, our understanding of youth gangs and how to work with them is often hampered by our inability to understand their behaviors and their importance to their members. A client who describes the behavior can cause us to want to learn more about it (who is most likely to engage in it, how it got started, what police have done to prevent it, and so forth). We may identify one or several areas where knowledge is incomplete or missing altogether—potential research problems.

Other potential research problems sometimes emerge in case supervision. For example, a social worker, seeking assistance, may ask her supervisor a question about some client problem, its incidence, (descriptive knowledge), what is most likely to happen if some intervention is attempted (predictive knowledge), or what intervention will produce the desired results (prescriptive knowledge). The supervisor, being candid, admits that she doesn't know, but that she will try to find out. She reports a week later that the answer to the social worker's question does not appear to be out there within our professional body of knowledge. A potential research problem has just been identified.

Sometimes, just in casual conversation, two or more coworkers may recognize that they share the same sense of frustration because the knowledge seems to be unavailable that would help them to be as effective in their practice as they would like to be. For example, a group of hospice social workers may feel frustrated in being unable to be as helpful to "stressed out" family caregivers as they would like. So they first try to determine if the knowledge needed to assist them is already available. An Internet search and/or a brainstorming session may be used to accomplish this and to better articulate the problem. It is of course possible that, as with all of the previous examples, they will discover that the knowledge they lack is available, and they were just not aware of it.

However, it is also possible that they will conclude that there exists little knowledge about the need for certain types of self-care among caregivers and which type of caregiver support groups have been found to be most effective in addressing them. If so, they may have identified a potential research problem.

Setting Problem Priorities

Not all knowledge gaps that confront the social worker can be regarded as either equally important or equally well suited to social work research. In determining whether we can justify our attention and limited research resources, certain issues and related questions should be addressed.

In the ideal world of unlimited research resources, any knowledge gap that might be hindering social workers' capacity to help others would be a problem suitable for study. But in the real world, certain knowledge gaps must be regarded as higher priorities than others. In addition to other questions related to priorities, we must be prepared to ask the basic question: Among those potential research problems that exist and that are of current concern, which are most in need of a solution?

Identifying a gap in knowledge as a higher or lower research priority can be a complicated process. In addition, it is not a task that comes naturally or comfortably to many social workers. It seems to go against some of our practice values to have to conclude that, although some knowledge gaps are very real and are a source of frustration for some people, they currently do not justify the expenditure of our limited research resources. It is helpful to remember that, in making this determination, we are not saying that potential research problems of lower priority are unimportant or should be ignored by social workers. We also are not saying that we absolutely will not conduct research on them. As in any decision that employs EBP principles, we would combine our knowledge of the problem (for example, who is most affected by it, how severe it is) with such other factors as our practice experience, social work values and ethics and even a little compassion and decide that certain research that by purely objective standards appears to be "low priority" cannot be conducted now.

In attempting to set priorities, we are just acknowledging that in a world of limited research resources, we sometimes must opt to get the greatest possible benefit out of our time and efforts. What sorts of questions can we ask to help us to objectively assess the research priority of a potential research problem? They might include the following:

Is the problem really an important one? Somewhere early in the research process, we need to demonstrate that the research problem selected for study ranks high in priority. This is especially important if a formal proposal must be written and submitted to a potential research sponsor or for review by an IRB (Chapter 2). After the research has been conducted, we also would like to be able to demonstrate to potential critics, as well as to those favorable to their research, that the problem studied was important, more important than others that might have been studied.

The question of what makes one potential research problem more important than another can be complex. It relates to a wide array of factors, such as the scope of the problem, which people are most affected by it, how badly knowledge is needed, and the potential value of the variety of products that can evolve from the research process that it sets in motion. The question also overlaps somewhat with other priority issues we will discuss.

Sometimes, the real importance of a research problem and the research that examined it cannot be fully appreciated until years after the research has been completed. Sometimes, the fact that the findings of research are widely publicized, widely cited, or widely used seems to add importance retroactively to a research study. Sometimes, a study's importance may relate less to its findings than to some other product of the research. For example, a standardized data collection instrument (Chapter 11) that is developed in order to help in understanding a problem and that gains widespread usage in other scientific inquiry may ultimately be considered a research project's greatest contribution to knowledge. It may help to legitimize the researcher's efforts, even if the findings of the original study were of limited value.

It is difficult to assess the ultimate importance of a proposed research problem. How can one envision all possible difficulties that could depreciate the value of the research? Or how can one accurately predict the final judgment of others as to whether the research effort was truly worthwhile? Fortunately, we can use certain guidelines to help us in wrestling with the issue of problem importance. We know that there are certain characteristics of research problems that seem to suggest that they are of higher priority than others. For example, problems may be considered high priority if they: (1) reflect a widely felt and critical knowledge gap; (2) relate to a difficulty that affects many people; (3) have the potential to generate specific recommendations rather than highly abstract knowledge; or, (4) are likely to produce by-products that will benefit other researchers conducting scientific inquiry on a wide variety of topics.

Do we already have enough knowledge about the problem? Some human conditions (for example, many social problems) have been thoroughly studied, often by people other than social workers, through major funding from government agencies or private foundations. Most knowledge gaps have already been filled. For example, we know that poverty and homelessness are social problems in the Western Hemisphere, and we have good data relating to their incidence. That does not mean, however, that some aspect of the problem does not have potential for social work research. Perhaps, we might conduct research to try to gain insight into either the unwillingness of a community's leaders to acknowledge their existence, or the values that may contribute to a reluctance to commit the resources needed to try to alleviate them. Research on either of these problems would be likely to generate new knowledge, knowledge that could be of immediate use to social work practitioners seeking social change strategies that have high potential for success.

Are people in other disciplines better suited to conduct research on the problem? There may be a need for research on a potential research problem, but it might be better to let others conduct it because they have specialized expertise that social workers lack. For example, social workers counseling children diagnosed with Attention Deficit Hyperactivity Disorder (ADHD) could benefit from knowing the long-term physical effects of a child taking certain prescription medications designed to treat it, but professionals with a better background in pharmacology or physiology might be better suited to conduct research on the problem. However, social workers might be the best people to conduct research designed to fill gaps in our knowledge about how use of the medications may affect the need for certain types of parenting behaviors or what patterns can be expected in a child's behavior in the evening hours after their influence on behavior has begun to wear off. Additional knowledge in either of these areas would be helpful to social workers in deciding how to work with children diagnosed with ADHD and with their parents.

What is the potential for utilization of any findings and recommendations that would be generated by the research? Who will care, and what is the likelihood that anyone with the power to use the knowledge that will be acquired will be moved to take recommended action? A study of a potential social work research problem that is not likely to result in needed change is of relatively little value.

The lack of any positive effect from research frequently results from financial and political obstacles to research utilization. People who might be able to use the research findings may lack either the necessary resources or the value commitment necessary to do what research indicates is needed. Sometimes both obstacles are present. For example, a community might have a problem of dangerous apathy among adolescents regarding the possibility of contracting a sexually transmittable disease. A lack of understanding of the apathy (and the lack of knowledge of how best to address it) could be the impetus for good, worthwhile, methodologically sound research that would both identify the source of it and generate recommendations as to how social workers could be effective in heightening adolescent awareness of the dangers involved. But because of certain conditions that are present within the community, research on the problem might be a waste of time. The research might result in recommendations that school social workers provide education on sexuality in the schools or at least run information groups in which the topic of sexually transmitted diseases (and how they are contracted) is discussed. But the probability of implementation of any such recommendations might be very small, even zero. It might already be known that a school board operating with a deficit budget might be unable to find the money to spend to purchase the educational materials needed to successfully offer this service. Or it might already be common knowledge that the powerful fundamentalist minister who chairs the school board would be almost certain to intimidate other board members into blocking what he has already publicly described as "instruction in sinning." Despite the need for research to study the problem, it may have to be regarded as lower priority because of the likelihood that research findings and recommendations would have little hope of utilization.

Am I sufficiently interested in studying the problem? The development of knowledge to benefit social workers and their clients can be an exciting activity. But research is also hard work. Certain necessary tasks can become very tedious at times. Not all potential research problems are of equal interest to us. Even a general interest in a research problem may not be sufficient to carry a researcher through times when necessary but less-than-exciting tasks must be performed. For example, entering research data into a computer collected from hundreds of participants, even when we are curious about the findings of our research, can be pretty boring. If we have no particular interest in what is found, it can be a truly dull job.

Is there a temptation for social workers to choose to study problems about which they have little interest? Unfortunately, yes. Various pressures from supervisors and higher level managers sometimes make it difficult to say no. On other occasions, the lure of grant money can help to convince them that they might be more interested in studying a research problem than they really are.

Conducting research on a problem where there is no real interest is usually a big mistake. It has the potential to affect negatively the quality of the research. It also can have a negative effect on the attitudes of the researcher about future scientific inquiry. All other factors being equal, a problem about which a potential researcher is interested and concerned should have higher priority than one in which the researcher's interest results primarily from political or financial motives.

What logistical obstacles are present? Some potential social work research problems may face major logistical obstacles to their study. It is probably correct to state that any problem can be studied. However, some, by their very nature are so complicated, would require so many resources, or would require so many methodological compromises that it would be virtually impossible to "do the job right." In determining if a problem is researchable on a practical and logistical basis, the following questions are worth asking.

- *Is the problem just too large?* Some problems are so widespread and pervasive that they would be totally unmanageable as the focus for a single research study. However, it might be possible to break off some small piece of the problem for study. For example, to attempt to understand the origin and extent of ageism within North American human service organizations would require a research study of such large scope that most social work researchers would lack the budget and other resources necessary to undertake it. (Research almost invariably ends up costing more than anticipated.) However, social work researchers with limited resources might be able to design research to study some aspect of the phenomenon, for example, what discriminatory methods are used for advertising supervisory job openings in not-for-profit organizations within their own state.
- *Can the needed measurement be accomplished?* As we shall discuss in more detail a little later, good measurement is absolutely essential to sound research. But some things are more easily measured than others. For example, behaviors, generally speaking, are more easily measured than attitudes or values. Although researchers have made great progress in the development of measurement for the latter in recent years, measuring many attitudes that might be of interest to us remains an imprecise art.

Which treatment interventions are effective and which ones are not, something that relates to many potential research problems of interest to social workers, provides special measurement difficulties. The success or failure rate in a job training program can be fairly easily determined by counting how many people who complete the program find and keep related jobs. However, the success or failure rate associated with a particular approach to marriage counseling can be much more difficult to ascertain. Was divorce indicative of success or failure? How are we to interpret the fact that a couple voluntarily terminated counseling? They could have stopped seeing the social worker because most of their difficulties had disappeared, or because they perceived that they were getting no help! Indicators of successful or unsuccessful treatment in such instances are limited to such untrustworthy data as notations in a case record or follow-up phone calls. Thus, any categorization of the success of an intervention as a success or a failure might be little more than a judgment call.

If studying a potential research problem would require the measurement of certain phenomena that seem to defy their measurement, the entire problem may not be regarded as researchable, and no amount of research can provide needed answers. A classic historical example of a nonresearchable problem is the debate that preoccupied some theologians several centuries ago. The problem of not knowing how many angels can dance on the head of a pin was not a candidate for scientific research then, and it would not be now. Some contemporary social work problems—for example, a lack of understanding of why some physicians seem to undervalue the professional education of social workers—may be only slightly more researchable than medieval philosophical questions. Physicians' respect for social workers' education might be so difficult to measure that the problem, if it is indeed a real one, may not be able to be studied. Besides, it may not be a high research priority, given the other criteria that we suggested earlier.

- *Do I have the necessary skills and expertise to conduct research on the problem?* Specialization is characteristic of people who conduct scientific inquiry. Some researchers are especially adept at certain specialized research tasks, such as use of the Internet, interviewing, questionnaire construction, or statistical analysis of data, and less competent to perform other tasks. Although it is possible to learn to do what is required or to hire a consultant to do it, this can represent a very costly use of limited research resources. If studying a research problem would require skill and expertise not currently possessed by a potential researcher—for example, the use of statistical analysis that cannot be contracted out or otherwise accessed—the problem may as well be considered unresearchable. Similarly, if the researcher's knowledge and skills lie in quantitative research methods, and studying the research problem would require a more qualitative approach, it might be best to let someone else study it.
- *Will I have access to needed data?* Some research problems that would seem like excellent candidates for study by social workers may not be researchable because the data that are needed to study them are not accessible. For example, sealed court records and patients' medical records are now safeguarded by law. Thus, it is generally impossible to use them for research purposes. Knowledge that could be acquired only with access to data that is beyond reach should probably be regarded as unattainable. Unless other ways of addressing the research problem can be found that will produce findings of comparable credibility, it might be better to find another research problem to study.

In the past, some very promising research studies have reached a costly dead end when researchers found out too late that they would not be allowed to conduct interviews with clients or staff or to review and record data from records that were assumed to be readily available. Similarly, some social workers have just assumed that it would be acceptable to record interviews with research participants but found out belatedly that permission was denied. Today, most researchers understand the importance of inquiring into the availability of needed data prior to the selection of a problem for study and prior to submission of a research proposal to an IRB. The IRB members will want to be assured that permission to access them has been received prior to their granting approval to conduct the research.

Identifying and Specifying the Research Problem

As we noted earlier, a careful identification and specification of a researchable problem has a way of keeping all the other steps in the research process on track. But any vagueness or ambiguity about the problem can haunt the researcher at many junctures in the research process and can result in a considerable amount of wasted effort. In this way, research is similar to social work intervention with individuals, families, groups, organizations, or communities. Much valuable time of social work practitioners has been wasted because they failed to obtain a clear understanding of the problem or accepted at face value the presenting complaint of a client or client group. In the role of researcher, this "barking up the wrong tree" phenomenon can be especially costly.

Years ago, one of the authors of this text was involved in an extended discussion that attempted to specify the research problem for a proposed project.[5] The process that took place still provides a good example of the effort involved in identifying and specifying a research problem. It took several hours and produced a considerable amount of frustration. But the time was well spent. The process was absolutely essential prior to the beginning of other steps in the research process.

The director of a county agency had proposed that the researchers (a group of social work graduate students) might conduct research on a problem that he had identified in his organization as their research practicum assignment. He had noticed that during the past year child protection workers were receiving many more reports of possible child abuse by local professionals than in previous years. A very large percentage of the cases were never opened for services because the worker assigned to investigate quickly determined that they were unfounded. From the director's perspective, this was an inefficient use of workers' time. They were spending much of their day dealing with reports where no abuse had taken place, while not having enough time to devote to those cases where abuse was probable. Simply stated, from his perspective, there were too many unfounded cases. He didn't know why this was occurring, and thus did not know how to act to address it.

Further discussion with the administrator allowed the students to compile a list of five possible explanations for what was happening:

1. Social workers in the community were making too many inappropriate referrals.
2. Inappropriate referrals were the result of inadequate training of social workers.
3. Child protection workers were erroneously declaring cases to be unfounded because they are overworked.
4. Cases were being declared unfounded for fear that a determination of founded would result in more work for child protection workers.
5. Certain workers were contributing to the large number of unfounded cases by determining that all or most of their cases are unfounded.

Note that each of these statements reflects what *might* have been occurring and, in some cases, even a possible reason for it. Each also suggests a different gap in knowledge that needed to be filled. If any one of them was indeed concluded to be what was happening, there was currently insufficient knowledge to understand better why it was happening and what could be done to address it (the best intervention). That is what research could have provided.

Often, through a combination of additional discussion and further investigation of existing knowledge and available data, it is possible to eliminate "bogus" explanations of some phenomenon and to identify the real one that needs to be studied. That is exactly what happened in our example. Following more inquiries and another meeting with the director, all but one of the preceding statements was eliminated. The great majority of the referrals were apparently quite appropriate, given what the literature suggested at the time about possible indicators of abuse. Their increased number was probably related in part to recent training that had emphasized recognition of conditions that might suggest that abuse had taken place and that a referral was in order.

Although some instances of child abuse might have been missed, there was no evidence to suggest that this was the case, at least not any more so than in previous years. Based on recent data within the professional literature, it was impossible to know whether the current rate of founded versus unfounded cases among his child protection workers was high, low, or about normal.

It also would be very difficult to measure accurately whether a case determination had been correct or incorrect, a measurement obstacle (see previous discussion) that was sufficient to preclude giving serious consideration to the third statement as the impetus for a research study. It was possible that the ratio of founded versus unfounded cases was about on target, but that the cases were being categorized incorrectly; there was simply no way to know. It also was learned that statement 4 was unlikely to be what was occurring in the organization. A policy existed whereby a case with a determination of founded was referred for follow-up services by another worker in another division of the organization. Thus, it resulted in no additional work for the worker who made the determination.

Based on the director's observations and a quick count of records, some workers seemed to have a much higher rate of unfounded determinations than others over the previous three years. Given the random assignment of cases and the large number of cases seen, such a disparity should not have existed. The director speculated that the identity of the worker assigned to a referral might have more to do with the determination of founded or unfounded than the facts of the case. Consequently, a variation of statement 5 was seen as the most plausible explanation for what was occurring.

To have used precipitously any of the first four explanations proposed by the research group as the research problem would have produced difficulties later on in the research. Much effort would have been wasted. The time spent in clarifying the exact nature of what was occurring was a productive and necessary exercise. It improved the overall efficiency of the scientific inquiry by saving much more time than it consumed.

Selecting Research Questions

A concise, well articulated problem statement is a good beginning. However, it is too broad to provide the needed focus for a research study. The process of narrowing must continue. Next, researchers generally select a potential group of broad research questions that relate to it, more than they could ever hope to address in a single study. In more quantitative studies, one or more of them may get answered during the extensive literature review that generally follows. The answers were there; the researcher just was not aware of them. Others may be eliminated as "unresearchable" or of relatively low priority. One or a few will be revised, usually made more specific, by what is learned from the literature review process and then a research design (Chapters 6–8) will be selected to attempt to arrive at their tentative answers. After that, the questions (and the plan for answering them) are essentially "set." Changes are unlikely to occur.

In more qualitative studies, the process of data collection often begins quite early, following a less extensive literature review. While some research questions may be answered or others revised by what is learned from the literature, the process of eliminating, revising and even adding research questions is ongoing. It is not limited to and does not end with the literature review. It continues throughout the data collection process. New questions are often added as the data suggest other important areas of inquiry. Others may be dropped along the way if they prove unproductive for knowledge building.

Box 3.1 provides examples of some research problem statements and some broad research questions that might relate to them. They are just examples; many other questions might be appropriate for each problem statement as well.

The broad research questions that ultimately are selected help to keep a researcher on track. For example, whether one is deciding what data must be collected, how to collect them, what statistical analysis to perform, or which research findings are most important to disseminate, the same question can be asked: How does that bear on the research question and contribute to its answer? Answers that can pass this test suggest an appropriate use of researchers' time.

What is the connection between a research problem statement and a research question? How do they differ? Researchers choose to focus on certain research questions because they believe that, if answers to them can be found, those answers will help to alleviate the research problem. Even if answers cannot be found, the knowledge obtained through the process of seeking them generally provides increased insight into the problem itself. Unlike a research problem statement, a research question always is followed by a question mark.

There are many different gaps in knowledge related to any research problem that could serve as the focus for the research. But they cannot all be studied. How many questions should a researcher attempt to study? What are the characteristics of a good research question? What makes one potential research question a better choice as the focus of our research than another one? Selection of research questions, like the selection of a research problem, is often a matter of priorities.

We observed in Chapter 1 that all scientific knowledge is tentative by definition. But the researcher still hopes to generate knowledge that is as definitive as possible. Therefore, as a general rule, it is better to do a good, thorough job of studying just a few research questions than it is to do a more superficial job of inquiring into the answers to many different ones.

Many of the criteria that are applied in selecting broad research questions for study are the same ones that we examined in selecting a research problem. The following questions are often helpful, both for limiting the number of questions to be studied and for producing a clearer understanding of just why the research is being conducted:

BOX 3.1   Some Research Problem Statements and Related Questions

Problem: The parents of children who die while committing violent crimes are also victims. However, we know little about how the parents experience this tragedy.

Q1. How do these parents perceive potential sources of support in their time of loss?
Q2. What obstacles to the grief process do they perceive?
Q3. What feelings do they have toward the families of the victims of the violence?
Q4. How have their relationships with friends and relatives been affected?

Problem: Homicide by children 8 to 12 is increasing. Social workers working with children this age often hear them talk about wanting to kill someone. There is little available knowledge to help them decide how to respond.

Q1. What behaviors of children immediately prior to homicidal acts might have indicated that the acts might occur?
Q2. What common experiences exist in the social histories of homicidal children?
Q3. What common experiences exist in the current life situations of homicidal children?
Q4. What have been the experiences of social workers who notified authorities when their young clients talked about homicide?

Problem: Welfare reform has dramatically reduced the number of families receiving public financial assistance. However, we have little knowledge about the impact of welfare reform on those people who are no longer on welfare rolls.

Q1. Have those no longer receiving welfare assistance found good jobs, or are they now relying on other institutions for financial assistance?
Q2. What has been the effect on children of former AFDC recipients who went to work after their benefits ran out?
Q3. Have day care facilities increased to meet adequately the needs of an increased number of working mothers?
Q4. How much have a strong economy and a low national unemployment rate (rather than welfare reform) contributed to the reduction in numbers of welfare recipients?

Problem: High unemployment has resulted in a recent reduction in charitable giving. We don't know how this has affected not-for-profit agencies and their clients and what we can do about it.

Q1. Has the funding led to the deletion of some valuable programs?
Q2. What are agencies doing to try to place reduced funding?
Q3. Have the United Way's new priorities for allocating funding caused some agencies to redefine their mission?
Q4. Have agencies become more competitive and less cooperative with each other?

Problem: Social workers are encountering an increasing number of middle and high school–age students who claim to be in "friends with benefits" relationships. They are uncertain how to address it in their counseling, or even whether to treat it as a problem.

Q1. Are these relationships really as widespread as some adolescents say they are?
Q2. If an adolescent is in such a relationship, how does he or she perceive it?
Q3. Do these relationships seem to occur most frequently among adolescents with certain problems or characteristics?
Q4. What long-term effects are these relationships likely to have on adult sexual relationships?

1. Which potential research questions would be most likely to contribute
   - New knowledge?
   - Knowledge for more effective practice intervention?
   - Knowledge that can be disseminated?
   - Knowledge that will make a difference?
   - Knowledge that other researchers will find useful?
2. Which potential research questions are most likely to have an answer that
   - Is attainable?
   - Would contribute the most to alleviation of the problem (the knowledge gap)?
3. Which potential research questions would require
   - Measurement of phenomena that can be easily measured?
   - Access to information that is likely to be available?
   - The use of research methods that are considered ethical?
   - The knowledge and expertise possessed by the researcher?

Each of the preceding questions reflects an important issue in the selection of a research question. To see how they might come into play in the selection of a research question, we will return to the example used in our discussion of problem specification. Having settled on what apparently was happening (some child protection workers had a much higher rate of unfounded cases than others), the students began to identify possible research questions, the answers to which might help to explain and/or alleviate the problem. Some of the many possible ones that were seriously considered included the following:

1. What laws and regulations govern child protection workers' decisions about whether a case is determined to be founded? Could ambiguity contained in them be producing different reporting rates (founded versus unfounded) among workers? Could recent changes in reporting procedures somehow be affecting whether a case is regarded as founded?
2. Could different working conditions in some way help to explain the different rates?
3. Could differences in education and training of workers somehow relate to the different rates?
4. Do co-workers perceive that some workers are more conscientious in their investigation than others?
5. How great an influence is supervision in worker determinations regarding reports of suspected abuse?
6. Are community professionals somehow influencing the decisions of some workers more than others? If so, how is this occurring?
7. Do some workers perceive rewards for either founded or unfounded cases that other workers do not perceive?
8. How might the work experience of the child protection worker affect the way that a case is perceived?
9. Does burnout somehow contribute to the different rates of founded cases among workers?
10. Are the different demographic characteristics of workers (for example, age, race, sex, or parenthood) related to their determinations?

What can we observe about the preceding questions? First, they all relate to the research problem in the same way. Each, if answered, could contribute to its alleviation. All the questions also relate to factors that may influence the decision making of child protection workers. However, each suggests a very different focus of inquiry. Note, too, that all of them are stated in a way that suggests that the cause for the different rates is unknown. This kind of noncommittal wording is very appropriate for this stage of the research process. It suggests that the researchers were keeping an open mind and not beginning the research with any preexisting biases.

All of the questions are quite broad. As we shall discuss later in this chapter, the tasks of refining broad research questions, making them more specific, and, when possible, even proposing tentative answers to them all come later in the process, in more qualitative studies, often considerably later.

Because researchers hope to be able to acquire as much relevant knowledge as possible in a research study, it is often desirable to select those questions that can be combined with other possible questions. As long as the research does not become too unmanageable or lose focus, combining questions can be an efficient use of time. It is exactly what occurred in the research that we have been describing.

Most of the original questions (including many that are not in the preceding list) were rejected for reasons related to the issues that were discussed earlier. For example, question 4 could not be examined because it was concluded that obtaining the required data would be difficult without damaging working relationships among staff members. All the caseworkers were found to share the same supervisor and to work under virtually identical working conditions, so questions 5 and 2 were discarded. Question 6 was summarily answered without the need for further study. It was learned that another study had just examined this question and found no evidence of any such influence.

Question 1 was concluded to be just a little too complex to study within the time available and with available resources. To study it would have required extensive interviews with the workers and the development of methods to test their job knowledge. The director stated that he could not permit workers to take enough time off from their regular duties to participate in a series of extended interviews or other similar forms of data collection. The use of question 6 also presented logistical obstacles. To answer it would have entailed collecting data from more than 100 individuals in the community who frequently make referrals, a formidable and costly endeavor. In light of the small amount of knowledge related to the problem that would be generated, the effort involved did not seem justified.

Some variation of question 10 appeared to be the best choice. The answer to it seemed obtainable. No one in the group had ever seen it discussed within current professional literature. What's more, questions 3, 7, and 9 could easily be answered along with it by adding a short personal interview designed to collect some of the needed data. The research question was restated as: Are characteristics of workers related to their determinations of whether a case is judged to be founded? The question was quite general, but it was specific enough to guide the student researchers during the next step in the research process: a review of relevant literature.

Summary

In this chapter, we examined the earliest tasks in the research process: problem identification and selection of broad research questions. We devoted an entire chapter to these tasks because we regard them as critical to a thoughtful, organized approach to knowledge building. They are also the first steps in all research (quantitative and qualitative), or at least they should be. After they have been completed (as noted in Chapter 1), quantitative and qualitative research studies generally head off in somewhat different directions.

A distinction was made between problems in general (such as social problems or the problems of an individual social worker, client, or client system) and potential social work research problems. A research problem can be thought of as a gap in our knowledge that interferes with our practice functioning and that makes our decision making more difficult. Potential research problems are sometimes identified when we find ourselves thinking to ourselves, "I wish I knew something that I don't know." Other times our interaction with clients uncovers some phenomenon that we don't understand or, perhaps, didn't even know existed. A potential research problem may also emerge from discussion with our colleagues or with our supervisors. However, not all gaps in knowledge that are identified in these ways are good candidates for research. The needed knowledge may exist, and with a little effort (like an Internet search), we can easily acquire it. Even if we learn that there really is an important knowledge gap, it may not be a good candidate for social work research because of priority issues that were discussed in this chapter and/or its suitability for the application of scientific methods.

Broad research questions evolve from and are closely related to a social work research problem. If answers to them can be found, those answers will help to reduce the knowledge gap that constitutes the research problem and thus have potential to alleviate the problem. We offered guidelines to assist in selecting the best research questions to study from among those that might be studied. A continuation of an earlier example illustrated both the importance of identifying and articulating the "real problem," and how a long list of possible research questions can be reduced to a manageable number.

For Discussion

1. Why should a research problem always be stated as a declarative sentence? Why might it be best to keep it short and not overly complex?
2. Would a problem statement in a more qualitative study be likely to be more or less specific than one in a more quantitative study? Explain.
3. What is the difference between a social problem and a social work research problem? What is the goal of most social work research?
4. Why are many social problems more appropriately studied by people from other disciplines such as sociology, anthropology, or social psychology?
5. What are some social work research problem statements relating to our work with people who are victims of terrorist attacks or natural disasters?
6. Based upon the priorities outlined in this chapter, which of the research problems identified in response to the previous question should receive highest and lowest priority for our research efforts? Why?

7. How can a failure to correctly identify the research problem cause a researcher to waste time and resources? Give an example of how this might happen.

8. What is supposed to be the relationship between a research problem statement and broad research questions? How can we determine if a research question is likely to accomplish its purpose?

9. What would be some broad research questions that might be appropriate for a research study designed to fill the knowledge gap reflected in the problem statement, "To date, few social work interventions are known to have been effective in the treatment of people who are convicted of crimes of pedophilia"?

10. Would the *research questions* in a more qualitative study be likely to be more or less specific than those in a more quantitative study? Explain.

Endnotes

1. Rubin, A., & Babbie, E. (2008). *Research methods for social work*, 6th ed. Belmont, CA: Brooks Cole, 129.

2. Frankfort-Nachmias, C., & Nachmias, D. (1992). *Research methods in the social sciences*, 4th ed. New York: St. Martin's Press, 51.

3. Rothery, M. (1993). Problems, questions, and hypotheses. In R. M. Grinnell, Jr. (Ed.), *Social work research and evaluation*, 4th ed. Itasca, IL: F.E. Peacock, 17.

4. Shontz, F. (1986). *Fundamentals of research in the behavioral sciences*. Washington, D.C.: American Psychiatric Press, 27.

5. Bellomy, P., Berstein, H., Bickley, S., et al. (1989). *Factors affecting child protection workers' decision-making in Sumter County*. Unpublished MSW research project. Columbia, SC: University of South Carolina, College of Social Work.

4

FINDING AND USING
EXISTING KNOWLEDGE

Reference to existing knowledge can occur at many different points in the research process. Researchers often use it to assist in selecting and specifying a social work research problem, and they use it again to narrow their list of possible research questions (Chapter 3). Answering questions about, for example, how widespread a problem is or whether some phenomenon is easily measurable also may require a quick trip to the library or an Internet search. However, the use of existing knowledge does not stop there. We use it to see if there are already partial answers to our research questions and (at least in more quantitative studies) to help to formulate hypotheses about what we expect to learn. It also helps us to make important decisions about how best to conduct our research. After data have been collected, the literature can help us to interpret our research findings in light of the knowledge accumulated by others.

What Is a Review of Literature?

In research, the term "review of literature" is used in two ways. It refers to both an activity and a written product. As we already noted, the *activity* of reviewing relevant literature is a task that occupies the attention of the researcher to a greater or lesser degree at many points in the research process. However, there is generally one time period when the researcher focuses intensely on the accumulated work of others who have studied and written about the research problem or some related topic. In studies that are predominantly qualitative, this is most likely to occur after some or all data have been collected—when the researcher is attempting to interpret them in relation to existing knowledge. In more traditional, quantitative studies, it generally occurs prior to data collection and is used to help in planning for the rest of the research process that is to follow. As we shall see, "literature" is also somewhat of a generic term in research. It includes sources of knowledge that go far beyond the printed word.

Eventually, what was learned from the activity of reviewing the literature is organized and written up in summary form as a separate section or chapter of the research report. This is the *product* known as the "Review of Literature," "Relevant Literature," or something similar. It is written for the reader of the report and describes which existing knowledge was considered relevant to the current study, what the researcher learned from it, and how it influenced both the way the research was conducted and, ultimately, any conclusions drawn from its findings.

Even new problems or ones that for one reason or another have received little or no attention in the past always bear some similarity to those that already have been studied. Knowledge drawn from research on related topics can be productively brought to bear. For example, during the late 1980s and early 1990s, the problem of date rape belatedly received widespread attention in the media. There were conflicting opinions expressed about, for example, its incidence, the reasons for it, and how it should be addressed. This was a potential social work research problem because without a clear understanding of the dynamics surrounding it and how it was perceived by both perpetrators and victims, we could not know how best to provide successful intervention. When research on the problem began, there initially was limited knowledge about the specific problem. Yet a review of the literature still was extremely useful for acquiring both insight into date rape and how best to design research to study the problem. Research on this newly identified problem was greatly facilitated by an examination of reports of previous studies on literally hundreds of diverse topics. Each made a valuable contribution that helped researchers focus their attention on the best ways to advance knowledge areas about date rape. Among the major topic areas examined were the following:

- History of violence against women.
- Violence against women within different cultures.
- Legal parameters defining rape.
- Substance abuse and physical violence.
- Law enforcement and judicial handling of rape accusations.
- Sexual violence.
- Anger expression and management.

Another "new" problem, our lack of understanding of unwillingness of sexually active teenagers at risk for teen pregnancy to use free contraceptive injections, was identified in the late 1990s. Because such injections (and contraceptive implants) were not even available until the mid-1990s, it would seem on the surface that a researcher wishing to study the problem would be in the dark. But there is plenty of literature on related topics that would address the problem and questions that relate to it. Related topics might have included:

- History of contraception.
- Emerging prevention methods.
- Outcome studies of various methods of contraception.
- Attitudes about contraception among adolescents.
- Attitudes about pregnancy among adolescents.
- Distrust of health care providers.
- Obstacles to use of public health services.

In the first decade of the twenty-first century, problems such as cyber-bullying and cyber-exhibitionism emerged related to the increasing availability of the Internet. As in the previous two examples, social workers hoping to generate knowledge that will help in working with clients who have experienced either of these problems could find related knowledge that would be helpful. For every research problem and for its related research questions there is a relevant body of knowledge. Whenever researchers report that little or nothing is known about the problem or that no relevant literature exists on the topic, it says more about themselves than about whatever is the focus of their research. It is an indication that (1) they probably do not understand the nature and purpose of the literature review or (2) they probably did not invest sufficient energy and time in this important step in the research process. There are no research problems and no research questions for which there are no existing relevant knowledge. Although it is conceivable that no one may have previously studied the exact questions selected, there is *always* knowledge available that could help to enlighten and inform the researcher.

Purpose of a Review of Literature

Whenever it is conducted, a literature review is a recognition that knowledge building is a cumulative process that goes on over long periods of time, and that each study has (or should have) a unique contribution to make to that process. It has several complementary objectives. These are summarized in Box 4.1.

BOX 4.1 How Researchers Make Use of the Literature

When a problem is first identified to:
- Specify the problem.
- Determine its suitability for study.
- Select broad research questions related to it.

Prior to data collection to:
- Learn more about the history, origin and scope of the research problem.
- Learn what methodologies have been applied successfully (and unsuccessfully) to study related research problems.
- Learn what answers already exist for their broad research questions.
- Decide what is the best way to acquire needed data, who or what might best provide them, and how best to analyze them.
- Refine and better specify their research questions.
- Identify variables that will need to be measured and learn what methods already are available to measure them (quantitative studies).
- Construct operational definitions of key variables (quantitative studies).
- Propose answers to their research questions in the form of hypotheses (quantitative studies).

After data collection to:
- Attempt to explain differences between current findings and existing knowledge.
- Identify ways in which current findings are consistent with and support existing knowledge.
- Interpret the data in light of existing knowledge.
- Specify how current findings advance knowledge.
- Develop additional theories and formulate hypotheses for future research studies to test.

Potential Sources

For researchers, the term *literature* really means *relevant knowledge.* This knowledge can be found in many different places and forms.

What qualifies a source of information for inclusion in what we have called the product known as "the review of literature"? It should enlighten and inform the researcher (and the reader of a research report). It also should be credible. The issue of credibility is often debatable. Even the best of sources are sometimes vulnerable to political or economic influences.

The most common sources (some of them clearly more credible than others) for a review of the literature include (but are not limited to) the following:

- Professional journal articles.
- Trustworthy websites.
- Books.
- Personal interviews with authorities.
- Research reports and monographs.
- Research presentations at conferences.
- Newspaper articles.
- Standard reference materials.

Professional Journal Articles

Articles within social work professional journals, such as *Social Work Research, Social Work,* or *Journal of Social Work Education,* usually represent a sizable and important portion of the knowledge that is brought to bear on a social work research question. Generally, they have undergone an anonymous peer review process that, although it gives no guarantee of scholarliness, at least suggests that others believe that they are worthy of publication. However, even these sources cannot always be trusted and must be examined carefully.

Journals in social work and related fields have proliferated in recent years. Some publications that purport to be professional journals are not refereed; that is, they do not use a blind review process that ensures that a friendship or the name of the author and/or his or her prestigious affiliation will not influence publication decisions. Even some of those that are refereed now receive so few submissions that they publish the majority of all submissions that are received. A reference book published by NASW in 1997[1] reported on the percentage of article submissions that were accepted for publication among nearly two hundred social work and social work–related journals that were in print at the time. The high rate of acceptance of some refereed journals was enlightening. Are they simply receiving mostly good, publishable submissions? Or are they "taking what they can get" in order to have enough articles to publish an issue?

If, just because a journal is refereed that is no guarantee that all of its content reflects the highest levels of scholarship, how can we tell the difference between a scholarly journal and one that is not so scholarly? Box 4.2 may be helpful in this regard.

Libraries have limited budgets for purchasing journals, either in paper form or through on-line subscriptions. Since journals are expensive (many journals actually charge

BOX 4.2   Evaluating Professional Journals as a Literature Source

- Does the goal of the journal seem to be to seek to disseminate important knowledge so that others can benefit from it?
- Are any research methods described in sufficient detail that the reader is able to judge whether they were methodologically sound and ethical?
- Is the journal published by a professional organization or respected university or teaching institution? Is it widely cited in the professional literature?
- Is the journal more "serious looking" than other, less scholarly publications? Does it contain tables, graphs, and the results of statistical analyses rather than pictures or colorful graphics?
- Do articles consist of mostly reports of primary research (original research conducted for the first time) and far fewer compilations of research results previously published elsewhere? If the journal contains any replications of previous studies, is the justification for the replication clearly articulated and convincing?
- Do articles contain some technical jargon that is specific to the discipline for which it was written, since there is the assumption that anyone interested enough to read them has some scholarly background in the area?
- Do the authors of articles have credentials (advanced degrees, but also work experience, reputations and/or previous publications in the topic area) that qualify them as scholars or authorities? (An Internet search by the author's name can help to confirm this.)
- Does the style of the writing of articles reflect objectivity, rather than an effort to try to win over the reader to the author's position?
- Do the articles contain footnotes and bibliographies to suggest that the authors did not just present their own beliefs or theories, but tied it to the work of others?

libraries more for subscriptions than they do individual subscribers), difficult choices must be made. Not surprisingly, librarians have shown a special interest in the scholarliness of professional journals and have devoted whole reference books[2] to the evaluation of their quality. These books are frequently available for our use in the reference section of both university and public libraries, should we have questions about the credibility of some journal that is unfamiliar to us.

It sometimes seems as if the topic of a journal article (it was "hot" at the time of publication) or its use of a particular research method or statistical procedure may have had more to do with its publication than its scholarliness. Sometimes the findings of research may be a major factor in the decision to publish. Undoubtedly, some findings are more popular than others, especially if they are consistent with popular opinion or seem to be supportive of our profession rather than critical of it. Another question we might ask is, "Is it possible that the topic of the article, the research methods used, or research findings, rather than the quality of the research, resulted in publication of the article?"

Relevant literature can be found in professional journals in many other fields besides social work (for example, psychology, nursing, sociology, education, health, anthropology, public administration, or public health). The journal may have been published anywhere in the world. If it is written in a foreign language, English translations will need to be found or undertaken if the work is considered critical to understanding the problem being investigated. Bilingual and bicultural students in the helping professions at nearby universities may be a good resource for both identifying relevant literature and for translation.

Especially when conducting certain forms of research, special care must be taken so that the literature that we choose to use in a literature review informs rather than misleads other researchers and the readers of our reports. When a researcher is conducting a study with a different ethnic or cultural group or within a cross-cultural context, literature that helps the researcher to better understand the manifestation of the target problem or research issue within that particular cultural framework is especially useful. Additional effort may be required to locate journal articles written by either indigenous social scientists or social work researchers and practitioners who possess special expertise in conducting research within a specific culture.

Trustworthy Websites

Not surprisingly, the Internet is a popular source for existing knowledge. For many people, it is now the first place to look when they want information about most anything. Its easy accessibility and the breadth of information available on it can greatly expedite a literature search. Unlike books, journal articles, or other commonly used reference materials that often are out of date before they are available in print, data on the Internet can be updated as frequently as is necessary. The ease with which knowledge can be put on the Internet is, at the same time, its greatest weakness. Individuals can put anything they want on it—no verification is required. Freedom of speech also permits individuals to play loosely with facts or to just plain fabricate.

If the Internet is so vulnerable to misinformation, why do we include it as a source of literature? Along with websites that we would never want to quote from in a review of literature, it also contains some very useful ones for the social work researcher. The latter group is sometimes referred to as "reliable websites." The adjective *reliable*, as used in this context, comes closest in meaning to the word *trustworthy*, which is the term we prefer to use, since the term reliability, when used later in this book in discussing measurement (Chapter 10), has a somewhat different connotation.

Many of the other sources of literature described elsewhere in this chapter are now accessible via the Internet (for example, the *Congressional Record*); more undoubtedly will follow. Some websites are specifically dedicated to facilitating access to reliable knowledge for social workers. For example, a common place to begin searching the Web for resources related to social work practice or education is the frequently visited Social Work Access Network (SWAN). It is a popular link to many other Internet sites (also administered by dedicated social work practitioners and academicians) that are generally acknowledged to be reliable sources of knowledge. SWAN also offers a listing of websites for social work journals. The links include some with full text articles (from electronic journals), but also some containing just abstracts or tables of contents.

Websites come and go, addresses are subject to change, and even the content and credibility of specific sites tend to vary based upon the preferences and biases of their current webmaster. Thus, when conducting an Internet literature search it is better to first go to SWAN or a similar site that we trust to maintain the integrity of its links and then follow them, rather than to try to go directly to an "old favorite" that might have changed considerably since the previous visit. However, we cannot always find what we need in this way. Then what? How can we distinguish trustworthy information obtained from the Internet from that which cannot be trusted and should not be cited in a review of literature? The question of what is a trustworthy website is itself widely discussed on the Internet. Box 4.3 contains some of the more commonly mentioned indicators that reflect on a website's credibility.

Books

Books remain a popular source for literature reviews. The reports of some major research studies are published in book form. Other books contain scholarly presentations of carefully researched theories. Of course, books also can contain material that falls far short of the standard of scholarliness that is expected for citation in a literature review. Just because something is in print, that is no guarantee of its trustworthiness. Much of what is published in book form has not undergone rigorous review and scrutiny. Even major textbook publishers have to consider potential sales along with quality issues and other factors when they make the decision to publish (or not to publish) a book. Checks on the accuracy of the content often are delegated to a few academicians who receive only minimal compensation for their reviews and who may be less than thorough in their efforts. There are also "vanity presses" that will publish virtually any material in book form

BOX 4.3   Evaluating Websites as a Literature Source

- What does the URL tell you? Does it contain a personal name, often an indicator that it is a personal webpage rather than one of an institution or organization? If it does not appear to be a personal webpage, what is the domain? Is it where you would expect to find the knowledge that you are seeking, e.g., *.gov* or *.us* for data collected by governmental organizations, *.org* for information relating to problems addressed by not-for-profit organizations, *.edu* for research conducted in colleges or universities, and so forth.
- Are there links that would allow you to verify the credibility of the site and the author of the material it contains? More reputable sites will contain links that, for example, take us to description of the organization that sponsors it and its mission, goals, and philosophy or to the author's professional vitae or biography, If there are links to other websites such as "additional sites," they should not just be those that reflect the same positions as that of the current one. Their credibility should also be examined. The links should work. When was the site last updated?
- What are the author's (or the organization's) claims to expertise in the area? Credentials are important, but look at the content of the webpage. Is it what we should be able to expect from a true scholar? Does the content seem to be little more than an opinion, a diatribe, or an attempt to "sound off" about some issue? A rambling discourse is not characteristic of scholarly writing. Scholars are well organized and concise; they rarely repeat themselves, unless it is for emphasis.
- Does the page seem to have been put there as a service to the scientific community or to other professionals? Or does it seem like it was put there to try to influence others to adopt the author's ideas or to sell them on his or her way of viewing things? Is it possible that it contains deliberate exaggerations and misstatements or was just meant to be funny or outrageous or to shock others in order to get some reaction?
- How well documented were statements that were made? How credible are they? Could citations have been taken out of context or the position of those cited otherwise distorted or altered in order to make a point?

(including a professor's course notes and other writings) if the author is willing to pay enough to become a published author.

In deciding whether to use what is in a book to influence one's own research or to include a citation from it in the literature review section of a report, it is desirable to ask certain "credibility" questions. Many of them are very similar to those we would ask in evaluating any source's credibility. We have listed them in Box 4.4.

Personal Interviews with Authorities

Some of the other usual sources should be approached with even more caution. Unless they are examined critically, researchers can be misled by assertions that are questionable, while simultaneously damaging the credibility of their own research efforts. Sometimes they should be included, and other times they should be omitted. Often the questions must be asked: Where do I draw the line? What constitutes usable knowledge and what does not?

The reader will recall that authorities were one of the nonscientific sources of knowledge that we described as untrustworthy in Chapter 1. So why would we include them as a possible source of knowledge? Because sometimes authorities *do* know something important! The principal problem surrounding content drawn from interviews with authorities is lack of consensus regarding who is an authority. Unfortunately, in some parts of Western society, authority frequently has been assumed to reside in all individuals with certain academic credentials (or in anyone who travels a distance of more than fifty miles and carries a briefcase). For the social work researcher, an authority whose comments are worth quoting in a literature review is someone who has in-depth knowledge of some aspect of the research problem or who has arrived at (at least partial) answers to certain research questions, preferably through the use of scientific methods. This greatly limits the number of authorities who should be quoted in a report of a review of literature.

A researcher in colonial America might have had some justification for quoting a community leader or member of the clergy on virtually any topic, because the limited

BOX 4.4   Evaluating Books as a Literature Source

- Does the author have a reputation for scholarly integrity? What are his or her credentials? With what professional institution is he or she affiliated? Is it considered reputable? Does it have any unusual beliefs, values, or commitments? Is the author frequently cited by others as an expert on the topic?
- Does the author's position in the book seem to be based on well designed research, either original or a scholarly review of the work of others?
- Does the author seem most intent on the advancement of knowledge, not on pursuing some personal or political agenda?
- Was the book published by a reputable, well established publisher with a reputation for quality and selectivity such as a major university press or widely used publisher of textbooks in the field?
- Is the book a recently revised edition? If it was published some years ago, is it considered a "classic" in its field that contains material of historical significance?
- Are reviews of the book generally positive? What strengths do they identify, and do they relate to those parts of the book that you plan to cite?

amount of available knowledge was concentrated within just a few people. But today's researcher should not make any assumptions about any individual's claims to knowledge based solely on academic or other formal credentials. There are no Renaissance men or women alive today who have knowledge in virtually every area. It would be erroneous to assume that, for example, a quotation from any physician is appropriate on a medical question or that one from a lawyer will provide needed knowledge on a legal one. The physician may see primarily older patients; thus, her position on a problem related to child rearing may have no basis other than her experiences as a child or as a mother and may even be distorted through interaction with a biased sample of patients. The lawyer may specialize in contract law and may speak more out of personal opinion than out of knowledge in discussing needed changes in child abuse reporting laws. This is not an indictment of these or other professions; it is only a recognition that the base of knowledge within most professional fields (including social work) and even their subspecialties has grown dramatically during the past century, to the point where no one can possibly know it all.

Use of a few, carefully chosen quotations from interviews with authorities in the review of literature section of a research report usually will not harm the credibility of the researcher's efforts. On the contrary, it may suggest balance and thoroughness in the final product. However, it might be wise to prevent any possible challenges to the credibility of authorities by including brief descriptions of the source of their expertise in the narrative. For example, a descriptive statement such as "one medical researcher, who has conducted National Institute of Mental Health (NIMH)–funded research on the possible relationship between the use of party drugs and suicide among young men, has concluded that . . . " would help to justify why that particular physician was cited in the literature review section of a research report.

Research Reports and Monographs

Research reports and monographs generally are intended to be honest communications of a researcher's methods and findings. Although the findings are only as good as the methods used to produce them, the fact that a researcher's methods are open to public critique and the possibility of replication increases the likelihood that a report or monograph will be credible. Of course, if the research was funded by some organization or special interest group that may have exerted undue influence over what was found and/or reported, such sources also cannot be trusted. For example, the credibility of research findings about the benefits to society of "payday loans" or "title loans" which were sponsored by companies that have much to gain by their continued legality would be highly suspect. They would not be suitable to cite.

Research Presentations at Conferences

While there is a great amount of knowledge disseminated at conferences and symposia, there is also a good amount of unsubstantiated opinion and misinformation shared. A presentation may be selected using a blind review process, but this is not always the case. Often, the reputation of the presenter or the topic (if it is a popular one) is a major factor in its selection. Frequently, a conference presentation may have no basis in research at all. It may be little more than a show-and-tell description of what the presenter has done and why he or she thinks it was good.

Most presentations at annual conferences, such as those sponsored by the NASW, the SSWR, the CSWE, or the Child Welfare League of America, have undergone a fairly rigorous screening procedure. Only a small percentage of proposals submitted are accepted for presentation. But the proposals usually consist of a brief abstract that is reviewed by volunteers who may have little interest in the topic and may not have the knowledge and skill to review the quality of a presentation on it. These gatherings also give program space to invited speakers whose past expertise in a subject area has been recognized by one or more members of their planning committee, but who may not have been active in the field for years. Personal friendships, quid pro quos, or other political concerns sometimes influence the decision to invite these individuals.

Many other professional gatherings that call themselves national and international conferences and symposia have far less credibility. (After all, any group can describe its conference as "national" or "international" if it chooses.) Some of the most suspect of these consist of a small group of individuals who share some specialized interest. They get together annually to present to each other (sometimes even on the same topic as the previous year) at geographically desirable locations. Participants take turns hosting the annual gathering and inviting each other to present their work. Although some knowledge is undoubtedly shared, there also is a liberal amount of networking, rest and recreation, and sight-seeing. The conference is viewed as more of a "perk" than the fulfillment of a professional responsibility to remain knowledgeable in one's field of specialization.

Presenting at conferences does not always require prior access to networks. Many national and especially international conferences that sound highly prestigious welcome new participants and will accept nearly any program proposal submitted if the person submitting it agrees to show up and pay the registration fee. Conference registration fees represent a major source of revenue for some organizations; they could not exist without well attended conferences at which high registration fees are required.

Information acquired at regional, state, and local conferences also varies widely in its credibility. Before placing too much credence in what is presented at them, inquiries should be made as to the selection process for presentations and the credentials of the presenters. Of course, a critical assessment of the research methods used also should be made.

Newspaper Articles

Newspapers, either in print form or on-line, can be a valuable source of knowledge. Some of the better ones (for example, *Christian Science Monitor* or *New York Times*) are frequently cited in a literature review. They provide news of general interest, and are written for educated readers. However, it should be remembered that even the better newspapers depend on commercial success for their continued existence. Newspaper sales and/or a large number of Internet hits at their websites are good for newspapers. Data on them can be used to help to sell print advertisements, and on-line links which can generate the needed cash to survive. Thus, what will "sell" sometimes has higher priority than carefully researched contributions to knowledge.

Newspapers acquire some of what they publish from such generally credible sources as reports of government-sponsored research. But they also publish findings (sometimes selectively) from research of questionable quality. They regularly publish guest editorials written by invited "experts" who may have more name recognition than expertise. When a topic is believed to be of widespread interest, it sometimes seems that getting the facts is less important than producing a timely piece that will be widely read.

Except when an article can be determined to possess a carefully researched origin and contains only firsthand information, it probably is best to use knowledge drawn from newspapers with extreme caution. Often, they are best used to learn about the *existence* of the knowledge-building work of others. It is then possible to seek out the original source, obtain a full report, and evaluate its merits based on the description of the researcher's methods.

Standard Reference Materials

For relevant knowledge that is available in written form, the various abstracts publications (e.g., *Social Work Abstracts, Sociological Abstracts, Psychological Abstracts, Dissertation Abstracts International,* or *SAGE Urban Studies Abstracts*) are always a good place to start a literature search. Listed by topic area as well as by author, they provide a good overview of where recent publications on various topics can be found. Quotations from abstracts publications should not be used in the report of a review. They are not meant to be a substitute for the original source, just a convenient way to learn about the existence of a publication that may (or may not) prove to be helpful.

Historically, standard reference materials have contained verified facts that can be cited in a report of a review of literature. They have tended to possess higher credibility than, for example, data obtained from the Internet because they have undergone a more thorough review and verification process. They may be called almanacs, encyclopedias, atlases, statistical abstracts, directories, annuals, yearbooks, compendia, or some similar title. With the advent of the Internet, however, they are disappearing in their printed form. They are increasingly available electronically, where they can be kept up-to-date much better than in print. There is no need for a periodic new edition or supplement—just make the needed changes as they are required and they are immediately available.

The Internet has also produced another phenomenon related to standard reference materials. In the past, volumes such as encyclopedias and almanacs were compiled and published by specialists who worked full time, year after year, carefully verifying and reverifying the content that went into them. In recent years, websites have emerged that also claim to be standard reference materials and are regarded as such by many people. Yet they lack the quality controls that we expect in a standard reference. Whether or not they possess the knowledge or expertise, anyone can contribute to them and even edit the contributions of others. Currently *Wikepedia,* "the people's encyclopedia," is the best known example of this trend. It is now one of the first links that appears when we do almost any web search. Can it be trusted? Like most of the other sources of knowledge described in this chapter, it undoubtedly contains many useful facts, submitted by knowledgeable people. However, it also undoubtedly contains misinformation and falsehoods, at least until a more knowledgeable contributor comes along and corrects them. At some point in time, it may become a trusted resource that should go relatively unquestioned and can legitimately be cited in a research review of literature. However, that time has not come yet. For now, its primary usefulness might be as a place to locate links to other, more trustworthy knowledge (such as research monographs or high quality professional journal articles) that can be used in a literature review.

One standard reference commonly used by social workers to get their literature search underway is the NASW publication *Encyclopedia of Social Work.*[3] It is a good place to begin a search of the literature, but because of the breadth of topics covered, and the fact that there are generally several years between publications of editions and supplements it is not too useful beyond that function. While some topics remain pretty much unchanged, others (including best practices for intervention with certain types of problems) do not. To accomplish the objectives of a literature review, it often is necessary to venture into other areas of the literature that are more current or detailed such as frequently trusted Internet websites.

Progress in technology for the storage, retrieval, and transfer of standard reference materials is rapidly escalating the amount of knowledge that is accessible to researchers. It is becoming ever more comprehensive.

Most university libraries now possess extensive databases that are electronically accessible through CD-ROMs. Although in the past they contained mostly descriptive information, such as census data, they are increasingly being expanded to contain much more, including the findings of research conducted almost anywhere on earth. CD-ROMs contain thousands of journal articles, book chapters, and dissertation abstracts within a given discipline. For example, the National Clearinghouse on Child Abuse and Neglect offers social organizations and institutions a CD-ROM database on child abuse and neglect cases within the United States. There also are CD-ROM databases for certain government documents and major newspapers. CD-ROM databases are updated on a regular basis, typically either yearly or quarterly.

CD-ROM databases are accessed electronically through computer terminals. Appropriate citations and abstracts are located through an electronic search process by specifying key words. Sources thus located are viewed on the computer screen and can be printed out in hard copy if desired. Conducting an electronic literature search is becoming a very user-friendly task. Although procedures vary somewhat by database and institution, generally once one has conducted one CD-ROM search, others are quite simple and can be highly productive. Like standard reference materials, computerized databases often are used early in the literature review process. They provide an excellent overview of what is out there.

Even various abstracts publications such as *Social Work Abstracts* (SWAB), *Sociofile*, and *PsychLIT*, are now available on CD-ROM. There also are dozens of others that address particular specializations within social work and related disciplines.

Other reference materials such as public documents and records of public gatherings also can be useful resources. For example, a researcher wishing to understand the values and thinking underlying current or pending legislation can learn a great deal by studying testimony of various individuals and interest groups that appears within the *Congressional Record.* Of course, because they are open to the public, these documents sometimes contain more posturing and efforts to appear politically correct to a legislator's constituents than they do knowledge. In fact, much of what gets entered into the Congressional Record is never verbalized in debates and discussions; it is entered, just so it will be there. Other public documents and records of public gatherings may also have undergone a certain creative revision that often leaves their credibility as a source of knowledge somewhat suspect.

Other, Even More "Questionable" Sources

What we have just described are those sources that, if used selectively, tend to be among the most credible sources of literature. However, there are others that, while they possess even less credibility, appear in literature reviews from time to time. We mention them here, not to encourage their use, but to caution why they should be used only when better sources are unavailable or cannot be found, and then only after a careful check on their credibility.

Content of Workshops

Workshop content may be based on empirical findings; often it is not. Frequently workshop leaders have been contracted with (paid) to deliver content in a way consistent with the wishes of whomever is paying for it (often, an organization). This leaves the knowledge contained therein vulnerable to influence and distortion. The researcher may need to explore whether what was said was based on the best knowledge available or was simply reflective of what the workshop's sponsoring organization wanted its participants to hear. If it is the former, workshop content may be appropriate for inclusion in a research literature review. However, it would still be better to go to the original sources that the presenter may have relied on in putting together the presentation.

Radio and Television Broadcasts

There is a great amount of knowledge and advice shared gratuitously by network radio and television talk show hosts and their "authority" guests. Very little of it, if any, would be likely either to enlighten the researcher or to convince others of the scholarliness of a literature review.

Occasionally, news specials and documentaries on major networks and on public radio and television are well researched and present excellent sources of information. However, the proliferation of certain types of television journalism and pseudo–news specials in recent years and the revelation that some of what was reported on documentaries was falsified or "staged" have cast increasing doubt on the credibility of television news broadcasts. Frequently, they now appear to be designed to entertain and to appeal to the lower interests of viewers and listeners. Special care and discretion should be used in separating knowledge from content that, if cited, would only weaken the researcher's scientific credibility.

Magazines and Periodicals

Magazines and periodicals vary widely in how much knowledge they publish, as opposed to how much pure fiction they include in order to sell subscriptions and single copies in supermarkets and other outlets. They run the gamut from informative and generally trustworthy (for example, the *Scientific American*, *Economist*, or *National Geographic*), to popular but unscientific (for example, *Reader's Digest*, *Parents*, or *Cosmopolitan*), to sensational (for example, *Star*, *Globe*, or *National Inquirer*). Only the first group is occasionally cited in a scholarly literature review without jeopardizing the researcher's credibility. Some newsmagazines and pop science seem to walk a thin line, attempting to appear scholarly and scientific while selecting topics and presentation formats (e.g., short, topical articles featuring provocative pictures) that clearly reflect an eye on sales figures rather than on the knowledge needs of their readers. They may even reflect a pragmatic mixture within a single issue; for example, a fairly scholarly article written by a respected researcher juxtaposed with another bit of "fluff" that would be an intellectual insult to anyone with more than a superficial knowledge of the topic. The message to the social work researcher conducting a literature review on a research problem or question should be obvious—think very carefully before you rely on such publications for knowledge. You may subscribe to it, read it religiously, learn some things that are helpful to you in your work, and even display it on your coffee table without embarrassment. But that does not mean that it is a potential source of knowledge that can be cited with confidence.

The popularity of a magazine or periodical is certainly no guarantee that its contents are the product of scientific inquiry or that they are worthy of citation in a literature review. In fact, we might speculate whether very high sales and financial success are not negatively correlated with the amount of scientific rigor that is required in what is published.

Some magazines and periodicals make no pretense of scholarliness. Their readers, who may want to believe that they possess an inquiring mind, often seek nothing but recreational reading or amusing diversion. Consequently, they are less likely to purchase a periodical whose articles tend to be based on scientific research than ones that are based on the flimsiest of inquiry, if not outright fantasy. They would probably not buy (or read in the checkout line) a publication with a lead article entitled "Posttraumatic Stress Syndrome among Returning War Veterans," but they might purchase the tabloid that promises a four-paragraph analysis of such fantasies as "Elvis Is Working as a Bartender in Cheektowaga" or "Despondent Twin Shoots Brother by Mistake."

Is there ever a place for acknowledging within a social work researcher's review of literature such unscholarly publications that occur at the extreme end of the credibility continuum? Not in the usual way. However, these publications have one thing in common: high sales. Their owners and editors maintain high sales by maintaining a finger on the pulse of what is of interest to the general public. A social problem that is in some form the topic of virtually every magazine at the supermarket checkout stand during a certain period (e.g., spousal battery or the activities of the press) can be assumed to have reached a certain level of public consciousness. The observation that, during the week of August 8, 2008, nine of the ten most popular magazines in America carried at least one article on the use of medication to increase libido among post-menopausal women might be a useful contribution to a literature review, even though the sources cited might make some scholars cringe. The researcher would certainly not be saying that everything (or even anything) within the text of the articles can be construed as knowledge, only that the fact of its publication in popular magazines attests to the topic's popular interest.

We have chosen an extreme example of how far the researcher occasionally may go in seeking and using information for the review of literature. Obviously, even a single use of some of the more suspect sources of information that abound could seriously harm the researcher's credibility and others' assessment of the findings and recommendations generated by the researcher's methods. They should be used rarely, if ever, and only for the limited purposes described. If more scholarly sources would accomplish the same purposes, they should be used instead. Our example makes an important point, however. Any source that relates to the research problem and to a research question *may* have the potential to inform the researcher in some way, even if the knowledge it contains may have no credibility whatsoever.

Organizing the Product of a Literature Review

After a search of existing knowledge, researchers usually find themselves with a great deal of information. It may consist of a stack of file cards with useful quotations on one side and the full citation (including all page numbers, volume numbers, and other necessary specifics) on the back or some computer-assisted variation of it. A good first step in making sense out of all of this knowledge is to sort it into several broad topic areas. These may have been identified prior to embarking on the literature review, or they may simply suggest themselves during the sorting process. An example will help to illustrate how this can be done.

Suppose that a researcher has conducted a literature review on the question: How has the increasingly chronic nature of HIV affected the role of caregivers and the demands made upon them? The variety of relevant knowledge that was collected could be sorted and organized using an outline format like the following:

   I. Terminal and Chronic Illnesses
      A. Definitions and Examples
      B. Interventions
      C. Caregiver Roles
        1. Terminal Illness
        2. Chronic Illnesses

   II. HIV/AIDS: The Early Years
      A. Confusion, Fear and Misunderstanding
      B. Beginning Insights
        1. Diagnosis
        2. Symptoms
        3. Course of the Disease
        4. Methods of Transmission
        5. Those Most at Risk
        6. Prevention Options
        7. Treatment Options
        8. Role of the Caregiver
      C. Judgments and Accusations
      D. Social and Political Responses

   III. Changes and Developments
      A. Increased Social Acceptance

B. Pharmacological Advances
   1. Ethical Issues
   2. Economic Issues
C. Incidence
   1. Traditional Populations
   2. Third World
   3. Nontraditional Groups
D. Longevity

IV. HIV as a Chronic Disease
A. Perceptions of Those Who are HIV-Positive
   1. Self
   2. The Community
   3. Friends and Relatives
B. Current Services
   1. Hospital
   2. Out-Patient
   3. Hospice
C. Caregiver Requirements
   1. New Stressors
   2. Relationship Issues
   3. Economic Impact

Organizing the products of a literature review into an outline containing broad topic areas can serve a number of useful purposes. Some knowledge that has been collected may not seem to fit perfectly within any of the areas. It may be concluded that it is not as relevant to the research problem or questions as had originally been assumed. Thus, it may be discarded. Or, if it seems to stand alone but clearly does enlighten some aspect of the research problem or questions, new topics may be added to incorporate it, and it may have to be expanded with some additional literature. It may be necessary to go back to the sources of literature to seek out additional references.

If it appears that there is no logical sequence to the topics (note the logical progression of the preceding topics) when a broad outline is constructed, additional topics may be required to link those already identified. When all topic areas and their subtopics have been developed, they should reflect a logical flow, often from the more general to those most closely related to the current research question or questions. The topics frequently are used as headings and subheadings when the report of the literature review is written.

Writing the Report

What are the characteristics of a good literature review section of a research report? How can the researcher's compilation of existing knowledge be organized and presented so that it will be of maximum benefit to the reader? Entire books have been written on this topic.[4] We will address only the major issues here.

Direction and Flow

In the literature review of a research study that is primarily quantitative, the reader should expect to find topics (identified by subheadings) of general relevance to the research questions near its beginning. For example, in a research study seeking an answer to the broad research question. Is there a relationship between use of party drugs such as ecstasy and adolescent suicide?, early sections of the literature review might be devoted to a historical overview of substance abuse, a summary of what is known about adolescent drug usage and a description of statistical trends in the incidence of adolescent suicide in North America. Knowledge that is more directly related to the research question—for example, a summary of the results of suicide autopsies conducted on recent cases of adolescent suicide or results of other studies that examined the relationship between other substance abuse and adolescent suicide—should appear later. Reports of research that studied the same questions or very similar ones should be summarized and discussed near the end of the review, so that the current research will appear to be a logical extension of previous scientific inquiries.

Thus, the flow of the literature review is reflective of deductive logic, a characteristic of quantitative studies in general. It reflects both direction and a logical progression, from the general to the specific. It demonstrates how the quantitative researcher used existing knowledge to refine their thinking about their research problems and questions, and how more specific questions and, often hypotheses, evolve from it.

In reports of qualitative research studies, there is also a review of literature section in which the researcher describes how existing knowledge relates to the current study. By convention (since that is the way it is done in quantitative studies), this section is often found early in the report, just before the methodology section. However, it is probably more appropriate to place it after a description of the data or to have two literature reviews, one brief one before the methodology section and another after presentation of the data. This would be more consistent with the ways that the literature is used—often to learn just enough to "get going" with the data collection and then to attempt to interpret the data in light of existing knowledge.

Use of Quotations and Citations

Direct quotations should be used sparingly in a literature review. It is the *substance* of what others have to say rather than their specific words that are important to the researcher. Excessive use of quotations may mislead the reader because quotations are always taken out of context. In addition, because all writers have their own style, quotations can make the flow of the text uneven while providing more detail than the reader requires.[5]

If facts such as statistics are included, it is always appropriate to provide citations. They allow the reader to verify the accuracy of what was included. But, like quotations, they should be included only if the work cited truly contributed something to the literature review, not simply as evidence that the researcher was thorough.

There may be a natural tendency to want to include every bit of knowledge that has been discovered. After all, finding it took a considerable amount of effort! But, if ten articles present essentially the same position, there is no reason to cite them all—that would be overkill. One or two will make the point and be less likely to disrupt the flow of the text.

How relevant should knowledge be in order to be cited? How much detail of others' work is needed or desirable? Daryl Bem has provided some useful guidelines:

> Cite only articles pertinent to the specific issues with which you are dealing; emphasize their major conclusions, findings, or relevant methodological issues and avoid unnecessary detail. If someone else has written a review article that surveys the literature on the topic, you can simply refer your own readers to the review and present only its most pertinent points in your own report. Even when you must describe an entire study, try to condense it as much as possible without sacrificing clarity.[6]

Are some types of citations better than others? Yes. But a good mix often is desirable. The best citations to use (all other factors being equal) may be those that refer to recent, well designed research (as opposed to those that may be a little dated or that may be methodologically flawed). But it is perfectly acceptable to include some older citations (especially if the contribution was a major influence on subsequent thought on a topic or issue). Older citations can also be very useful for providing a historical perspective on a problem or event. They reflect the state of the art of knowledge, beliefs, and attitudes at a point in history.

It should be clear by now that the quotations and citations included in a report of a literature review are there to help explain how the researcher went from point A to point B. They are not there to impress others with how much relevant information was examined. If anything should impress the reader of a good research report, it should be the researcher's objectivity and open-mindedness.

Objectivity can be demonstrated in a number of ways. For example, it can be seen in a willingness to include the conflicting opinions and conclusions of other researchers, which almost invariably exist. It is not unusual for two scholars to express beliefs and conclusions that are diametrically opposite. The inclusion of references to literature that reflects both sides of an argument suggests that the researcher has been both thorough and objective in the literature review. Similarly, open-mindedness can be demonstrated by sometimes including the ideas and opinions of others that are controversial or generally not consistent with mainstream beliefs and the reasoning behind them.

Role of the Researcher

We do not mean to suggest that the researcher should always remain well behind the scenes in a literature review or express no opinions or conclusions. In fact, the opposite is true. Although biases should not be evident in a good literature review, the researcher's *thought processes* should be both obvious and open to critique. The reader should be able to sense the presence of the researcher in the text. A good literature review is a carefully woven mixture of knowledge and how it was used by the researcher.

The role of the researcher in a review of the literature section of a research report has some similarities to that of a travel guide. Suppose you are visiting a city like San Francisco for the first time and you only have one full day to take in the sights. You could spend hours or days surfing the Internet before your travel, plan an itinerary based on what interests you, and then rent a car to get around when you arrive. Or, you could simply sign up for a city tour in a van or bus with a travel guide to drive and take you to the most commonly visited tourist attractions, while giving you some background on them. The latter choice might cost a little more and some of what you see may not interest you too much, but the savings in time and effort will be well worth it. Like a travel guide, researchers have identified and organized what they believe is of interest and relevant to the research problems and questions related to it. This is a real time and effort saver for readers—relevant knowledge has been distilled down into an organized, well written narrative. But there is more to the analogy. A travel guide would not tell you that you must be very impressed by the Golden Gate Bridge or that Coit Tower is really disappointing. He or she would simply provide access to a number of potentially interesting sights and let you decide for yourself if you share his or her opinion of them. Similarly, researchers do not *tell* the readers of a review of literature what to conclude or how to interpret it— they merely summarize what they derived from it (perhaps, a hypothesis or a design for answering their research questions) and readers are free to disagree with some or all of their conclusions.

In a well written literature review, the researcher helps the reader to navigate through existing, relevant knowledge, stopping along the way to pull together conclusions and to evaluate just where (in the researcher's opinion) the literature seems to be leading. The researcher tries not to exert too much influence on the reader, whenever possible letting the literature speak for itself. In a well written literature review, the reader generally will come to the same or similar conclusions as the researcher and will agree about what the literature has to say about the research questions and how best to study them. The researcher's conclusions should contain no surprises. They will have been anticipated by the reader based on the evidence (the literature) that has been presented.

If we perceive the researcher's role as similar to that of a travel guide, neither of the two problems that frequently characterize literature reviews is likely to occur. One fairly common problem exists when the researcher's own thinking dominates the literature review and appears to be invulnerable to influence by it. The reader is left with the suspicion that existing knowledge had little influence on the conclusions that were drawn. Even if a fair number of citations are present, they do not reflect balance. It appears that the researcher selectively used only that literature that would support existing biases and did not grow in an understanding of the research problem or questions. The researcher emerged from the literature review with unchanged beliefs. The reader, sensing this, is likely to doubt whether other stages of the research process were conducted in an unbiased manner.

Sometimes another problem can occur. The development of the researcher's thinking is barely evident in the literature review, but for a different reason. The literature review seems to be little more than a long series of quotations, included in the research report because they are expected. They lend a scholarly appearance, but have no other apparent purpose. There is no way for the reader to evaluate the researcher's thought processes. There is not enough evidence that the knowledge assembled by the researcher was even assimilated.

In the above scenarios, the researcher has not made productive use of the accumulated literature. Credibility may be hopelessly damaged. But if the author assumes the role of guide, the proper mix of quotations reflecting relevant knowledge and the use of that knowledge to refine thinking about the research topic will be in evidence. The literature review will be a unified whole that seems to take the reader somewhere.

Summary

The term *literature review* refers to both a process of referring to existing knowledge at different points in the research process and to a product, namely, a section or chapter of the research report. A body of knowledge exists for any research question. The process of reviewing existing knowledge about a research question can shape our thinking about the question and its possible answer. We discussed the other reasons why we look at what is already known relative to a question, that is, what the literature review is supposed to accomplish.

The pros and cons of including various potential sources of knowledge in the review of literature section of a research report were discussed, with special focus on how the selection of a source can affect the credibility of the researcher and the research findings. Practical suggestions also were given for organizing a wide array of knowledge into a logical and coherent report of what is known relative to the research problem and the questions chosen for study. While not a perfect analogy, we proposed that the writer of a research report functions much like a tour guide. The writer compiles relevant knowledge and presents it to the reader along with his or her interpretations and conclusions drawn from it. The writer encourages the reader to critique these conclusions and the thought processes that produced them and to agree or disagree with them.

For Discussion

1. What are some newly identified problems that a social work researcher might wish to study? What are some areas of existing knowledge that might be appropriate in conducting a literature review on them?
2. How is a review of the literature helpful in deciding how to collect data or to perform other research tasks?
3. Why is "relevant knowledge" a better description of the sources examined in a literature review than the term "the literature"? What does it include?
4. Why are refereed journal articles considered to be more trustworthy sources than non-refereed ones? Why are they still sometimes "suspect"?
5. Has an increase in the number of on-line social work professional journals in recent years been a good thing for researchers conducting literature reviews? Why or why not?
6. Why is it not a good idea to rely solely on the Internet for sources in a literature review (or in writing a term paper, for that matter)?
7. Can all social work textbooks be considered trustworthy sources of knowledge? Why or why not?
8. Who would be considered a good authority to interview on the effects of the work requirements of welfare reform on public perceptions of welfare recipients?
9. How do politics and economic issues affect the credibility of the content at professional conferences and in newspapers?
10. How is the role of the researcher in a review of literature different from that of a student writing a term paper? How is it similar?

Endnotes

1. NASW (1997). *An author's guide to social work journals*, 4th ed. Silver Spring, MD: NASW Press.
2. LaGuardia, C. (Ed.) (2003). *Magazines for libraries*, 12th ed. New York: Bowker.
3. NASW (1995). *Encyclopedia of social work*, 19th ed. Silver Spring, MD: NASW Press.
4. See, e.g., Galvin, J. (2006). *Writing literature reviews*, 3rd ed. Los Angeles: Pyrczak Publishing; or Hart, C. (1998). *Doing a literature review*. Thousand Oaks, CA: Sage Publications.
5. Pyrczak, F., & Bruce, R. (2005). *Writing empirical research reports*, 5th ed. Los Angeles: Pyrczak Publishing, 41.
6. Bem, D. (1991). Writing the research report. In C. Judd, R. Eliot, & L. Kidder, (Eds.), *Research methods in social relations*, 6th ed. Fort Worth, TX: Harcourt, Brace, Jovanovich, 453.

5

FOCUSED RESEARCH QUESTIONS AND RESEARCH HYPOTHESES

As we noted in the previous chapter, researchers rely heavily on existing knowledge (the literature) to assist them. When they consult it prior to data collection, it helps them in selecting the most appropriate design for their research (Chapters 6–8). It also helps them to specify better the research questions that will be examined in their research. Depending on the amount of knowledge available and what is learned, they may even be able to predict what answers will be found. These two latter products of literature reviews, focused research questions and hypotheses, are so important to research that we will devote this chapter to them.

Focused Questions

Selecting broad research questions (Chapter 3) is a useful exercise. It reduces a study of a research problem to a manageable size. As we suggested, no one study could possibly do a thorough job of examining all questions that might relate to a research problem; some choices must be made. However, broad questions such as those in the examples in Chapter 3 do not provide a specific enough focus to guide the researcher in performing such necessary tasks as identifying the most appropriate people or objects to study, determining what needs to be observed and/or measured, or determining how best to do it. Broad questions also provide little or no guidance for selecting the methods to sort and analyze data. Before these tasks can be undertaken, further refinement and specification of the research questions are required.

What is the difference between a broad research question such as those discussed in Chapter 3 and the more specific questions that are likely to be a product of the literature review? How does a review of existing knowledge help the researcher to move from the former to the latter?

To illustrate the difference between broad and focused research questions, we will return to the example used in Chapter 3,[1] when we discussed which broad research questions might be most productive to examine. The reader will recall that after eliminating other options, the student researchers who were looking into the problem of large numbers of unfounded child abuse determinations settled on one broad question: Are the different demographic characteristics of workers (for example, age, race, sex, or parenthood) related to their determinations? This was a good start. The question provided a beginning focus for the study and helped to narrow their literature review to a manageable number of topics. It committed the researchers to gaining a better understanding of the decision (founded /unfounded) that child protection workers must make when they receive a referral for possible child abuse or neglect. It provided a research focus—exploration of a possible relationship between one factor (social worker characteristics) and those decisions. But the question was still too general to provide any real direction to the researchers as to the best way to go about seeking an answer to it.

At this point in the process, it also was not known to what degree answers already existed to the question, what methods had been used to study it, or what other researchers had learned in the process of conducting research on the question or on related questions. For example, without reviewing the literature, it was not possible to know which worker characteristics would or would not be promising to examine.

Before conducting their literature review, the researchers also were left with a very impractical and vague idea of how to proceed with their research. One group member suggested facetiously that they should just find some child protection workers and ask them to write a description of themselves and how they make decisions. She and the other members knew there had to be a better way to proceed, but what was it? Until they consulted the literature, they could not know what it was.

When they began to search the literature, the researchers soon confirmed what they had suspected—they were not attempting to build knowledge in a vacuum. For example, it was learned that other researchers had been studying professionals' decision making for many years; some had even used human service workers as research participants. Other literature (conflicting federal laws and procedures) confirmed their hunch that there was a lack of consistent clear federal procedural guidelines and that the definitions of what constitutes child abuse were vague. A review of state policy manuals suggested that state guidelines were no less ambiguous.

The researchers found one article that was especially helpful in suggesting how to study their research question. It described the relative merits of different research methods that were used to learn what factors seem to influence social workers' decision making in a variety of settings (but not in child protection).

As they continued to search the literature and talked more with child welfare administrators, group members began to compile a list of personal characteristics that, based on past research, might be related to the decisions that they make. Several appeared to be especially good prospects. They included level of educational achievement, discipline methods used in the workers' homes of origin, feelings about their jobs, and whether they were parents themselves. All had been found to be related to social workers' decision making in one or more other research studies. They decided to collect data on each of these and not to gather data on certain other worker characteristics (for example, age, health status, or gender) that, based on past research, probably would not be related to decision making about cases referred for possible child abuse or neglect.

Some of what the researchers learned from their literature review could be described as inconclusive or even conflicting. For example, the human behavior literature suggested that parenting practices in the home of origin would be likely to have some effect on adult attitudes toward the ways that others treated their children. But personnel data also indicated that the child protection workers had undergone both formal education and special training for their jobs. Wasn't it logical to conclude that parenting practices in their home of origin might no longer influence their decision making to any great degree? Maybe, but remember (Chapter 1), logic is pretty untrustworthy as a source of knowledge.

The literature review produced focused research questions that would have been impossible to formulate prior to finding out what was already known about the problem, what related questions had been studied, and what answers had been found. Because of it, the researchers were able to take their broad research question and to reformulate it into two more focused (more specific) questions:

- Is there a relationship between disciplinary practices in child protection workers' families of origin and their decision making about cases referred for suspected child abuse or neglect?
- To what degree do workers perceive that their formal education and training in child protection services has influenced their decision making about cases referred for suspected child abuse or neglect?

With these and other focused questions to work with, the research took on a clearer focus. As a result of conducting the literature review, it was now possible to know what data about workers and their decisions should be gathered and, by learning from the experiences of other researchers, to have a good idea about the best ways to go about gathering it. Box 5.1 provides additional examples of broad research questions and a corresponding focused research question that might be produced through reviewing relevant scientific literature.

BOX 5.1   Examples of Broad Research Questions and Focused Research Questions

Broad Research Questions	Focused Research Questions
A. Are people with developmental disabilities unhappy working in sheltered workshops?	A. What working conditions contribute most to dissatisfaction of workers in sheltered workshops?
B. How do value conflicts affect client services when social workers are supervised by nurses?	B. When nurses supervise social workers, why are patients less likely to refuse painful life-extending treatment?
D. Why do social work students dislike courses in research and statistics?	C. Is there a correlation between the increase in day care facilities and reports of abuse or neglect?
C. Have day care facilities increased to meet the needs of families denied extended benefits since welfare reform?	D. Is the rate of math phobia higher among social work students than in the general population?
E. What obstacles to the grief process do parents of children who die while committing violent crimes perceive?	E. Why do parents of children who die while committing violent crimes often withdraw from contact with their communities?

Research Hypotheses

In most qualitative research, a brief search of available literature prior to data collection helps to formulate a plan for conducting the research (a design) and to narrow and refine the research question or questions. But it goes no farther. It does not suggest answers to the questions. Thus, data collection begins without being able to predict what will be found, just a little clearer idea of the questions to be examined. However, in more quantitative studies, the research problem or a similar one may have been studied for some time, and a considerable amount of related knowledge about it may have accumulated. Then a literature review may do even more. It may suggest what will be found after data are collected and analyzed. Then it is possible to formulate one or more research hypotheses.

A *research hypothesis* is a tentative answer to a research question. It is based on existing knowledge (and sometimes, to a lesser degree, on practice experience) and is a prediction of what the researcher will find. It generally takes the form of a statement of a relationship between or among certain variables. In research studies, that are primarily quantitative, data that have been collected are examined using statistical tests to determine whether support for research hypotheses was found. As previously noted, researchers usually do not seek support for research hypotheses in more qualitative studies. Relevant variables often are not even identified when data collection begins—it would be impossible to predict a relationship between them. However, the final product of a qualitative study may be one or more theories or *hypothesis statements*. Other researchers may subsequently adopt them as their research hypotheses and then attempt to learn if there is support for them, often using more quantitative methods.

Research hypotheses generally are stated in either the present or the future tense. In rare instances, such as in the case of historical research (Chapter 8), the past tense is used. They also are stated in the form of declarative sentences, never as questions, because they are (tentative) answers to research questions.

Related Definitions

To understand fully just what research hypotheses are and how a literature review can be helpful in formulating them, we will first need to define certain key research terms.

Variable.   We have already used the term *variable* several times. It is impossible not to do so because the study of variables is essential to research. A *variable* is an attribute or characteristic that differs in quantity or quality among different persons, objects, times, places, and so on. In our earlier example, the different parenting experiences of child protection workers within their homes of origin would be a variable. If all the workers had been parented in the same way, parenting experience would not be considered a variable; it would be a *constant*. In research, constants usually are of less interest than variables.

Demographic Variable.   A demographic variable is a type of variable. The term *demographic variable* really is a generic term that is used most often by researchers to refer to those commonly measured variables that give researchers (and, when reported, readers of research reports) a clearer understanding of the general characteristics of research participants. Some of the variables generally referred to as "demographic" include age, gender, income, religious affiliation, education, and marital status. Demographic variables sometimes are collectively referred to as *bio-data.*

Although certain demographic variables frequently are included in questionnaires and other research data collection instruments, there is no rule that says that they must be. Unless researchers have reason to believe that a demographic variable is related to the research question in some way (as determined through the literature review) or that the readers of their research report will require information about it (e.g., to determine if their clients are similar to researchers' participants), there is really no justification to measure it. In fact, unless one of these justifications exists, there may be some good ethical and practical reasons not to measure it. Some demographic variables (e.g., age, religious affiliation, marital status, or income) may be considered sensitive and personal. Collecting data about them when the researcher has no practical use for them is an unnecessary invasion of the participants' right to privacy. Besides, requesting unnecessary data from participants who are less than eager to provide them can jeopardize the collection of other data that are really needed.

Value Label or Value. The terms *value label* or *value* (as used in research) mean essentially the same thing. They are (respectively) the name or number assigned to a specific measurement of a variable.

A value label is a word or words used to denote a form that a variable can assume. (Some people prefer to use the term *attribute,* as in "the different attributes a variable can assume.") For example, for the variable "parenting style in home of origin," different value labels might be "autocratic," "democratic," "laissez-faire," or some other group of words that reflect the differences in parenting style that existed within child protection workers' homes of origin. Note that the differences reflect different kinds or qualities (rather than quantities) of the variable. A value also is a specific measurement of a variable, but it is expressed as a number reflecting the quantity of the variable present. For the variable "number of siblings," different values would likely be 0, 1, 2, 3, 4, and so on, indicating the actual number of siblings who were present in the home.

Whether we use the term value label or value is a function of just how precisely a variable can be measured (see Chapter 10), and whether its different measurements reflect only a difference in kind or have a more quantitative connotation. Thus, the variable "parenthood" might use value labels like "yes" or "no" to denote whether each worker is a parent. However, if we were to ask exactly how many biological or adopted children under age eighteen resided with the worker, 0, 1, 2, 3, or 4, and so forth would be referred to as values, since they reflect quantitative differences among research participants.

Frequency. *Frequency* refers to the number of times that a given value label or value was found to exist among the persons, objects, and the like (referred to as *cases* in a given research study) that were studied. If five workers were found to have been reared in homes that used autocratic parenting styles, we would say that the value label "autocratic" had a frequency of 5. If democratic styles existed in nine homes of workers, the value label "democratic" would have had a frequency of 9, and so forth.

Dependent Variable and Independent Variable or Predictor Variable and Outcome Variable.   Often, in an attempt to communicate clearly what a researcher is predicting within a hypothesis, one of two possible pairs of terms is used. The terms *dependent variable* and *independent variable* are one such pair. When they are used, the term dependent variable is assigned to the variable whose variation the researcher is most interested in understanding and explaining. In social work research, the different degree of treatment success that occurs among clients is a common dependent variable, but a dependent variable can be any other variable that the researcher has declared to be the one whose variations are of primary interest.

The label dependent variable is not applied to a variable unless at least one other variable (independent variable) has been hypothesized to be at least a contributor to its variations. The term independent variable is then applied to the variable or variables that the researcher believes may produce at least some of the variation that exists within the dependent variable. If, for example, the variable degree of treatment success among clients in a hypothesis is labeled the dependent variable, the independent variable might be method of treatment, degree of family involvement, or fee paid by the client. It also could be some other variable that the literature and practice experience have indicated as likely to contribute to the variations in the degree of treatment success that clients experience.

Ideally, an independent variable is introduced and/or manipulated in some way by the researcher so that its effects on the dependent variable can be monitored and recorded. Of course, this is often either ethically or logistically impossible. As long as the researcher is asserting that one variable is believed to influence the values of a second variable (and not vice versa), it is appropriate to refer to the first variable as the independent variable and to the second as the dependent variable.

The terms dependent variable and independent variable are used together or not at all. Another pair of terms sometimes is substituted, *predictor variable* (in place of independent variable) and *outcome variable* (in place of dependent variable), when they more accurately describe what is believed to be the relationship between variables. Like the term dependent variable, the term outcome variable communicates which variable is of primary interest to the researcher.

Predictor variable and outcome variable are the terms of choice when the researcher has no control over the variables and the best that can be learned is whether they are associated or correlated (discussed later in this chapter). For example, in a research hypothesis that predicts the relationship between gender and age of first sexual experience in a certain culture it would be appropriate to describe gender as the predictor variable and age of first sexual experience as the outcome variable. To use the terms independent variable and dependent variable would be misleading, since the researcher cannot assume or hope to demonstrate conclusively that gender causes or is even a contributor to variations in age of first sexual experience, even if the two variables are found to be related.

The terms dependent variable (or outcome variable) and independent variable (or predictor variable) are specific to a given piece of research. That is, they describe the focus of one researcher's investigation and the nature of a relationship between variables believed to exist within it. Another researcher is likely to have a different focus and/or to suggest a different relationship. Thus, in different research studies, different labels may be used for the same variable or variables. For example, a social worker seeking to explain different success rates among couples in marital counseling (the dependent variable) would label type of treatment used as the independent variable. Within the same organization, a social work administrator may conduct other research in which type of treatment is the variable primary interest (outcome variable) and may label some other variable, such as the school of social work attended by counselors, as the predictor variable.

The terms dependent variable, independent variable, outcome variable, and predictor variable should be regarded simply as convenient labels. They help the reader of a research report understand the focus of the researcher's area of inquiry and better understand exactly what the researcher believes to be the nature of a relationship between or among variables. They also suggest the type of research methods used and the type of statistical analysis most likely to have been applied.

Sometimes neither pair of labels is appropriate. In some research that predicts the existence of a relationship between variables, it may not be possible or appropriate to identify one variable in a hypothesis as clearly dependent (or outcome) and another as independent (or predictor). For example, the literature may suggest that alcoholism and unemployment are related, but in a study of the relationship between the two social problems, it may not be possible to make a case for applying the label "outcome" (or "dependent") to one variable any more than to the other. The researcher may be more interested in studying their interaction than in understanding variation in rates of one or the other, or in examining to what degree (if any) one may be influencing the other. Or the research goal may be simply to hope to learn the extent to which one problem tends to be found with the other. If either is the primary research focus, the terms dependent (or outcome) variable or independent (or predictor) variable would not be used. Then the hypothesis should be stated so that it is clear that the researcher is not communicating that one variable is of any greater interest than the other, or that it is believed that one variable is contributing to the different values of the other variable, simply that they *covary* (they vary together in a certain pattern).

Other Related Terms.   We know from our knowledge of human behavior that the relationship between two variables is rarely a simple one. For example, the decision to join or not join a youth gang is not solely a function of whether or not there is a father figure in the home. Many other variables come into play that can easily confuse us about the true relationship between these two variables. Researchers have names that they use to describe the other variables.

The term *confounding variable* is frequently used in a generic way. It refers to any variable that somehow can mislead the researcher about the true relationship between dependent and independent variables. A term that is used similarly is *extraneous variable*. The term *intervening variable* also is sometimes substituted. However, this term really has a more specific usage relating to the time when a variable's influence on the relationship between an independent variable and a dependent variable was believed to occur. In this more narrow usage, a variable could be considered potentially intervening only if it may have influenced the dependent variable after the independent variable occurred. For example, sexual experiences during adolescence might be considered an intervening variable if a researcher wished to study the relationship between the presence or absence of sexual abuse as a child (independent variable) and current sexual satisfaction (dependent variable) of adults. The independent variable (the presence or absence of sexual abuse as a child) may have influenced the intervening variable (sexual experiences during adolescence), which in turn influenced the dependent variable (current sexual satisfaction).

There is other, more specific terminology that more precisely describes the specific way in which one or more other variables might have the potential to mislead the researcher about the true relationship between the dependent and independent variables. For example, the term *antecedent variable* is used to describe a third variable that preceded both the dependent and the independent variables and influenced both of their variations. Or the term *obscuring variable* is used to describe a variable that interacts with the dependent and independent variables in such a way as to make them appear less closely related than they really are. In an introductory book like this one, these distinctions are not too important. We will use the term confounding variable in its generic sense to refer to any variable that has the potential to distort or misrepresent the true relationship between the dependent (or outcome) and independent (or predictor) variables, no matter how (specifically) it does or in which direction it has the potential to mislead the researcher.

Social work practitioners are aware of and work with confounding variables all the time, although the label may be an unfamiliar one. In practice as in research, we would hope to control confounding variables and to minimize or eliminate their influence, but this often is not possible. For example, as practitioners, we might wish to know to what degree our treatment is influencing a client's social functioning. But we may be concerned about how the attitude or behavior of a spouse or of the client's employer (potentially confounding variables) might influence the level of success that may be achieved in our treatment. We sometimes must acknowledge that our treatment may be less a factor in the client's social functioning level than either of these other variables. Either may have a major influence on what on the surface may appear to be the relationship between our treatment and our client's social functioning. The interaction between the spouse's and the employer's behaviors and attitudes and any number of other possible confounding variables can muddy the water as we attempt to determine the relationship between our treatment and the client's level of social functioning.

Fortunately, researchers have devised ways to minimize or at least to help sort out the influence of variables that are potentially confounding in attempting to understand the relationship between dependent and independent variables. When this is possible, we no longer refer to a variable as confounding or extraneous or by any of the other terms that denote the specific way the variable may be affecting the primary relationship between independent and dependent variables. We refer to it as a *control variable* (sometimes called a *moderating variable*), a potentially confounding variable whose influence has been controlled. This can be done using one of several statistical tests, employing mathematical formulas designed for this purpose. When the apparent relationship between the independent variable and the dependent variable disappears when the measurements of the control variable are introduced into the formula, researchers describe the original relationship as *spurious*. Of course, the introduction of the control variable can also have the opposite effect—it can reveal an apparent relationship between the independent and dependent variables that was not previously in evidence. This suggests that the control variable was really an obscuring variable.

Types of Relationships between Variables

A research hypothesis, as we noted, states that we believe (based on existing knowledge as revealed in the literature and our experience) certain variables are related. The presence of the research hypothesis sends notice that we are seeking additional evidence for this presumed relationship. In addition, a research hypothesis generally goes a little further. It also states the *nature* of the relationship between the variables. Certain types of relationships are commonly stated in hypotheses (see Box 5.2). Some reflect a very subtle distinction; others are more dramatic. We will mention the three most commonly used ones.

Association.   A research hypothesis that states a belief in an association between variables is really a pretty conservative assertion. It asserts that certain value categories of one variable (usually one that cannot be measured with much precision) tend to be found with certain value categories of another variable.

To describe a relationship between variables as an association is to acknowledge that the influence of one or more confounding variables is likely and that they probably have not been adequately controlled. It also acknowledges both the limits of measurement of the variables (see Chapter 10) and the limits of the statistical analysis (see Chapter 12) used to determine the likelihood of a true relationship between the variables. A research hypothesis is likely to be stated so as to reflect only an association between variables (and nothing more) if

- The variables can be measured so that their values reflect only qualitative differences (differences of kind) and not the precise quantity of the variable present.
- Statistical analysis that produces only an indication of degree of association is all that can legitimately be used.
- The researcher was unable to introduce or manipulate the predictor variable in any way or to exert control over potentially confounding variables.

An example of a research hypothesis that suggests a relationship of only association is: Among adolescent patients, those who receive group treatment are more likely to be rehospitalized than those who receive individual treatment. Note that, in this hypothesis, all three of the preceding conditions are present.

Research hypotheses that state beliefs about association between or among variables are quite common in social work research. Although an association between variables gives researchers less information about the relationship than they might like to have,

BOX 5.2   Relationships between Variables Expressed in Hypotheses

Association	Certain value categories of X are found with certain value categories of Y.
Causation	Values or value categories of X cause values or value categories of Y.
Correlation	Higher values of X are found with higher values of Y and vice versa; or, higher values of X are found with lower values of Y and vice versa.

knowledge of an association between variables still can be useful to the social worker. For example, if researchers were to learn that there is an association between gender and child protection decisions, this might represent very useful information, even though it would fall short of saying that being male or female alone causes one to make certain decisions.

Causation.   A research hypothesis that states a belief in causation goes out on a limb. It states that the values or value categories of the independent variable *produce* different values or value categories of the dependent variable. It leaves no room for the possibility that one or more confounding variables or any other phenomenon (such as a biased sample or chance) may have produced this apparent relationship within cases that are studied. An example of a hypothesis that states a relationship of causation between variables is: Among adolescent psychiatric patients, group treatment produces lower rates of rehospitalization than individual treatment. In order to demonstrate support for this relationship, three conditions would have to be present:

- The treatment must have occurred before the rehospitalization/nonrehospitalization.
- There must be an association between the independent and dependent variables.
- All other explanations for rehospitalization or nonrehospitalization (besides the type of treatment given) must have been ruled out.

The first two conditions might be met. However, the third one would be extremely problematic. It would require a research design that would be logistically difficult and, perhaps, unethical. The requirements of such a design will be discussed in Chapter 6.

Not surprisingly, research hypotheses that suggest a belief in a relationship of causation between variables (also known as a cause–effect relationship) are relatively rare in social work research. If the dependent variable is a behavior or human condition (which often is the case), we would not likely conclude that it is caused by the influence of any one other variable. That would be in direct opposition to our belief that behavior or conditions have many interrelated causes, a major tenet of social systems theory. For ethical (Chapter 2) and logistical reasons it is often impossible physically to control potentially confounding variables that are likely to influence the relationship between the dependent and the independent variables. We might be able to control statistically for their influence, but we would first have to identify all of them, an impossible task. For these reasons, most research designs used in social work research do not presume to identify cause–effect relationships between variables.

Correlation.   A correlation might be regarded as a special type of association. If a research hypothesis predicts a correlation between variables, it implies a little more about their relationship than just a simple association. But a prediction that variables will be found to be correlated still falls far short of saying that the values of one variable will be shown to have caused the values of the other to occur, just that they will be found to covary. As in the case of association, inadequately controlled confounding variables (or some other cause) may be producing any apparent relationship between the variables. A hypothesis is likely to be stated so as to reflect a correlation between or among variables if

- The variables can be measured so that their values reflect different, precise, and measurable quantities of the variables.
- Certain statistical analyses designed to determine the strength and direction of the relationship will be used.
- The researcher was unable to introduce or manipulate the predictor variable in any way or to exert control over potentially confounding variables.

Unless it is specifically stated otherwise, when a correlation between variables is predicted in a research hypothesis, it refers to a linear correlation. (There are other types that are discussed in statistics books.[2]) A *linear correlation* between two variables is a relationship in which one of two patterns exists. Either high values (indicating large, quantitative measurements) of one variable are found (disproportionately) with high values of the other variable, and low values of the first are found with low values of the second (described as a *positive correlation*). Or high values of one variable are found with low values of the other variable and vice versa (described as a *negative* or *inverse correlation*). These patterns of a relationship can be seen in a graph called a *scattergram* which portrays simultaneously the measurements for both variables for every case. In a scattergram, strong correlations will be reflected in a pattern of dots that approximate a straight line, hence the term linear correlation.

An example of a research hypothesis that predicts the existence of a linear correlation between two variables is: Among adolescent psychiatric patients, there is a negative correlation between number of group treatment sessions attended per week and length of hospitalization. Note that the hypothesis predicts a negative correlation. It predicts that former patients who attended the most group sessions per week will have spent less time hospitalized than those who rarely attended, and vice versa. A hypothesis that predicted a positive correlation between the predictor and criterion variables would have been illogical, assuming that the group sessions were believed to be making a positive contribution to patients' recovery.

In the most common usage of the term, a correlation is just a little more precise statement of a relationship between variables (based on their measurement and the type of statistical analysis used) than an association. Like association, it does not prove causation. Many variables are highly correlated, yet the different values of one variable do not cause the different values of the other. In a research hypothesis that predicts a relationship of correlation, researchers generally use the labels predictor variable and outcome variable (rather than independent variable and dependent variable) to describe the relationship between variables. This occurs when it is believed that values of one (the predictor variable) are a better predictor of values of the other (the outcome variable) than the other way around, or when the values of one (the predictor variable) occurred before the values of the other (the outcome variable).

Types of Research Hypotheses

If a researcher predicts that variables will be found to be related (association, causation, or correlation), it is possible to express that relationship in one of two ways within a research hypothesis. Either a directional or a nondirectional hypothesis may be appropriate, depending on what was learned from the literature review.

In a *directional* (also called *one-tailed*) *research hypothesis,* the researcher not only asserts that the variables will be found to be related, but also predicts the direction of their relationship. In contrast, in a *nondirectional (two-tailed) research hypothesis,* the researcher asserts that the variables will be found to be related, but does not wish to hazard a guess as to the direction in which they will be found to be related.[3] An example of a directional hypothesis is: Among adolescent psychiatric patients, those who received group treatment will reflect a higher rate of rehospitalization than those who received individual treatment. An example of a nondirectional hypothesis using the same two variables is: Among adolescent psychiatric patients, there will be a difference in rehospitalization rate between those who received group counseling and those who received individual counseling.

Sometimes variables are commonly believed to be related, but the researcher, based on the literature review and practice experience, has become convinced that they really are unrelated. Then a research hypothesis would be stated in such a way that it reflects the prediction that the variables will be found to be unrelated. An example of a hypothesis that predicts no relationship between variables is: Among adolescent psychiatric patients, those who received group treatment will have the same rate of rehospitalization as those who received individual treatment.

Notice that, in this example, the two variables were described as having no association. If they are not even believed to be associated, they could not be correlated, or a relationship of causation could not exist. Box 5.3 provides another example of the differences among these forms of research hypotheses.

Notice too that the third type of research hypothesis is really just the opposite of the other two types. It states that two variables are unrelated; if they somehow appear to be related, that is because of one or more other explanations, for example, the influence of some confounding variable or some other flaw in the design of the research. The appearance of a relationship might exist because we deliberately or unintentionally drew an atypical sample of cases to study (Chapter 9) or simply because we just drew an unusual sample—samples rarely look exactly like they would if all possible cases were to be studied. This latter phenomenon is why the third type of research hypothesis is sometimes (mistakenly) referred to as the "null hypothesis." However, they are not exactly the same, which is why we have chosen to use another term. First, the null hypothesis (discussed in more detail in Chapter 12) is not a *research* hypothesis per se. It is more hypothetical than real. Besides, it relates *only* to the tendency of samples to naturally differ from each other and from the population from which they are selected, and the degree to which that may have produced an apparent relationship between variables. It says nothing about all of the other reasons (including those just mentioned) why variables may appear to be related when they really are not.

BOX 5.3   Three Types of Research Hypotheses

1. Directional   "Males learn computer skills faster than females" *or* "Females learn computer skills faster than males."
2. Nondirectional "Males and females learn computer skills at different speeds."
3. No relationship "There is no difference in the speed at which males and females learn computer skills."

When Are Research Hypotheses Appropriate?

As noted previously, the literature may suggest that any tentative suggestion about the answer to a research question (that is, a hypothesis) would be very presumptive on our part. There may just not be enough known about the area to justify making a statement about how certain variables might be related or even which variables are relevant to the research problem, as in the case of many qualitative studies. Or, if an answer is suggested, the literature, research ethics, and/or our knowledge of social work practice may reveal that it would be impossible to test that answer. If either of these is the case, a testable hypothesis might not be appropriate.

If previous efforts have been made to study the research question, if at least some tentative statement about the relationship between variables seems justified, if finding or not finding support for such a relationship would be a valuable contribution to knowledge, and if it appears that a method can be devised to test that relationship, then one or more hypotheses may be in order. Whether a research hypothesis should suggest a belief in causation, correlation, an association, or no relationship between or among variables is a bit of a judgment call based on the researcher's assessment of just how much is already known about the answer to the research question and what type of measurement of variables, control of potentially confounding variables, and data analysis is believed to be possible. Existing knowledge (and the researcher's belief in its credibility) as well as personal observations would be used in deciding whether the research hypothesis should be stated in its directional or nondirectional form.

There is one additional general guideline that should be used in formulating a research hypothesis. At this point, it should be obvious but probably bears mentioning anyway. When a hypothesis is tested, the results should produce a reasonable extension of existing knowledge as found in the literature. Finding support or nonsupport for it should never fail to increase our knowledge about a problem; it should do more than simply confirm what we already know. On the other extreme, it is extremely rare that the knowledge generated by hypothesis testing represents a quantum leap from what we already know. The findings of most research make a relatively small contribution to filling a knowledge gap. Most good research hypotheses reflect this realistic expectation.

Although we might like to demonstrate support for research hypotheses, it is not essential to the goal of advancing our understanding of a research problem. One of the beauties of research is that, if it is conducted according to principles of scientific inquiry and we thus have reasonable confidence in our findings, we stand to advance knowledge by demonstrating either that variables probably are related or that they probably are not. For example, a researcher might hypothesize that one treatment intervention designed to reduce clinical depression is more effective than another method. But if it is learned that both methods are really about equally effective (nonsupport for a directional research hypothesis), this knowledge can still inform practice decision making. An unsupported research hypothesis is just as valuable as one for which support has been demonstrated. Among other benefits, an unsupported hypothesis can tell other researchers what hunches *not* to bother to pursue in their own research.

Wording of Research Hypotheses

It should be obvious by now that the way a research hypothesis is stated is very important. We want it to communicate exactly what we are predicting will be found, and nothing else. There are some helpful guidelines that have evolved within the scientific community,[4] based on researchers' recognition of the importance of clear communication. The following additional criteria are generally considered important.

Consistency of Conceptualization.   The variables within the hypothesis, the dependent (outcome) and independent (predictor) variables, should be stated at approximately the same level of abstraction or concreteness. For example, the research hypothesis— People who hold college degrees have a high level of self-awareness—fails to meet this criterion of a good hypothesis. The first variable, education level, is easily measured and would fall on the concrete end of the continuum of conceptualization. The other variable, self-awareness, is far more abstract and difficult to measure with precision. A restatement of the research hypothesis that reflects greater consistency of conceptualization would be: People who hold college degrees will be more likely to receive a score of more than 80 on the Smith and Jones Scale of Self-Awareness than those who do not hold a college degree. Or, by moving education to a more abstract level, we could state: People with high achievement will have a higher level of self-awareness than those with low achievement.

Relevance to the Problem.   Good hypotheses, when tested, will generate knowledge that has the potential to contribute to the alleviation of the research problem. This criterion seems obvious. Why would a researcher ever state and test a research hypothesis that is unrelated to the problem? It can happen, usually unintentionally. Sometimes, in the process of reviewing the literature, researchers can get sidetracked, losing sight of why they wanted to study it in the first place. They emerge with some very justifiable and logical research hypotheses that unfortunately have little or no relationship to the problem or its solution. This generally occurs because the broad research questions were not well formulated and did not provide enough focus. With good, broad questions, the problem is less likely to occur. This criterion should be thought of as a reminder, a check to make sure that the researcher did not forget about the problem while immersed in the literature.

Completeness.   A research hypothesis should be stated as completely as possible. The person reading it should not wonder about the researcher's meaning or if it is missing key words. A sure indicator that a hypothesis is incomplete is the use of words that suggest comparison without the presence of a reference point. For example, the research hypothesis— Women under age thirty are more assertive—lacks completeness. It leaves the reader in doubt about what exactly the researcher believes to be true about the assertiveness of women under thirty. Are they more assertive than women over thirty, than men under thirty, than all men, or than whom? A research hypothesis that would be considered more complete is: Women under age thirty are more assertive than women thirty and older. Phrases like "faster," "more frequently," and so on are useless in communicating the researcher's beliefs unless a reference point (for example, a comparison group) is included in the hypothesis.

Specificity.   Specificity is closely related to completeness. Both criteria emphasize the importance of the researcher's saying exactly what is meant in a research hypothesis. Specificity requires that the words chosen to describe the variables in the research hypothesis and the relationship believed to exist between them should suggest only one meaning to the reader of the hypothesis. Many words and phrases in our language have more than one meaning; the researcher has the responsibility to ensure that a research hypothesis is stated so that no misunderstanding can possibly result. For example, the hypothesis—Poorly timed marital counseling will reflect a low success rate—lacks specificity (in addition to having other problems). The expression "poorly timed marital counseling" probably refers to other factors that may exist in a couple's life at the time that they seek counseling. But we cannot be sure. It may also refer to social workers' tendency to let their appointments run over the time scheduled for counseling sessions. Similarly, the word *reflect* in the hypothesis also contributes confusion regarding the researcher's meaning. It is one of those words that sometimes are used as synonymous with "have," and other times it is used to say that factors appear to be related when they really are not. Further confusing matters, it even has a special clinical meaning to social workers—an interviewing technique designed to help clients consider the meaning of what they have said. Given the context of the word in the research hypothesis, it is impossible to tell which meaning of the word is intended. The researcher's belief could be expressed with more specificity if the hypothesis were restated. For example, it could have been worded: Couples undergoing bankruptcy proceedings are less likely to judge their marital counseling successful than those couples who have less severe financial problems.

Potential for Testing.   In order to examine a possible relationship between or among variables, it is necessary to measure those variables with reasonable precision. Different cases must be able to be sorted into different groups (assigned value labels or values) in such a way that each case clearly falls into one and only one group. Some variables seem almost to defy objective measurement and therefore are inappropriate for inclusion within research hypotheses. For example, teachers and students continue to disagree on what constitutes effective teaching or on what the characteristics of good leadership are. A research hypothesis that states: Good teachers will exhibit leadership within the classroom, would be a difficult one to test until we can achieve better agreement on how to measure both good teaching and leadership. Like beauty or a good personality, they remain a little too subjective to be able to test the hypothesis objectively. However, another research hypothesis—Teachers who post office hours are more likely to receive higher teaching evaluations than those who do not post office hours—is more testable. Here both variables are easily measurable.

The "Perfectly Worded" Research Hypothesis

The preceding five criteria for the wording of a research hypothesis tend to overlap a little. Sometimes meeting the requirements of one criterion helps the researcher meet the requirements of a second one; sometimes it can have the opposite effect. The perfect research hypothesis, one that meets all criteria and that does it in one or more clear, concise statements is probably an unachievable goal. The criteria should be viewed as guidelines to help the researcher improve the way a hypothesis is stated, even if perfection is not possible.

Research hypothesis construction, like problem identification (Chapter 3), is one of those steps in the research process that all too often is addressed hurriedly or taken lightly. A well worded hypothesis can facilitate decision making at all other stages of the research process that follow; a research hypothesis that is vague or otherwise sloppy can cause later difficulties for the social work researcher. Time spent on hypothesis construction is rarely wasted; in the long run, it is a time saver.

Use of Subhypotheses

One other technique sometimes can be used to help research hypotheses communicate more effectively what the researcher is saying. It is a good idea not to try to say too much in a single hypothesis. If a relationship between variables is believed to exist but is a difficult one to explain in a simple declarative sentence, several different subhypotheses may be needed.

Subhypotheses often are helpful if there is an overall pattern of relationship between variables, but the pattern does not hold up for all case values or even reverses itself at some points. (Statisticians sometimes refer to this as a *nonlinear relationship* between variables.) For example, social workers working in hospice settings might be hypothesized to exhibit certain patterns of degree of involvement with patients and their caregivers at various stages in the course of the patient's terminal illness. We might predict that they generally tend to be more involved when the patient first seeks hospice care and as the patient approaches death than during the time periods in between. The relationship between their degree of involvement and the stages of illness of their patients cannot be stated simply in one brief research hypothesis. Any overall pattern believed to exist could be stated first as the central hypothesis, for example: Hospice social workers exhibit different degrees of professional involvement with their patients that are related to the stages of the patient's illness. Then many different subhypotheses could be formulated to describe any other trends within the central pattern. A series of simple statements expressing what we believe to be the relationships between the variables is always preferable to a single research hypothesis that is so complex that few readers could understand it.

Overall, social work researchers should strive for simple, clear communication in stating research hypotheses. If they are successful in this effort, their hypotheses should be more than adequate to guide the subsequent stages of the research process.

Summary

In this chapter, we examined two of the important products that may emerge from a search of existing knowledge. In both qualitative and quantitative studies, the researcher uses it to be able to state the research question or questions more precisely, reflecting a more specific focus of the research. In quantitative research (and much more rarely in qualitative studies) existing knowledge suggests a possible answer to one or more of them. Then the researcher goes even further and draws conclusions from the literature in the form of one or more research hypotheses that will be tested.

Social workers and other researchers have developed their own language (and sometimes used existing language) to communicate certain key concepts. They use it both for clarity and efficiency of communication. In this chapter we introduced many research terms and described their specific meanings for the researcher.

We defined those terms that are essential to the understanding of hypotheses. The meanings of *variable, demographic variable, value label* or *value, frequency, dependent variable, independent variable, outcome variable* and *predictor variable* were explored in some detail. Other terms used to describe the specific effects that other variables may have on the relationship between the principal variables of interest were also introduced. In future chapters, we will use the most generic of these terms, *confounding variable* to describe any variable that might confuse us about the true relationship between the independent (or predictor) and dependent (or outcome) variables.

A research hypothesis was defined (among other things) as a prediction of a relationship between or among variables. It generally goes even further in predicting the way in which they will be found to be related. Terms used to describe the nature of a relationship between variables (*association, causation,* and *correlation*) were differentiated, and the forms that a research hypothesis can take (*directional, nondirectional,* or *no relationship*) were explained.

The importance of wording in hypothesis construction was emphasized throughout this chapter. Criteria for evaluating the quality of the wording of a research hypothesis were proposed, and the appropriate use of subhypotheses was discussed.

For Discussion

1. Why would it be unwise to select a single broad research question before conducting a literature review? Is it possible to start out with too many broad research questions?
2. Why do qualitative studies usually not test research hypotheses?
3. Why is it more acceptable to change focused research questions or to add new ones during data collection in a qualitative study than in a more quantitative one?
4. Why is a research hypothesis never in the form of a question?
5. What factors determine whether one or more research hypotheses are appropriate in a research study?
6. Why are the terms *independent variable* and *dependent variable* sometimes not accurate for describing the variables in a research hypothesis?
7. Confounding variables can make two other variables appear to be more (or less) strongly related than they really are. What are some examples of how this might occur?
8. Would it be more accurate to predict in a research hypothesis that gender and scores on a statistics exam will be associated or correlated? Why?
9. A researcher hopes to find support for her conclusion (from reviewing existing knowledge) that men and women are equally successful as managers. What form of research hypothesis should she construct?
10. What is wrong with the wording of this research hypothesis? "Younger people are less likely to show respect for authority unless they have attended military school or had a fundamentalist religious upbringing." How could it be reworded?

Endnotes

1. Bellomy, P., Berstein, H., Bickley, S., et al. (1989). *Factors affecting child protection workers' decision-making in Sumter County.* Unpublished MSW research project. Columbia, SC: University of South Carolina, College of Social Work.

2. See, e.g., Weinbach, R. W., & Grinnell, R. M., Jr. (2007). *Statistics for social workers.* Boston: Allyn and Bacon, 143–144.

3. Ibid., 88.

4. See, for example, Goldstein, H. (1969). *Research standards and methods for social workers.* Northbrook, IL: Whitehall Company, 55–57.

P A R T **III**

RESEARCH DESIGNS

6

TERMS USED TO DESCRIBE
THE GENERAL CHARACTERISTICS
OF A RESEARCH STUDY

In the previous chapter, we discussed how existing knowledge is used prior to data collection. In both qualitative and quantitative research it is used to develop well articulated, focused research questions. In quantitative studies it often allows the researcher to develop research hypotheses as well. In all types of research it also helps the researcher to make decisions about how the research should be conducted, what is generally referred to as the research design.

What Is a Research Design?

A literature review reveals what is already known about the research problem and the methods that have been used to study it. It thus suggests to the researcher what specific research methods and strategies are best suited to conduct further inquiry—a design for the current research study. A design is a plan to attempt to find answers to the researcher's questions and/or to test any hypothesis or hypotheses that were formulated.

The design of a research study is a response to a series of questions. The major ones that it addresses are

- Where and when should the research be conducted?
- What data should be collected?
- From whom can they best be obtained?
- What would be the best way to collect them?
- How will research participants be located or selected?
- What information will be sought?
- What variables will need to be measured?

- How should they be measured?
- Are there other variables that will need to be controlled?
- If so, how should this be accomplished?
- What unavoidable methodological limitations will exist, and how can their effects be minimized?
- How should the data be organized and analyzed?
- How should research findings be disseminated?

The research design serves as a plan for the latter stages of the research. The answers to the preceding questions are not arrived at independently of each other. The decision-making process is made easier by the fact that these questions and their answers are inter-related. Having determined the answer to one or more of them, the answers to other questions often become quite obvious. For example, the selection of certain individuals to provide research data is likely to influence the general method of data collection that will be used. Similarly, the way variables are measured and the way that research participants are selected generally suggest the most appropriate type of statistical analysis to use. If one examines the ways that research has been conducted in the past, the interrelatedness of the preceding questions becomes readily apparent. Certain patterns emerge.

Design Nomenclature

The terminology used to describe the design of a research study can be confusing. That is because the design of a given research study can be (and often is) described in a number of ways and at several different levels. We discussed two of the most general of these back in Chapter 1. Describing research as either "basic" or "applied" communicates how and when the knowledge derived from a study is intended to be used. It says that the findings of a study are designed to either (1) contribute to our professional knowledge base (basic), or (2) to be of immediate use for addressing some problem, answering some question, or making some pending decision (applied).

Another way to convey the general characteristics of a research design that was discussed in Chapter 1 is to describe it as either predominantly "quantitative" or predominantly "qualitative." When applied, the terms suggest reliance on certain research methods, the nature of the data that are collected, and how they are analyzed as well as other distinguishing characteristics. We described them in Chapter 1 and have alluded to them elsewhere several times, but they are used so frequently in the chapters that follow that they are summarized again here in Box 6.1.

Other terms (also adjectives) help to describe research methods in broad terms. We will examine them in this chapter. They offer additional understanding of how and why the research was conducted, for example, how many times key variables were measured, what general methods for acquiring data were used, or what type of knowledge was sought.

Still other commonly used terms are labels for designs have been developed and used effectively in past research and are often a good way to address some current research need. They have become "standards" or models for answering certain types of research questions. They can be displayed graphically to reflect certain key features of the design,

BOX 6.1   Qualitative and Quantitative Research

Qualitative Research	Quantitative Research
• Is admittedly subjective.	• Seeks to be objective.
• Seeks to understand.	• Seeks to explain, predict.
• Uses inductive logic.	• Uses deductive logic.
• Produces hypotheses.	• Tests hypotheses.
• Data analyzed as received.	• Data analyzed after collected.
• Researcher is the instrument.	• Reliance on standardized instruments to measure.

such as the number of research samples (Chapter 9) that are used or the sequence in which certain events are supposed to take place. However, even they do not provide a detailed description of how a given research study should be conducted. They merely describe a general framework on which to build the specifics needed to conduct the research. The researcher still needs to supply the specifics.

Still other terms that help to describe a research design will be discussed in Chapter 8. They are primarily labels for specialized methods for conducting research. These methods rely heavily on certain types of research activities to acquire and analyze certain types of research data.

It is often necessary to use several different terms in order completely and accurately to describe the design of a research study. Some may be very general and some more specific, but each allows some other researcher or the reader of a research report to get a little clearer picture of exactly how the research was conducted.

Cross-Sectional, Pretest-Posttest, or Longitudinal

One way to describe a research design in general terms is to state the number of times observations or personal contacts will occur and/or certain key variables will be measured and, to a lesser degree, the length of time over which the research is conducted. Three terms are frequently used for this purpose and they are defined and discussed in the following paragraphs.

Designs that are described as *cross-sectional* do this just once (with all variables measured as simultaneously as possible). The researcher seeks to acquire "a snapshot in time," and then to draw conclusions about what has been observed. Conclusions may include a description of the distribution of certain variables (for example, how many people experience one problem as opposed to another one or how severe a problem is today). They may also be used to answer questions or test hypotheses about the relationships between variables (for example, are age and attitudes about marriages between people of the same gender related?). Cross-sectional designs are common in social work research, so common that unless the terms pretest-posttest or longitudinal are used, it is usually safe to assume that the design is cross sectional.

In *pretest-posttest* designs (sometimes called "before and after" designs) the researcher conducts observations, or interviews, or measures key variables in some other way twice, generally before and after some event. In evaluation research, the "event" is likely to be a service or social program that is offered to clients or some other life experience to which people are exposed. The presence of a pretest measurement allows us to determine just how much change occurred in the interim between the first and second measurements. That can be important information in, for example, helping to determine the effectiveness of social work intervention.

If a research design is described as *longitudinal,* that means the researcher conducts observations, or interviews, measures key variables, and so forth more than twice, often many more times, and sometimes over a long period of time. All longitudinal research designs share a single characteristic—they entail the repeated study and/or measurement over time at predetermined intervals. Longitudinal studies are designed to study change. But they try to find out more than simply if change occurred or how much change took place. They seek to identify exactly when change occurred and what phenomena were associated with it. Only longitudinal research can provide this type of useful knowledge. For example, in a qualitative longitudinal study, a researcher might study a group of people who survived a natural disaster such as a flood or hurricane by interviewing them annually over ten years to learn how their perceptions of the event change over time and what might be associated with these changes.

Three additional adjectives are often used in describing longitudinal research. They reflect differences in the way that a sample of research participants is selected. One variety, the *trend study,* entails drawing a sample of participants on several different occasions from a group (pool) of potential participants. The pool tends to change over time. For example, a group of students may be selected at random from a social work program each year to participate in a study to assess changes in attitudes toward research. Although some students may be included in more than one stage of data collection (for example, they may appear in the sample selected during two or more different years), the sample of students will be different each year from the sample selected any other year. An overall trend in changes in attitude within the program (but not within individual students) thus can be observed.

In a second variety of longitudinal research, the *cohort study,* the pool of potential research participants does not change, but the specific cases selected for study will differ during stages of data collection. For example, in a cohort study, a class of full-time students might be measured regarding their attitudes toward research over an academic year. Assuming that the class suffered no attrition or added no new members during the year, the class would be known as a cohort. Participants would be selected at random from the class on several occasions. No two groups selected for study would likely be identical in terms of which students would be included, but each group selected would represent the class at the various points of data collection.

In the third variation of longitudinal research, the *panel study,* the same group of research participants would be studied over time. In our example of a study to examine changes in student attitudes toward research, the same randomly selected students would be studied over their student careers to monitor any changes in their attitudes. Only attrition would result in any change in the composition of the group. The infamous Tuskegee studies described in Chapter 2 provides another example of a longitudinal study that used the panel method.

Longitudinal studies can last for a few days or a few weeks. More typically, they are conducted over a period of years. Some have gone on past the lifetime of the researchers who originally designed them and have been carried on by others, for example, studies on the status of women in the United States.

Most longitudinal studies are designed to document change. But they are also well suited to the needs of researchers who wish to document and learn more about the existence of a certain pattern of behavior and what is associated with it. Good examples of longitudinal research of this type are the studies of a large number of terminally ill patients that were conducted by Elizabeth Kübler-Ross[1] and her associates over several decades. The researchers were able to identify five predictable stages in the dying process and to describe them in detail. As a result, hospice social workers and others who work with people who have a terminal illness now possess greater insight into their patients' behaviors and are better able to help them come to successful resolutions relating to their impending death.

The findings of other longitudinal studies in the area of grief and loss[2] have similarly proven invaluable to the social work practitioner. For example, we now know that the time around the first anniversary of the death of a loved one often is accompanied by depression and that anger at a deceased relative is a very predictable phenomenon at certain stages of the grieving process. Consequently, counseling now can focus on helping clients to anticipate and to deal with anniversary depression and to verbalize, better understand, accept, and work through their anger toward the deceased.

Longitudinal designs can acquire knowledge not readily acquired using other designs. Slowly developing changes and up-and-down fluctuations in behaviors and phenomena might be missed using cross-sectional or pretest-posttest designs. But they can be identified and plotted by using repeated measurements over long periods. Longitudinal designs alone are able to tell us when changes occur and to help us to predict their occurrence with reasonable accuracy.

The major drawback to using longitudinal designs is their cost. Researchers often are unwilling or unable to make the expensive, long-term commitment that is necessary to properly conduct them. Because they take so long to complete, researchers who hope to build an academic or scientific career around publication of numerous research papers or professional journal articles tend to shy away from them. One can spend a decade on a longitudinal study that can result in a single published scientific paper. However, such studies may be more substantive and often produce more definitive answers to research questions than cross-sectional or pretest-posttest studies.

Exploratory, Descriptive, or Explanatory

Still another way to characterize a research design in general terms is to use one of three other labels—exploratory, descriptive, or explanatory. They describe the primary type of knowledge that it seeks to acquire and suggests the primary methods that are used for acquiring it.

Knowledge building in a given problem area is a cumulative process. As we suggested in Chapter 1, uncovering and disseminating knowledge is a systematic process that occurs over time. It is rarely (if ever) the work of one individual. That's why we tie our research to existing knowledge by reviewing the professional literature. We want to build on the work of others, and our findings will in turn help to facilitate the work of subsequent researchers.

BOX 6.2   The Knowledge-Building Continuum

Exploratory   → Descriptive   → Explanatory

Sometimes the process of movement toward answers and at least partial solutions to problems occurs relatively rapidly, but more typically, progress in knowledge building is slow work. It entails the use of a variety of methods (designs) that occur most often in a certain logical sequence.

When very little is known about a problem and there are many more questions than answers, certain types of research designs are indicated. As knowledge accumulates, other designs are both possible and indicated. They are in turn replaced by other designs that have the potential to provide more definitive answers to certain types of questions. Because there is a logical sequence in which different designs are employed in the study of a research problem, they can be placed on a continuum such as that shown in Box 6.2.

As Box 6.2 suggests, as a general rule, exploratory research designs tend to be the first kind of research conducted on a problem or question. They then form a basis for descriptive designs, which precede explanatory ones. At least that is the way it is supposed to happen. In the real world, the situation may be quite different. For example, in social work, our understanding of the phenomenon that is the focus of much of our research, human behavior, will always remain quite incomplete and fragmented. Consequently, much of the research that we conduct continues to be of the exploratory and descriptive types, no matter how long some type of behavior has been studied and no matter how many studies of it have been conducted.

Even if a sound base of research knowledge exists about a problem or question, we sometimes still find ourselves unable to move much further along the continuum for other reasons. We may never be able to conduct the most methodologically rigorous explanatory research studies. These designs (at least those that use human participants) are not always feasible for investigating certain questions, because to employ them would violate research and professional ethics (Chapter 2). Some questions—for example: What happens when clients are denied access to all help?—might best be studied by denying help to a randomly selected group of clients applying for our services and asking other organizations also to deny them assistance. Of course, such a practice would not and should not be tolerated. An alternative way of studying the question might be the best that we could do, despite the fact that existing knowledge about the question might suggest that we are ready for explanatory research on it.

Orderly progress along the continuum is perhaps more of an ideal than a description of reality. There are numerous situations that suggest the need for exceptions. Sometimes, we mistakenly conclude that we have learned more about a problem than we really have. Explanatory research is conducted, and it presents us with surprises. It causes us to question the state of existing knowledge about a problem or question. Thus, we conclude that a return to descriptive or even exploratory research is indicated. Often, since historically the emphasis has been on conducting quantitative research, this means going back and conducting more qualitative studies (which tend to fall most often in the exploratory and descriptive areas). Their findings can then be used to "fill in the gaps" or attempt to explain some of the "surprises" that more quantitative studies have produced.

An important task for the researcher reviewing existing knowledge is to locate just where on the continuum one's own research should fall. For example, if a review of professional literature reveals that virtually all of the past research on a problem has been of an exploratory nature, then a more rigorous design, such as explanatory research, is clearly premature. Research that is designed to improve on the current description of the problem and the conditions that surround it would be more appropriate. Conversely, if our professional literature contains some reports of research that used explanatory designs to successfully isolate the cause of the problem, additional exploratory or descriptive research would not seem appropriate. The existing level of knowledge would suggest that such research would be unnecessary and redundant and that, perhaps, it is time to conduct research designed to test the effectiveness of methods of intervention (prevention or treatment) in order to attempt to make a contribution to evidence-based practice.

Examples of Exploratory Designs

Exploratory research is appropriate when problems have been identified but our understanding of them is quite limited. It is conducted to lay the groundwork for other knowledge building that will follow. Exploratory designs are predicated on the assumption that we need to know more about something before we can begin to understand it or attempt to confront it using intervention methods with high potential for success. In exploratory research, we often don't even know what it is we need to know!

In an exploratory study, the researcher begins his or her inquiry without much insight into the research problem, as is often the case in more qualitative studies. But it is hoped that the research will narrow the list. Because the relevant variables cannot even be specified, there can be no hypotheses to test. However, a frequent goal of exploratory research is to derive hypotheses for future research endeavors.

Similarly, selection of research participants or cases for study is usually not a very rigorous or exacting procedure when exploratory research designs are used. There may be few cases studied, or a large number may be selected in order to learn as much as possible about the problem. In either instance, there are no legitimate claims to their being representative of others not selected for study.

We do not wish to imply that persons who conduct exploratory research employ a more haphazard approach to knowledge building than those who use other designs. Good exploratory research is always carefully planned and conducted using specific methods and according to established guidelines. But researchers who conduct exploratory research must work with less "preknowledge" than within other research designs.

Thus, exploratory designs are employed to begin the process of knowledge building about a problem or focused question. For example, prior to the 1960s, exploratory research was used appropriately for studies of child abuse. In the early 1980s, it was used for studying spouse abuse and the problems of people with HIV infection. In the 1990s it was used to study the phenomenon of bullying within school settings. Early in the twenty-first century, cyber-bullying was the focus of exploratory research, as we were just beginning to recognize the existence of a problem that did not exist before the widespread availability of electronic communication. Exploratory studies often simply try to conceptualize exactly what a problem is, the degree to which it is recognized as a problem, what forms it takes, and what variables might relate to it. As knowledge begins to accumulate, exploratory designs are no longer appropriate for studying these problems, but they are appropriate for studying other, more recently identified ones.

We will describe three designs that are widely used in exploratory social work research. They (and the other designs that are commonly used in descriptive and explanatory research studies which are described in the sections that follow) are widely used in research in many fields. Although they were developed for purposes of quantitative research, they may be equally appropriate for qualitative studies, but only if the conditions for using them be met. We will use standard notations to describe them. In quantitative research they signify as follows:

X = Exposure to the independent variable or treatment condition
O_1 = First measurement of the dependent variable
O_2 = Second measurement of the dependent variable
R = Random assignment of persons to a group

1. The One-Shot Case Study.   The one-shot case study design, also called the one-group, posttest-only design, is the most basic of all research designs. Schematically, it is noted as

$$X\ O$$

where X represents exposure to some variable (such as a program or intervention) and O represents measurement of a dependent variable among participants. Let's look at an example of how this design may be used in a social work research study.

Suppose a social worker in a neighborhood community center wishes to determine if eight weeks of English classes are helpful for teaching the English language to a group of Spanish-speaking residents who are seeking employment in an industry where a certain level of English fluency is required. The social worker identifies interested participants and arranges for them to receive the instruction. When the course is completed (eight weeks later), the group takes a brief paper-and-pencil test that measures knowledge of the English language. The social worker scores the tests and calculates the percentage of people who pass it. This provides the measurement of the dependent variable *(O)*.

The major advantage of the design is simplicity. However, it does not provide any comparisons (for example, how much of the English language participants actually knew before exposure to the class, with how much they knew following the eight-week course). Thus, it is difficult to conclude from this design that the program itself (and not something else) brought about any change in the participants' knowledge of English.

2. The Cross-Sectional Survey Design.   The cross-sectional survey design entails measurement of some characteristic in a defined sample or group at a given point in time. It is diagrammed rather simply as

$$O$$

where O represents one measurement of the dependent variable. For example, let's say the associate dean of a school of social work wishes to know what particular social work electives students might wish to take during the summer semester. A brief survey instrument describing proposed elective courses is developed and mailed to students to complete. A large percentage of these students complete the instrument and return it. The associate dean determines from their responses which courses should be offered during the summer semester *(O)*.

The cross-sectional survey design, as used here, provides information about what individuals may want, feel, or believe at a given time. This is its primary usefulness. The alternative would be to guess what students might want for summer course work and run the risk of offering courses that no one is interested in taking or not offering courses that students may want or need.

3. The Longitudinal Case Study Design. In the longitudinal case study design, research participants are exposed to some event or they are introduced to the independent variable (for example, they participate in some social program) followed by several repeat observations, interviews, or measurements. Thus it is a form of longitudinal research. It may be diagrammed as follows:

$$X \; O_1 \; O_2 \; O_3$$

Using our first example again, suppose the social worker wanted to determine if the knowledge of the English language possessed by participants declines, is retained, or continues to grow over a six-month period. X represents the eight-week language course that participants take. O_1 is the first measurement of their knowledge of English taken immediately following the course. O_2 is the second measurement of their knowledge of English taken three months later, and O_3 is the third measurement of this same variable at a six-month follow-up. From this design the social worker is able to determine both (1) what happens to participants' knowledge of English over time; and (2) what else is happening at the times when changes occur.

Examples of Descriptive Designs

The accumulation of the findings derived from exploratory research makes it possible to use descriptive designs. In more qualitative descriptive studies, the researcher often seeks to describe the *variety* of ways that people experience or perceive something, for example some trauma, or other event or life experience. In descriptive research that is more quantitative, measurement and description of relevant variables (those identified using exploratory research designs) and the distribution of their values is usually the goal. For example, research on the problem of child abuse moved beyond exploration and into description by the late 1960s and early 1970s. Studies sought to measure its patterns of incidence and severity, and to chronicle its different forms. The major relevant variables had already been identified through exploratory research; it was now possible and desirable for researchers to measure how they were distributed and to see if there were any patterns of relationships between and among them.

Quantitative descriptive research also sometimes seeks to better understand and measure *how* variables are naturally distributed. However, it does not entail introducing or manipulating variables to see how other variables are affected. Thus, support for a relationship of causation between variables would not be possible using descriptive methods. Although seeking support for relationships between variables is not a major objective of most descriptive research, we sometimes see hypotheses tested in quantitative descriptive research designs. When we do, they generally predict a relationship of association or correlation.

Even when hypotheses are not formulated prior to data collection, a relationship between and among variables sometimes appears to be obvious, especially in large-scale descriptive studies. For example, in one common type of descriptive study, the census, it is often possible to detect apparent associations or correlations that appear promising and are worthy of additional study. Statistical analysis can be performed to attempt to determine the mathematical probability that the apparent relationship is the work of chance or sampling error (Chapter 12). It can be performed by the researchers who actually collected the data or by others who later have access to them.

In quantitative descriptive research, the researcher hopes to generalize from cases studied to those that are similar but were not part of the research study. Thus, it is critical that the researcher select and study cases that are typical of the entire group. Accuracy of measurement of variables also takes on great importance. Thus, case sampling and measurement (the topics of later chapters) absorb a considerable amount of the time and attention of the researcher.

Quantitative descriptive research is only as good or as bad as the representativeness of the sample of cases that are studied and the accuracy of the description that it produces. Just describing, if performed well, is an exact science that requires a great amount of knowledge and skill. There are rules and procedures that govern the conduct of good quantitative descriptive research, just as in all other types of research.

In more qualitative descriptive studies, acquiring a representative sample of research participants is less important than in more quantitative studies. What is often sought instead is diversity, for example, the widest possible variety in the way participants experienced some event such as family violence, how they perceived it, the range of meanings attributed to it, and so forth. Accurate measurement is believed to be an impossible goal since so much of what is examined (the data) is assumed to be subjective.

Three different descriptive research designs are widely used in social work research. They are:

1. One-Group Pretest-Posttest Design.   The one-group pretest-posttest design represents an improvement over many exploratory designs, as it adds an opportunity to compare pretest and posttest measures of the dependent variable. It is symbolized as follows:

$$O_1 \ X \ O_2$$

O_1 represents the first measurement of the dependent variable, prior to exposure of participants to the independent variable (X). Afterward, participants are again measured on the dependent variable, and their scores are compared. It is hoped that there will be a difference between performance at O_1 and O_2 and that this change may be attributed to the program or intervention (X). Let's look at our previous example and apply the one-group pretest-posttest design to it.

Using a paper-and-pencil test to measure knowledge of the English language in a group of Spanish-speaking clients at a neighborhood center, the social worker asks them to complete the test before the first session of the eight-week class (O_1). Following completion of this course, the participants complete the inventory again (O_2). The social worker then may make a comparison of how much change there was in knowledge of the English language from measurement 1 to measurement 2.

Because of the pretest measurement (O_1), it is possible to know how much change in the dependent variable actually occurred over the course of the intervention. This is the major advantage of the one-group pretest-posttest design.

2. The Static Group Comparison Design.   The static group comparison design allows the researcher to compare two groups on their measurements of a dependent variable, following exposure of one group to the independent variable. It is symbolized as follows:

$$X \ O_1$$
$$O_1$$

A brief example illustrates the usefulness of this design. A social worker wishes to compare two groups on their levels of anxiety following a behavioral treatment program designed to reduce the anxiety symptoms in otherwise healthy adults. Group 1 consists of those people who are selected for inclusion in the treatment program, a cognitive behavioral approach to treatment that lasts three months. Following completion of the program, the participants are measured on their level of anxiety using a standardized measuring instrument designed for this purpose. For comparison purposes, a group of similar adults who did not complete this program (perhaps they are on a waiting list for receiving this service) is measured using the same instrument. Then a comparison is made between those who completed the treatment and those who did not. If the group receiving the treatment shows a lower level of anxiety than the comparison group, then it may be concluded that the treatment had the desired effect. However, because there was no pretest for either group, we really do not know if the treatment group had a lower level of anxiety to begin with than the comparison group. This is the major limitation of the static group comparison design.

3. Time Series Design.   In the time series design, several measurements are taken on a dependent variable over time, typically before and after exposure to the independent variable (another longitudinal approach). A typical time series design looks like this:

$$O_1 \ O_2 \ O_3 \ X \ O_4 \ O_5 \ O_6$$

These symbols indicate that three measurements of the dependent variable were taken prior to exposure of the group to the intervention. Following intervention, three more measures (over time) were taken of the dependent variable. An example will help illustrate the usefulness of this design in social work research.

A group of men meet weekly at a local mental health center to work on issues related to anger expression. During week 1, week 2, and week 3, the level of expressed anger is measured using a standardized measuring instrument designed for this purpose. The social worker introduces a new model of treatment at week 4. The model requires several weeks of group process. When enough time has lapsed for the new treatment to have taken effect, the men's expressed anger is again measured for three consecutive weeks.

Several comparisons are possible using a time series design. First of all, the three pretest measures allow the researcher to establish a baseline measurement of the dependent variable. Baseline measures taken in this way allow a researcher to measure a variable as precisely as possible before intervention. The baseline measurement would be the average expressed anger score of the group over the three-week period prior to the introduction of the intervention in week 4. It probably would be a more accurate measurement of the dependent variable than a single measurement of it on just one day because the variable is likely to fluctuate naturally over time.

Following the intervention, the repeated measures allow the researcher to make at least two comparisons:

- *Comparison 1:* From the average pretest measure to an average posttest measure, to see if the intervention may have produced changes in expressed anger in the desired direction.
- *Comparisons 2 and 3:* From O_4 to O_5 and from O_5 to O_6, to see if any changes that occurred in the desired direction endured over time.

In summary, descriptive designs allow the researcher to go beyond exploring and permit comparisons between groups on their measurement of the dependent variable, typically before and after participation in some intervention. Although they are an improvement over exploratory designs, they still fall far short of being able to tell us if the independent variable actually produced changes in the dependent variable.

Examples of Explanatory Designs

At some point, the knowledge about a problem may advance to a point where it is possible to justify the use of explanatory designs. Exploratory and descriptive designs seek primarily understanding of a problem and of factors that are associated with it. Some design variations give us hints as to which solutions might be effective. However, by using explanatory research, it is possible to arrive at more definitive answers as to what might cause the problem and what intervention methods are effective in treating or even preventing it.

When explanatory research designs are used, the researcher uses hypothesis testing to try to verify possible relationships between variables. When explanatory research is conducted, the dependent and independent variables have already been identified through exploratory research, and their distribution has been described through descriptive research. Cases are selected for study with the goal of making them as representative as possible of all cases, including those not studied. The researcher hopes to be able to verify the presence of important relationships between or among variables. Whenever possible, other (confounding) variables that might somehow serve to misrepresent the true relationship between dependent and independent variables are controlled. This is accomplished through randomization, their physical manipulation, or through statistical methods. If they cannot be controlled, every effort is made to determine the degree to which they may have obfuscated the relationship between the independent and dependent variables.

Explanatory designs seek to uncover causal relationships between variables. As we indicated in the previous chapter, causality is a special kind of relationship. It goes beyond association and even simple correlation. In a causal relationship, exposure to an independent variable (and to its different quantities or qualities) actually brings about changes in the other (dependent) variable. As noted previously, there are three conditions that must be present in relationships in order to conclude that one variable (x) causes the changes in the other (y). These conditions are that

1. x must actually precede y in time order.
2. x and y must consistently covary.
3. All other explanations for changes in y must be ruled out.

All three of these conditions must be present in order to determine that x caused or produced the changes in the value categories or values of y.

Experimental Research.   There are two types of explanatory research designs, experimental and quasiexperimental. Experimental designs are the most widely known and are the ideal ones. We will discuss them in considerable detail. Like all forms of explanatory research, seek to explain the variations (different values) of a dependent variable in relation to one or more independent variables. But when reputable researchers use the word *experiment* to characterize their research, they are stating that their research design has several specific features.

Unfortunately, the word *experiment* has crept into the vernacular. It is tossed around rather loosely and sometimes used to describe almost any research or quasiresearch endeavor. For example, we sometimes hear social workers talk about the experimental use of a new treatment method when what they really have done is simply to substitute the new method for another one. Sometimes *experiment* is even used to describe any action that a person performs deliberately just to see what happens. For example, we hear people talk about performing an experiment when they don't make the morning coffee one morning, in order to see if their roommate will make it or will wait for it to be made. Neither of these examples comes close to what true experimental research is.

An experimental research design is very rigorous. Its requirements make it the ideal design for generating cause–effect knowledge. However, these requirements also frequently preclude its use for logistical and ethical reasons. Why? In a true experiment, the following very demanding requirements must be met:

- *The independent variable(s) are introduced or manipulated, one at a time, by the researcher.* This means, for example, that the researcher wishing to study the relationship between enrollment in a specific job training program and success in seeking employment must control who is enrolled in the program and who is not. Or another researcher studying the effect of hours of treatment time on recovery in an inpatient psychiatric facility would have to control tightly the exact number of treatment hours given patients participating in the study.
- *There are one or more control groups that are not exposed to the independent variable.* In the first example just described, the researcher would also select a group of individuals who would not enroll in the job training program (a control group). They would be identified, but not given the training. Their success rate in finding employment (the dependent variable) would be measured along with that of those selected

for the program, for comparison purposes. In the second example, a control group would also be selected. Their number of hours of treatment time would not be influenced in any way by the researcher.

• *Research participants are randomly selected and then randomly assigned to experimental and control groups.* In other types of research (for example, a quantitative descriptive survey of clients who are HIV-positive) a sample of research participants is often randomly selected from possible research participants. However, it is the random *assignment* requirement of an experiment that sets it apart from other designs. Random assignment means that, in the first example, nothing (other than random assignment to the groups) would influence whether potential trainees would be enrolled in the job training program (experimental group) or selected for the control group. In the second example, assignment to either the experimental or the control group would also have to be totally random.

Why is random assignment so important in an experiment? When experimental research designs are used, random assignment of research participants to experimental and control groups often is the primary vehicle used for control of confounding variables. Random assignment relies on the laws of probability and what is likely to occur in the long run. It depends on the equalization effect that occurs naturally within groups (subsamples) drawn from the same pool as more and more cases are added to them. As more cases are added to the two groups in a random manner, the groups become increasingly similar. In our first example, if the researcher assigned cases to the experimental and control groups randomly and if the two groups were reasonably large, the groups should be similar in all respects. This means that variables that we have reason to believe may affect success in finding employment, such as motivation level, work experience, health, intelligence, physical appearance, or verbal skills, will tend to be similar in the two groups when they are viewed in toto.

But what if the literature review failed to reveal one or more other confounding variables that might affect success in finding employment? They may be neither logical nor obvious, something that we might not have guessed to be potentially confounding variables (for example, number of siblings or birth order). Can these variables also be controlled through random assignment of cases to relatively large experimental and control groups? Can a researcher assume that if the experimental and control groups are fairly large, they will reflect comparable distributions of them? Yes. A highly desirable effect of random assignment is that, if performed correctly, it will control for the effects of all confounding variables, even those whose existence we have no reason to suspect! This is why random assignment is such an important feature of experimental designs.

The process of randomization is so useful a method for controlling confounding variables that researchers frequently devise methods to use it in other ways within experimental designs. In our example of an experiment designed to measure the effectiveness of a job training program, the researcher might randomly select (from among available trainers) those who will be used in the program. This would increase the likelihood that it was the program and not the skills of the trainer that were evaluated. The researcher might also randomly select times of day to offer the training, rooms to be used, or any other potentially confounding variable that can be randomized without affecting the nature of the program being evaluated.

Even in nonexperimental research, randomization is sometimes used to improve the research design. Many potentially confounding variables can be randomized even if the researcher cannot control them physically. For example, a researcher can randomly select days or times to conduct measurements of client attitudes such as depression or anger, in order to minimize the likelihood that such factors as health conditions, seasonal influences, or family events might bias the measurements.

Experiments are the only research designs that possess the preceding combination of characteristics and requirements. They use the best methods available to help the researcher rule out the possible effects of confounding variables. Consequently, among the basic designs we have described, experimental designs do the most convincing job of providing evidence that a cause–effect relationship between variables exists. They can help the researcher conclude with reasonable certainty that the presence of a certain value of the independent variable caused a certain value of the dependent variable to occur. Because the independent variable was either introduced or manipulated by the researcher, it could not have been the other way around. Experimental designs also can prove that different values of the dependent variable could not have occurred because of one or more other (confounding) variables.

Because all true experimental designs require rigorous control over certain conditions (assignment of people to groups, exposure to the independent variable, and so on), it sometimes can be difficult to implement them because of ethical concerns. In human services, we are committed to delivering the best possible services to each client, regardless of what a research design may indicate as desirable. Research must be of lower priority than service. However, with careful planning, experiments can be designed and implemented within human service organizations. We will describe three experimental designs that are sometimes used in social work research.

1. The Classical Experimental Design.   The classical experimental design, also called the pretest-posttest control group design, does a good job of controlling for the possible effects of confounding variables. It is portrayed as follows:

$$\text{Group 1 } R\ O_1\ X\ O_2$$
$$\text{Group 2 } R\ O_1\ O_2$$

In this design, individuals are randomly selected and then randomly assigned to one of two groups: an experimental group or a control group. The dependent variable is measured for both groups (O_1). The experimental group (group 1) is exposed to the independent variable, such as participation in a social program. Following completion of the program, the dependent variable is again measured for both groups (O_2). Then the following comparisons can be made:

- *Comparison 1:* The researcher examines the O_1 scores for both groups, anticipating that these measures will be essentially equivalent. (They should be if randomization has been successful.) In addition, these measurements will be useful to compute changes in each group from O_1 to O_2.

- *Comparison 2:* The researcher examines the O_2 scores for both groups, anticipating that O_2 for the experimental group will have changed in a predicted direction, whereas O_2 for the control group will not, or will change much less, because this group was not exposed to the treatment program. Assuming the researcher finds the expected change in O_2 for the experimental group, with no or much less change in the control group, it can be concluded with some degree of certainty that the change is due to exposure to the independent variable rather than to some other factor.

The classical experimental design requires that the researcher has the authority to randomly assign research participants to one of two treatment conditions. It also requires that both groups are pretested and posttested. Finally, the design requires that individuals in the control group not receive the intervention being tested—a requirement that might be regarded as professionally unethical and therefore unacceptable.

2. The Solomon Four-Group Design.   The Solomon Four-Group design is very similar to the classical experimental design, but instead of using two groups, it uses four. The additional two groups are used to determine if the use of a pretest may have contributed to changes in the dependent variable. The design is symbolized as follows:

Group 1 R O_1 X O_2
Group 2 R O_1 O_2
Group 3 R X O_2
Group 4 R O_2

Although the design may appear complicated, it is actually quite simple. Groups 1 and 3 are both experimental groups; each receives exposure to the intervention. However, group 3 does not receive a pretest. Groups 2 and 4 are both control groups; neither receives the intervention. In addition, group 4 does not receive a pretest; in fact, the only thing group 4 receives is a posttest. Then at least four comparisons can be made:

- *Comparison 1:* O_1 and O_2 for both experimental groups. What the researcher hopes to find is a change in both experimental groups, with no difference between scores of the two groups. If there is a difference, it might indicate the effect of a pretest.
- *Comparison 2:* O_2 for both control groups. These measures ought to be similar, because neither group received the intervention.
- *Comparison 3:* O_1 for groups 1 and 2. These measures ought to be similar as well, because random assignment has been used to assign people to groups, and no one at this point had received the independent variable.
- *Comparison 4:* O_2 for all four groups. If the intervention was successful, scores for the two experimental groups should be better than scores for the two control groups. However, unless the results of the first three comparisons showed the desired results, conclusions about the intervention's causing changes in the dependent variable probably cannot be justified.

3. The Posttest-Only Control Group Design.   The posttest-only control group design, sometimes called the randomized posttest-only control group design, uses random assignment of persons to either an experimental or control group to equalize them; neither group is pretested. The design is symbolized as follows:

$$R \, X \, O_1 \, R \, O_1$$

O_1 is the first measurement of the dependent variable, which in this design is a posttest. The design allows the researcher to compare posttest measurements of the dependent variable by group. Specifically, the researcher is interested in discovering if the posttest measurement for the experimental group is either higher or lower than for the control group. It should be, if the intervention had an effect. Even though there is no pretest to ensure equivalence of the groups prior to exposure to the independent variable, random assignment theoretically takes care of this. Pretests are required, however, when the measurement of the amount of change from pretest to posttest is important for the purpose of the study. In addition, pretesting is necessary if the groups are so small as to render random assignment ineffective in creating equivalent groups.

Quasiexperimental Research.   *Quasiexperimental* research designs are explanatory designs that are similar to experiments but that fail to meet one or more of their requisite conditions. Many quasiexperimental designs have one or more control groups, but they are not *true control groups,* groups that have been constituted by random assignment to them along with their experimental group counterparts. The control groups then are referred to as *nonequivalent control groups.* There may be compelling ethical reasons for not creating true control groups, such as the need to assign clients to experimental or control groups based on the judgment of professionals that they will likely benefit from (and not be harmed by) them. In other situations, true control groups may be logistically impossible because, for example, some interaction between members of control and experimental groups is inevitable or even desirable. Whole books have been written on various experimental and quasiexperimental research designs. The classic remains a 1963 volume[3] by Campbell and Stanley and its subsequent revisions.

What Is a "Good" Research Design?

The fact that explanatory research is characterized by rigorous hypothesis testing and methods that attempt to control for the effects of confounding variables often has led to the erroneous conclusion that they are always appropriate or are a standard by which to judge other research. Historically, there has been a pronounced bias in this direction. High school science teachers still sometimes denigrate any student research proposals that lack a control group when they are entered in science fairs (also known as "Annual Parents' Science Competitions"). The knowledge sought may suggest the need for an exploratory or descriptive study, or for a more qualitative approach to knowledge building, but the student who uses one may pay the price for using a design that is still regarded by some as "unscientific" or otherwise inferior. Similarly, social workers seeking funding for their research from private foundations and government institutions have struggled to compete with others who submit research proposals describing experimental or quasiexperimental designs. Qualitative studies (even though they may be exactly what are needed to address a research problem) face especially difficult odds when grants are awarded.

Our profession has suffered from an explanatory bias, too. It is the impetus for much of the criticism that has been leveled at social work research and the questioning of social work research findings. There is relatively little social work explanatory research; therefore, our research isn't worth much, so say critics both within and outside our profession. Admittedly, more explanatory research could be done with a little extra thought and effort. But such criticisms often fail to acknowledge the methodological and ethical difficulties (though certainly not the impossibility) of conducting such research within social work practice settings. The common use of the terms *higher level* (for explanatory designs) and *lower level* (for exploratory or descriptive ones) over the years has been unfortunate and only helped to perpetuate the bias. This terminology has often been construed as an indicator of quality in evaluating a research design, with lower level designs viewed as sloppy or lacking in rigor. But the choice of a design should be based on the type of knowledge needed and the degree to which it is already present. Any one type of design is not inherently better than any other. All can reflect rigor and the careful use of scientific methods. All have their uses and make valuable contributions to our knowledge building and to empirically based social work practice.

It should also be observed that some very good research designs seem to sit on the edge; they fall somewhere between two general categories. When this happens, a researcher might describe the general nature of his or her design using compound terms such as exploratory–descriptive or descriptive–explanatory to reflect the fact that a design does not quite fit cleanly into a single design category and that it contains elements of more than one.

Other broad descriptions of research designs (basic or applied, cross-sectional or longitudinal, and quantitative or qualitative) sometimes are not a perfect fit. Basic research sometimes can have immediate applicability, even if it was unintentional. Much research that is basically cross sectional has one or more pretest-posttest or longitudinal components. As noted in Chapter 1, it is also not at all unusual to have a sound research design that is a hybrid of quantitative and qualitative methodologies. The two components can be complementary, each serving to confirm or refute the other's findings. As long as there is consistency (see the following discussion) within the various components of a design, a hybrid design is acceptable, if not desirable. The researcher may simply be attempting to take advantage of the special features of different methods of knowledge building within the same study or to attempt to verify the research findings in various ways.

General Characteristics of a Good Research Design

The design selected by the researcher is described in the research report, generally in a separate "methodology" section. Thus, it is vulnerable to critique. As we indicated in Chapter 1, this is a desirable characteristic of the scientific method, since it allows the reader to critique the researcher's design and makes replication of the research possible.

Although no design is ever perfect (compromises are inevitable), the researcher strives to come up with the best design, given unavoidable limitations. The advantages of different design features must be considered. For example, the popularity of many cross-sectional designs is based in part on their potential to control several of the threats to internal validity (described later in this chapter). They can be eliminated when a single measurement of all variables takes place at the same time.

Generally, an appropriate design can be recognized by the presence of certain characteristics:

- *It is based on a review of existing knowledge.* It should be obvious why the design was selected. The reader of the review of literature section of a report should not be surprised by any part of the research design. It should suggest that the researcher has learned from the methodological successes and failures of others. A design may have come directly from a recommendation of the "Suggestions for Future Research" section of another recent study, or it may represent a needed replication of research conducted years earlier.

- *It is appropriate for the level of knowledge that exists.* The design should promise to advance knowledge about a problem or question. As such, it will generally fall at or slightly to the right on the research continuum of other recent scholarly research in the area. It should not threaten either to "reinvent the wheel" or represent a quantum leap by, for example, attempting experimental research on a problem that has barely been identified and adequately described. The design should suggest that the researcher has found the appropriate place on the design continuum.

- *It is internally consistent in each of its components.* As suggested earlier, certain design types can be recognized by groupings of characteristics. A design or design component should contain features that belong together, not a little bit of one and a little bit of another. For example, if a design claims to be both quantitative and descriptive, and attempts to generalize from research participants to others, it should reflect careful attention to selection of a research sample that will represent the group being studied. The use of a group of participants selected less carefully (as they might be in more qualitative, exploratory research) would not be appropriate. An experimental or quasiexperimental design would be expected to test hypotheses and contain methods for control of confounding variables. One expects to find certain design features with certain designs or design components and not with others. When the researcher settles on a design type, the decision provides help in resolving such issues as the importance of obtaining a representative sample or the degree to which control of potentially confounding variables is critical in conducting the research.

- *It is feasible.* The ideal research design may be impossible to implement because of economic, political, ethical, or logistical obstacles. It may have to be compromised in order to deal with the realities that exist within the context of social work research. For example, descriptive research on gang members' initiation rites that is otherwise well designed probably will have to rely on other sources of data rather than firsthand observation. A feasible alternative might involve the substitution of interviews with community leaders or police officers who are closely affiliated with gang members. Such secondary sources, although probably not as good, would reflect a reasonable compromise; The research design would be "doable."

Assessment Criteria for Different Types of Designs

What we have just described are general criteria for assessing design quality. However, depending on the type of research that is undertaken, other more specific criteria are often used.

Quantitative Descriptive Designs.   What if the research is more accurately categorized as both quantitative and descriptive? Different assessment questions might be appropriate. For example:

- Were the most meaningful variables measured?
- Did the methods used for measuring variables seem to produce accurate measurements?
- Was the sample of cases that provided data a representative one?

Qualitative Designs.   Qualitative research is usually exploratory and/or descriptive. By definition, it would rarely (if ever) be considered explanatory because (1) it is not intended to determine if there is support for hypotheses about relationships between variables, and (2) it does not meet the requirements to do so. For example, it generally lacks control groups, does not use random selection of research participants, and so forth. If a study is primarily qualitative, there are certain questions that often are appropriate for assessing the quality of its design: For example, we might ask:

- Did the research participants reflect sufficient diversity in relation to whatever is being examined (perceptions, coping styles, and so forth)?
- Did the data collection methods that were used seem to encourage research participants to share their perceptions and experiences openly and candidly?
- Did the data collection methods yield data that reflect "richness"? (For example, they might have elicited direct quotations from research participants that accurately convey their perceptions or how they experienced some phenomenon.)
- Did the research identify variables that may relate in some way to the problem?
- Did the research design have the potential to produce credible theories or hypotheses that might contribute to our understanding of the research problem?

Explanatory Designs.   Suppose the research design is explanatory. Efforts are made to find support for a cause–effect relationship between certain variables of interest. How can we evaluate how well this was done? Assessing the quality of an explanatory design focuses primarily on the degree to which the findings that it produced possess two characteristics—internal validity and (sometimes to a lesser degree) external validity.

Internal validity refers to the amount of confidence we have that exposure to the independent variable produced changes in the dependent variable, and that there are no other explanations for these changes. Obviously then, internal validity is critical to any conclusions about causation drawn from explanatory research (but not for exploratory or descriptive studies). For example, suppose that a researcher asserts that, based on research findings, "in counseling victims of rape, counseling method A produces a higher rate of success than counseling method B." We will agree with this conclusion only if we are convinced that, based on the research design used, it is justifiable. We will be convinced only if the design seems to have internal validity; that is, if the differences in success rate that were observed appear to have been caused by the two counseling methods and nothing else. It was not client age, marital status, varying skill level of the social workers who counseled them, or any of the millions of other potentially confounding variables that produced the different rates of success. The research was designed so that they were all controlled in some way.

There are many factors that are generally acknowledged to threaten internal validity.[4] The following are among the most common ones.

- *Testing effects.* As we suggested in one of our earlier examples, the use of a pretest to measure the dependent variable may actually result in a change in measurements of the variable. So, theoretically, can any other measurement that is required. Participants can learn from or be otherwise influenced by the process of completing a questionnaire or other measurement procedures. If feasible, the use of two or more experimental and control groups (as in the Solomon Four-Group design described in Chapter 6) can help the researcher assess the extent to which testing effects might represent a threat to internal validity.

- *Maturation or passage of time.* Some behaviors and problems seem to have a logical life cycle, or change naturally over time. For example, grief over the death of a loved one tends to subside over time with or without counseling. Any conclusion that the presence of long-term bereavement counseling may have resulted in improved survivor functioning would thus have to be tempered with an assessment of the degree to which time (the threat to internal validity) might have contributed to apparent treatment success.

- *History.* Events sometimes occur during the course of research that might have a major effect on the dependent variable. It may be a much greater effect on it than that of the independent variable. Such a historical event may never make the newspapers. For example, it may be the firing of a popular coworker or the implementation of a new personnel policy that affects the job satisfaction of a group of social workers much more than the presence or absence of a new attitude adjustment hour (the independent variable). Or the event may be truly historical in scope, such as a tsunami or a terrorist bombing. We could sympathize with researchers who, for example, might have been attempting to prove that "type of counseling affects anxiety level of clients" if one of these disasters occurred in the community during the course of treatment. The internal validity of their findings would almost certainly be questioned.

- *Statistical regression to the mean.* Sometimes it is desirable to select research participants who exhibit only the most extreme measurements of some variable. We might do this in order to be certain that our participants are those most in need of intervention and/or that they truly possess certain characteristics that we want to try to affect (for example, low assertiveness or a high level of hostility). Based on some measurement of the (dependent) variable, they will have exhibited the most dramatically high or low measurements of it. Following the introduction of intervention (the independent variable), the dependent variable generally would be measured again. The second measurement is likely to be less extreme than the first one. Would that mean that the intervention was successful? Maybe, but maybe not. Even if the intervention had no effect whatsoever, a less extreme measurement of the dependent variable might have occurred simply because participants were unlikely to repeat their extremely high or low measurement of the variable. There would be little room for their measurement of the variable to become more extreme, but plenty of room for it to moderate just based on its normal fluctuations.

The tendency of extreme measurements to regress or to become more moderate over time can obscure and obfuscate the results of research that uses participants who were selected because of their extreme measurements of a variable. If feasible, a control group consisting of others possessing equally extreme measurements can be used to determine whether statistical regression threatened the internal validity of research findings. If changes in the control group are found to parallel those in the experimental group, it was probably statistical regression and not the independent variable that affected the dependent variable.

- *Instrumentation.* If there has been a pretest and a different version of the instrument was then used as a posttest, the researcher must be certain that any differences in the experimental and control groups did not result from differences in the instruments used. Were the pretest and posttest measurements equal in difficulty or otherwise comparable? Were the experimental and control groups given different versions, and were they comparable? Did they favor one group or the other? If not, any differences may have been caused by the different instruments used, not by the independent variable.

- *Lack of sample comparability.* No comparison of an experimental group with a control group following the introduction or manipulation of an independent variable is fair if the two groups were not comparable to begin with. As noted, we use randomization in true experiments to improve comparability. But in quasiexperiments or other explanatory designs, we often must use experimental and control groups in which participants were not randomly assigned. The samples may deliberately or unintentionally have been constituted in such a way that one group might have a higher likelihood of success (if that is the dependent variable). For example, what if we compare clients who attend a substance abuse counseling program with those who do not choose to participate after being referred for counseling? The counseling offered (the independent variable) may not explain the fact that those people in counseling had a lower rate of recidivism. Perhaps they were just more highly motivated, or some other factor might better explain both their wish to seek counseling and their lower recidivism rate than it would for those who did not attend.

- *Experimental mortality.* The fact that research participants or objects are lost to the researcher in the course of research can offer a threat to internal validity. This is particularly true in some forms of longitudinal research (discussed earlier in this chapter) but it can occur in other types of research as well. If the reasons that cases are lost are somehow related to the dependent variable, the results can be misinterpreted, and the findings may lack internal validity. For example, in a study of the effectiveness of a new method of addiction counseling, a control group (one that receives the usual treatment) could be used. Clients could be randomly assigned to one type of treatment or the other. At the time of the posttest interview, the experimental group (those who receive the new treatment) might reflect a much higher rate of success. But the experimental group has lost 40 percent of its cases (those who are no longer available to be interviewed), whereas all clients in the control group agree to participate in the posttest interview. The lost 40 percent may reflect the same rate of treatment success as the remaining 60 percent in the experimental group that was interviewed. But they also may not. They may have dropped out of treatment because the treatment was so successful that it became unnecessary. That is probably an overly optimistic interpretation of their behavior. It is also possible that they left because they concluded that their treatment was doing them no good, and they decided to devote the time that they had been wasting to better pursuit of their addiction! If so, the conclusion that the experimental treatment was more successful than the usual treatment would be lacking in internal validity because of experimental mortality.

- *Ambiguity about direction of causation.* Sometimes in preexplanatory research designs it could be argued that it was really the researcher's dependent variable that produced different values of the independent variable, rather than the other way around. For example, a researcher might observe that couples who completed a ten-week marital enrichment seminar have a higher level of marital satisfaction (the dependent variable) than those who dropped out before the seminar was completed. Does that mean that the seminar enhances marital satisfaction? Maybe. But perhaps satisfaction affected completion, rather than the other way around. Perhaps those who completed the seminar had fewer problems, making it easier for them to complete it, whereas those who had more problems had to drop out. (In this example, the threat to internal validity is closely related to the previous one.)
- *Diffusion or overlap of intervention methods.* If we hope to compare the effectiveness of two intervention methods, it is best if they are discrete and bear little or no similarity to each other. Unfortunately, this is not always the case. In the real world, blurring takes place over time, often because features of one intervention become imitated by practitioners of the other intervention method. Thus, any comparison is not a clean one.

    For example, suppose a researcher wanted to find out whether support or confrontation is more effective in counseling spouse-abusing clients. Would the social workers assigned to use confrontation methods be able to stick to the method assigned to them? Would their treatment have elements of support? Would those assigned to be only supportive of clients occasionally lapse into a little confrontation? Perhaps both groups of social workers offering treatment will have learned over the years that certain elements of the opposite treatment method can be helpful on occasion and, consciously or unconsciously, they will inject them into their interventions. Then how will we be able to say that it was the treatment intervention (support or confrontation) that produced the different treatment success rates of the two groups of clients? Or if no difference in success rates were to be found, how do we know that the similarity between the two intervention methods used did not hide a real difference in the effectiveness of the methods?

These threats to internal validity should be regarded as the most common problems to be aware of, rather than a complete list. Explanatory research is designed to control them. Experimental designs are those most likely to produce findings with acceptable internal validity than other designs because they use true control groups consisting of people or objects that are randomly selected and randomly assigned to them.

When it is concluded in an explanatory study that a research finding appears to have a high level of internal validity, it is possible to conclude that the values of the independent variable (and not something else) may have caused the values of the dependent variable among cases (persons) studied. But how far can we generalize this relationship between variables? To all cases that were not selected for study? To all persons within the state who are similar in some way to those studied? To all persons everywhere who are similar? These are issues of external validity.

External validity refers to the extent to which findings are believed to apply beyond cases that were actually studied. Internal validity alone is not sufficient to guarantee its presence. To a great extent, external validity relates directly to the characteristics of the cases that were studied and to what degree they can be assumed to be representative of other cases that were not studied.

To illustrate the concept of external validity, we might consider a hypothetical study of the effect of the career goals of child protection workers (the independent variable) on the quality of services that they deliver (the dependent variable). Let us assume that a carefully designed and implemented explanatory study of a sample of workers within Erie County in western New York State produces the finding that career goals of the workers in the study appear to directly affect the quality of child protection services within the county. On careful scrutiny of the researchers' methods, we conclude that the finding probably has internal validity; other variables and factors that might have caused the variations in the dependent variable were well controlled. To what degree does the finding have external validity? Is the relationship between the variables likely to be present among all child welfare workers (including those working in adoptions) within Erie County? Among all public welfare social workers in Erie County? Among all public welfare workers in all counties in New York State? Would it hold up for any county organization with a heavy urban population, for both BSW and MSW social workers, for staff whose average age is fifty-two years or older, for those with no formal social work education, or for some other group of workers who may differ from those actually studied in some other way? These are all questions that relate to the external validity of the findings of the research.

Assessing the external validity of research findings and the design that produced them entails a judgment about the research sample that was studied. Specifically, it requires a conclusion about who (besides the people or objects in the research sample themselves) might also have the same characteristics of the people or objects in the sample. This is the issue of sample representativeness (discussed in detail in Chapter 9).

Obviously, good external validity (also referred to as broad *generalizability*) is important to the utility of explanatory research, which attempts to identify relationships between variables within research samples and provide evidence that the same relationships exist beyond those samples. If it is considered quite limited, research findings lose value. However, external validity is also often important to researchers conducting quantitative descriptive research studies, because they often study what they hope is a representative sample of people or objects in order to learn something about some larger group. In a descriptive study, a sample that is unique (biased) in some way can tell us little or nothing (or even mislead us) about the characteristics of people or objects not actually studied. But a descriptive study with good external validity can be very useful to the social worker. It can provide tentative knowledge about clients or other people who may never themselves have been studied by researchers.

External validity is not nearly as important in exploratory studies as it is in explanatory or quantitative descriptive ones. In fact, many exploratory studies make no pretense of studying a representative sample of people or objects, often because one simply is not available. (Internal validity, of course, is also a nonissue, because exploratory studies generally do not seek to find support for relationships between variables.) In the designs of program evaluations (Chapter 13) that seek to learn if a program achieved its desired outcomes, internal validity is very important. We need to know if the program (and nothing else) produced desirable changes in some problem. However, since most programs are relatively unique, the external validity (generalizability) of any findings is usually expected to be quite limited.

As with internal validity, there are many threats to the external validity of a research finding. Many different phenomena can serve to make research participants unique. Any findings about relationships between variables found among them may not be generalizable to others. Their experience as participants in the research (for example, the attention given to them as research participants) may itself have made them different from persons who might otherwise be regarded as similar to them. The issue of just how much external validity a research finding possesses is not easily resolved. Certain methods of case sampling (Chapter 9) and the use of large samples can increase the likelihood that a research finding will have good external validity. But few, if any, research findings constitute universal truths.

Research studies involving racial and ethnic groups raise some special concerns with regard to external validity. One issue is the use of generic labels when describing racial and ethnic groups in the United States. As the diversity of the American population continues to increase, the use of such labels in social work research is and will become increasingly problematic.

The term *Hispanic* is essentially a linguistic designation that refers to people from countries where Spanish is the dominant language and where cultural aspects such as religion, music, art, dance, and food are influenced by traditions emanating from Spain (usually as a colonial power). However, findings from studies on one Hispanic group may not be generalizable to other nationalities or ethnic groups that are included in this designation. There are distinct idiomatic differences, belief systems, and cultural patterns among and between groups, such as Cubans, Puerto Ricans, Dominicans, Mexican Americans, and Latin Americans, who make up the Hispanic mosaic in the United States. The failure to recognize these differences may lead to overgeneralizations from one group to another.

Within-group differences related to variables such as nationality, social class, education, religion, language, immigration patterns, and degree of acculturation influence responses in research and thereby determine the degree of external validity of a given research study. A similar issue must be addressed when using the term *black non-Hispanic,* which refers to people of African descent in the United States, South America, Africa, and the English-speaking Caribbean. The terms *American Indian* or *Native American* generally are used to describe 512 federally recognized tribes, who speak more than 200 dialects. *Asian, Pacific Islander* refers to more than 60 separate racial and ethnic groups. The desire of demographers and researchers to reduce this vast complexity into a few easily applicable labels can lead to a false sense of security in generalizing findings across and within racial and ethnic subgroups. Researchers are expected to help others assess the external validity of their research findings. In the research report, a detailed description should be provided of one's research participants and exactly how they were selected.

Any conclusions about the degree to which the findings of a research study possess both internal validity and external validity are always a bit subjective. Ultimately, they are based on one's individual judgment of the quality of the research design and the limitations that it contains. The responsibility of the researcher is to describe a research design honestly and completely, and let others (such as the reader's of the research report) draw their own conclusions about it.

Summary

A research design was described as a plan for conducting research. It is the way that a researcher responds to certain questions about how the research is to be conducted.

The general characteristics of a research design can be conveyed in a number of different ways. As we noted earlier, research can be described as basic or applied, or as primarily qualitative or primarily quantitative. It can also be described as either cross-sectional, pretest-posttest, or longitudinal, suggesting (among other things) how many times people were observed or interviewed or certain key variables were measured and what questions the researcher was attempting to answer. Or, it can be described as exploratory, descriptive, or explanatory, suggesting (among other things) the kind of knowledge that was sought and how the researcher went about seeking it. Box 6.3 summarizes some of what was discussed here and in Chapter 1.

Sometimes it is possible to use an existing design framework that has been used many times before and has even acquired a label that is widely understood. They exist for exploratory, descriptive, and explanatory research studies. We examined a number of them in this chapter, including the best known one, the classical experiment. Of course,

BOX 6.3   General Terms Used to Describe Research

Term	Major Differences	Decision Criteria
Basic/Applied	Purpose, application of findings	Knowledge requirements
Qualitative/Quantitative	Methods used; data and its analysis	Knowledge sought
Cross-Sectional/Pretest-Posttest/ Longitudinal	Number and time of measurements	Knowledge sought
Exploratory/Descriptive/Explanatory	General nature of the research	Current knowledge level

even when using an existing design framework, it must still be "fleshed out" to meet the specific requirements of a given research study. Thus, every research design is different, tailored to answer the questions that are unique to the study.

Research designs are never perfect. They are limited by logistical, ethical, legal, monetary, political, time, and other factors. However, given these constraints, some designs are still better than others. We discussed some of the criteria that can be used in evaluating the quality of various types of preexplanatory (including qualitative) and explanatory research designs—what is important to their success. We examined in considerable detail the most common criteria that are used in evaluating the quality of explanatory research designs—the degree to which they produced findings that possess internal validity and external validity. The external validity (generalizability) of findings is usually an important criterion for evaluating descriptive research designs as well.

For Discussion

1. What can longitudinal research designs tell us that other designs cannot? Why do you suppose they are not used more frequently in social work research?
2. Why would it be inappropriate to conduct exploratory research on such questions as "How does family violence affect children?" or "Do children who are adopted sometimes have problems related to their adoption?" What types of research might be more appropriate?
3. Why do we see qualitative research methods most frequently in research that could be described as exploratory or descriptive? What would be an example of a quantitative descriptive research study?
4. What can an experimental design tell us that the other types of design cannot? Why is this possible?
5. What is the difference between an experimental design and a quasiexperimental one? Why are experimental designs not used more frequently in social work research?
6. What do the specific design labels (and the symbols used to represent them) in this chapter (e.g., "time series," "Solomon Four-Group," etc.) tell us about how the research study is conducted? What do they fail to tell us?
7. How does an experimental design control for threats to internal validity? Why is this effective?
8. Why is internal validity of greatest importance in explanatory research designs? Why is it irrelevant in an exploratory design?
9. How does reporting the characteristics of research participants or of the setting of the research help the reader of a research report to make a judgment about the external validity of any research findings?
10. How might cultural factors affect the external validity of a descriptive study of patterns of spouse abuse among a particular ethnic group?

Part III • Research Designs

Endnotes

1. Kübler-Ross, E. (1989). *On death and dying.* New York: Macmillan, 38, 137.
2. Benoliel, J. (1985). Loss and adaptation: Circumstances, contingencies, and consequences. *Death Studies, 9,* 217–233.
3. Campbell, D., & Stanley, J. (1963). *Experimental and quasi-experimental designs for research.* Chicago: Rand McNally.
4. See, e.g., Singleton, R., & Straits, B. (2005). *Approaches to social research.* New York: Oxford University Press, 159–162, 195–196, 434–435.

7

METHODS FOR ACQUIRING RESEARCH DATA

One of the common characteristics of all types of research (such as those discussed in the previous chapter) is that it seeks to increase our knowledge through the analysis of data. Data can come in many forms and have many different origins. Some research designs (such as those used for evaluating social programs) require access to many different data sources. Others, including some that employ the specialized research methods described in the next chapter, rely on just a few or only a single source.

There is no one best data source. Each has advantages and limitations that are considered in answering the important research design question—what data source or sources would be most appropriate for my research study? In this chapter, we will examine the options that are most frequently used in social work research.

Secondary Data Analysis

Sometimes the time-consuming and expensive task of collecting original data for research studies is unnecessary. Many research questions can be examined using data that already exist, often without leaving our place of employment. The reanalysis of selected data that were collected and stored for some other purpose is known as *secondary data analysis*. For reasons that will be evident, it is much more likely to be a viable option as a data source in quantitative studies than in qualitative ones.

Sources

Human service organizations store great amounts of information about their clients and programs. They can sometimes be used to examine research questions and to test hypotheses using quantitative methods. Extensive data banks exist within public social agencies, both to meet government requirements and to facilitate service delivery to clients. Smaller

BOX 7.1   Common Methods for Acquiring Research Data

Method	Definitions/Description
Secondary data analysis	Uses data collected for some other purpose.
Oral histories	Recorded, firsthand descriptions of people who "were there." (Can be a source of secondary data or can be considered "original data.")
In-person interviews	One-on-one conversations; structure varies.
Group interviews	Several individuals provide data simultaneously; structure varies.
Systematic observation	Watching, observing, recording (may include participation).
Telephone	Data collected via phone or fax.
Electronic communication	Data collected via computer through e-mail, instant messaging, instant chats, etc.
Mailed questionnaires	Data collected via postal service.

private and sectarian organizations also store a substantial amount of information about clients and client functioning. Increasingly, information is stored and retrieved via computer data information systems. However, in some smaller organizations, it still is maintained manually in the form of written files and records.

There also are many sources of research data within the public domain that can be useful to social workers for conducting research. For example, census data are a rich source, collected at great expense to the taxpayer. Generally, they tend to be underused by researchers. The public documents section of libraries stores a wide variety of other statistical data, some of which were listed in Chapter 4. Labor statistics and public health statistics are available through computer access and in public and university libraries. Federal grant reports and reports of demonstration projects also are available as documents, and frequently contain useful data.

More and more data that were collected for some other purposes are appearing on the Internet each year. Often the product of well funded research studies by governmental agencies, they relate to human conditions and problems that are often the focus of social work research. Organizations such as the National Science Foundation, the National Institute on Alcohol and Alcoholism, the National Institute on Child Health and Human Development and the National Institutes of Health (NIH) now make data from their research available and encourage others to use it for their own research. It has been suggested that this has occurred, in part, because of the recognition that the high cost of federal research studies can be better justified if the data they produce can be "mined" to answer other research questions besides those originally addressed.[1] Regardless of the reasons for the proliferation of trustworthy research data on the Internet, it presents some excellent opportunities for social work researchers. However, as we noted in Chapter 4, it is worth remembering that not all data that appear on the Internet (perhaps not even most) can be trusted. Thus, it is always wise to "consider the source." Data that are within the public domain may be used (with appropriate citation from their sources). Researchers do not need permission to analyze census data or data published by the National Center for Health Statistics and other federal agencies. They can be used, for example, to chronicle social changes such as the rise and decline of various occupations, urban migration, or the increased presence of women in the workplace over the past century.

The NASW, the CSWE, and other professional organizations also annually collect data about their members. Social workers interested in conducting research using selected characteristics of professional social workers, educators, schools, and students can obtain permission to reanalyze these data.

Different Uses

Secondary analysis is used in both descriptive and some explanatory quantitative studies. It is a component of many program evaluations (see Chapter 13). It is not used in experiments because, by definition, they require that the independent variable is either introduced or physically manipulated by the researcher. This would be impossible because, in secondary analysis, data usually were collected by someone else for some other purpose. Some examples of use of social agency data may help to demonstrate the wide variety of ways that secondary analysis can be used in research if ethical and legal requirements can be met.

- In a private psychiatric in-patient facility, a researcher may wish to describe the participation of institutionalized clients in making discharge plans. A secondary analysis of data drawn from available case records might be used.
- In a child protection agency, case record data could be used to compile a picture of the disposition of cases that are referred for investigation of possible child abuse. They could be used to create a composite picture of patterns of service delivery.
- As part of a program evaluation of a battered women's shelter, agency record data could be used to learn if clients served by the organization are representative of the community in age, income level, ethnicity, and so forth. Data could be compared statistically to county- or community-maintained data on the same social indicators.
- In an alcohol rehabilitation facility, secondary data analysis also could be used to seek support for the hypothesis that there is a positive correlation between clients' participation in a given program and changes in some aspect of their functioning. Data analysis might involve calculating the strength and direction of correlation between the two variables.

When data can be accessed by computer, it can be tempting for researchers to select data on many variables and to seek any relationships between them that can be found. We recommend caution in using this approach as a method of secondary analysis. For both ethical and statistical reasons (beyond our discussion here) variables should be selected and analyzed only after the researcher has justified hypotheses about their relationships (based on the literature review). The computer should be used for statistical analysis of relationships believed to exist, not to engage in a fishing expedition.

Tasks Required

There are a number of activities that require special attention in research that employs secondary analysis of data. They include the following:

- *Operationalizing of variables.* Methods used to measure variables in the original data collection should be identified, and if at all possible, the same operational definitions should be applied in the current study. Also, some estimate of the degree of reliability and validity (Chapter 10) of the original measurement should be made.

- *Specifying the sampling plan used.* The source of data (case record, personnel file, monthly statistical report, and so on) and the strategy for selecting a sample of cases should be specified and justified.
- *Developing a data collection instrument and coding scheme for data collection.* Typically, this is accomplished by using a data collection instrument that has been developed specifically for the research. Data are drawn from the original documents and recorded on the instrument. The researcher may decide to have more than one person read and record the same data from the original source. If this is done, an estimate of the reliability of the data-gathering method can be made (Chapter 10).
- *Analyzing the data.* The appropriate level of measurement for each variable must be determined (based on information about how it was originally collected) before statistical analysis (Chapter 12) can be conducted.
- *Identifying the limitations of the study.* Although most research reports typically include a section describing limitations of the study, the inclusion of a limitations section is particularly important in secondary analysis. Due to the nature of the data being analyzed (they were measured and recorded for some purpose other than the current study and usually by people other than the researcher) there is a greater-than-usual likelihood that the data will have limitations.

Advantages

Secondary data analysis is appealing to social workers for a number of reasons. First, the financial costs associated with it often are minimal compared with other data collection methods. Second, it generally requires less time than other forms of data collection and analysis. The data are already collected and recorded; the researcher needs only to develop a sampling method and an instrument for coding and recording them. If the data are already available in a form that is compatible with statistical analysis software, analysis can begin almost immediately following the literature review and the development of focused questions and/or hypotheses.

When legally and ethically feasible, secondary analyses are less intrusive than other methods that collect original data from participants. Permissions may not need to be secured, as people are not interviewed or observed in person by the researcher. However, when agency record data are used, clients' permission may be required because data were provided for use in treatment, not for research. Problems related to anonymity may not be an issue if data are stored by case number or some other method that ensures that the researcher cannot possibly know who provided which data when it was originally collected. As a rule, one is less likely to encounter bureaucratic obstacles to conducting secondary analysis than when conducting other types of research that entail the collection of original data from clients or staff.

Limitations

Given the many advantages of conducting secondary analysis, why is it not used more frequently? For one thing, even when data are available for secondary data analysis they often are quite limited. When planning to collect original data, researchers generally learn from the literature review (Chapter 4) what variables need to be studied. Then they simply collect whatever data are needed. In secondary analysis, the existing data may fall short of providing all that is required to answer a research question or to provide support or nonsupport for a hypothesis. If measurements of a variable are not in the record or document, the variable generally cannot be examined (unless it is possible for the researcher to go back personally and measure it). The researcher's plans for studying a question or testing a hypothesis may need to be modified to fit existing data.

Another potential problem with the use of secondary analysis relates to the quality of measurement that was conducted. If the data are lacking in credibility, no amount of secondary analysis will improve their quality. A thorough examination of the context in which data were originally collected can help the researcher to determine whether they can be trusted. Some assessment of their quality should be made. Questions might include, for example: Who gathered them, using what kind of recording method? What hidden agenda may have influenced what was recorded and what was not? If the people who originally recorded the information are available to the researcher, they should be consulted on these and other issues.

Most of the kinds of secondary data that are in the public domain or are otherwise available for research tend to be relatively "sterile." Thus, they cannot provide answers to the questions that are the focus of many social work research studies that seek an in-depth understanding of such phenomena as human emotions, perceptions, or behaviors. A notable exception is oral histories.

Oral Histories

One way to learn what it was like to experience some event or phenomenon is to ask people to describe it in their own words (and to preserve what was said). That is how people create oral histories, written, audio or video recordings of people discussing an experience or life event from their perspective. Later, these recordings can be analyzed using a variety of research methods (for example, content analysis as described in Chapter 8) in order to attempt to answer a variety of research questions.

Oral histories are firsthand accounts, what would seem to be, on the surface, a very trustworthy data source. Who better to describe something than someone who "lived it?" However, when using oral histories as a data source, it should be remembered that what an oral history describes most accurately is how someone perceived or experienced something, not necessarily how it actually occurred. Even descriptions of perceptions and experiences may not be totally accurate if much time has lapsed. Preresearch meetings with participants (sometimes called *narrators*) are often used to develop comfortable relationships and to determine which questions might be most productive to ask when histories are conducted. Then, the interviews are conducted and recorded, often during many sessions. Consequently, the person compiling an oral history can easily influence what the participant says. For these reasons, oral histories are generally regarded as "qualitative data." When they are analyzed, "qualitative analysis" is conducted.

Oral histories preserve history. Thus, they enable us to learn from people who may no longer be with us or who are here now, but will not always be around to tell their stories. For example, oral histories exist in which veterans of World Wars I and II, survivors of Nazi concentration camps, participants in the American civil rights movement, early labor union organizers, and people who worked in President Franklin Roosevelt's New Deal programs describe what these events were like from their perspective. Oral histories have recently been compiled in which people who lived through the events of September 11, 2001 in New York and Washington, D.C., describe their experiences.[2] Others seek to learn what relatives and friends of people who died in the attacks remember about their loved ones.[3]

There are many different examples of oral histories within our literature. Oral histories sometimes are used in ethnographic studies (described in Chapter 8). For example, the oral history data collection method was used in a study that examined life themes of native Hawaiian female elders.[4] The elders, known as *kupunas* to native Hawaiians, play important roles in native Hawaiian culture. Three themes selected for emphasis in the study were relationships with people, relationships with nature, and spiritual and religious beliefs. The data developed in interviews were transcribed and then analyzed according to the themes, and prepared in draft form for review by participants to aid in correcting any misinformation. Following the reviews, they were bound and preserved by the Center for Oral History at a university.

In another study, Martin conducted in-depth interviews of elderly African Americans living in a community in the southeastern part of the United States. She gathered and recorded oral histories from members of fifteen families.[5] The study evolved from Martin's concern with how the relative strengths of African American families are portrayed. It documented African American family adaptation systems.

Martin's interviewing schedule was an adaptation of Hartman's eco-map. A copy of the map was provided to all participants as a stimulus for discussion. The map was later used to help organize the oral history data that Martin had gathered.

Martin made extensive use of individual narratives to preserve the stories of her participants. All interviews were audio-taped and later transcribed. Themes related to adaptation, survival, and growth were identified in analyses of the transcriptions. The data were presented both in tabular form and thematically. Whenever possible, the respondents' own words were used to highlight important findings.

In the first phase of a more extensive project, in 2007. Logan interviewed and recorded the experiences of ten African American women who were involved in the civil rights movement in South Carolina. Each participant's life narrative was captured in both booklet form and DVD.[6]

In these oral histories and in many others, participants were encouraged to "tell their story," to interpret what it meant to them, and even to describe their emotions and feelings surrounding it. However, oral histories also can be used to create an historical record of most anything else where participants were present. For example, members of the original board of directors of a social agency can be asked to describe their recollections of early meetings and discussions that occurred. Their oral histories can be used at some later time to provide insight into why the organization began, what it hoped to accomplish, and how its mission evolved.

The examples that we have cited help to illustrate the many different uses of oral histories. They also suggest why it is difficult to say exactly what an oral history is. Is it a product of some activity, an original data source, or a secondary data source? The answer to this question is that it can be all three!

For many people who compile and preserve them, oral histories are the end product of their work, a recorded description of how people experienced some life event, preserved for posterity. When this is the case, compiling and preserving them is an activity, but it is really more the work of an historian than a researcher. It is a valuable contribution to society, but it does not require most of the knowledge and skills that researchers use.

If the person compiling oral histories is more interested in answering research questions of immediate interest or, less frequently, determining if there is support for their research hypotheses (that is, he or she is functioning more as a researcher), they can be regarded as an original data source. For example, a researcher could compile them in such a way as to seek answers to a question such as, "How do people from the Middle East perceive that they have been treated differently in North America following the terrorist acts of the twenty-first century?" The histories that are compiled can be analyzed in search of an answer, using the skills of the researcher.

No matter why or by whom (historians or researchers) oral histories are created, once they exist, they become a potential secondary data source for researchers who come along later. They can be used to seek answers to research questions that those who compiled them may have had little interest in or may never even have contemplated.

It is probably most accurate to simply state that oral histories are a good data resource for researchers. They may be either a source of secondary data *or* an original data source.

In-Person Interviews

Interviews with research participants are an important and widely used data source for social work researchers. They have always been popular methods of data collection and are likely to remain so.

Differences between Quantitative and Qualitative Interviews

Interviews are essential to most all qualitative research but often perform a valuable function in quantitative studies as well. However, quantitative and qualitative research interviews differ in several important ways. Box 7.2 summarizes some of the most important ones.

Goal and Objective.   Of course, the primary purpose of all social work research interviewing is to collect data about some human phenomenon. In quantitative research, the researcher uses the interview most often to attempt to accurately describe a behavior, attitude, belief, or knowledge level by measuring one or more variables that are indicators of them. He or she wants to get accurate, factual information that will allow for the testing of research hypotheses.

In more qualitative studies, the data sought are generally different. The researcher is likely to be attempting to learn more about, for example, how research participants experienced some event, how they perceived it at the time, and what it currently means to them.

Reason for Use.   In quantitative studies, interviews often are not the primary method of data collection. They are often used to verify the accuracy of data acquired in some

BOX 7.2   In-Person Interviews in Quantitative and Qualitative Research

Goal	Qualitative Studies	Quantitative Studies
	Test hypotheses	Elicit perceptions, subjective meanings
Immediate objective	Accurate measurement	Insight, understanding
Reason for use	Verification, necessity	Method of choice
Relationship: participants	Detached, objective	Close, supportive, even therapeutic
Emotionality	Discouraged	Encouraged, supported
Structure	Highly structured	Unstructured, conversational, responsive
Discussion of sensitive issues	Avoided or delayed	Sought, encouraged early, supported

other way, such as through the use of a mailed questionnaire. The interview may just be a follow-up attempt to verify or explain information provided by the primary data collection method.

In quantitative research, interviews also are used for data collection when there is a need for data that only can be obtained through oral communication or a combination of oral communication and first-person observation. Characteristics of research participants sometimes suggest that research interviews are the best way to obtain data. For example, very young children, some older people, people with learning disabilities, or other people with no or minimal literacy skills all may require the use of an interview.

Aspects of specific cultures also may favor the use of the in-person interview. Because cooperation in interpersonal interactions is important in cultures that are more collectivistic, research participants who adhere to these values may respond more favorably to in-person data collection approaches than to less personal data collection approaches, such as questionnaires or telephone surveys. In many Hispanic cultures, *personalismo* is valued; that is, time is taken for people to get to know one another and trust is established before information (especially that of a sensitive nature) is shared. The in-person interview is more conducive to this type of interaction and may increase rate of compliance with research protocols among people who hold this cultural perspective.

In qualitative research, interviewing is often the primary or even the only method of data collection. Through it (and the observations that accompany it), the researcher hopes to find out how people experienced some phenomenon or event, to learn its meaning or its essence for them. The data that are provided are thus subjective. In addition, there is also a second layer of subjectivity present—the researcher's *interpretation* of its meaning. Consequently, since there is little pretense of objectivity, "richness" rather than factual information is sought, often through development of relationships of candor and trust with the participant. There is little attempt to avoid influencing the data; it is unavoidable.

Relationship with Research Participants.   In a research interview in a predominantly quantitative study, the researcher is cordial and respectful, but does not seek to form a close or supportive relationship with research participants, and may consciously try to avoid one. Thus, in a quantitative research interview, the researcher strives to not influence the responses of research participants by his or her choice of words, behaviors, facial expressions, and so forth. When a participant responds to questions, there is no indication provided in the form of either positive or negative reinforcement that would suggest that one response is preferable to another. Special attention is even paid to dress, mode of communication, manner of presentation, and overall demeanor. The researcher works to eliminate personal characteristics that may offend, intimidate, or otherwise influence the responses of participants. Of course, they cannot alter certain of their personal characteristics, such as age, gender, or ethnicity. However, they remain sensitive to them and attempt to determine how they may have influenced data collection.

In quantitative interviews, only required data are sought; any additional exchange of information is viewed as unnecessary and even undesirable. One common problem encountered is that requests for advice or other forms of assistance often occur, especially since the research participant generally knows that the researcher is a social worker. For example, it is difficult to collect factual data about participants' methods of child rearing without advice being sought at some point during the interview. To a quantitative researcher, promptly responding to such requests could compromise the role of "objective researcher" — it can affect the participant's subsequent responses. It also can disrupt the flow of data collection, making it difficult to get the interview back on track. The researcher may feel a professional obligation to provide assistance, if able, but probably would not do so during data collection. A reply that "I will be happy to talk about that with you after we complete our interview" is appropriate and usually tends to be accepted by the participant. Naturally, such promises should be remembered and kept. Assistance may entail actually giving advice (but only after data collection) or, more commonly, making a referral to an appropriate organization or helping person.

In contrast, in a qualitative research interview, the relationship with participants is likely to be close and even therapeutic, when needed. This type of relationship represents no particular problem because, as previously noted, there are few pretenses of objectivity in data collection and therefore little concern that it might be compromised. Interpersonal exchanges such as questions about the researcher's family or educational background or requests for assistance are considered natural and expected. So the researcher responds to them when they occur. Providing requested help "on the spot" is viewed as both an ethical responsibility and desirable from a research perspective, since it will likely increase the likelihood that a participant will trust the researcher and thus be more open and candid in the conversation that follows.

Attitudes toward Emotionality.   Emotionality in a more quantitative interview represents a problem for the researcher. Even when measurements of attitudes and feelings are sought, emotional responses are assumed to provide unreliable indicators of them. Besides, emotionality in a research interview can seriously interfere with the collection of other needed data.

In qualitative research, displays of emotion by participants are not uncommon. In fact, sometimes the researcher encourages emotionality to help better understand how the participant is experiencing or has experienced some phenomenon. They may be helpful in achieving the researcher's objectives.

Structure.   In more quantitative research interviews, major digressions by the participant are generally viewed as undesirable. The researcher exerts fairly tight control over the flow of the interview. Too long or too frequent digressions can interfere with the completion of data collection. Research interviews that run overtime can result in fatigue for participants or the researcher; either may threaten the quality of data acquired. Unnecessarily long interviews can also cause other appointments to be missed or other potential participants to be in a less receptive mood for data collection.

Usually, qualitative research interviews tend to involve relatively little structure and control by the researcher. Digressions by participants are expected and are generally regarded as useful because they lead into topics that often are more productive than those that the social worker might have introduced. Getting participants back on track is required only if it becomes apparent that they are avoiding topics that need to be discussed and that are believed to be within their emotional tolerance for discussion.

Discussion of Sensitive Issues.   Both quantitative and qualitative interviews are likely to include discussion of behaviors or feelings of a personal or sensitive nature. Because this can provoke discomfort for participants, placement of such content within the interview is often an issue. In more quantitative types of research, discussion of sensitive matters occurs only if necessary; that is, only if it relates to the research question and/or hypothesis. In such instances, it usually is planned near the end of the interview. Placed too early, there is a risk of losing potential participants who may decide that they have had enough, terminating the interview before much data have been collected. But if placed near the end of the interview, there is sufficient time for debriefing and for the interview to end on a less emotionally charged note.

In a qualitative research interview, sensitive content is often elicited early in the interview, when there will be plenty of time to explore them and to provide support. The researcher does not like to see discussions about sensitive issues begin as the interview is about to draw to a close, and therefore does whatever possible to get to those issues early.

Advantages

Besides the fact that they allow the researcher to collect data from participants who might be unable to complete written data collection instruments, there are a number of other important advantages to collecting data using in-person interviews. As should be obvious from our previous discussion, they are generally more relevant to qualitative studies than to more quantitative ones.

- *Opportunity to probe.* While talking with research participants, the researcher is able to initiate clarification about their responses by making such comments as "I wonder if you could tell me more about that?" or "What led you to that conclusion?" These comments provide participants with the opportunity to expand on responses more fully, thereby allowing the researcher to acquire more in-depth, accurate data. It may thus be possible to understand and measure an individual's attitude about an issue and perhaps even determine the origins of that attitude. This type of insight is less likely to occur if a mailed instrument or other method that does not allow for interaction between the researcher and the participant is used for data collection.

- *High completion rate.* Interviews usually permit researchers to secure a completed return. If participants agree to be interviewed, then interviewers usually are able to get them to complete the interview.
- *Access to supplementary data.* Interviewers are able to observe participants while they are responding to questions. Nonverbal communications may provide important data. They can indicate the participant's ease in responding, evasiveness in answering questions, or how seriously the participant seems to be taking the interview. They can be carefully observed, recorded, and used as part of later data analysis.
- *Opportunity to individualize data collection.* Interviews can be individualized as needed to facilitate data collection or to aid in obtaining complete data from participants. Of course, the more interviews differ, the more difficult it becomes to compare responses of participants.
- *Use of interviewing skills.* Interviewing is a natural for social work researchers whose professional education prepares them to conduct interviews about a wide range of topics. Thus, interviewing takes advantage of their strengths.

Disadvantages

If interviews were the perfect data source, no other methods would be needed. But there are some major problems inherent in research interviews, especially in quantitative research. Although careful preparation can minimize them, it cannot totally eliminate them.

- *Influence of the interviewer.* The fact that the researcher is present and is posing questions directly to the participant may influence the responses of participants. (Qualitative researchers, we will recall, regard such influence as inevitable anyway.) In some cases, participants may choose a response that they believe is sought by the interviewer. This type of distortion in responses is known as an *expectancy effect.* Participants also may choose a socially desirable response rather than provide their true response. Erroneous conclusions on the part of the interviewer can result.
- *Potential for recording errors.* The accuracy of data collected in an interview also may be negatively affected by the manner in which responses are recorded by the interviewer. Participants may provide truthful and accurate data, but if they are forgotten, distorted, misinterpreted, or recorded in error by the interviewer, data quality will still be low. Careful preparation for data collection that addresses how data are to be gathered and recorded can reduce the potential for recording errors. If interviewers other than the researcher are to be used, they should be carefully trained in order to have a thorough understanding of the expected role and demeanor of the interviewer and the purpose of the study and its overall design. They should be given supervised practice in use of any interview schedule that is to be used, and the correct manner of recording data.

  Interviewer training can be expensive, but its cost is justified. If two or more interviewers are to be used, consistency in recording is enhanced if interviewers are trained together. They should be provided with the opportunity to ask any questions about the study that they may have. Interviewing simulations and role play can be part of the training package.

  Audio- or video-recording of interviews can greatly reduce recording errors and is a common practice in qualitative research studies. The recordings can be reviewed later, as many times as necessary, until the researcher is reasonably certain what was said or expressed. Others can also listen to or view the recordings (while respecting confidentiality) in order to verify or refute what was believed to have transpired. Recording of interviews is generally more feasible in qualitative studies than in quantitative ones in which there may be more reluctance by research participants to allow it (less of a trust relationship) and researchers may have greater concern about how it might affect the truthfulness of responses.

- *Errors caused by demographic differences.* When interviewers and research participants are from different language, racial, cultural, or even socioeconomic groups, the possibility of flawed data due to either socially desirable responses or unwillingness or fear of providing frank answers to questions may be increased. This is especially likely to occur when the research topic touches on areas related to the nature of differences between investigator and participant (for example, racial prejudices and attitudes toward other groups). Under certain conditions, it may be preferable to match interviewers and participants according to language, culture, and even socioeconomic status. Use of same-ethnic data collectors can increase rapport and trust. Communication also is enhanced when bilingual interviewers are used for participants who are not native English speakers. Bilingual and bicultural interviewers are more likely to be aware of idiomatic variations among particular ethnic or nationality groups, as well as subtle differences in meaning for the same or similar words. They are also more likely to recognize and understand nonverbal forms of communication, which may be more critical than what participants actually say.[7]

Butler[8] cautions that simply matching interviewer and participant by race or ethnicity may be insufficient to guard against problems relating to demographics of the researcher and research participants. She notes, for example, that many African American professionals are from the upper and middle classes or are trained in mainstream educational settings that remove them from the realities of fellow African Americans from different socioeconomic circumstances.

Interviewing Protocol

Whenever in-person interviews are used for data collection, researchers contact potential participants and acquire their permission to be interviewed. Then the interview is conducted at a time and a place that is mutually agreeable to both interviewer and participant.

Interviews can be conducted in a human service organization, a public place, or the participant's own home. If participants are interviewed in their home, additional data can be collected and later analyzed. For example, observations can be made about the home environment and about their interaction with significant others. These kinds of data can provide the researcher with additional (in some cases, serendipitous) data which may help to explain the participant's other responses more fully.

There are some other practices that researchers try to follow to ensure that data received through interviewing are as complete and usable as possible. They include the following:

- *Provide complete identification.* Interviewers should appropriately identify themselves and remind the participant of the purpose of the study and of their agreement to be interviewed. An appropriate introduction helps to confirm that the study is legitimate and thus helps to make the participant more desirous of providing all requested data.

• *Promote pleasant interaction.* Respect and courtesy, of course, are appropriate in all research interviews. They are especially essential when interviews are conducted in the participant's own home, where the researcher is a guest. Research participants often give much more than they hope to receive; an interviewer's demeanor should reflect an appreciation of this fact.

• *Use data collection instruments.* Because quantitative research interviewing tends to be more structured than interviewing used in qualitative research, data collection instruments (sometimes referred to as *interview schedules*) generally are used. In interviews in which a high percentage of items are designed to be read to participants, the specific wording of an item and the sequence in which items are covered take on great importance. Any deviation from the wording or from sequencing of items could influence the responses that are received and could invalidate any comparisons made between research participants. In less structured research such as many qualitative studies, a schedule serves as only a general outline; wording and sequencing of items is less critical.)

• *Record unobtrusively.* The style of recording of research data and observations will vary from one interviewer to another and from one study to another. For some studies, it may be essential to circle the appropriate responses on a data collection instrument or to record verbatim what the participant says. As noted earlier, recording of interviews may be possible and desirable, especially in more qualitative studies. However data are recorded, it should be done as unobtrusively as possible in order not to disrupt the flow of the interview.

• *Specify the progress of the interview.* As the interview progresses, the interviewer should periodically let the participant know about what percentage of the interview remains to be completed. This may help participants avoid becoming frustrated about the time required, help them remain focused, and give them a feeling of better participation in the interview process. Interviewers might say something like "Now we have reached the halfway point," "We have just two more questions to go," or "We're nearly through now."

Group Interviews

Another useful method for acquiring research data is the *group interview*. It can occur inperson or on-line, and can be an efficient (economical) way of collecting research data.

Focus Groups

A common form of group data collection in social work research (and one that is especially wellsuited to the skills of social workers) is the *focus group*. Focus groups are more likely to be used in qualitative studies than in quantitative ones. They also are used widely in program evaluations (Chapter 13) to gain insights from clients, staff, and others who have formed opinions about a social program.

How does a focus group work? People who share a similar problem or who have experienced a similar life experience may be invited to participate in a group discussion led by the researcher. For example, a focus group of openly gay teenagers could be formed to discuss how they experienced the attitudes of teachers and other high school students, or a group of Native American students might meet with a researcher to describe their perceptions of how they think they have been treated in a predominantly white community.

Focus groups also are sometimes intentionally comprised of individuals who do not share the same experiences, beliefs, values or demographic characteristics. For example, a researcher might lead a focus group of very diverse people (ethnically, socioeconomically, educationally, and so forth) in order to assess the degree of support in a community for a proposed group home for people with developmental disabilities.

It is believed that a focus group has certain advantages over one-on-one interviews with researchers. Particularly if the experience is one that is difficult to talk about, the group can be a source of emotional support. Members are especially likely to be candid among others who have had similar experiences or who have similar values or opinions. The group also can be a stimulus for individual participants in another way. Members can be helped to think about and respond to issues (brought up by other members) that they might otherwise not consider. Are there negatives associated with collecting data in a group of research participants? Yes. A major one is that the influence of the group can easily produce data of questionable merit. It is difficult to know when participants are speaking honestly about their own experiences and perceptions. In focus groups of people who are similar to each other, they may be just joining in and revealing what they think the other group members expect them to offer. In diverse focus groups, they may just be so outraged by what others say that they overreact and say things that may not be correct or reflective of their true opinions. Because of the possibility of group influences on individuals, data collected in focus groups must be used cautiously.

The role of the leader (often called a facilitator) in a focus group is a little different from the role that the leader plays in other types of groups in which social workers participate (such as treatment groups) and different from the role researchers play in either qualitative or quantitative one-on-one in-person interviews. Leading a focus group to collect research data entails providing some degree of structure and direction to the discussion in order to acquire what is needed. At the same time, the researcher does not want to limit discussion excessively or to lead it too much, thus missing out on some unanticipated, valuable insights that participants might otherwise provide. This requires a difficult balancing act.

Other Group Data Collection

While focus groups are a common method of acquiring data in groups, they are not the only one. Not all groups are focus groups, and other types of groups (for example, social groups, meetings) offer potential data sources as well, either through interviewing, observation, or (most often) some combination of the two. Even treatment groups have this potential, but if they are to be used, additional ethical obstacles such as the presence of dual relationships (Chapter 2) must be overcome.

Finally, not all group data collection involves interviewing at all. In some studies that rely on standardized instruments or questionnaires (Chapter 12) for data collection, a researcher may use a group setting for their completion. When it is logistically feasible to gather a number of research participants in one place (for example, in a social agency or at a college or university), group administration can be a cost-efficient way to collect data. In addition, there is the advantage of the researcher's presence—if any questions or items are unclear, participants can receive clarification, the same clarification that is provided to everyone else in the room.

Systematic Observation

When conducting either one-on-one interviews or conducting group interviews such as focus groups, researchers have the opportunity to observe research participants. These observations often yield additional, unanticipated data for their research.

Sometimes researchers observe some behavior or phenomenon in a more planned way. Then it serves as their primary method of data collection and is called *systematic observation*. It is used in both qualitative and quantitative studies, but it tends to be less structured in qualitative research than when used in more quantitative studies.

Observation is sometimes made in a created or contrived situation. The Zimbardo studies (Stanford prison experiment) of college students assuming the role of prisoner or prison guard (Chapter 1) are an example of this type of research. The created situation may also involve deception, such as in the "ethically challenged" Milgram electroshock studies discussed in Chapter 2. However, most observation is conducted in a "natural," setting, one that is not created for purposes of the research.

Unstructured Systematic Observation

There are many instances in social work research where we may use observation as a data source. For example, we may wish to know more about parent–child interactions, group process, or task completion. Or, as part of a program evaluation, we may wish to learn what it is like to be a client in the program. If so, systematic observation can constitute a valuable source of data.

Unstructured observation is characterized by a lack of formal data-gathering instruments. Typically in unstructured observation, the researcher is either a passive observer or a participant observer (actually takes part in some activity). These methods are appropriate when the phenomenon being studied cannot be clearly specified in advance and when it is important to observe participants in their own environments rather than in a laboratory setting. For example, researchers who are interested in studying behavior of a group such as Weight-Watchers or Alcoholics Anonymous might choose to join the group and make observations over some period of time. Researchers in anthropology and social psychology have used unstructured observational methods in their studies of street gangs, homeless people, and various non-Western cultures.

In areas of inquiry where knowledge is limited, it often is best to observe behavior in an unstructured manner. In so doing, the researcher is not constrained by categories or checklists and is open to viewing all behaviors (or components of behaviors) that are displayed. Unstructured observation really falls somewhere between exploratory and descriptive research. It is often used to learn more about a behavior, culture, or environment of interest, often to lay the groundwork for subsequent studies that are more structured.

Unstructured observation requires researchers to maintain field notes. Usually they either make mental notes for later recording or maintain a recorded running account or description of behaviors during the observation period. Developing and maintaining some kind of note-taking procedure is crucial; otherwise, at the end of the observation study, researchers would have to depend on their memory to recall what they observed.

Because unstructured observation tends to yield data that are primarily qualitative in nature, certain methods for presentation are generally used. Information collected often is presented in narrative rather than statistical form. Running accounts, case vignettes, and anecdotes are often used. Direct quotations from participants are frequently included.

We will use an example to demonstrate how unstructured observation might be used in social work research. Suppose that a researcher is interested in developing an understanding of the psychosocial needs of family caregivers of older people. Unstructured observation might be used to study caregivers and the older people to whom they offer care in their homes. During periods of observation, the researcher could carefully observe the needs and demands of older people, as well as the responses of their caregivers. The interactions between the two would be observed and characterized. The activities and emotional responses of the caregivers would be particularly noted. The application of an unstructured observational method would allow certain kinds of questions to be addressed. They might include:

- Do caregivers seem able to perform the tasks required to provide needed care? If not, what are their emotional responses to not being able to meet their relatives' needs?
- Do caregivers have opportunities to meet their own needs? What sacrifices do they appear to make in order to care for the older person? How able are they to verbalize anger or frustration because of the demands of caregiving?
- What assistance is available to caregivers? Are there other people who are part of the caregiving network? If so, which ones appear to be most helpful to caregivers, and why?

Advantages.   Unstructured observation is characterized by flexibility. During the observation period, researchers may take note of behaviors, reactions, or environmental features that may relate to the phenomenon being studied. Trained, sensitive observers are able to record data about many variables of potential impact on it. During the course of an unstructured observation, researchers may become aware of the influence of other phenomena that were not originally identified or conceptualized. They may make the decision to include observations of them in their study or to make them the focus of some subsequent research study.

Findings from studies using systematic observation often can be generalized beyond those research participants who were studied. Especially in naturalistic observation— that is, in studies where data are gathered by observing participants in their own environments—external validity can be quite good. In systematic observation that occurs in the field (as distinguished from the laboratory), the researcher can be relatively confident that the behavior observed is characteristic of what people (at least in that setting) actually say and do. This is not always the case in other research designs, for example, in those that use questionnaires or other self-report measures that permit participants to tell researchers only what they wish us to know.

Limitations.   Of course, external validity in any research design is greatly dependent on the representativeness of the participants studied. In systematic observation, it also is affected by participants' *reactivity,* that is, the degree to which they modify their behavior in response to the presence of the observer. The possibility of reactivity's affecting the measurement process should be carefully considered in the design of a study that relies on observation as a data source. It may be possible to select an observer role that will at least minimize the impact of reactivity while still providing the needed access to data.

Other disadvantages inherent in the use of unstructured observation (besides reactivity) relate to the consistency and objectivity of measurement procedures. Both can seriously damage the credibility of one's research findings.

Consistency of data collection is a primary concern because, in unstructured observation, data collection is not standardized to any degree. When more than one observer collects data, variation in data collection procedures may be especially great. This is the issue of interobserver agreement (Chapter 10). The reliability of data can be enhanced by employing two or more observers to conduct the same measurement. Interobserver agreement can be assessed by using a form of statistical analysis that estimates the percentage of agreement between two observers.

Fatigue or boredom can also negatively affect the quality of the observations that are made, because observation generally occurs over an extended period of time. The potential for this problem can be reduced by using several observers, with each responsible for relatively short time segments of observation.

Because observers must be sensitized to a behavior before it is described and recorded, the likelihood exists that selective perception will play a part in which data get noted or in the interpretation of what a behavior means. Training observers to increase sensitivity to the nature of the behavior of interest, to use appropriate observational techniques, and to use appropriate methods of recording data will minimize the major sources of measurement bias inherent in observation studies. However, subjectivity must be assumed to exist in all data collected using unstructured observation (and in other qualitative research studies as well). That is why it is generally more suitable for use in qualitative research than in quantitative studies.

Structured Observation

In quantitative research, experimental and quasiexperimental designs are often not feasible or desirable for one or a variety of reasons. Sometimes, they simply would not be effective in acquiring the kind of data we require. Especially if our goal is to accurately describe some behavior or phenomenon, other methods would be more effective. Structured observation is sometimes used for this purpose.

Structured observation requires identifying a specific behavior or set of behaviors and systematically observing them over a given time period. A data-gathering instrument is used. Because of the structure imposed by this method, data are more similar (on a case-by-case basis) and therefore more easily sorted and analyzed than those collected using less structured observation methods.

In designing any form of observation, researchers must decide on the nature and degree of involvement with research participants that are best. The most appropriate role for a given study depends on the purpose of the study, the researcher's assessment of how the most accurate data can be obtained, and legal and ethical issues. Observer roles may be understood as being located on a continuum from complete observer to participant observer. Possible observer roles might include:

- Concealed, nonparticipating (complete observer)
- Concealed, participating
- Not concealed, nonparticipating
- Not concealed, minimally participating
- Not concealed, participating (participant observer)

The two variables, concealment of the observer (usually the researcher and his or her true purpose) and degree of participation, can affect the quality of the data collected. When the presence of an observer is not concealed, participants may consciously or unconsciously alter their behavior. But when the presence of an observer is concealed from participants, they are more likely to behave in their usual manner. So why not simply conceal the fact that the researcher is an observer collecting research data? As was noted in our discussion of research ethics in Chapter 2, not allowing participants to know that they are being observed may be considered unwarranted intrusion on their privacy. It might not be permitted by an IRB on ethical grounds because participants had not voluntarily agreed to be part of the research. Even if participants had agreed to participate in research, but had not been told that they would be observed without their knowledge, that could be unethical. But if they voluntarily agreed to participate and were told that they would be observed but would not know exactly *when* they were being observed, this would not constitute deception and would probably be considered ethical.

How would the various roles be operationalized in social work research? An example might be helpful. Suppose a team of researchers is interested in studying the quality of interviewing skills of beginning social workers in a human service organization. If the researchers elect to observe the interview sessions of new workers from behind a one-way mirror, then they would be considered to be "concealed, nonparticipating." If the researchers observe from behind the mirror while using equipment that would enable them to prompt the interviewers, then the observers would be "concealed, participating." They also could choose to observe a sample of client interviews conducted by beginning-level workers by actually sitting in on the interviews. If the researchers only record behaviors and do not influence the direction of the interview in any way, then they are "not concealed, nonparticipating." But if the researchers provide occasional suggestions to the workers, suggest approval or disapproval of the workers' interviewing methods through nonverbal communication, or otherwise subtly influence them to conduct the interview differently, then the researchers are "not concealed, minimally participating." However, if the interviews are conducted jointly by researchers and workers, and the workers' skills are later evaluated, the researchers would be "not concealed, participating."

Sometimes the choice of an observer role can greatly affect the quality of the data that will be acquired. If researchers wish to gather data that will not be affected by their presence, then the observer should be concealed and nonparticipating. However, if the data are unlikely to be adversely affected by the observer's presence, then the observer need not be concealed.

There generally are seven steps in implementing a structured observational design. They are the following:

1. *Define the behavior or list of behaviors to be studied.* In structured observation, the researcher decides what behaviors to study based on the literature review. They are those behaviors considered critical to an understanding of the research problem and to answering research questions and/or testing hypotheses. Operational definitions of the behaviors are developed; they provide the basis for observation. Characteristics of the behaviors to be measured are also specified, for example, their frequency, duration, intensity, and so forth.

2. *Identify a time frame during which the behaviors will be observed.* The researcher has to know when specific behaviors are most likely to occur. This knowledge also comes from a thorough understanding of the behavior under investigation derived from the review of literature and personal or professional experience. For example, if we are interested in studying verbal abuse by caregivers of older people, the researcher should have learned which times of day are most stressful for caregivers. In addition to identifying a specific time during the day (or week or month) to observe, the literature review might also suggest a time interval during which the observation should occur. Will the observer observe for one hour at a time, for three hours, or for five minutes each hour? A time sample should be selected based on the nature of the behavior under study (when and how frequently it is most likely to occur) and on the physical and emotional capacities of observers to gather accurate data. If observers are required to gather data for long periods of time, the quality of the data may suffer (referred to as *measurement decay*). Observers get tired or bored; they require breaks and relief from their work.

3. *Develop a data collection instrument.* In structured observation, instruments typically take the form of behavioral checklists or category schemes. They are designed so that, when a behavior is displayed, its characteristics can easily be recorded. The instrument may also include demographic data on participants being observed, such as name, age, gender, or other identifying characteristics. As is true for other new data collection instruments (Chapter 11), the instrument should be pilot tested before use. This is done to see how effective the instrument is in describing the behavior.

4. *Select an observer role.* The observer role most appropriate to the behavior being studied is selected. Logistical and ethical issues (as previously mentioned) are addressed.

5. *Train observers.* Structured observation requires the use of trained research personnel. Unless the researcher is conducting all observations personally (a potential source of bias), others usually are recruited or hired to observe. They need to be trained by the researcher in the method of observation to be used, and they need to gain experience with the use of the data collection instrument. Observers need to know what to look for, when to observe it, how to know if behavior is occurring, and how to record it using the instrument.

6. *Conduct the observations.* Observers apply the observational method, recording the data as they are obtained.

7. *Verify the data.* Data are checked for accuracy. It may be possible to use videotaping (with participant permission) to record behaviors. If so, an observer need not be present, and a team of trained reviewers can view the recordings and arrive at a consensus as to what occurred. If this is not possible, a second observer may be used. If there is a serious discrepancy between the data collected by two observers, the disputed data generally are discarded.

Advantages.   A major advantage of a more structured approach to observation is that the data thus acquired tend to be measured in a consistent manner and may also be more accurate. They also tend to be better organized and in a more consistent format. It is easier to code them for computer analysis. Thus, quantitative analysis is possible, including statistical testing of research hypotheses.

Limitations.   The "down side" to data thus acquired is that, of necessity, they tend to be more sterile than data collected in less structured ways. Observations tend to be more limited in scope. Potentially valuable observations may not become part of the data if planning for them was not conducted beforehand. Thus, structured observation is a more appropriate data source for quantitative studies where accurate measurement of a limited number of variables and examining possible relationships between them is important, than in qualitative studies where the researcher is required to be more open to receiving and processing the unexpected.

Telephone Interviews

The telephone and its relative, the fax machine can sometimes be used for collecting data, even though it has more limitations than advantages. If the amount of data required is small and it is not too personal, and if the research participants have some connection or positive association with the researcher or some group that he or she represents, they can be an economical way (the primary advantage) to collect data from a large number of participants.

Two common examples of research that often use telephone interviews surveys are client satisfaction surveys in human service organizations and alumni follow-up surveys in schools of social work. If an administrator is interested in determining to what degree a sample of clients is satisfied with services recently received, the phone can be used to contact former clients. Securing their responses to five or six questions can be performed quickly and inexpensively. Similarly, current students or faculty members can conduct a survey of a sample of a school's graduates to learn, for example, if they had difficulty in finding employment, what courses they found most useful in their practice, what curriculum changes they might recommend, and so forth.

When should telephone interviews be conducted? Common sense and experience would suggest that it is a poor idea to call between 5:00 P.M. and, say, 7:00 P.M., when many people are returning from work or having dinner. Similarly, calling either late in the evening or very early in the morning is often resented by potential participants. Although these times are especially inconvenient for people to provide data over the phone, most any time that the researcher calls is likely to find potential participants doing something that they would prefer to do. Perhaps in earlier times people enjoyed unanticipated phone calls, but few do today. Finding a time that is convenient is a difficult but important task in telephone interviewing. Therefore, it is prudent to schedule telephone interviews with participants in advance whenever possible.

Even if a phone call comes at an ideal time, any simple requests for information are now suspect. Telephone interviewers must overcome the annoyance and normal suspicions that people display when they receive a call from someone purporting to conduct legitimate research. The researcher can almost expect to hear "I don't have time for this!" or just a hang-up unless his or her credibility has been established in some way prior to a call.

Unfortunately, pseudoresearch has been used as a device to make a sale or, even worse, to collect personal information to be used by the researcher for some self-serving (or even illicit) purpose. Telephone requests for information, even from a known reputable source such as a university or social agency, now often meet with suspicion. Although virtually anyone can memorize a few questions to collect telephone data, overcoming resistance to providing information over the phone is the hardest part of telephone interviewing. It requires all the interviewing skills of the social worker.

Most of the same principles that apply to in-person interviews apply to the telephone interview as well. However, because participants may be naturally suspicious of why they have been called and of the true purpose of a caller whom they cannot see, telephone researchers have an especially hard sell. It is necessary that interviewers identify themselves and tell what organization is supporting or endorsing their research. They should also ask permission to conduct the interview. If a participant indicates that the call has come at an inconvenient time, a request to reschedule the interview should be made.

An important limitation of data gathered through telephone interviews and fax is the difficulty of obtaining a group of participants who are representative of the group being studied. Therefore, the external validity of research that uses them often is regarded as poor.

Any time of day when telephone interviews are conducted has the potential to interfere with sample representativeness. For example, people employed outside the home tend to be unavailable during daytime hours. But representativeness of the sample can be hindered in other ways, too. An organization administrator might have access to all case records (containing phone numbers) to conduct a follow-up client satisfaction survey. But some former clients may have moved or had their phones disconnected and would thus be unavailable to be contacted. And they may be (disproportionately) the very people who either are doing very well and have moved out of state or are having the most problems and are most dissatisfied with their services. Similarly, an alumni follow-up survey might get the participation of only those alumni who are most satisfied with their education (and want to show their appreciation) or those who are most dissatisfied (and want to take the opportunity to vent about it). The alumni who are more neutral may have little vested interest in providing data. They are more likely to refuse to provide it and therefore will be underrepresented in the data collected.

Often, the researcher who lacks access to current agency or university records is even less fortunate. If it is necessary to punch numbers at random or select them randomly from a phone directory, a biased sample is almost certain to result. A telephone directory is not a very good source from which to draw a research sample. The phone book automatically excludes people who use only their cellular phones, or who either simply do not have telephones, or who do not have listed numbers. In addition, the widespread use of voice mail and answering machines (often used to screen calls) has made it difficult to get through to even many of those who have listed home phone numbers. All of these factors can severely bias a sample in relation to occupation, gender, ethnicity, socioeconomic class, and other related variables that may be important to the research. Of course, many of these same variables are related to access to fax machines.

Despite the likelihood of sampling bias, telephone interviews continue to be used for research data collection. The arrival of "unlimited minutes" for long-distance calls has made them an even more economical alternative than most other methods. When they are used, certain rules can be applied (for example, asking the person in a household who most recently celebrated a birthday to provide data) to at least minimize sampling bias and even to calculate the true response rate.[9]

Electronic Communication

The widespread use of electronic communication (e-mail, voice-over IP, instant chats, on-line groups and instant messaging) make them tempting alternatives as methods for data collection. Data can be collected quickly and at minimal cost. Many people (especially younger ones) rely heavily on the use of electronics (try taking them away!) and would rather "write" or otherwise communicate by computer or cell phone than by, for example, completing a written questionnaire on paper and mailing it back to the researcher.

Like the telephone or fax, electronic communication has a major problem relating to sampling bias and the external validity of some findings. Some people still do not have regular access to a computer or cell phone, or if they do, they may not have e-mail or instant messaging. Others have them, but still lack computer skills or are uncomfortable using them. Differences in relation to gender, ethnicity, and age are not as pronounced as they once were, but they still exist. Thus, the likelihood of acquiring a representative sample in relation to such variables is likely to be reduced when using electronic communication as opposed to some other methods. Of course, as suggested earlier, some people's preference for communicating electronically may leave them disinclined to participate in research that requests data in any other way.

Because of obvious limitations, electronic communication is used most effectively as a method for data collection when certain conditions exist. For example:

1. A reasonably complete list of potential research participants is available, along with their electronic addresses.
2. The majority of potential participants are likely to be people who regularly use their computers or cell phones as a primary method of daily communication.
3. Variables that are believed to relate to differences in computer or cell-phone ownership and usage are unlikely to be relevant to the research questions that are being examined.
4. The data sought are such that they lend themselves to a questionnaire format and are not very personal (do not arouse suspicions about viruses or "spoof mail").
5. The research is primarily quantitative.

Of course, electronic communication (like the other methods for acquiring data that are discussed in this chapter) can also be used in conjunction with other methods, as preliminary to one or more of them, or as a follow-up to them. For example, an e-mail survey can be used to identify potential participants who have certain characteristics and are willing to participate in an in-person interview, or to seek bits of data that may have not been collected for some reason during a prior interview.

Mailed Questionnaires

Data collection by mailed questionnaire is widely used in quantitative social work research, especially in descriptive surveys (Chapter 8). A mailed, self-administered questionnaire can reach large numbers of participants quickly and at relatively low cost. However, for data thus acquired to be valuable, the questionnaires must reach the appropriate people, they must be completed correctly, and participants must return them as directed. What sometimes happens instead is that many mailed data collection instruments are either misplaced by recipients, discarded as junk mail, completed but never mailed back to the researcher, or completed incorrectly to the point that they must be discarded.

In order to increase the number of usable responses, it often is necessary to use a second or even third mailing of the data collection instrument. In order to reduce costs, instruments are precoded with an identifying number prior to the first mailing, so that when they are returned, the researcher can tell who has returned them and who has not. Then a second mailing is sent to those who did not return them. Given the virtual necessity of second mailings, data collection by mail is more costly than it might first appear. The costs of printing the instrument, of preparing the mailings, and of the postage required for two or more mailings can be appreciable. The major advantage of using mailed instruments is access to potential research participants. When they are used, large numbers of people who might otherwise be inaccessible for financial and/or logistical reasons can provide data.

There also are several other problems associated with the use of the postal system to collect data. We will discuss some of the major ones in the next chapter when we examine the pros and cons of survey designs.

Summary

Chapter 7 presented some of the most common ways that social work researchers acquire the research data that they hope will provide answers to their research questions and/or allow them to test their hypotheses. It should be obvious by now that some of these methods are more suited to some types of research design (for example, quantitative or qualitative; exploratory, descriptive, or explanatory; and so forth) than others. That is because each method has certain advantages and disadvantages that can either make it well suited for a particular type of research or present major problems. They are summarized in Box 7.3.

Each option presented in this chapter should be viewed as a data source to be considered. Together, they form a kind of menu from which to select one or more. Each can

BOX 7.3   Common Methods for Acquiring Research Data: Primary Advantages and Disadvantages

Source	Primary Advantage	Primary Limitation
Secondary data analysis	Cost	Validity issues, sterility
Oral histories	Access to firsthand observations	Subjectivity, bias
In-person interviews	Response rate, researcher availability	Cost, measurement bias
Group interviews	Efficiency, group support	Group pressure
Systematic observation	Less reliance on others	Distortion
Telephone	Cost	Sampling bias, suspicion
Electronic communication	Cost	Sampling bias, suspicion
Mailed questionnaires	Accessibility of participants	Response rate, response bias

be the only method used to acquire data, but they are often used in combination as well, as we shall see in the next chapter.

This chapter digressed somewhat from our overview of research designs per se. The selection of one or more methods for acquiring data is just one piece of a research design—just one design question to be addressed. However, we included this content here rather than later because it introduced terminology that is essential to understanding the specialized types of research that will be discussed in the next chapter. In it, we will introduce more labels that researchers often use to describe how and why they conducted their research, that is, other ways to describe the characteristics of their research designs.

For Discussion

1. What groups of people would be most underrepresented in research that used U.S. census data? What are some research questions that could not be answered?
2. How have recent laws restricting access to medical and school records made the use of secondary data more difficult for researchers? Is this good or bad, overall?
3. What are some other groups of people (besides those mentioned in this chapter) whose oral histories would be useful to preserve? What research questions might future researchers try to answer through access to them?
4. Why do researchers using more quantitative methods attempt to avoid helping relationships with participants during in-person interviews? Why do more qualitative approaches to data collection see them as less problematic or even desirable?
5. What are some observations that a researcher can make when conducting an inperson interview in a participant's home? Can they be considered "accurate"?
6. What does what we know about group processes suggest about the value of any data collected from a focus group consisting of victims of childhood sexual abuse? What might be a better data source?
7. What ethical and legal issues would a researcher have to address in deciding which role to assume in conducting a descriptive study of substance abuse among college students by using structured observation as a data source?

8. Would structured or unstructured observation be more effective for collecting data on the social patterns of people who are homeless? Why?

9. When using data collected from telephone interviews, why is sampling bias an even greater problem today than it was in 2000?

10. What might influence you to complete a request for research data that you receive by e-mail? What might influence you to not complete it, or to not even open it?

Endnotes

1. Sales, E., Lichtenwalter, S. and Fevola, A. Secondary analysis in social work research education: Past, present, and future promise. *Journal of Social Work Education XLI*I (3) (Fall, 2006), 545.

2. September 11th, 2001, *Oral history narrative and memory project* (ongoing). Columbia University, R. Kleinman, project coordinator. www.columbia.edu/cu/lweb/indiv/oral/sept11.html.

3. Jones, C. Oral history project opens new chapter. USA today.com/nese/nation/2005-07-12-9-11-oral-histories_x.htm.

4. Mokuau, N., & Browne, C. (1994). Life themes of native Hawaiian female elders: Resources for cultural preservation. *Social Work, 39* (1), 43–49.

5. Martin, R. (1995). *Oral history in social work: Research, assessment, and intervention.* Thousand Oaks, CA: Sage Publications.

6. Logan, S. (2007). *In Their Own Voices.* (*10 Voices: Ten African American Women who Made a Difference*). Columbia, SC: University of South Carolina College of Social Work, I. DeQuincey Newman Institute for Peace and Justice.

7. Marin, G., & Marin, B. (1991). *Research with Hispanic populations.* Newbury Park, CA: Sage Publications.

8. Butler, J. P. (1992). Of kindred minds: The ties that bind. In OSAP, *Cultural competence for evaluators.* Washington, D.C.: U.S. Department of Health and Human Services, 23–54.

9. See, e. g., Risley-Curtiss, C., Holley, L. and Wolf, S. The animal–human bond and ethnic diversity. *Social Work*, LI (3) (July 2006), 260.

8

OTHER WAYS TO DESCRIBE RESEARCH METHODS

In Chapter 6 we presented some labels that frequently are used to describe the broadest characteristics of a research design, for example, how many times measurements of a variable are made or what type of knowledge it hopes to acquire. However, there are still other more specific labels that are applied to research designs. They are nouns (not adjectives this time) and convey certain design characteristics. Thus, when we see these labels applied correctly, they communicate a considerable amount about the research methods that the researcher uses. For example, they suggest the data sources most likely to be used (Chapter 7), the methods most likely to be used to collect data, and the ways that data are most likely to be analyzed. For the sake of clarity, it would be nice if there were no overlap among them but, as we shall see, that is not the case.

The Survey

Surveys have always been a very important part of social work research. In program evaluations, some sort of client satisfaction survey is almost always a requirement (even though, it should be remembered, client satisfaction is not always synonymous with program success). Most surveys are (1) cross sectional, (2) used to collect quantitative data, and (3) descriptive. They are important tools in both basic and applied research that are used to measure, for example, the demographic characteristics of people along with their opinions, preferences, and beliefs.

A good survey can answer many research questions. However, a poor one can lead us to erroneous conclusions and actually be counterproductive toward achieving the goal of evidence-based social work practice. Planning to conduct a survey can be a painstaking process. It involves making many important decisions about, for example, sampling (Chapter 10) and how data will be analyzed. It also requires a very exacting process of word selection. Unless a previously developed, proven data collection instrument can be used with confidence, a new instrument has to be developed and pilot tested (Chapter 11). Developing the instrument is not simply a matter of deciding what answers are sought and quickly writing a group of questions to elicit answers to them. The planning process entails much more work and thought than that.

Common Problems

Even the best planned surveys that use carefully constructed data collection instruments can produce misleading findings. This is especially true in surveys that rely heavily on data acquired by telephone or electronic data collection methods or in surveys that rely heavily on mailed questionnaires. However, it also can occur when acquiring data through in-person interviews. The problem lies in the difficulty of getting a truly representative group of responses when conducting surveys. We next discuss what can happen when mailed questionnaires are used.

Potential for Distortion.   Distortion is likely to occur when any self-administered data collection instrument is used, but especially when data are collected by mail. When instruments are mailed to research participants, researchers do not know whether or not participants understood what was asked or if they responded honestly. A participant who does not need to face the researcher may be more likely either to inadvertently or deliberately misrepresent reality than one who participates in in-person interviews. That is why it is so important to word questions and statements very carefully. Books written on survey research generally focus on mistakes to avoid in constructing surveys.[1] Box 8.1 lists some of the more commonly noted ones, along with examples of "how not to do it."

BOX 8.1   What to Avoid When Constructing Survey Questions*

Avoid	Example of a Poorly Worded Item
Leading questions	Should innocent children have to do without needed medical care?
Prestige bias	Do you agree with the Juvenile Diabetes Association that stem cell research should be expanded?
Vagueness	How often do you do things that risk your health?
Double-barreled questions	Do you favor national health care supported through a tax increase?
Impossible questions to answer	If you had not become ill, would you have finished college?
Jargon, acronyms	Do you think the NASA has finally jumped the shark?
Emotional language	Have abuses by welfare cheats and deadbeat fathers contributed to outrageous Medicaid costs?
False beliefs	When did you first learn that HIV is not a terminal illness?
"Loaded" responses	Would you rate your current health care as OK, inferior, or very inadequate?

*Some of the poorly worded items may contain one or more additional problems.

If inaccurate data are provided because of poorly worded questions or statements, researchers may not be able to detect it. They may also have no way of knowing if the participant filled out the instrument carefully and thoughtfully or just put down anything to complete it. They do not know if its completion took an hour, or two minutes. They also have no way of knowing the state of mind of participants when the instruments were completed. They may have been extremely conscientious in completing them. However, they may also have "just put down anything," or even deliberately provided false information. Returned data collection instruments that contain clearly facetious or impossible responses can simply be discarded. But it is more difficult to determine what to do with a completed instrument that contains responses that are just a little unusual—it may contain valid data, or it may not.

Identity of the Participant.   When using a mailed instrument, it may be impossible to know if the person to whom it was sent completed it. Did it fall into the hands of a mischievous child? Or was it deliberately delegated to another for completion? The identity of the respondent is almost certain to be a problem with some groups of people. For example, if a mailed questionnaire is sent to physicians, any research respondents are likely to be clerical staff members who work for the doctors and who complete all of their paperwork.

Return Rate.   A common problem with data collection by mail is a low rate of return of completed instruments. It is just too easy for potential research participants to discard a request for data or, with all good intentions, to set it aside and forget about it. The researcher who uses mailed data collection asks much and offers little. There is no potential for a pleasant interpersonal exchange with the researcher, only a letter from a person who is most likely to be a stranger and whose motives for seeking participation in the research are likely to be suspect.

Although some research naturally draws a higher rate of return (for example, research on emotionally charged topics or requests for data sent to college alumni or people who are fellow members of religious or civic organizations), a typical rate for data collection instruments mailed to strangers and using at least one follow-up request is 30 to 40 percent. A return rate somewhat higher than that is considered good. A much higher response rate should be viewed with suspicion. For example, the researcher may have requested "interested volunteers" to complete a questionnaire. The implausibly high response rate reported may be misleading to the reader if this is not clearly stated in a research article or report. In fact, the researcher's findings may be more biased than another survey with a more typical return rate.

One obvious implication is that if a sample of responses of a given size is needed, the researcher should either (1) send out at least three times that many instruments to ensure having enough completed ones for data analysis or (2) go to extraordinary lengths to attempt to increase the usual, expected rate of return. As we shall discuss, the latter method is the preferred one.

- *Keep it short.* The potential value of a well designed study can be quickly negated if the researcher cannot generate a sufficiently high response rate. Excessive length probably results in more discarded instruments than any other cause. Few potential participants will complete a ten-page instrument, no matter what the topic or their interest in it. Ten pages worth of questions jammed onto both sides of four or five pages, or use of small print, will not fool anyone or fare any better. Such attempts at deception just make potential participants angry. Generally, if an instrument is longer than a few normally spaced, easily read pages, it probably is trying to collect too much data at a single time. The researcher also should use as many fixed-alternative items (see Chapter 11) as possible. People are more likely to make a check mark or an X than to write one or more words.

- *Avoid bad times.* Although there is no ideal time to ask research participants to complete an instrument, some times of the year have been found to be worse than others. The December holidays should be avoided. Among student participants, midterm and final examination times (and spring break) are not likely to result in a high response rate.

- *Provide incentives.* A small cash payment or some other small gift as payment for participation will almost always result in more instruments being completed and returned. A promise of a reward after a completed instrument is received will be less effective in improving the response rate than an incentive mailed out with the instrument and cover letter. Why are incentives not used more frequently? The costs of providing them may be great, and the costs may be more than just monetary. They may influence the responses received. Are participants who are paid for their responses either consciously or unconsciously more likely to provide those responses that they think are being sought by the researcher? The answer to this question is almost impossible to determine. Another type of incentive that can increase the response rate is an offer to share an outline or summary of the major research findings. If it is used, any requests for the summary (there are usually relatively few) must be honored, despite the cost of the additional correspondence. Not to do so would be unethical.

- *Provide postage-paid, preaddressed return envelopes.* People are unlikely to return an instrument unless they can do it simply and with no cost to them. Given the usual rate of return for mailed instruments, it generally is more economical to use metered envelopes than to affix a stamp to the return envelope. The postage for each response will be a little higher than if a stamp were provided, but one is charged only for those that are mailed back. Postage also affects return rate in another way: Generally, more expensive mailing methods yield higher rates of response. First-class mail is more likely to result in completed instruments than third-class mail. High-priority methods such as overnight delivery yield relatively high rates of response, but their cost can be prohibitive.

- *Use a carefully worded cover letter.* The cover letter should tell potential participants how they were selected to receive the instrument and that their response is important to the success of the research. Especially if the research deals with sensitive matters (for example, sexuality, religious or political beliefs, or behaviors that are either illegal or not socially approved), potential respondents will need to know how the researcher got their names and how data will be used, and they will need to be assured that any confidentiality or anonymity promises will be kept.

The cover letter should reflect the researcher's genuine interest in the research problem and the assumption that potential participants may share that interest.

Potential respondents also will need to be convinced that the instrument is not just being sent to millions of people and that their responses are important to the success of the research. If the researcher personally signs each cover letter, this will help to reinforce this impression.

Like the survey itself, careful wording of the cover letter is very important. The wrong type of appeal for participation actually can reduce the rate of response. For example, a statement such as "I am a social work student who needs to collect data to meet my research course requirement" suggests that (1) the researcher probably is not really interested in the problem; (2) the researcher would not be conducting the research if it were not required; and (3) the findings are unlikely ever to be used for anything other than for helping a professor to assign a course grade. Why would anyone want to take the time to respond favorably to such an appeal?

• *Use return addresses and letterheads.* The return address on an envelope used to mail out a data collection instrument and the inside address on the cover letter can affect the rate of return of mailed instruments. A home or business address can lend credibility to a research study; generally, a post office box number can harm it.

• The use of some agency return addresses and inside addresses can help to increase the return rate; the use of others can decrease it. When an organizational affiliation is likely to increase the response rate, permission to use agency envelopes and stationery should be sought; they suggest written endorsement of and support for the research. However, some organizations such as state departments of social services, or state departments of mental health or corrections, evoke certain emotional responses. Using their envelopes and stationery might negatively affect return rate and can even bias the data that are received.

Response Bias.   It can easily be determined if a researcher has received a satisfactory return rate. But a second and more difficult question that must be answered is whether the data that are available for analysis were collected from a representative sample of participants. Although a high percentage of responses to a mailing of an instrument (for example, 50 percent) is likely to produce a representative sample of those who were requested to participate, there is no guarantee that it does. The 50 percent who failed to respond may differ from the 50 percent who did, in some important way that could still have produced a biased sample. Conversely, although not likely, even a very low rate of return (for example, 25 percent) theoretically could have produced a sample that is representative of the population being studied. The problem with using mailed instruments is that it is difficult to know whether those who did not return the instrument are similar to or different from those who did in some important way. Some follow-up calls to determine why the former group did not respond are sometimes informative. They can provide at least some insight into whether or not a response bias exists. However, they also can be perceived as harassment by those people who already indicated their unwillingness to be research participants when they did not return their data collection instruments.

In some research situations, a response bias is quite predictable. For example, a follow-up survey to assess the vocational success of people denied admission to a job training program would be expected to prompt a disproportionately high rate of return from three groups: (1) those who have been very successful and who wish to gloat about their success; (2) those who are still unemployed and who wish to blame their denial to the program for their failures; and (3) those who receive the instrument, perceive that it means that they are still being considered for admission to the program, and therefore are careful to complete and return it. A lower rate of return might be expected from other people who are employed, but have not been very successful in their careers or otherwise have less emotional investment in completing the data collection instrument.

A descriptive study of hazing rituals (emotional and physical abuse of students attempting to be admitted to membership in some group or organization) among high school and college students[2] provides a good example of how response bias can operate. In August 2000, many major newspapers reported that a large percentage of students had been victims of hazing. Although this conclusion was based on a study in which mailed questionnaires were completed and anonymously returned by a large number of students, the questionnaires represented only a 12 percent return rate; that is, only 12 percent of the questionnaires mailed out were returned. The low return rate was reason enough for us to question the external validity of any findings drawn from returned questionnaires. However, we also should ask who was most likely to return the questionnaires and who was not. Wouldn't students who had experienced hazing be more likely to take the trouble to complete and return them than those who had had no experience with hazing and thus had no particular interest in it? It would probably be safe to assume that generalizations from this sample (at least any about incidence of hazing) are very suspect.

When it appears that the use of the mail for data collection would be likely to result in response bias, other methods of data collection such as in-person interviews should be considered. A smaller (but more representative) sample of participants is almost always preferable to a larger, biased one.

Surveys are invariably flawed somewhat (like all research designs), no matter what method of acquiring data is employed. Nevertheless, they are likely to remain a popular method for conducting certain types of research. What is a desirable stance to take in regard to them? We can recognize their limitations (primarily questions about their external validity), not assume that their findings are 100 percent accurate, and acknowledge their many contributions to our knowledge base. For example, they often provide useful (if tentative) insights about some problem or phenomenon that we wish to understand better.

Recently, there has been discussion of how traditional methods of conducting large-scale national surveys could be revised to yield high response rates and better data. One researcher has proposed that a carefully selected, representative sample of 1,000 American households might be identified and provided with a laptop computer and high-speed Internet access to allow them to participate in a 30-minute secure survey every month.[3] The time blocks with these "professional research participants" could then be sold to researchers such as political pollsters or others who seek to measure American opinions and trends. Undoubtedly, the twenty-first century will see other innovative approaches to survey research, as the full capacity of the Internet has not yet been fully realized.

The Case Study

A case study is descriptive and more qualitative than quantitative. It combines observations of behavior with observations of attitudes and perceptions of research participants. It employs methods of data collection that rely heavily on the interviewing skills of researchers and their capacity to establish relationships of trust. As we shall see, there are some good reasons for the case study's continued popularity among social work researchers.

Case studies have often been misunderstood and sometimes maligned. Misunderstandings about case studies have sometimes led to a belief that they are less than scientific methods for knowledge building. Part of this misunderstanding may be attributable to misapplication of the label to research that is poorly designed and implemented. For example, sometimes researchers have conducted some other type of research using a very small sample of research participants. In order to deflect criticism of their work and the credibility of their findings, they have erroneously applied the case study label to their research design.

A case study is appropriate for situations in which certain interrelated conditions are present. These are that:

- *Little is known about the area being studied.* Topics for which there already exists a substantive body of relevant knowledge are better studied using other research designs.
- *The area studied generally involves illegal behavior or at least a form of behavior that is not socially sanctioned.* Thus, the behavior is not available for study using more traditional research designs, such as surveys. Participants may be fearful about being found out and are usually very concerned about the confidentiality of what they reveal about themselves or their situation.
- *It is impossible to draw a representative sample of participants.* Because the research generally involves the study of illegal or other non–socially sanctioned behavior, a master list of potential research participants does not exist. Consequently, participants are selected based on their availability and willingness to participate in the research. There is no way of knowing if they are typical of others who are involved in the same behavior.

Researchers conducting case studies collect their data from just one or a few cases. Usually the number does not exceed four or five. A case need not be an individual person; it can also be a family, a group, an organization, a community, or virtually any other system or entity that can be readily defined.

In a case study, interviewers must be receptive and nonjudgmental. They must be able to observe and interpret a wide variety of verbal and nonverbal communication, because data collected consist of both responses to preselected questions and the interviewer's observations of participants.

In a case study, acquiring the trust of participants is absolutely essential. Relationships of trust are not easily developed and nurtured because participants naturally tend to be guarded in what they say and to whom they say it. They have learned how to give evasive answers to sensitive questions and find it difficult to be candid. Social workers are ideally suited to conduct case studies. Their interviewing skills, nonjudgmental attitudes, and other professional values and ethics help to foster trust.

Suitable Topics

There are many problem areas that are well suited to a case study design. Different aspects of substance abuse, sexual deviance, white-collar crime, and other forms of antisocial behavior come readily to mind. Many other gaps in knowledge that are the focus of social work research are not suited to case study designs, primarily because they do not involve behavior that is illegal or not socially acceptable.

Because what constitutes illegal or non–socially sanctioned behavior tends to change over time, the list of problems that are suitable for study using a case study design is ever changing. One of the authors of this text supervised a case study of couples living together outside of marriage in the early 1970s. At the time and within the moral climate of the geographical locale in which the research was conducted, the case study was an appropriate choice of design. Just a few years later, research on the same topic could have and should have used other research methods because of a greater public acceptance of this alternate lifestyle. In 1988 he conducted a case study on "secret survivors," people who had experienced the sudden death of a partner in a long-term extramarital affair.[4] At that time, the case study was appropriate for a study of that problem. But less than a decade later, changing societal values and the accumulation of other exploratory studies of the problem or of similar ones (such as partners who die from AIDS) had moved our understanding of the problem beyond the point where a case study would be appropriate. In the early twenty-first century, a more appropriate focus for a case study might be people who deliberately seek to infect others with the HIV virus or people who commit fraud in order to seek government compensation for acts of terrorism. Every year, problems emerge that are appropriate for research using a case study design, whereas others are deleted from the list.

Strengths and Limitations

Case studies make it possible to achieve insights (such as how people feel about and experience certain phenomena) that are unavailable using more quantitative methods. They also are among the most interesting and gratifying types of research that can be conducted. A researcher conducting a case study can experience a feeling of being on the very cutting edge of knowledge building about a problem or question.

A major limitation of the case study is its inability to generate knowledge that could be described as definitive. Any conclusions should be carefully qualified. Because the number of participants is small and because they cannot be considered representative, few real conclusions emerge from case histories. Often, the most that can be said about data collected is something like "These are some of the problems that were found," "These are some of the ways that some people experience them," or "This is what some people think can be done about them." A case study does not allow the researcher to generalize beyond the research participants. Thus, the external validity of any findings is very low or even nonexistent.

Grounded Theory

Grounded theory is one of the best known (and one of the purest types) of qualitative research. It would fall in the exploratory–descriptive area. It is more likely to be cross sectional than longitudinal in the purest sense; however, data collection can occur over an extended period of time and entail the use of multiple interviews with the same research participants. It relies heavily on skillful interviewing and a specialized form of data analysis. Grounded theory research seeks to learn what meanings people give to certain events in their lives. Like most qualitative research, it seeks to generate hypotheses, not test them. Like many types of qualitative research, it also attempts to build theory from data (in contrast to quantitative research, which often tests theories using data). But it differs from other types of qualitative research in some important ways.

Researchers conducting grounded theory studies constantly monitor and reshape their developing theories. The method involves a recurring process of proposing (based on analysis of completed interview data), and checking and verifying what has been proposed (within subsequent interviews). In grounded theory research, sample selection, data collection, and data analysis occur simultaneously rather than in a preestablished sequence. Analysis of early data guides and shapes subsequent sample selection and the focus of future data collection. Researchers use emerging theoretical categories to influence both the ways in which subsequent data collection will be accomplished and from whom. For example, in early interviews, researchers may begin by asking general research questions based on whatever clues the literature may provide as to what they might find. If some questions turn out to be irrelevant or nonproductive, they are dropped in subsequent interviews. Other, new ones, suggested by what they learned in earlier interviews may be added. Similarly, if certain types of participants seem to be providing more enlightenment for their emerging theories than others, subsequent interviews may target only those people who show the greatest potential to verify (or refute) their theories.

Despite its somewhat unconventional approaches to data collection and case sampling, grounded theory is definitely not a haphazard or unscientific method of conducting research. It employs a systematic sequence of steps. For example, after one batch of data is collected (often, interviews are videotaped), the process of analyzing and conceptualizing it, referred to as *coding,* is begun. In the early stages of analysis, a process called *open coding* is used. It entails broadly conceptualizing what the data seem to mean and beginning to categorize them. It requires a careful dissection of interviews, sometimes word by word. Questions such as "What is this?" or "What does this seem to mean?" are common at this stage of the data analysis.

Later, two other types of coding (which are a little too complicated to explain in this overview), axial coding and selective coding, are used. Eventually, as proposed relationships between categories gain support as more data are collected, the researcher produces what is referred to as a *story line,* a brief narrative description of what was observed. This is analyzed and distilled further to form what is called a *core category.* Finally, a theory or hypothesis emerges as a product of the research. For example, in Taylor's research on parents who experienced the death of an adult child to AIDS (also referred to in Chapter 2), she developed the theory statement, "Parents of persons with AIDS employ a combination of spiritual strengths and self-talk, along with a network of social supports and confidants, to arrive at a level of acceptance and confidence."[5] Note that there are several terms in the statement (spiritual strengths, self-talk, social supports, confidants, acceptance, and confidence) that were codes that the researcher developed from the process of analyzing the interviews and conceptualizing what was heard and observed.

Grounded theory is based on the premise that the meanings that people give to events in their lives (for example, certain experiences or losses) are very important in understanding their responses and resilience to the events. It is based primarily on theories of symbolic interaction, which hold that people construct their own meanings for events based in part on their interactions with others. Grounded theory research thus seems especially well suited to acquiring the kinds of knowledge needed by social workers. Conducting it also requires many of the very attributes (interviewing skills, ability to form relationships, and so forth) that we possess.

Content Analysis

Content analysis is a systematic method for analyzing some form of human communication. It is very versatile. It has features that are typical of quantitative research, such as an emphasis on the use of representative samples and the accurate measurement of variables. It can be used to test for associations and correlations between and among variables However, it can be used in predominantly qualitative studies, for example, in analyzing audio- or videotapes of interviews in studies that use grounded theory methods. Content analysis is cross sectional, since the data are examined at one point in time. Yet, if those data were accumulated over a long period of time, it can be used to identify changes that occurred during the time that they were being accumulated, a feature usually associated with pretest-posttest or longitudinal research.

Content analysis can be used for analyzing the original data from a research study or, more frequently, for attempting to answer research questions using secondary data that are a form of communication. Communication can take many different forms, such as:

- Video- or audiotapes of in-person interviews.
- Oral histories.
- Documents such as newspaper articles, professional journals, or congressional records.
- Moving pictures or television programs.
- Minutes of meetings.
- Films or videotapes of social gatherings.
- Photographs.
- Recorded phone conversations.
- E-mail or text messages.

Human communication contains a rich archive of popular culture. When examined systematically, it can be very informative. Using content analysis it is possible to compare, for example, the portrayal of women and men, of Caucasians and people of color, of people with disabilities and other people, or of people across various sociocultural groups. The data can be analyzed, either qualitatively or, more commonly, quantitatively, using a variety of methods.

Content analysis generally entails a categorization and counting process. Questions that might be answered using quantitative content analysis might include:

- Has the media's representation of women changed over the past ten years?
- How many articles about people with disabilities does a journal publish?
- Are males more likely to be published than females?

A single type of communication can answer many different research questions using content analysis. For example, a researcher could use the previous five years of a university's student evaluations of instructors to answer any of these questions:

- Do students seem to be getting more critical of instructors?
- What are the most common strengths and weaknesses of instructors that are listed?
- Do part-time students make fewer negative comments about instructors than full-time students?

There are many good examples of past research that has used content analysis. We will mention briefly just a few of them that would fall under the category of feminist research (discussed later in this chapter):

- Quam and Austin examined the coverage of women's issues in social work journals from 1970 to 1981.[6] The authors first conceptualized and operationalized what they meant by women's issues and then reviewed a total of 3,991 articles published in eight journals.
- Pugliesi examined the medicalization of emotion, a concept related to premenstrual syndrome (PMS).[7] She performed a content analysis of ninety articles published in popular magazines from 1976 to 1990. Her study provided an analysis of the meaning of PMS in popular culture.
- Rothman, Powers, and Rothman used content analysis of 146 top-grossing films from 1945 to 1993 to test their hypothesis that films produced during the conservative Reagan and first Bush administrations were more sexist than those produced in other years.[8] The researchers demonstrated that since the 1960s there has been a marked increase in the representation of women in nontraditional roles and that, when they are, they tend to be presented in a sympathetic way. Thus, the researchers' hypothesis was not supported.

Content analysis used to be a very tedious process. The development of computer programs that can quickly scan various forms of human communication and, for example, count how often certain words or phrases appear, has made it much easier. As the technology for doing this continues to expand so that more and more types of communication can be examined by computer, content analysis is likely to continue to gain in popularity.

Historical Research

Another type of research that relies heavily on analysis of secondary data (sometimes including content analysis of human communication) is historical research. It employs many of the same methods that researchers in other fields (such as history, anthropology, or archeology) use in their efforts to recreate the past. While not as frequently used by social work researchers as some other types of research like surveys or evaluation research, when it has been used its findings have sometimes proven very helpful in our work.

Historical research is primarily descriptive. It may document changes in time or it may just seek to create an accurate picture of some time in the past. It can entail both quantitative and qualitative research methods. For example, a single study may rely on both a content analysis of old minutes of meetings from around the time when an organization was founded (quantitative) and in-depth interviews with some of its original employees (qualitative) in order to attempt to learn what the original mission of the organization was.

Historical research involves the systematic collection and analysis of a wide array of historical data relevant to a research question and/or hypothesis. It requires reconstructing the past in order to address some current knowledge deficit or to answer some question or questions. For example, an historical research design might be used to study the public statements of legislators in newspapers and the *Congressional Record* around the time that a piece of legislation was passed in order to try to learn what the legislation was designed to accomplish. Or historical research might attempt to ascertain the original meaning of a social work construct by examining its usage in the professional literature when it first appeared fifty years ago.

Historical research, as a process, requires the development of a research question or hypothesis that can logically be studied by the analysis of historical documents and other sources that may illuminate the past. Once the question is defined, the researcher identifies sources of historical data that will begin to address the research question and/or hypothesis. Sources of data that may be consulted include interviews with key individuals who were present at an earlier time (oral histories), letters, memoirs, public records and documents, newspapers, agency memos, and reports.

Firsthand information, such as that given by "survivors" or by their official records, is considered a primary data source. Secondary sources are those accounts that have been written by historians or other persons not directly involved in the historical event. Obviously, the source of the data used in a historical research study is a major factor in assessing the quality of its findings. Data that are biased or are of dubious quality make for poor historical research. Whenever possible, primary sources are preferred to secondary sources.

Once the data have been gathered, they are synthesized. The researcher determines what they mean in relation to the research questions and/or hypotheses. Are there historical or conceptual themes present? How strong and pervasive are they? The final research report generally is written as a narrative that identifies the research questions and describes the method of inquiry (including an in-depth discussion of sources of data used). It then attempts to place the research findings in historical perspective.

When conducting historical research, researchers generally believe that current problems and questions often have their origins in earlier times. They are attempting to obtain a better understanding of the present by gaining a clearer understanding of how things were. Sometimes the past that the researcher hopes to reconstruct for this purpose may have existed many years or centuries earlier. Often, there are no survivors who might be interviewed, so data collection must rely on written records and documents to provide needed information.

The historical researcher frequently sets out either to provide additional confirmation for theories about what is believed to be true about the past or to attempt to dispel a common misconception about what existed. One researcher, Byrd, attempted to do the latter. He used historical research to study the attitudes of people toward the poor in colonial America.[9] He had observed that a common assumption among many historians is that the English poor laws were simply transferred from England to the colonies with very little modification. Thus, it has also been assumed that many of the harsh and punitive approaches to the poor that characterized life in England at the time also existed in the colonies. Byrd doubted that this assumption was correct.

Byrd conducted an extensive review of the literature. He then collected his data by a systematic review of approximately 2,000 carefully documented case histories of persons who sought financial aid during the years 1732 to 1775. All had requested assistance at St. Philip's Church, the major source of help for the poor in colonial Charles Town (now Charleston, South Carolina).

As Byrd had suspected, the research findings bore little resemblance to what had been portrayed in history books. For example, he found that the poor were treated humanely and with dignity; no comments about their laziness or moral impoverishment were found. The poor also did not represent a distinct, stigmatized segment of colonial society. The community seemed to have accepted them and worked together to provide them with opportunities to achieve financial independence.

Existing laws in Charles Town apparently were far less punitive than the English poor laws. They had been considerably softened to reflect the charitable attitudes toward the poor that were present at the time. Even those laws that might have limited assistance to some people who did not meet residency requirements often were circumvented in order to help those in need.

Any contention that the conservative and even punitive federal policies of financial assistance in the United States during the 1980s were somehow just an extension of what has always been in existence in America (that is, they are typically American) just did not hold up in light of Byrd's findings. These stereotypes and the stigmatization of the poor that is associated with them are relatively new; they are certainly not a part of the original value system on which the United States was founded.

This example of research conducted many years ago points out one additional desirable feature of historical research—its findings do not become quickly dated like those of many other types of research. Unless subsequent historical research suggests that they are inaccurate, they can be used for years and even decades to, for example, influence social policy or dispel common stereotypes.

Ethnographic Research

Ethnographic research is primarily descriptive research. It is most likely to be cross sectional but is sometimes more longitudinal, that is, it is conducted over an extended period of time to record changes. Ethnographic research uses a combination of both quantitative and qualitative research methods to answer research questions about individuals within their social context. It entails observations and measurement of behaviors (more quantitative), but it also seeks to understand the beliefs, attitudes, values, social roles, social structures, and norms of behavior in social environments that are different from that of the researcher by using more qualitative research methods. It often relies on various forms of systematic observation (Chapter 7) to accomplish these goals.

Ethnographic methods were first developed in the field of anthropology to guide participant observation and qualitative field research of Western investigators studying behavior in primitive societies. However, ethnographic methods are now also used to understand subgroups within modern dominant cultures. Those subgroups may exist based on shared race, culture, class, religion, or some other characteristics that in some way differentiate the subgroup from the mainstream culture.

Two concepts embedded in ethnographic research methods are "emic" and "etic" perspectives. The *emic* perspective is that of the insider who is indigenous to the group being studied. This perspective is an experiential one based on an individual's having been socialized to daily living in the culture and participating fully in all its psychosocial aspects.

The *etic* perspective is that of the outsider—the stance traditionally assumed by researchers who study a culture that is not their own. An assumption of ethnographic research is that each perspective has advantages and disadvantages. For example, although the emic perspective permits an intricate understanding of even the most subtle cultural nuances, its familiarity with the cultural context may fail to raise critical questions about why things are the way they are or what maintains the status quo. Although the etic perspective may miss important cultural nuances, it allows researchers to raise questions of context and purpose that would never occur to an insider to ask. Ethnographic research attempts to blend these two perspectives by allowing the outside investigator to function as an insider, through participant observation and other methods that will enhance the understanding of the cultural context. As in other types of research that rely on participant observation, the extent to which the very presence of the outsider changes the natural order of the cultural dynamics of insiders (reactivity) is a potential source of distortion of data thus collected.

Goodson-Lawes[10] describes a particularly useful application of ethnographic methods in social work research. The researcher used ethnographic research to study families of Mexican and Vietnamese immigrants. Researchers lived with the families in order to understand the consequences of immigration for family functioning and family structure. They learned their language and took part in the daily life of the families. They became a normal presence in their homes. Events, reactions, emotions, and interactions were carefully recorded in detailed journals.

Although participant observation is the data collection methodology most often associated with ethnographic research, there now are other methodological approaches that can help investigators to understand different cultures. These include eco-mapping, GIS mapping, formal and informal interviews, life histories, kinship charts, and analysis of religious practices, myths, music, and other forms of folklore.

Because of negative historical and political encounters between ethnic communities and mainstream governmental or social welfare institutions, gaining access to study samples in ethnic communities may be problematic. Mistrust of motives for the research and fear of how the data may be used are frequently expressed concerns. Many ethnic communities have been used as study sites, with little or no feedback on study outcomes. Even when feedback has been given, it sometimes has not been in a form that is helpful in addressing community problems.

Many researchers conduct key informant surveys to assist them in conducting ethnographic research. They consist of unstructured interviews with knowledgeable individuals and community leaders or open-ended questionnaires mailed to them. They are used to gain the advice and support of people who can offer an insider's perspective on their research efforts. Such surveys may be especially useful when the researcher is undertaking exploratory investigation that requires an understanding of an unfamiliar research context or setting.

Who is a potential key informant? The answer to this question sometimes is hard to determine in ethnic communities. Leaders designated by funding sources or university advisory boards may not be regarded as leaders by the members of their ethnic group. Butler[11] notes, for example, that whereas funding sources may rely on academic credentials, work experience, or political connections to select leaders, members of the African American community are more likely to locate leadership in individuals who embody the community values of spirituality, wisdom, strength of character, and style. This suggests that key informants should be selected across social class strata in ethnic communities.

In conducting ethnographic research, key informants can be helpful in several ways. They can provide guidance on where to find information and resources on topics of study interest, how to access and gain participation of study participants, and how to interpret study findings. Key informant surveys are also a way of forging alliances with community leaders and influential citizens who can endorse the research enterprise.

Some ethnic communities have set up stringent review and approval procedures before permission to conduct research is granted. Notable among these are some of the Native American tribal groups. Any researcher wishing to conduct studies that are on tribal lands or that involve people who are members of their tribal group must be prepared to comply with their particular approval process. Typically, researchers must present a proposal before a tribal, community, or village governing body that frequently wishes to exercise some degree of control over the research process. Beauvais and Trimble[12] describe these as (1) assignment of a tribal or village member to monitor study implementation; (2) guidelines concerning respondent selection procedures; (3) community's right to review and edit questionnaires, interview schedules and field notes, and so on; (4) community's right to review and edit research reports and to restrict or prevent the circulation and distribution of findings; and (5) ownership of the raw data and findings granted to the tribe or village. There are a few tribes that forbid any outside research within their boundaries; as sovereign states, they can legally do so.

It is to the researcher's advantage to understand the specific historical and cultural traits of the target community to (1) anticipate the degree and nature of resistance to participation and (2) seek advice from knowledgeable individuals on overcoming resistance to participation. Kim and her colleagues[13] provide examples of recommended approaches in working with Asian American communities:

- Conducting data collection in private settings.
- Providing refreshments (because of the importance of food and communal meals in social gatherings).
- Using personal contacts, such as telephone calls or word-of-mouth invitations, to invite participation in the study, rather than sending letters for formal appointments.

- Compensating respondents for their time (because research and evaluation are less important to many Asian Americans than work in exchange for compensation).
- Providing transportation and child care (because many Asian American families are accustomed to having children present at semiformal gatherings).

What Kim recommends illustrates the importance of cultural sensitivity when conducting ethnographic research. However, as we have repeatedly emphasized (and will emphasize in the next section), it is essential to good research of any type.

Cross-Cultural Research

Cross-cultural research is somewhat related to ethnographic research. It is primarily descriptive research, and employs both quantitative and qualitative methods. However, it has its own unique focus—it seeks to describe cultural similarities (universalities that exist across cultures) and differences between and among cultures. It is being used more frequently than in past years due to a number of factors, including the opening of previously sealed international borders, large migration streams, globalization of the economic market, international tourism, increased cross-cultural communication, and technological innovations that make communication and scholarship in other countries possible.[14] In cross-cultural research, investigators face some unique methodological challenges usually related to definitions of theoretical constructs and their valid measurement in different cultural contexts. Other problems relate to obtaining a representative sample and accuracy of translation of data collection instruments into foreign languages. Some of these are methodological issues unique to cross-cultural research, which will be addressed in more detail in later chapters in this text.

Social workers wishing to conduct research and/or practice in foreign countries will be especially interested in cross-cultural studies of human behavior, family systems, and other social organizations, as well as epidemiological studies of health and mental health disorders, and their treatment in various cultural contexts. Some of their findings may also apply to the study of ethnic and racial groups within the North American culture.

Marin and Marin[15] offer several suggestions for researchers who plan to undertake cross-cultural research. They are designed to reduce the risk of *cultural encapsulation* (that is, depending entirely on one's own cultural frame of reference to formulate assumptions and define research constructs) and to increase *cultural relativity* (that is, the ability to understand behavior, attitudes, and values within the context of the culture in which it occurs). Suggested strategies include the following:

- Cultural immersion in the group to be studied.
- The obtaining of information directly from cultural minorities about values and normative behavior rooted in the culture (that is, what is normal and what is pathological for that specific culture).
- Collaboration with key informants from the culture to be studied on all aspects of the study design prior to initiating the study.

Feminist Research

Feminist research is distinguished primarily by two things—its focus and its purpose. It is research that seeks to build knowledge about women, specifically, about their unique problems and the social institutions that affect them. When the label "feminist research" is used to describe a research study, it does not convey very much about what research methods were used. That is because feminist research employs all available methods, often in combination. Feminist research runs the gamut in relation to the broad descriptions described in Chapter 6. It can be predominantly quantitative or qualitative; exploratory, descriptive or (less frequently) explanatory; or employ cross-sectional, longitudinal, or pretest-posttest designs.

Goals and Assumptions

In her work on feminist research,[16] Shulamit Reinharz points out that feminist research relates to "women's ways of knowing," a concept developed by others who have observed that women acquire knowledge differently than men. Feminist research is designed to hear the voices and other communications that more traditional, male-oriented approaches to knowledge building may miss. That would seem to suggest that (1) it is only qualitative research, and (2) it can only be conducted by women. Both of these assumptions would be incorrect. However, it is conducted by people (men and women) who generally identify themselves as feminists or at least are concerned with the status and well-being of women.

Feminist research should be regarded as research both for and about women. It is often a form of action research, that is, research designed to bring about change in women's lives by confronting sexism and attempting to alter those social institutions that may promote or perpetuate it. It results in consciousness raising and awareness of women's issues. The fact that feminist researchers study problems such as rape, sexual harassment, sexism, and salary equity stimulates reflection and discussion about these issues by others.

Feminist research rests on the assumption that the fact of gender is critical to understanding women and culture. Thus, gender is a central focus of it. It has produced a wealth of data about women. For example, within the past two decades, knowledge about domestic violence, marital rape, women's health issues, and women's work at home and in the community has been developed. Knowledge derived from feminist research is used to validate women's lives and experiences, and is useful for understanding their issues, problems, and strengths. It also has been used to suggest additional needed research relevant to women and to influence the development of social policy that directly affects women.

A Response to Traditional Research Methods

Knowledge that is developed through feminist research is often contextual and relative. This is justified by feminist scholars based on the assertion that traditional approaches to scientific research assume an objectivity about the world that is irrelevant to women's lives.

More traditional methods of inquiry are believed to ignore and distort women's realities. For example, many widely accepted measurement procedures were developed and standardized using males, thus making them of questionable value in understanding women's experiences. In addition, historically, many life experiences that are important to the lives of women, such as sexual harassment in the workplace, have been neglected by researchers using traditional research methods.

Feminist researchers have described the more traditional methods of inquiry (especially experimental designs) as being antithetical to the purposes of feminist research. For example, experimental research generally is conducted "in the laboratory" under tightly controlled research conditions. Feminists have argued that these types of designs have a sexist bias in the ways that questions are asked and answered and the way that data are interpreted. They assert that the artificiality of the research laboratory is not conducive to a true understanding of people and their relationships. In addition, it is asserted that traditional research methods have tended to exploit and objectify women.

Feminist research, with its emphasis on more egalitarian approaches to interacting with research participants, is believed to be less exploitive in its approach to data collection than traditional methods. It is more egalitarian; the relationship between the researcher and the person being studied is more one of equality. (That is why research participants often are referred to as "research partners.")

Feminist research is conducted within the context of an understanding of feminist perspectives of culture; it uses these perspectives to select methods for study of a research problem and for interpreting data. Feminist researchers also argue that their methods of conducting research allow them to critique knowledge developed by others using more traditional models of inquiry and to attempt to reconcile their findings with those of others. Doing this can put a whole new meaning on what a researcher learns directly, how the researcher interprets the findings of others, and how the data collection experience mutually affects the research participants.

Design Characteristics

Methodologically, feminist research has been described using such terms as *open, contextual, relative, interpretive, experiential, empowering,* and *social change–oriented.* These descriptors suggest the wide range of research designs used by and for feminist scholarship. Feminist research relies heavily on a variety of qualitative (and, less frequently, quantitative) techniques. Feminist research designs are often hybrids, combining features of two or more approaches to knowledge building. For example, both quantitative and qualitative design features can be used in a single study. A variety of quantitative data can be collected and analyzed. But then participants also can be asked if they would like to meet with a member of the research team to discuss their responses more fully in order better to understand their meaning to them.

Like some of the other forms of research described in this chapter, feminist methods are characterized by relatively open relationships between researchers and research participants. Researchers may get involved with the lives of participants by establishing relationships with them that go beyond simple data collection. They often serve as resources to participants by providing information about community resources, or may assist them in bringing about social change. The relationship between researchers and their participants is viewed as critical to the development of knowledge about women. Questions asked often emanate from researchers' own concerns and experiences, rather than out of some previously developed interview schedule or agenda. The knowledge acquired through this kind of interpersonal interaction leads logically to an interpretive approach to data analysis which makes no claims of total objectivity.

Feminist research usually does not emphasize the testing of prespecified hypotheses. It focuses instead on the development of a wide range of information and understanding. It has been described as emergent; it is not highly controlled. It often seeks to gather a wide array of descriptive, contextual information in order to provide data that are as complete as possible for analysis.

Examples

Virtually every research method described so far has been used in feminist research. Based on our description, it should come as no surprise to the reader that some of the qualitative methods described earlier in this chapter (for example, grounded theory) are frequently used.

On occasion, feminist descriptive research has used quantitative methods such as fixed-alternative surveys and more open-ended, semistructured interviews. Typically, large-scale surveys have been used to develop incidence data about a problem affecting women or to allow women anonymously to describe their attitudes, experiences, and beliefs about a women's issue that is sensitive in nature. After quantitative data have been generated and statistical analyses have been performed, findings may be publicized to attempt to promote social change.

Semistructured, open-ended questionnaires (administered by the researcher) are useful when the purpose of a study is to have participants respond to certain questions in their own words. Participants often become involved both in the interpretation of the meanings of their responses and in the refinement of data collection methods to be used in future research. Typically, this method of data collection entails the use of multiple sessions with participants. Because the researcher often cannot anticipate the type of information that will be shared, the interviews often are a process of discovery both for participants and for the feminist researcher.

What are some examples of past descriptive feminist research? How was it conducted?

- Survey research studies with a feminist focus were used to study date rape among college students. Prior to the mid-1980s there were few (if any) references to date rape in the social science literature. More quantitative studies on a variety of forms of abuse of women were developed partially as an outgrowth of earlier research and also because of changing societal definitions of what connotes permissible levels of violence. Two studies examining date rape as a form of violence against women were developed.
- In 1986, one of the authors of this book conducted a survey of over 600 college students at a large state-supported institution.[17] It produced incidence and prevalence data about date rape and compared the perceptions of men and women about the behavior. The study combined the use of a fixed-alternative questionnaire with a few open-ended questions. The fixed-alternative items were designed to develop

incidence data and to describe how force was used by men and experienced by the women. The open-ended questions permitted participants to more fully describe any incident of date rape in which they had been involved. The researcher also offered suggestions for how to get help with these issues. Referral assistance was offered to those women wishing to be in touch with community organizations offering rape counseling services.

The findings of the study demonstrated that there were sharp differences in how men and women define and report date rape, and in how they experienced the use of force. These were interpreted within a framework of discussion of stereotypical gender role differences and expectations for sexual favors.

- In another survey, 209 male and female students from an ethnically diverse environment were surveyed.[18] The study also sought to estimate the incidence of date rape and to compare victimization rates by ethnicity. Based on their findings, the researchers concluded that if they are to be effective, date rape prevention programs must be sensitive to cultural definitions of social role and to the different levels of acceptance of violence against women within different ethnic groups. Their recommendations were based in part on observations that Japanese women were less likely to label their victimization experiences on dates as sexual assaults than were Caucasian women.

- A study examined the work preferences and well-being among single African American working mothers. This population of women has largely been ignored by previous research on employment and welfare policy. Jackson (1993)[19] used semi-structured interviews and a brief self-administered instrument with 111 single working mothers to explore how they cope with the demands of jobs and parenting. The data from this study were reported in relation to role strain, emotional well-being, perceptions of children, employment preferences, working hours, educational attainment, and gender of the child. Sophisticated quantitative analyses were used to analyze the data. The author found that mothers whose formal educational attainment was at the level of high school or below experienced greater role strain, greater depressive symptomatology, least favorable perceptions of children, and lower ratings of overall life satisfaction than those with more formal education. The study was noteworthy both because of the population of women the researcher chose to study and the use of a multimethodological approach to the problems under investigation.

- A study examined the experience of pregnancy and its relationship to attitudes regarding diagnostic testing. It was conducted using intensive, in-person interviews with thirty-one women to explore their experiences and perceptions of their pregnancies. Gregg[20] found that women experience pregnancy and identify being pregnant very differently. The women she interviewed talked about the risks and choices made in their pregnancies, including the use of diagnostic tests. The author used statistical analysis to develop topical categories and responses. She concluded that the medical/physiological approach to understanding pregnancy was inadequate for understanding the pregnancy experience.

A more qualitative approach to data collection and analysis—naturalistic inquiry (a form of unstructured systematic observation)—attempts to document and understand women's behavior as influenced by their social contexts. Observations may be made in a variety of field settings, such as women's health organizations, women's work and social groups, and other groups and communities to which women belong. The data in naturalistic inquiries, as in most qualitative research, are typically rich in detail. In naturalistic inquiry, the researcher allows the patterns and themes contained in the data observed to emerge.

There are many excellent examples of naturalistic inquiries in the literature. Many of these studies have been conducted by feminist sociologists and anthropologists. One study sought to better understand wife abuse in a rural community.[21] Based on the findings from the researcher's naturalistic inquiry of violence and social control, she conceptualized three categories of control. She then used them to assert that domestic violence is dependent on culture and social structures that condone men's domination of women and that, without them, violence would be less effective as a means of social control.

We have mentioned only a few of the forms that feminist research can take. As we noted earlier, it is the specialized purpose and focus of feminist research that gives it its identity. It is designed specifically to develop needed knowledge about women and the social institutions that impact on them.

Meta-Analysis

In meta-analysis, the unit of analysis is not a case record or a person; it is a report of research. Meta-analysis examines the reports from research studies that focused on the same questions or tested the same hypotheses. Thus, it is a specialized form of content analysis—analysis of secondary data that consist of certain forms of human communication. The reports may be found in professional journals, research monographs, program evaluation documents, theses, dissertations, or anywhere else that research designs and findings are described in sufficient detail to be analyzed critically.

Most meta-analysis is cross-sectional and is regarded as explanatory research. Thus, designs generally include hypothesis specification and testing, and statistical analysis of data, characteristics of research that is more quantitative than qualitative. Designs can be highly rigorous and contain various methods to control for problems of design bias and confounding variables, some of which are unique to this type of research and some of which are common to other forms of secondary analysis.

Meta-analysis has made major contributions to evidence-based practice. A common use of meta-analysis is to try to ascertain if a method or model of intervention is effective for addressing some problem or condition. It is used to attempt to answer questions such as: When we look at *all* of the evaluations of publicly funded job training programs that served welfare recipients, have they been successful? Or, based on available research studies, is confrontation effective in treating clients who have been diagnosed as anorexic? Or, do sexual abstinence programs produce a reduction of unwanted teen pregnancy?

Because findings of meta-analysis are based on the reports of studies conducted by many different researchers in different settings, they are often based on data collected from very large numbers of research participants collectively. This has certain advantages. Although a particular design bias may have been in operation in one or two studies, it is unlikely to exist in all of them. Also, the large number of cases on which findings are based should make the likelihood of sampling error quite low. Thus, meta-analysis studies have the potential to possess a high level of both internal validity and external validity.

There are also several problems associated with the use of meta-analysis. Like all forms of secondary data analysis, meta-analysis studies are limited by the quality of data that are available. The report of one study may be very comprehensive; the report of another may be sketchy. This can cause problems in drawing conclusions about the credibility of their respective findings. Also, it is rare that two or more research studies that examined the same research question used exactly the same research methods. Because of this, the researcher inevitably ends up asking: How comparable must research methods be for me to include the report of a research study in a meta-analysis?

Another potential problem relates to the selection processes that sometimes influence what gets into print. Perhaps, as some people have suggested, professional journals may be more likely to publish articles where demonstration of support for directional or nondirectional hypotheses was found than those where variables were found to be unrelated. If this is true, it could result in a built-in bias within the data. Or when program evaluations are used in meta-analysis, they may be biased to show programs in a good light (or a bad one) if political pressure was applied. Certain statistical corrections and design features (beyond the scope of this book) have been developed to attempt to address the problem of bias in the use of meta-analysis.

Meta-analysis is growing in popularity among social work researchers. It is becoming more feasible as we begin to accumulate reports of research that are either replications of earlier research or are reports of research that are similar enough that they lend themselves to this type of analysis. The findings of meta-analysis have added greatly to our progress in becoming more evidence-based practitioners.

Summary

In Chapter 6 we presented several ways that researchers describe the design of their research in the broadest of terms. Chapter 7 described potential data sources—an important component of any research design. In this chapter, we presented a number of common labels that communicate to other researchers and to the readers of research reports and journal articles additional information about the type of research design that was used. Each is characterized by (1) a general purpose; (2) the data sources they rely on most frequently; and (3) the primary research activity that is employed. Box 8.2 summarizes the major characteristics of each of the design labels that were discussed in this chapter (evaluation research will be discussed in Chapters 13 and 14).

As the content of this chapter and that of Chapter 6 demonstrates, there is considerable ambiguity and overlap in the words that are used to describe research designs. They should be regarded as ways to help us to know "in general" what methods a researcher used when he or she went about conducting the research. However, they cannot convey exactly what he or she did, since every research design is unique. In the next three chapters, we will examine some important issues that, when addressed, provide needed details for completing a description of a research design.

BOX 8.2   Specialized Research Methods

Label	Purpose	Major Data Source(s)	Major Activities
Survey	Measure what exists	Questionnaires	Collecting, tabulating
Case study	Gain beginning insights	In-person interviews	Talking, listening
Grounded theory	Develop theories, hypotheses	In-person interviews	Conceptualizing, verifying
Content analysis	Identify patterns, relationships	Human communication	Drawing conclusions
Historical	Re-create the past	Artifacts	Uncovering, analyzing
Ethnographic	Understanding of a culture	Interviews, observation	Field research methods
Cross cultural	Identify cultural differences	Interviews, observation	Field research methods
Feminist	Empowerment/advocacy	Widely varying	Widely varying
Meta-analysis	Aggregate findings	Research reports	Data analysis and interpretation
Single system*	Evaluate individual practice	Client system data	Measuring, interpreting
Program evaluation*	Evaluate programs	Multiple	Collecting and analyzing data

*Discussed in Chapters 13 and 14.

For Discussion

1. Why do you think that surveys remain so popular in social work research? What are some research problems that can never be studied using surveys?
2. In the past, what has influenced you to complete or not complete a survey? What would have made you more likely to complete one that you just threw away?
3. How is response bias most likely to affect the findings of a follow-up survey of clients who were denied services by a social agency?
4. What are some problems and behaviors today that would be appropriate for a case study? What are some that were appropriate ten years ago, but are no longer?
5. Some research is described as grounded theory. Why would it be more accurate to describe grounded theory as the *product* of this type of research rather than as a research method?
6. How could we use content analysis to answer the research question, "Do professional sports broadcasts attempt to appeal more to male viewers than women?"

7. How could historical research on the attitudes toward family violence during World War II be used to help us to better understand current attitudes toward family violence? How could the findings be used to influence public policy today?

8. In an ethnographic study of a youth gang, why would the combined perspectives of researchers and of gang members provide a more accurate description of the gang's culture than either perspective alone? What other groups might provide additional understanding?

9. Are female researchers more qualified to conduct feminist research than males? Why or why not?

10. Based on your readings and discussions in social work practice courses, what are some research questions that probably could now be answered through meta-analysis?

Endnotes

1. See, e.g., Babbie, E. (2005). *The Basics of Social Research*. Belmont, CA: Thompson Wadsworth, 254–263. Or Bailey, K. *Methods of Social Research* (1994). New York: The Free Press, 106–118.

2. McQueen, A. (2000). Students humiliated by hazing. In *The State* (August 29, 2000). Columbia, SC, A1.

3. Trei, L. Social science researcher to overhaul survey methodology with $2 million grant. *Stanford Education News*, September 27, 2006.

4. Weinbach, R. (1989). Sudden death and secret survivors: Helping those who grieve alone. *Social Work, 34,* 57–60.

5. Taylor, L. (1998). Parents who lost an adult child to AIDS. In A. Godenzi (Ed.), *Abenteuer forschung*. University of Freiburg, Switzerland, 237.

6. Quam, J., & Austin, C. (1984). Coverage of women's issues in eight social work journals, 1970–81. *Social Work, 29,* 360–365.

7. Pugliesi, K. (1992). Premenstrual syndrome: The medicalization of emotion related to conflict and chronic role strain. *Journal of Social Relations, 18*(2), 131–165.

8. Rothman, S., Powers, S., & Rothman, D. (1993). Feminism in films. *Society, 303*(203), 66–72.

9. Byrd, M. (1973). *Ye have the poor always with you: Attitudes toward relief of the poor in colonial Charles Town.* Unpublished MSW thesis. Columbia, SC: University of South Carolina.

10. Goodson-Lawes, J. (1994). Ethnicity and poverty as research variables: Family studies with Mexican and Vietnamese newcomers. In E. Sherman & W. J. Reid (Eds.), *Qualitative research in social work.* New York: Columbia University Press, 21–31.

11. Butler, J. P. (1992). Of kindred minds: The ties that bind. In OSAP, *Cultural competence for evaluators.* Washington, D.C.: U.S. Department of Health and Human Services, 23–54.

12. Beauvais, F., & Trimble, J. E. (1992). The role of the researcher in evaluating American-Indian alcohol and other drug abuse prevention programs. In OSAP, *Cultural competence for evaluators.* Washington, D.C.: U.S. Department of Health and Human Services, 173–202.

13. Kim, S., McLeod, J. H., & Shantzis, C. (1992). Cultural competence for evaluators working with Asian American communities: Some practical considerations. In OSAP, *Cultural competence for evaluators.* Washington, D.C.: U.S. Department of Health and Human Services, 203–260.

14. Van de Vijver, F., & Leung, K. (1997). *Methods and data analysis for cross-cultural research.* Thousand Oaks, CA: Sage Publications.
15. Marin, G., & Marin, B. (1991). *Research with Hispanic populations.* Newbury Park, CA: Sage Publications.
16. Reinharz, S. (1992). *Feminist methods in social research.* New York: Oxford University Press.
17. Yegidis, B. (1986). Date rape and other forced sexual encounters among college students. *Journal of Sex Education and Therapy, 12*(2), 51–54.
18. Mills, C., & Granoff, B. (1992). Date rape and acquaintance rape among a sample of college students. *Social Work, 37*(6), 504–509.
19. Jackson, A. (1993). Black, single, working mothers in poverty: Preferences for employment, well-being, and perceptions of preschool-age children. *Social Work, 38*(1), 26–33.
20. Gregg, R. (1994). Exploration of pregnancy and choice in a high-tech age. In C. Reissman (Ed.), *Qualitative studies in social work research.* Thousand Oaks, CA: Sage Publications.
21. Gagne, P. (1992). Appalachian women: Violence and social control. *Journal of Contemporary Ethnography, 20*(4), 387–415.

9

SAMPLING ISSUES AND OPTIONS

In the previous chapters there were numerous references to two important components of research design, sampling (sometimes referred to as *case sampling*) and measurement. Because of their importance (especially in quantitative research), we will examine them in greater detail in this chapter and the two that follow.

In social work research a sample is often a group of people chosen to represent some larger group of people. For example, it might be a group of active clients with some problem who are chosen to represent all clients with that problem. In a program evaluation (Chapter 13), a sample is likely to be simply the clients in the program. Or it might be a group of staff members who are chosen to participate in a focus group. Samples can also be inanimate. Other examples of samples might be:

- A group of case records selected to estimate the extent of some problem, such as the error rate in service eligibility determination.
- A group of social agencies selected from among all agencies that serve a certain client population.
- A group of research reports that meet certain criteria and that are evaluations of a particular method of intervention in a meta-analysis (Chapter 8).
- A group of records of human communication such as the minutes of business meetings, recordings of oral histories, television programs, or Internet websites that are used for content analysis (Chapters 7 and 8).
- The measurements of a client target problem in one phase of a single system research study (Chapter 14).

In exploratory studies in which the researcher hopes only to begin to acquire a better understanding of some problem or other phenomenon, samples are often chosen more for their availability than anything else. There can be little pretense that what is learned from them can be generalized to cases not studied. This is also the case in many studies that are primarily qualitative and that, for example, seek to learn about the different ways that people perceive or experience some problem or event and the meanings they attribute to it. In many descriptive studies and in explanatory ones that attempt to test hypotheses about relationships between variables (studies that tend to rely more on quantitative research methods), sampling methods are used that increase the likelihood that findings from the sample can be generalized beyond it. In short, every effort is made to produce findings that possess good external validity.

The reason for sampling is efficiency. By using one or more research samples, researchers hope to learn something at less cost than would be involved if they had to learn it some other way that entailed studying many more people or objects. Whether the research is designed to determine if there is support for hypotheses, to describe some problem more accurately, to begin to understand it, or to achieve any other purpose for which research is conducted, the composition of a research sample is important. Not just any sample will do. We seek the sample or samples that will best accomplish our purpose.

Terminology

When used in a discussion of sampling, some terms take on very specific meanings. Let us look at some of the most important ones.

Case

A case (sometimes called an "element" if it refers to an inanimate object) is the basic unit of analysis in a given research study. If the unit of analysis is a person (as is often the situation in social work research), the term is used to denote each actual person who was selected for study. Collectively, those people selected as research participants for the study constitute the sample (see following). The term *case* may also refer to many different units of analysis, for example, a family, group, organization, community, or even nation.

Universe, Theoretical Population, and Accessible Population

The word *universe* is sometimes used in discussions of sampling. When it is, it refers to the entire collection of people (or elements) that share some defined characteristics, more often called the *theoretical population*. The universe or theoretical population can never really be known, since it includes cases from both the past and the future. It might consist of, for example, all incidents of child abuse among North Americans. Another term, *accessible population* (to which we will simply refer as "population" after this initial discussion) has a somewhat narrower connotation. It refers to only those cases that theoretically might be selected as research participants, those that are potentially accessible to the researcher because of geography, time, methods of data collection, and budget limitations or other constraints. For example, in one study a research population may be all of the clients served by a county mental health program. In another, it may be all students enrolled in accredited social work programs in a state or province. This is not to imply that a research population is always relatively small or geographically limited. It may be possible to select cases from populations that are very large and/or widely dispersed. If, for example, there is a comprehensive list of all cases (such as the CSWE's list of all accredited BSW programs in the United States), the research population may be both large and geographically dispersed.

Sampling Frame

A sampling frame is the actual listing of potential cases from which some are drawn. The researcher hopes that it will be at least a reasonable approximation of the population. But we all know that lists, no matter how meticulously they have been compiled, often are incomplete or contain some people or objects that should not be included. For example, if we are interested in studying some characteristic of social work students, then the population may be defined as all current BSW and MSW students at XYZ University, and the sampling frame may be an actual list of social work students supplied by the dean's office. It would not include all students who registered after the day the list was compiled, and it may contain the names of some students who recently have withdrawn from social work courses but have not completed the necessary paperwork or notified the dean.

A population is what we would like to use for selecting cases, whereas a sampling frame is an available list that is the next best thing to a population. Frequently, a sampling frame is all that is available. Then one has no choice but to use a sampling frame, knowing full well that it is not a 100 percent accurate representation of the population. When researchers study some problem that carries a social stigma or is illegal, use of a sampling frame is usually inevitable. The sampling frame may not even be a close approximation of the population. For example, suppose that a researcher in Mississippi wishes to interview victims of date rape during the past six months, to determine what percentage of victims seem to be suffering from post-traumatic stress disorder (PTSD). No list of date rape victims in Mississippi for the time period may be available. But a sampling frame containing the names of at least some victims could be compiled with the help of local law enforcement officials within the state if they could be convinced that the researcher would protect participants' confidentiality and conduct the research ethically. The researcher might elect to use this sampling frame despite the fact that it probably differs in some important ways from the population of cases from which cases could be selected. For example, it would not contain the names of date rape victims who did not go to the police or refused to press charges against their attacker.

Sample

We have used the term *sample* many times in this book. What exactly does it mean? A sample is a subset of cases selected for study from among people or objects within a defined population. It is chosen to represent the population. If there are two or more groupings of cases within a sample, they are referred to as *subsamples*.

Generally, researchers conclude that it is unfeasible or unnecessary to study the entire population or all potential cases. The population may be too large and/or too costly to study. Or researchers may conclude that it is possible to learn almost as much (and at far less cost) by studying only a portion of the population (or sampling frame). So they select a sample of cases.

Representativeness

In the previous chapter, we mentioned the importance of using a representative sample in quantitative research. It impacts both the internal and external validity of research findings (Chapter 6). Although it is desirable in all research, representativeness is less critical in most qualitative studies, which often do not seek support for hypotheses (so internal validity is not an issue) or otherwise hope to generalize their research findings from the sample to its population (so external validity is less of an issue).

Representativeness is one of two criteria generally applied in evaluating the quality of a research sample. It refers to the degree to which a research sample is similar to the population from which it was drawn. Thus, representativeness should be regarded as a relative term. Ideally, researchers would like to study cases that are identical in all respects to the members of the population from which they were selected. Of course, the only way that this can happen is if they do not sample at all, but study the entire population instead. But if they did, the major benefit of sampling (conservation of research resources) would be lost. Fortunately, perfect representativeness in every respect within a sample is not really necessary—a sample can be sufficiently representative of a population if it resembles the population as a whole with respect to a limited number of relevant variables, most often the dependent, independent, and any potentially confounding variables.

In Chapter 6, we mentioned three different sampling methods that are used in longitudinal studies. Generally, sample representativeness is very important in this type of research. It entails costly and time-consuming study of participants who, it is hoped, will provide an accurate picture of changes that occur within the population. A special problem in panel studies (which study the same group of participants over time) is the likelihood that participants may drop out or otherwise become unavailable as the study progresses. Because of death, participant mobility, or other forms of attrition ("experimental mortality"), the number of participants who are available over the entire course of the study often is much reduced from those who initially agreed to participate. If the causes for dropout are not related to central research questions, the problem can be handled by anticipating sizable participant loss and beginning with enough extra participants to absorb it. However, the participants who drop out may leave because of factors relevant to the central focus of the research. If this occurs, their presence can be missed and can affect the credibility of any research findings.

Size

The second criterion that is considered in assessing the quality of a research sample is size. It has a special, narrow meaning within the context of sampling. Sample size refers simply to the number of cases it contains, not to the percentage of the population or sampling frame that it contains. This is an important distinction and one often misunderstood. Although it seems logical that a sample that includes only a small percentage of the population could not possibly be a good sample, this is not necessarily true. Political pollsters using large (1,800 to 2,200) samples have been remarkably successful in recent years in predicting the results of most close national elections. Yet their samples consistently include far less than 1 percent of registered voters. Why have they been so successful? A sample of 1,800 to 2,200 is large in the absolute sense. In addition, those cases within their samples were carefully selected using methods designed to increase the likelihood of the sample's representativeness.

In sampling, size and representativeness are interrelated. A sample's size affects its potential to be representative. For example, if we draw two samples, one larger than the other, and use the same method for drawing them, the larger sample is more likely to be representative of the population than the smaller one. However, the relationship between sample size and representativeness is not usually that simple and is not as direct as we might logically assume.

When is a sample considered to be large? When is it so small that it is almost surely not representative? While these would seem like easy questions to answer, they are not. There is no general rule; no absolute definition of what is a large sample or a small one. To use one would be to rely on tradition, and as we discussed back in Chapter 1, that would be dangerous. No, numbers cannot be assigned; a small sample is not always less than 30, less than 100, and so forth; the same applies to what is a large sample. In short—it depends. However, there are several principles and factors that have been identified that address the issue of sample size and its relationship to representiveness. They assume that a sample is a random one (discussed later in this chapter). They relate to (1) the size of the population from which a sample is drawn (which it is possible to describe as large or small), and (2) the amount of variability within it. These principles can be helpful in deciding what sample size is most likely to produce the degree of representativeness that we require. However, they still do not produce a formula for determining the correct sample size to use. Here are a few of the principles:

1. If the number of people or elements in the population is small (for example, under hundred or even smaller), even a relatively small increase in sample size is likely to make the sample more representative. Conversely, if the population is large, adding a few more cases to the sample will most likely have little effect on its representativeness. A point of "diminishing returns" will have been reached.
2. If the number of people or elements in the population is small, the sample may have to include a fairly large percentage of the population (referred to as *sampling ratio* or *sample to population ratio*), perhaps 25 or 30 percent, to be sufficiently representative. If the population is very large (in the hundreds of thousands or even millions, as in the example of political polls mentioned earlier), a very small sampling ratio, less than 1 percent or even less, should provide a sufficiently representative sample.
3. If the population varies widely in relation to the variables being examined, a larger sample may be required in order to achieve sample representativeness than if the population is more homogeneous.

Another factor to be considered in evaluating whether a sample size is appropriate for a given research study is the statistical analysis used. A sample can be considered too small if it or one or more of its subsamples is smaller than the size for which a statistical test was designed. Conversely, it is too large if it is larger than the size recommended for a given statistical test. If a sample is concluded to be an appropriate size (for the statistical analysis used) and has been selected in such a way that it produces a high likelihood of representativeness, it is likely to be considered a good one, especially if the researcher hopes to produce findings that possess a high degree of external validity.

Sampling Error

There are two reasons why a sample may differ from its population (Box 9.1). The difference that occurs naturally when a sample is drawn from a population or sampling frame is referred to as *sampling error.* All samples, but especially smaller ones, are likely to differ from the population from which they were drawn. Even two or more identically sized samples drawn from the same population (for example, two samples drawn independently from a class of social work students) are likely to differ regarding any variables that we may wish to study. The concept of sampling error is critical to an understanding of how certain types of statistical testing work (see Chapter 12). And it is often what can make variables appear to be related when they really are not. It can also hide true relationships between or among variables.

The relationship between sample size and the amount of sampling error present in a sample can be easily demonstrated by thinking of a class of fifty social work graduate students. Suppose the average age (referred to as the "mean" in statistical analysis) of the class is thirty, with most students being between twenty-seven and thirty-three. The oldest is thirty-nine, and the youngest is twenty-one. The ages of the students might form a bell shape, or normal distribution, if we were to form a frequency polygon of everyone's ages.

If we were to draw a sample of five students from the class, we would not expect the average age of the sample of five to be exactly thirty. It might be twenty-eight or thirty-two or even twenty-five or thirty-five. The difference between the mean of the sample and the mean of the class (population) would be the amount of sampling error in the sample. If we drew many repeated samples of five students from the class, most of the samples would not have a mean age of exactly thirty. The average ages of the respective samples of five students would differ from the class mean (thirty) and from each other. Thus, most of the time, the mean age of any sample would be a poor estimate of the age of the class—the sample would not be very representative of the class for the variable age.

Now suppose that we had drawn samples of fifteen students from the same population (class) of fifty. We would still expect that the mean ages of most of the samples would not be exactly thirty. However, we would expect that more of them would be closer to thirty than when we drew only samples of five. Why? Because with samples of fifteen, the law of averages would be more likely to take over than with samples of only five. A sample of five might contain, for example, five of the oldest students in the class. Then the sampling error might be large. In sampling fifteen students from the class, our first five selections might be the same five older students. But as we select more cases for the sample, the likelihood of drawing younger than average students (to balance off the first five) would now be increased, because the average age of the remaining pool of students would now be less than thirty. As samples get larger, they begin to look more and more

BOX 9.1   Two Reasons Samples May Differ from the Population from Which They Were Drawn

1. *Sampling bias.*   The intentional or unintentional systematic distortion of a sample.
2. *Sampling error.*   The normal tendency of a sample to differ from its population.

like their population. So, if we had drawn samples of forty-nine students each, we could expect that the samples might vary somewhat from the class average age of thirty and from each other, but not by very much. If we selected the entire population of all fifty students, there would be no sampling error. But this would defeat the purpose of sampling, which is to build knowledge in the most efficient way.

Since samples are likely to vary from their populations, we cannot simply assume that measurements of a sample's characteristics are the same as those of its population. But how much do they differ? We can assume that there is some degree of similarity between a sample and its population because the sample consists of cases drawn from the population. An estimate of the similarity of a sample to its population can help us gauge to what degree a drawn sample is sufficiently representative of the population in relation to one or more variables. But how similar can we expect a given sample to be to its population?

There are methods and formulas[1] to help us determine the minimum sample size that will produce an acceptably low sampling error. It is important to remember that it is the number of cases in a sample and the amount of variability within its population (and not simply the percentage of the population that a sample represents) are important in estimating the amount of sampling error within a sample.

Sampling Bias

Even if a sample is relatively large and tables and/or statistical analysis seem to suggest that the amount of sampling error is estimated to be quite small, the sample still may not be adequately representative. It may contain too much sampling bias. *Sampling bias* refers to the systematic distortion of a sample. It can occur either intentionally or unintentionally. It is caused by such factors as the methods used to select a sample or when and where a sample was selected. A biased sample contains overrepresentation of some types of cases and underrepresentation of others (relative to the population from which it was drawn).

Especially in more quantitative studies, a biased sample can seriously limit the usefulness of the data collected by the researcher. If a sample does not represent its population, nearly anything we find out about cases in the sample will be of limited value. We may know a great deal about a particular (biased) group of cases, but we will be unable to generalize this knowledge to the population from which the sample was drawn. Thus, the external validity of findings generated by a study of a badly biased sample (or of one containing too much sampling error, for that matter) is low.

Some samples almost invariably contain sampling bias. For example, client satisfaction surveys tend to contain a disproportionate number of responses from clients who are most satisfied with services. However, there generally are ways to decrease the likelihood that sampling bias will occur. By paying special attention to how and under what conditions a sample is selected, using strategies discussed later in this chapter, we can increase the representativeness of research samples.

Statistic and Parameter

The terms *statistic* and *parameter* are closely related. Statistics are descriptions of the distribution of variables within samples. Parameters are descriptions of the distribution of variables within populations. In more quantitative research studies, we often secure statistics from our sample data that we hope will tell us something about the parameters of the same variables within the population that the sample is supposed to represent. For example, we may calculate the mean (average) age of people within the sample (a statistic) and hope to be able to use that statistic as an estimate of the mean age of the population (a parameter). In those less common situations in which we attempt to study the entire population, we would summarize the findings of the research study as parameters. For example, if we conducted a thorough analysis of active case records in a human service organization and then summarized the demographic characteristics of those clients currently being served, we would refer to our summaries as parameters.

Random Selection

Random selection entails drawing the cases for a sample or subsample using methods to ensure that all cases have an equal probability of being selected. It is designed to preclude sampling bias and to produce a more representative sample than would be produced if it were not used. By enhancing sample representativiveness, random selection can increase the external validity of research findings.

Random selection should not be confused with *random assignment* of cases that were selected to two or more subsamples. Random assignment relates more to design issues (Chapters 6–8) than to our discussion of sampling. It is used to increase the internal validity of research findings by controlling for the most common threats to it.

In a research study, it is possible to have random selection without random assignment and vice versa. In experimental designs (Chapter 6) both are present.

Random Sample

A random sample is a sample or subsample that is drawn using random selection. There are distinct advantages to random samples. They control for sampling bias by making it impossible to distort the sample in some systematic way. In addition, although random samples cannot eliminate sampling error, with a random sample we can use the laws of probability to produce an estimate of the amount of sampling error within the sample and to statistically determine the probability that certain relationships between variables within the sample were the work of sampling error.[2]

Random samples are used in social work research when a representative sample is important. However, several factors explain why they are not used more frequently. To draw a random sample, we must have access to a list of cases in a population or to a sampling frame that is a good approximation of the population. Even if a good sampling frame is available, the cost of acquiring a random sample may be prohibitive. Many organizations that maintain such lists charge researchers who may wish to use a list of cases drawn at random from them. Or it may simply be too expensive to collect data from cases in a random sample when cases are geographically scattered and in-person interviews are the data collection method of choice.

There may also be ethical reasons why random samples are not used. For example, we could draw a random sample of current clients to receive an experimental treatment, but our knowledge of certain clients in the sample might suggest that they would more likely benefit from some other treatment or that they might likely be harmed by the experimental treatment. Ethically, such clients could not be included, and thus our sample would no longer be considered random.

We can now summarize how the preceding terms relate to each other in the context of research sampling:

> *Universe* or *theoretical population* refers to the entire collection of people (or elements) that share some defined characteristic(s) that a researcher wishes to study. A *population* is that portion of it that is realistically accessible to the researcher. A *sampling frame* is an available list that approximates a population but is likely to differ from it in some ways. A *sample* is a group of *cases* drawn from a sampling frame that is actually studied in some way. The purpose of selecting a sample is to have available for study a group of cases that (to a greater or lesser degree) represent a larger number of cases within the population. Two criteria used to evaluate the quality of a sample are its *representativeness* (the degree to which it resembles the population) and its *size* (the number of cases that it contains). Samples may tend not to be representative of the population because of (1) *sampling error*, which is the natural tendency of a sample to differ from its population or (2) *sampling bias*, which is the systematic distortion of a sample because of a variety of factors. In analyzing data collected from a *random* sample, the researcher may calculate sample *statistics* and conduct statistical analysis as a way of estimating population *parameters* or, in explanatory studies, to determine the likelihood that sampling error might have produced a relationship between variables within the sample.

Probability Sampling

There are two general categories of sampling methods available to researchers: probability sampling and nonprobability sampling. Probability sampling uses some method of random selection. With probability sampling, it is possible to calculate the statistical probability that any case within a sampling frame or population will be selected as part of the research sample. There are several methods used to select a probability sample.

Simple Random Sampling

Simple random sampling is the most well known type of probability sampling. It entails randomly selecting some predetermined number of cases from the sampling frame or population. A researcher wanting to select 25 people from a sampling frame of 100 would write each person's name on an individual 3" × 5" file card and then randomly select 25 cards from some container. If the cards were identical except for the names on them and they were mixed in the container in a way that each had an equal probability of selection, a simple random sample would result.

For drawing larger samples, the researcher could consult a table of mathematically generated random numbers[3] to assist in the selection of cases. To use a table of random numbers, each case is first assigned a consecutive number. Then the researcher enters the table at some random point (selecting any number off the chart arbitrarily) and moves through the chart systematically. For example, the researcher might decide to work down a given column of numbers until the required number of cases has been selected. The cases that are selected would be those that have the same numbers as those corresponding to the ones picked from the chart.

Another common method for selecting a simple random sample is to use computer software designed to select numbers at random. Many statistical software packages now offer a random numbers function. All cases in the sampling frame or population are assigned consecutive numbers. Then the researcher enters the size of the sampling frame or population and the number or percentage of cases that will constitute the sample. The software produces a sample of random numbers as output. The researcher then selects the cases that have had those numbers assigned to them.

Systematic Random Sampling

Systematic random sampling is popular because of its simplicity. No table of random numbers is needed, and no computer programs are required. It uses a three-step process. An example will help to explain how it works.

Suppose that a researcher wishes to conduct a client satisfaction survey using a 25 percent sample of all 100 active clients in a human service organization. That would be 25 cases. The case records for the active clients (the sampling frame) are stored in a locked file drawer or as a computer-generated file. The first 25 case records in the file could be selected, but they would not constitute a probability sample. Such a sample might be biased. For example, because files are stored alphabetically, the first 25 cases could include only those cases whose last names start with a letter early in the alphabet— that might produce a bias in terms of ethnicity. So, a systematic random sample would be preferable.

How would a systematic sample be drawn? First, the necessary sampling interval (referred to as k) would have to be computed. The sampling interval is found by dividing the number of cases in the sampling frame by the number of cases needed for the sample. Because a sample of 25 would be 1 case out of 4 (100 divided by 25 = 4), the sampling interval (k) would be 4.

Next, the researcher would randomly select a number from 1 to 4 (k). Let us say that it is 3. The number thus selected (3) would be the starting point—the third case in the file would be selected. Then, the researcher would select every fourth case after that; that is, the seventh case, the eleventh, the fifteenth, the nineteenth, and so forth.

The initial, random selection of a starting point is an important step, and it cannot be ignored. It is necessary so that every case in the file would have had an equal chance of selection when the sampling commenced.

Stratified Sampling

Stratified sampling can be used (1) to reduce the amount of sampling error when using a simple random sample or a systematic random sample, or (2) simply to ensure that there are enough cases within different value or value label categories of a variable for comparison purposes. For either purpose, a two-stage sampling method is used.

Stage 1 of stratified sampling requires the researcher to divide the population into homogeneous categories, or strata. That is, people or objects are placed in one of two or more strata (subgroups of the population or sampling frame) based on their measurement (value or value label) of a variable. Thus, within strata, members are homogeneous with regard to this variable (for example, all social workers in one stratum and all physicians in another stratum for the variable "profession," or all females in one stratum and all males in the other stratum for the variable "gender"). In the second stage, the desired number of cases is selected from each stratum by either simple random sampling or systematic random sampling.

There are two different types of stratified random sampling. They reflect (respectively) the two uses of stratified sampling that we mentioned previously. In *proportionate stratified random sampling,* the researcher elects to stratify based on a variable that could distort the research findings if not proportionately represented in the research sample (that is, one that is a potentially confounding variable). For example, a researcher wishing to study the effectiveness of treatment intervention on a group of clients who have been diagnosed as clinically depressed might have good reason to stratify the sample by gender. There might be concern that client gender may be a confounding variable that relates to treatment success. Thus, a method is needed to ensure that the sample does not consist of a disproportionate (relative to the sampling frame) number of either men or women.

Let us assume that the sampling frame from which the sample is drawn consists of 1,000 cases, of which 900 are female and 100 are male. A 5 percent sample (consisting of 50 cases) is to be drawn. To draw a proportionate stratified random sample, the cases would first be sorted into two strata or groups consisting of (1) the 900 females and (2) the 100 males. Then 5 percent of the females (45 cases) would be selected at random, and 5 percent of the males (5 cases) would be selected at random. The sample, like the sampling frame, would thus be 90 percent female—perfectly representative regarding gender. The sample thus produced might be biased in some other respects, but it is definitely not biased regarding gender. And every case in the sampling frame had an equal likelihood of being selected (0.05, or 5 percent), so the sample is considered to be a random one.

But what if the researcher wished to determine if the treatment intervention is more effective with males or with females? If a proportionate stratified random sample were used, it would require comparing the clinical depression level of one subsample of 45 females (probably an acceptable size) with the other subsample consisting of only 5 males. The researcher might be uncomfortable with allowing only 5 males to represent all male clients. Could only 5 cases be representative of males? Five is a very small subsample; the likelihood of sampling error might be high, and certain potentially useful forms of statistical analysis that require larger samples would have to be eliminated.

An alternative method of sampling that also relies on the use of strata (homogeneous subgroups) is *disproportionate stratified sampling*. It can be used to produce subsamples of comparable size for comparison purposes by over-sampling from one group and under-sampling from another. For example, the researcher in the previous example might randomly select a subsample consisting of 25 females and another of 25 males from their respective strata. In the total sample (females and males), there would be a disproportionate number of males (relative to the sampling frame). In the sample, 50 percent of the cases would be male, but in the sampling frame the percentage of males is only 10 percent. Males and females clearly would have a different probability of being selected for the research sample. But it is still possible to calculate the likelihood of their being selected for the research sample—thus, the sample would still be a probability one (but not a random one). Any male client would have a very high probability of being selected for the sample (25 out of 100, or 0.25); for any female client, the probability would be only 25 out of 900, or less than 0.03.

Cluster Sampling

Cluster sampling involves a multistage process of listing and then randomly sampling groups of cases rather than individual cases. It is more likely to be used in large-scale surveys or in studies that involve cases that are geographically distant from each other than in small, organization-based studies. There are some research situations where it is extremely useful for putting together a sample that is both representative and sufficiently large, while conserving the resources of the researcher.

In cluster sampling, researchers identify clusters of cases. Next, they randomly select a predetermined number of clusters. Then all cases (or sometimes a random sample of all cases) within each of the selected clusters is selected to constitute the research sample.

The following example should help clarify how cluster sampling is accomplished. Suppose a researcher wishes to identify and collect data to develop a description of the characteristics of a random sample of battered women in residence at spouse abuse shelters within a state. For various reasons (including their safety), there is unlikely to exist a master list of these women. Thus, a simple random sampling method could not be used. However, a list of all shelters within a particular state may exist. Each shelter can be thought of as a cluster of cases. A random sample of these shelters (clusters) can be conducted or, if the size of the shelters varies widely, we might want to group the shelters first, based on their size, and then randomly select shelters from within each grouping. The numbers selected from each grouping might be proportionate to the percentage of all shelters that the grouping represents. Then the administrators of the shelters selected could be asked to provide a list of all persons currently in the shelter (using numbers instead of names to preserve the clients' confidentiality). The list of numbers from each of these shelters could then comprise the research sample, or if the number of cases thus obtained were still too large, some form of random sample of the numbers could be selected.

Sometimes, even if a master list of potential research participants can be compiled, cluster sampling may still be the sampling method of choice. A major advantage of cluster sampling is that it allows the researcher to collect data in a timely and cost-efficient way, while not greatly increasing the likelihood of sampling bias. It allows a researcher to collect data on a large number of cases quickly and at relatively little cost. In our example, the researcher would be able to collect data about a large number of people in just a few locations (those shelters that were selected) using cluster sampling. Yet even if a simple random sample of all cases currently active in the shelters could have been drawn, a considerable amount of time and money would have been spent requesting assistance in acquiring data or even traveling around the state to collect data on just one or two cases in each of many different shelters.

Nonprobability Sampling

In a nonprobability sample, it is not possible to calculate the likelihood that a given person or element will be selected. It does not involve random selection, so we can assume that some cases will have a greater likelihood of being selected than others. However, we cannot know how much greater. We also cannot estimate how much sampling error a sample contains using what statisticians call confidence intervals.

In many research studies, the method that produces a probability sample (random selection) cannot be used. This happens most frequently when no population list or even sampling frame is available from which to draw the sample. In such a situation, it would be impossible to calculate the likelihood of a given case's being selected. This was the situation when one of the authors was involved in an exploratory study of women who delayed childbearing until after age thirty. No sample drawn could possibly be a probability one, because the population could not be identified or specified and no acceptable sampling frame was available.

Even when it is possible to draw a probability sample, it might not be the best sample to use to study a given problem or research question. A nonprobability sample may be preferable. In some of the types of research that we described in Chapter 8, sample representativeness is not as important as other sample characteristics. For example, in research studies where the emphasis is on exploring the nature and impact of a problem, it may make sense to study only individuals who are likely to have the best in-depth understanding of the problem, whether or not they represent a cross-section of the population experiencing it. In this type of study, the researcher might deliberately exclude from the study those who might otherwise have been randomly selected as participants, but who may contribute little or nothing new to an understanding of it.

Four commonly used nonprobability sampling methods have proven useful to social work researchers. All of these methods are suited to situations in which the researcher either (1) would prefer a representative sample but is unable to compile a population or sampling frame from which to draw one using probability sampling methods or (2) has decided that representativeness is less important to sample composition than one or more other characteristics.

Convenience Sampling

One type of nonprobability sampling plan entails a very unscientific approach to sampling. *Convenience sampling* (sometimes called "accidental sampling") entails selecting cases for study primarily because they happen to be readily accessible to the researcher. It is this type of sampling that is most likely to have been used when we hear on the evening news that a "random sample" of residents of our community was interviewed about their opinions regarding some news event. In fact, the sample was not at all random! Generally, the people interviewed were all in the same shopping mall or were on a street corner near the television studio. They were selected mainly because of convenience. Clearly, some potential participants (those most readily available) had a greater likelihood of selection than others.

As is true of any sampling method, convenience sampling may produce an acceptable level of representativeness, but it is the method that is probably least likely to do so.

The usefulness of convenience samples in social work research is limited. If the researcher is beginning to explore a new area of inquiry and it is hard to locate people with certain characteristics or obtain their permission to be research participants, it may be the only feasible alternative. But convenience samples present a major difficulty for researchers. How can they interpret the findings of their research? To whom do they apply? Under what conditions? Research designs that rely on convenience sampling have little or no claim to external validity. Findings generally are believed to be applicable only to those people or objects that were studied.

Purposive Sampling

Sometimes cases are selected because they are believed to be able to give the researcher access to some unique approach to a problem or situation or a special perspective, insight, expertise, experience, characteristic, or condition that we wish to understand. For example, suppose we wish to know more about the variations in coping strategies used by people diagnosed with early-stage Alzheimer's disease. Although we might be able to produce a sampling frame of people who have recently been diagnosed and to draw a random sample from it, the sample thus selected might not be what is needed for our research. For our research objective, a purposive sample actually might be preferable to a more representative one. It would be more likely to help us describe the wide variety of coping methods used.

How would we acquire a purposive sample of people recently diagnosed with Alzheimer's disease? From informal conversations with medical staff, we might learn of a number of people being treated at clinics and hospitals who employ what staff members perceive as unique coping strategies. We might then select those twenty people with what seem like the most unique ways of coping and ask them to voluntarily take part in in-depth research interviews. Our sample would not be representative of the population or even of the available sampling frame. It would not contain the same distribution of coping strategies (percentage-wise) that exists within the population of people with Alzheimer's. For example, we might estimate that 40 percent of the people might all use the same coping strategy, but we might select only one person for our sample of twenty (5 percent) who use that strategy. Because we would be seeking to learn about the diversity of coping strategies used by people (heterogeneity), there might be little value in interviewing more than one person who uses any one coping strategy. That would be redundant.

There are other variations of purposive sampling that are used less frequently in social work research. One, *expert sampling*, selects cases based on the criterion that they have a certain desired expertise. Thus we might select and bring together a panel of researchers, all of whom have studied the problem of weight-based discrimination or a group of primary care physicians who have set up their practices using a fee-based system (a system in which patients pay a fixed amount per year and are then promised certain services at no additional charge). These "panels of experts" can then be surveyed, brought together in a focus group, and so forth to attempt to tap their experience and expertise.

Sometimes, we might prefer a group of people who are "typical" in some way. Then we would use a type of purposive sampling known as *mode instance sampling*. For example, in conducting a needs assessment (Chapter 13) for a proposed social program, a researcher may want to assemble a sample of typical clients who might use the proposed program's services to collect their opinions or assess their needs.

Still another form of purposive sampling is the opposite of mode instance sampling. It is *deviant case sampling*, and it seeks the most atypical cases for study. For example, in an exploratory qualitative study, a researcher might wish to use a sample of investors who profited the most and/or who lost the most money by lying on home loan applications to acquire real estate that they planned to resell ("flip"). They might then be interviewed in order to learn how they were ethically able to justify their illegal behavior.

Snowball Sampling

One method of nonprobability sampling does not select a sample at one point in time. It bears some resemblance to both convenience sampling and expert sampling. When using snowball sampling, the sample is compiled as the research progresses. First, one or just a few people are identified as potential research participants. Then they are asked to provide the names of people they know or know about who, like themselves, have experienced some problem or who in other ways meet the necessary criteria for inclusion in the research study. The next potential participants are contacted by the researcher to determine if they are indeed eligible for inclusion in the sample and whether they are willing to participate in the study. They may then be asked to provide the names of other possible participants. The process is repeated until enough participants agree to take part in the study.

Snowball sampling is often used in the case studies such as those described in Chapter 8 and in the previously mentioned research study that interviewed a sample of women who had given birth to their first child after age thirty. In the latter example, an initial sample of women was identified by placing an ad in the paper (hardly a random selection procedure). Women who responded to the ad were interviewed by a member of the research team to ensure they met the necessary criteria to be part of the research study and to attempt to complete an early draft of a research data collection instrument. At the conclusion of the interview, they were asked if they knew of other women who, like themselves, had borne their first child after age thirty. These prospects were then followed up by the research team. The use of snowball sampling was appropriate because (1) the purpose of the study was to develop a research instrument for a subsequent study of delayed childbearing and (2) the researchers were not attempting to describe accurately the population of women who delay childbearing.

In exploratory studies designed to learn more about either a new problem or one that has only recently been identified, snowball samples are often used. The problem or behavior need not be illegal or carry some social stigma (as is characteristic of case studies). For example, a useful sample of adolescents who are recent victims of "cyberbullying" (harassment by peers using e-mail or other electronic communication) could be compiled by first identifying one victim and then asking him or her to provide the names of others who they know that have had similar experiences. Of course, as this problem grows and more and more victims of it are identified, a sampling frame of victims will be able to be compiled. Other, perhaps better methods of acquiring research samples then will be used.

Quota Sampling

Another type of nonprobability sampling method is used to obtain a sample that is (1) as representative as possible in relation to potentially confounding variables and (2) of a specified size (quota). The most common type of quota sampling, *proportional quota sampling* begins with establishing an estimate of the characteristics of the research population regarding selected variables. This description is built into a matrix; that is, a table displaying the percentage of people in the population believed to share each combination of characteristics. Then people are selected for study who have all of the characteristics described within each specific cell of the matrix. Sampling continues until there is a final sample of people selected that represents each of the cells. Then the people in each cell are assigned a "weight," a number based upon what is believed to be the portion of the total population that they represent. Quota sampling is the method of sampling that is generally used by political pollsters conducting exit polls. It has produced some accurate predictions but also some embarrassing, wrong ones. However, when the latter has occurred, it has usually been attributed to other factors, not some flaw in the sampling method used.

Sometimes it is logistically impossible (cost, time, geography) to use a large research sample. However, the researcher still wants to be sure that certain variables are adequately represented in the sample. If proportional quota sampling were to be used, characteristics of cases that occur relatively infrequently might not be adequately represented. For example, the sample might contain only one person who is a Pacific Islander and has a disability. This one individual clearly cannot represent all people who have this combination of demographic characteristics—it would be better to have at least two or three cases. Then it might be preferable to use a less common sampling method, *nonproportional quota sampling*. It is considered the nonprobability equivalent of disproportionate stratified sampling. It entails determining the minimum number of cases required for each category or combination of characteristics (cell) and then sampling until that minimum is attained.

The use of nonproportional quota sampling, like many choices we make in research, is a trade-off. It is based on the assumption that sacrificing a little representativeness in the sample as a whole is preferable to the risk of having a category or combination of characteristics with a very small number of cases and, thus, a high probability of sampling error within it.

There is one major problem that frequently precludes the more frequent use of quota sampling of either type. It is the absence of accurate estimates of the characteristics of the population of interest needed to develop a quota matrix. If some data are missing or are not believed to be very accurate, a sufficiently representative sample cannot be obtained by quota sampling. Quota sampling should be used only when (1) the researcher has confidence that the data needed to establish a quota matrix represent reasonably accurate estimates of the characteristics of the population and (2) some unbiased (ideally, random) method of selecting participants within each cell can be implemented after a matrix has been constructed.

Selecting a Good Sample

The sampling methods that we have just described might be regarded as options, or a menu of sampling alternatives. Sometimes we simply select the one best suited to our needs and use it to draw a sample. Often, sampling is a little more complicated. We employ a *sampling plan*, a sequence of steps or stages that makes use of two or more of these methods. For example, in a study of the job satisfaction of social workers' in large outpatient mental health clinics, we might first (using systematic random sampling) select the names of twenty clinics from a statewide directory. The social workers in these clinics would then serve as a cluster sample. However, rather than selecting all of the social workers employed there to participate in our research study, we might draw a 20 percent simple random sample of them. After interviewing them we might select 10 social workers who are the most dissatisfied with their jobs (mode instance sampling) to participate in a focus group to discuss the reasons for their dissatisfaction. This multistage sampling plan would be designed to take advantage of the features of all of the different sampling methods used.

When selecting the sampling method or methods to be used and determining the appropriate sample size, a number of important, interrelated issues must be addressed. Some of them relate to practical matters that are easily understood; others are a little more technical. The major issues that the researcher needs to consider are (1) available resources for securing the sample, (2) the overall design and purpose of the study, (3) the type of statistical analysis that will be used, and (4) the relative importance of sample representativeness.

Available Resources

If the study is being funded by a human service organization or some other organization that has contracted to have it designed and implemented, the size of the sample to be used may already have been specified. If this is not the case, the researcher is free to use judgment in selecting an appropriate research sample.

In general, larger samples are likely to be more representative of the population than are smaller ones. As previously illustrated, when larger samples are chosen, sampling error is reduced. But even in quantitative studies where sample representativeness usually is critical to the credibility of the research, there is a point of diminishing returns. A researcher gets to the point where an increase in sample size does not appreciably reduce the amount of sampling error that may be present.

Using large samples can be costly. As stated previously, the processes of compromise and trade-off are ongoing activities in conducting social work research. Resources spent collecting data from a large number of research participants leaves less time and resources for performing other essential tasks in the research process. But if a smaller sample is used, some of that time and those resources can be used to perform those other tasks. The overall quality of the research study might actually be better.

Overall Design and Purpose of the Study

Generally, we expect to see different size samples (and different sampling methods) with certain types of research. For example, qualitative research studies often use smaller samples than more quantitative designs and nonprobability sampling methods. Often a representative sample is impossible to obtain because of the absence of an adequate sampling frame. And it may not be considered important anyway if the research is primarily exploratory. In contrast, large-scale descriptive studies that are primarily quantitative often use large samples (to reduce sampling error) and strive for representativeness by using random sampling methods, because the external validity of findings is considered very important. If, for example, the purpose of a study is to describe accurately the characteristics of some client population such as older people who have admitted to having been victims of financial abuse and a good sampling frame is available, then a randomly selected sample consisting of several hundred cases may be used in order to ensure the likelihood of a sufficiently representative sample.

Other types of research use samples of various sizes, usually depending on financial resources available to support the research and the number of cases available for study. Research whose objective is primarily to develop measurement instruments to be used in subsequent research studies may use relatively small samples but may use many different samples representing different subpopulations and/or different times and settings for measurement. If a researcher wishes merely to pilot-test a research instrument that will be revised and used to collect data, then a small nonprobability sample is likely to be used.

It is sometimes helpful to consult reports of other similar research and note how many cases were used. This kind of information can be used as a general guide, but it should be remembered that errors in sample size selection are quite common. We would not want to repeat another researcher's mistakes. For more in-depth discussion of sampling methods and issues, a text that is devoted solely to the topic of research sampling[4] should be consulted.

Statistical Analyses to Be Used

In qualitative studies, statistical analysis usually is not an important consideration in designing a sampling plan. There currently are methods of analyzing qualitative data (primarily content analysis) that convert words to numbers that can then be analyzed statistically. However, since the sampling methods most frequently used (purposive, snowball, or even convenience) rarely produce samples that can be considered representative, there is usually little value in conducting statistical analysis. Any conclusions regarding, for example, relationships between or among variables would be highly suspect.

In primarily quantitative studies, the size of a research sample and the type of sampling method used are important factors in the selection of the form of statistical analysis to be used. But sometimes it works the other way around. In some instances, the researcher knows in advance what analysis will have to be used—as, for example, when conducting grant-sponsored research that specifies which statistical tests are acceptable or when replicating the research of others who used a specific form of statistical analysis. Then the size of the sample as well as the sampling method used (for example, probability or nonprobability) is tailored to the requirements of the statistical analysis that must be used.

The relationship between types of statistical analysis and the most appropriate sample size are beyond the scope of this text. However, we should remember that sample size guidelines for various statistical analyses exist for a purpose. If a specific statistical test has been designed for a certain sample size, the sample size selected should be within the specified range. It should be neither smaller than nor exceed it. Samples that are either smaller or larger than recommended for a given statistical test can result in misleading conclusions regarding relationships between variables.

The Importance of Sample Representativeness

As we noted earlier, quantitative studies place great importance on the the selection of representative samples. There is a concentrated effort to avoid sampling bias and to determine (statistically) the mathematical probability that sampling error may have produced any relationships between variables that are identified or that it might have obscured real ones. Thus, whenever possible, quantitative studies rely on probability samples and random sampling methods to increase the likelihood of representativeness within research samples.

In more qualitative studies where representativeness is often impossible anyway, nonprobability sampling methods generally provide an adequate sample of cases. Both representativeness and size are less important than criteria such as the "richness" of data that a sample provides or the diversity (of perceptions, meanings, experiences, and so forth) contained within it.

Summary

In this chapter, we focused on sample selection and its relationship to good research. Key terms relating to sampling were defined. Representativeness and size were identified as the two criteria most frequently used in evaluating the quality of a sample, at least in more quantitative studies.

Sampling methods were characterized as either probability or nonprobability, depending on whether it is possible to calculate the mathematical probability that an individual person or object will be selected to be a case within the research sample. Random samples are often regarded as superior to nonrandom ones because they are more likely to be representative of the population from which they are selected and allow for the use of certain types of statistical analyses. Four types were described in this chapter: simple random sampling, systematic random sampling, cluster sampling, and proportional stratified random sampling.

For some research studies, probability samples may be neither feasible nor desirable. In some qualitative studies, for example, nonprobability sampling methods may yield samples that are exactly what is needed. Four common nonprobability sampling methods were described: convenience sampling, purposive sampling, snowball sampling, and quota sampling.

Finally, we discussed four major issues that the researcher needs to consider when deciding which sampling method to use and how large a sample is needed. They are (1) available resources for securing the sample, (2) the overall design and purpose of the study, and (3) the type of statistical analysis (if any) that will be used, and (4) the importance of sample representativeness to the research.

For Discussion

1. Why is sample representativeness much less a concern in qualitative studies than it is in more quantitative ones?
2. When would any sampling not be desirable when the population is very small, for example, when the research participants are the previous editors-in-chief of the journal *Social Work*?
3. When is a sampling frame most likely to be substituted for a population in drawing a research sample? What are some other examples of sampling frames?
4. What is the relationship between sample size and representativeness? How does each affect the external validity of research findings?
5. Why are random samples less likely to be biased than nonrandom ones?
6. Why do even random samples contain sampling error? Can it ever be totally eliminated? What can be done about it?
7. What is the importance of first determining k when using systematic random sampling? How would simply choosing the first case in a file and then going on from there cause the sample no longer to be considered random?
8. Why do researchers sometimes trade off representativeness for diversity or some other attribute in selecting a sample? Of what types of sampling is this characteristic?
9. How is randomization sometimes used in sampling methods that are considered to be "nonprobability"? How does it increase the likelihood of creating a more representative sample?
10. Is your class a representative sample of social work students? Why or why not? How have sampling bias and sampling error affected its representativeness?

Endnotes

1. See, for example, Weinbach, R., & Grinnell, R., Jr. (2007). *Statistics for social workers*. Boston: Allyn and Bacon, 114–118. Or Rosenthal, J. (2001). *Statistics and data interpretation for the helping professions*. Belmont, CA: Wadsworth/Thomson Learning, 236–239.
2. See for example, Weinbach and Grinnell, op. cit., 89–97.
3. See, for example, Neuman, W. L. (1997). *Social research methods: Qualitative and quantitative approaches*. Boston: Allyn and Bacon, 484–487.
4. See, for example, Jollifee, F. (1986). *Survey design and analysis*. New York: Ellis Horwood. Or Converse, J. (1987). *Survey research in the United States: Roots and emergence*. Berkeley, CA: University of California Press. Or Levy, P., & Lemeshow, S. (1999). *Sampling of populations: Methods and applications*. Wiley Series in Survey Methodology. Wiley-Interscience Publishing. Or Thompson, S. (2002). *Sampling,* 2nd ed. New York: Wiley-Interscience Publishing.

10

MEASUREMENT CONCEPTS AND ISSUES

Once having decided on which people or objects will provide the needed data (sampling issues), researchers generally focus on measurement issues. Specifically, they decide (1) what data will need to be collected and (2) what instruments or methods will be used to collect it.

In quantitative research, accurate measurement is of paramount importance. Whether the goal is to create a description of some problem or phenomenon (as in descriptive designs) or to test to see if two or more variables probably really are related in the population from which a research sample was drawn, any research findings will be misleading if key variables are not measured accurately. For example, how could we know if a report of the incidence and severity of family violence in a community is accurate if it is unclear what exactly was meant by family violence, or if the methods for measuring its severity appear to be highly subjective? Or, how can we trust a researcher's conclusion that motivation and degree of success in counseling are positively correlated if motivation was determined solely on clients' own assessments, or success in counseling was measured based solely on the subjective impressions of their social workers?

In qualitative studies, measurement is still important. However, people conducting qualitative studies acknowledge that their measurements may be biased by their own presence or other factors and will necessarily have a certain degree of subjectivity; they expect that. But that does not absolve them of the responsibility to (1) measure even highly subjective variables such as impressions, perceptions, or the meaning of certain events to participants as accurately as possible, and (2) measure more easily measured variables such as their participants' demographic characteristics or behaviors accurately. Thus, while this chapter and the next one may seem to relate mostly to quantitative research, much of their content is equally applicable to more qualitative research designs.

It is sometimes suggested that measurement issues should be resolved and decisions about how to measure certain variables should be made before research sampling occurs or data sources are selected. Although there are compelling arguments for this sequence of events, we believe that it makes more sense to make measurement decisions after sampling issues have been resolved and the sources for data have been selected. Until it has been decided who or what cases will provide data and how they will be providing it (for example, using written questionnaires, in-person interviews, direct observation, and so forth), it is difficult to know what type of measurements are possible and the best ways to obtain them.

What Is Measurement in Research?

Most of us think we understand what measurement is all about and how it works. After all, we have used it almost all of our lives. But just to be sure we all agree on what it means, let's review it. In research, *measurement* is the process of sorting and, when possible, quantifying information in some systematic fashion. It entails collecting data in relation to certain variables and assigning the appropriate value categories or values to individual cases. In the social work literature, there is disagreement as to how precisely it is possible to measure certain variables. Some writers have taken the position that, with enough effort, virtually all variables can be accurately measured.[1] They believe that most variables can be *quantified*, that is, a number can be assigned to describe accurately the exact amount of the variable present within a case. Other writers, especially those who espouse qualitative research methods, point out that because of the nature of many of the variables that are of interest to social workers, they cannot be quantified using standardized measurement techniques. Our position in this chapter is that for most (if not all) variables, a measurement strategy can be developed that will yield useful knowledge for researchers. However, we also acknowledge that many variables of interest to social workers do not readily lend themselves to quantification.

Preparation for Measurement

Before any measurement can take place, two interrelated activities must take place. They are referred to as *conceptualization* and *operationalization*.

Conceptualization

Conceptualization entails (1) selecting and specifying what we believe to be the most important or relevant variables to measure and (2) stating the value categories or values that each variable can assume. It also involves (3) specifying as precisely as possible exactly what we will mean by those variables. In performing these tasks, we rely on both available knowledge (the literature) and our practice knowledge and experience. For example, the literature may have suggested that abuse (or nonabuse) of medication by terminally ill patients may be related to whether or not hospice care is given. It may have suggested the hypothesis that "Terminally ill patients who receive hospice care will be less likely to abuse medication than terminally ill patients who do not receive hospice care." Two variables that clearly would need to be measured are (1) involvement (or noninvolvement) with hospice care, and (2) the presence or absence of medication abuse.

Specification of the predictor variable (hospice involvement/noninvolvement) would be no problem. But we would need to specify exactly what we mean by medication abuse (the outcome variable). Would it be any use of medication—accidental or intentional— other than exactly as prescribed? Should it include taking less of a medicine than prescribed? What about the use of additional nonprescription medication?

All of the preceding questions (and more) would need to be addressed before data collection could begin, so that cases could be correctly and consistently assigned to value categories for both variables. There are no right or wrong answers to the questions. A researcher can answer them any way that seems logical. Sometimes, the answers are summarized at this point in what is referred to as an *operational definition.* An operational definition tells the reader of a research report exactly what criteria were used in measurement in the current study; other researchers might apply different operational definitions to the same term in their research. An operational definition says, in effect, "When I use a term in this research, this is what I mean by it." For example, a researcher might construct the following operational definition:

> *Medication abuse = The intentional misuse of a prescribed, controlled narcotic substance on at least three occasions by a terminally ill person.*

Generally, several operational definitions must be constructed. Operational definitions then are presented as a group (along with definitions of other terms that may need to be defined) at the end of a literature review or near the beginning of the methodology part of a research report. In our example, it would also be necessary to define operationally such terms as *terminally ill and hospice services.*

Operationalization

Operationalization is closely related to conceptualization and is the last step in preparation for measurement. It refers to specifying the actual measuring devices or methods that will be used to measure key variables. Thus, it further clarifies their meaning.

Generally, there are many different ways that a variable can be measured. For example, measurement of the variable "medication abuse" might entail actual observations by nurses, social workers, caregivers, or aides; it might also include social workers' impressions based on mental alertness or other symptoms of medication abuse, self-reports of patients, or something as specific as a count or measurement of the patient's available medication at regular intervals.

We noted that operational definitions of a term may vary from study to study. Similarly, different researchers may actually measure the same variable in different ways. Unless the researcher is replicating the research of others (in which case the same method of measuring the variable should be used), that is fine. The only requirements for operationalization of a given variable are that it should be logical and justified (usually through the literature). Sometimes researchers choose to include the method of measurement (operationalization) of a variable[2] in their operational definition of the variable. For example:

> *Medication abuse = The intentional misuse of a prescribed, controlled narcotic substance on at least three occasions by a terminally ill person **as reported by the patient's primary caregiver.***

Cultural Sensitivity in Operationalization.   Certain theoretical concepts may have different meanings for research participants, depending on their different ethnic and cultural backgrounds. When this is the case, every effort should be made to operationalize a variable in a way that is consistent with the culture of those individuals who are providing research data. For example, what if a researcher needs to measure the educational attainment of a group of research participants? Traditionally, "years of formal schooling completed as reported by the research participant" is the operational definition of educational attainment. This definition, however, may underestimate the actual educational experiences and degree of knowledge attainment in certain groups of people. For example, for some African Americans, especially those from rural backgrounds, formal systems of education have not always been accessible. However, many (especially older) African Americans achieved both enhanced knowledge and skills through some combination of mentoring, apprenticeship, craftsmanship, and entrepreneurship. An accurate assessment of their educational attainment should include some measurement of these less formal avenues of education.

Levels of Measurement

Levels (sometimes called "scales") of measurement refer to the degree of precision with which a variable is believed to be measured. Researchers must decide at what level each variable has been measured, sometimes based on the nature of the variable itself and more frequently on the method of measurement used. Determining what level of measurement a researcher has generated is an important decision. It is essential in deciding the most appropriate methods for statistical analyses of data (Chapter 12). Researchers determine which of four labels is appropriate to apply to their measurement of a given variable. They represent a hierarchy of measurement precision.

Nominal-Level

Nominal-level is the most basic form of measurement. It involves the use of a measurement scheme that simply sorts cases into different, mutually exclusive value categories of a variable. To be considered nominal-level, a case must fall into one category (and only one) of the variable. The different value categories of a variable reflect only a difference in kind, not a difference in the amount of the variable present within a given case. Even if a number is used as a label for a value category, the number has no quantitative significance. For example, in measuring the variable "gender," the researcher may use the number 1 for males and the number 2 for females, or the other way around. In either case, the numbers do not reflect a quantitative difference—just a qualitative one. They are merely labels, substitutes for words.

In measuring many variables, nominal measurement is all that appears possible. Variables such as gender, whether one voted in the last election, whether one owns a car, undergraduate major, or religious affiliation are nominal by their very nature. (One might be interested in measuring the number of cars owned or degree of religiosity, but those are different variables, ones that have the potential for other, higher levels of measurement.)

Ordinal-Level

Ordinal measurement meets all the criteria for nominal measurement. In addition, the value categories possess a logical rank-ordering. The term ordinal-level is appropriately assigned to variables that have been measured using a range of categories, such as "always," "sometimes," "rarely," and "never"; or "not improved," "slightly improved," "somewhat improved," and "greatly improved." Note that these categories can be rank ordered—we would all arrange them in the same sequence to reflect the different quantities of some variable that each represents. But the value labels are not very precise. For example, although we would all agree that "somewhat improved" reflects more improvement than "slightly improved," we cannot say exactly how much more.

Ordinal measurement is seen quite frequently in social work practice and research. For example, social workers may be interested in measuring the degree of cooperation displayed by families that have been court ordered to receive treatment. They might categorize degree of cooperation as (1) highly cooperative, (2) cooperative, or (3) uncooperative. Of course, it would be necessary to specify the criteria by which a rating (1, 2, or 3) would be assigned. Note that the distance between successive points of measurement on the scale is not fixed. In other words, the distance between ratings of 2 and 3 on the scale is not assumed to be equal to the distance between ratings of 1 and 2. The numbers simply represent ranks.

Examples of variables in social work research that may be regarded as ordinal-level include many sociodemographic variables such as age (when measured using the value categories elderly, middle-aged, young adult, adolescent, preadolescent, and child); social class standing (upper, middle, lower, and so on); and degree of educational attainment (when measured by the highest degree completed). Many psychosocial variables that are measured using newly developed instruments, even if they produce a score that is a number, can also be claimed to generate only ordinal-level measurement. Examples may include degree of frustration, coping capacity, ability to use social support systems, or level of social functioning.

Interval-Level

Interval-level measurement meets all of the criteria for ordinal-level measurement and one additional one—the exact distances between categories (values) of the variable are known and are equal to each other. Many standardized tests, especially those that have been refined over many years, are believed to produce interval level measurement. For example, IQ tests, Scholastic Assessment Tests (SATs), or Graduate Record Exams (GREs) are constructed so that they are believed to contain equal intervals. In theory at least, the difference between two equal interviews on an IQ test (say, between scores of 115 and 110, and between scores of 87 and 82) should reflect equal quantities of the construct (intelligence) that the test is assumed to measure.

Interval-level measurement may use a zero as one of its values. Some scales (Chapter 11) that measure people's attitudes are constructed so that, for convenience of interpretation, scores range from zero to 100. In others, scores may even assume negative values. However, in either instance the zero represents just a point on a range of measurement, not the total absence of the variable. The point may be an arbitrary one or it may have some importance to the construct, such as the point where the construct can no longer be meaningfully measured.

Whether a measurement produces interval-level data is often debatable. (The same could be said for the other levels of measurement.) Generally, as long as the distance between successive points on the scale is fixed and equal, interval measurement can be assumed to exist. Depending on how precisely they can be measured, the same psychosocial variables used as examples in the previous section to demonstrate the use of ordinal-level measurement (degree of frustration, coping capacity, ability to use social support systems, and level of social functioning) might be considered to be interval level. A newly developed method of measuring them would most likely produce measurement that could only be considered ordinal-level. But over time and with repeated evaluation and refinement, an instrument might be developed that could be assumed to produce interval-level measurement.

Ratio-Level

Ratio-level measurement meets all of the criteria for interval measurement—values can be rank ordered with fixed, equal distances between them. However, the ratio scale is characterized by an additional feature—zero has an absolute meaning; that is, it is used to indicate a point where there is no measurable quantity of the variable. Unlike interval-level measurement, no value can be less than zero (negative). For example, if the variable "income" were to be operationalized as the actual gross earned annual income of clients as reported on their prior year's income tax return, the variable could be regarded as ratio level. A value of zero would mean no earned income. In addition, a person with an income of $60,000 could be said to have an income three times that of another person with an income of $20,000. We could not make such statements about variables that are nominal-, ordinal-, or interval-level.

In social work research, we might be interested in measuring how many children people have, how many social workers work on a case management team, or how many other organizations have offered services to clients. Each of these measurements could be regarded as ratio-level since a value of zero would be a "true zero," that is, it would reflect zero or none of the variable.

More on Levels of Measurement

The level of measurement of variables is often not a "given" in social work research. With many variables, the level of their measurement is often dependent how we ask a question or solicit data. For example, if we wanted to learn about research participants' life experiences with marriage using a self-administered questionnaire, we could ask, "Have you ever been married?" (yes or no). That would produce nominal-level measurement. Or, we could ask married people the question, "How likely would you be to marry again?" (very likely, somewhat likely, not likely, very unlikely). That would produce ordinal-level data. A standardized data collection instrument that measures marital satisfaction included as part of the data collection instrument might produce interval-level data. Or we might ask, "How many times have you been married?" That would produce ratio-level measurement.

In general, we seek to measure a variable at the highest level possible, that is, as precisely as possible. Among other reasons for doing so, this allows for a wider range of statistical analyses. However, there are times when we might sacrifice precision for other priorities. Why would we ever do this? Sometimes an estimate of a measurement is all that we require or can hope to receive, perhaps, because participants might not remember the exact, correct answer. It might be better to obtain an accurate estimate than an incorrect precise answer. Or, we might need to measure variables that are considered quite "personal." For example, income, number of marriages, or number of illegal substances that have been used probably could be reported on with reasonable accuracy and would yield interval- or even ratio-level measurement. However, to ask about them very directly and require specific numbers might result in some potential research participants refusing to provide any data. Thus it might be preferable to provide ranges for responses (which would produce ordinal-level data) instead. The ranges provide for a little more privacy, and thus might increase the percent of participants who would provide needed data. So, we might choose to trade off measurement precision for a higher response rate—often a good trade-off.

Some variables that would seem to be inherently nominal-level (gender, religious affiliation, and so forth) do not have to remain so. For example, the variable gender can be converted into a new variable that we might call "femaleness." Then a female research participant would be assigned the value 1, and a male would be assigned the value 0. If we chose to make the new variable "maleness," a male would be assigned the value 1 and a female would be assigned the value 0. Any new variables thus created (called *dummy variables*) are really measurements of the same variable or construct, but they are now considered ratio level for purposes of statistical analysis. Researchers sometimes do this in order to include the original variable in certain statistical analyses (tests) that require the more precise level of measurement.

The level of measurement of variables (as the reader has probably already surmised) is a major determinant in the type of statistical analysis of data that can be employed. However, the level of measurement of a variable is sometimes little more than a "judgment call." Nominal-level variables are easily identified. However, distinguishing between ordinal- and interval-level measurement is often difficult. It often comes down to a judgment of whether or not the intervals reflected in the measurement are really equal in size. Not surprisingly, even researchers sometimes disagree as to whether a data collection instrument or a certain type of scale (Chapter 11) yields interval- or ordinal-level data.

Distinguishing between interval- and ratio-level measurement also can be difficult sometimes. (Should age be interval- or ratio-level?) Fortunately, for statistical purposes, the distinction is relatively unimportant. In fact, in books on statistics, the conditions for using certain types of analyses (tests of inference) often do not even make the distinction between interval- and ratio-level measurement. In describing the level of measurement requirements for using certain statistical tests, the terms nominal, ordinal, and interval/ratio are frequently used.

Criteria for Good Measurement

In Chapter 6, we discussed two criteria used in evaluating many research designs (external validity and internal validity). In the previous chapter we presented two criteria for assessing the quality of a research sample (representativeness and size). There are also two criteria that are used to assess measurement quality (see Box 10.1). They are reliability and validity.

BOX 10.1   Indications That the Measurement Is Good

1. It is *reliable:* We can demonstrate that it produces consistent results (96, 96, 96, and so on) in a variety of situations and under different conditions.
2. It is *valid:* We can demonstrate that it actually measures what we claim that it measures (96 = high level of aggression, not of assertiveness, anger or some other construct).

Note: A measurement that is valid is both reliable and unbiased. Thus, a measurement that is valid is always reliable, but one that is reliable may not be valid.

Reliability

Reliability is most closely related to the concept of consistency.[3] It asks the question: Does a measurement produce the same results under various conditions? If the object or person being measured by it has not changed, a good measure should not produce different results under different conditions. For example, one indicator of reliability (test-retest, discussed in the next section) has to do with the extent to which a measurement produces the same results when it is conducted at one time as opposed to some other time. If there is no reason why a research participant's measurement of a variable (such as attitude toward capital punishment or sexist beliefs) should have changed, then measuring a person a second time using the same method as the first time should yield the same or nearly identical results. If not, the mathematical measurement is not considered reliable.

The degree to which a measurement is reliable is usually expressed in what is referred to as a *correlation coefficient,* a mathematical indicator of how much a measurement of a variable agrees (correlates) with a second measurement of the variable. A correlation coefficient reflects both the strength and the direction of the correlation between the two measurements. It consists of a number and a sign (– or +). Correlation coefficients range from –1.00 to +1.00. In using correlation coefficients as evidence of reliability, the researcher hopes to be able to produce correlation coefficients that are very high and positive (for example, .85, .92, and so forth).

High, positive correlation coefficients would result when (1) people or objects are measured twice (on two different days, by two different researchers, and so forth) using the same method of measuring the variable, and (2) the measurements for all or at least most people or objects are the same or nearly the same on both occasions. For example, if we claimed to be measuring assertiveness, a high positive correlation coefficient would result if people tended to receive the same or nearly the same assertiveness score when measured on Monday and again on Friday. That would demonstrate the reliability of our method of measuring assertiveness.

Probably no method for measuring variables such as human attributes is universally reliable. It is generally limited to certain groups or segments of the population. For example, some methods for measuring characteristics such as assertiveness or hostility may be considered reliable when used with men, but not with women. Others may be reliable within one socioeconomic class, ethnic group, or culture, but not within another, or with people above a certain age, but not younger than that age. That is because the indicators of an attribute, what we use to measure a variable, tend to be more or less appropriate (they vary) based on gender, socioeconomic class, ethnicity, culture, age, and so forth. For researchers, the message is this: Be sure that the methods of measurement that you choose have been found to be reliable with *your* research participants.

The reliability of measurement can be demonstrated in several ways. Each provides an indication of a different indicator of reliability. In any given research study, we are usually interested in the degree to which our measurement possesses just one or, perhaps, two of these indicators of reliability. The others tend to be less relevant.

Fortunately, in recent years, a great amount of time and energy has been devoted by researchers[4] to developing better ways to measure variables that are of interest to social work researchers. Part of this process has involved "reliability testing," determining the various indicators of reliability that a method of measurement of a variable possesses and the degree to which it possesses them. We can now find whole books of such measurement instruments as indexes and scales[5] (Chapter 11) along with estimates of the amount of reliability that they possess (in the form of correlation coefficients) within different subgroups of people or in different settings. Often, it is possible to find exactly what we need—a measurement instrument that has been demonstrated to possess the kind of reliability that we need. Even if none is quite appropriate, they can give us some beginning ideas for developing our own methods of measurement.

How do researchers estimate reliability of different indicators? What does each indicator mean? When is each of greatest concern? To understand the answers to these questions we need to examine the five basic indicators of reliability individually.

Test-Retest Reliability. An estimate of test-retest reliability (mentioned previously) requires testing the same participants twice, using the same measuring instrument to measure a variable both times, and then comparing the two pairs of measurements for each case. A correlation coefficient suggests the amount of agreement between the two sets of scores. The higher the (positive) correlation derived, the higher the reliability estimate.

Test-retest reliability tells the researcher how consistently an instrument performs at different times. A time delay may occur between the first and second measurements of the variable, or they may be scheduled immediately after each other. If a delay between measurements is to be used, it can be as great as a week or even several months. Longer delays are most often used if (1) there is reason to believe that participants' measurements of the variable do not change naturally over time, and (2) the researcher is concerned with a testing effect, that is, the extent to which participants' second measurement of the variable might be influenced by the experience of the first measurement if the two measurements occur too closely to each other.

This indicator of reliability is often an important criterion in assessing the quality of measurement in social work research and, ultimately, the quality of the research itself. For example, suppose the research entails the measurement of variables such as personality traits or certain psychiatric diagnoses, variables that should not change over a reasonably short period of time. Unless their measurement can be demonstrated to have test-retest reliability, any findings about the relationship between them or between them and other variables such as success in treatment, length of treatment, and so forth will have little credibility. The lack of evidence of test-retest reliability would suggest that people may not have been accurately categorized in the first place.

Parallel Forms Reliability.   An estimate of parallel forms reliability (also called "alternate forms reliability" or "equivalent forms reliability") involves the administration of two forms of the same test to the same participants. They are administered with or without a delay between administrations. If the scores on the two forms of the same test are identical or nearly identical, parallel forms reliability has been demonstrated.

Parallel forms of a test are available for many standardized achievement and knowledge measures (for example, IQ tests, SATs, or GREs) as well as for tests designed to measure many attitudes or perceptions. They have been developed so that, no matter which form (variation) of the test a person completes, the score should be about the same. In theory, a student also can take one form of a test such as an SAT, and the persons sitting to the right and left could have different forms of the same test. None of the three would have an advantage over the others; their respective scores would provide accurate measurements of the variable.

When parallel forms of a measurement instrument are used, proof of their statistical equivalence is generally expected. This is accomplished by demonstrating that the different forms produce measurements that are comparable. For example, the researcher might report that the different forms all produce distributions of scores that have the same or very similar means (averages) and the same amount of variability.

While a demonstration of parallel forms reliability is very important to people who develop and market standardized tests that require different forms of the same test, it is usually of less concern to social work researchers. However, it can be important. Suppose a social worker is conducting longitudinal research to attempt to learn when and under what conditions changes occur in clients in an intensive anger management treatment program. He or she might need to measure anger management skills of clients on a weekly basis. To use the same instrument for measuring the variable each week might be problematic. Clients would eventually learn the "best" or socially desirable answers from being asked the same questions every week and possibly discussing them with other clients or family members. However, if different forms of the instrument (perhaps containing different but similar scenarios) could be found or developed, the problem might be avoided. Parallel forms reliability would become important. Unless it could be demonstrated to exist, the measurement of the variable would be suspect. The use of the different forms (not the intervention) may have produced any apparent "change."

Split Half Reliability.   An estimate of split half reliability entails dividing a single measurement instrument into two equal parts and correlating the score on one half with the score on the other. The two halves may be derived by, for example, placing the even-numbered items in one group and the odd-numbered items in a second group. The reliability estimate derived from using the split half method is really an estimate of the internal consistency of the measure, that is, the degree to which half of the measurements within an instrument are correlated with the other half. It can suggest the degree to which the instrument provides a consistent measurement of the variable, but it does not provide an estimate of its consistency over time. Split half reliability estimates have been popular in the past, primarily because of the simplicity of their calculation. They are quickly and easily calculated by hand.

Professors who develop short answer tests designed to measure knowledge of some subject are often interested in an estimate of split half reliability. It can suggest the degree to which the test is consistent in its level of difficulty. If individual students' scores on one half of the test are about the same as their scores on the other half, split half reliability is high; if they vary considerably, it is low.

In social work research, this indicator of reliability is most likely to be a concern if a variable being measured is the research participants' level of knowledge of some kind and the researcher wants the indicators of it to reflect equal difficulty. We might, for example, wish to measure social workers' knowledge of child abuse reporting laws by developing and administering a test to our research participants. It might consist of a series of forty true/false statements about current laws. The number of correct answers (out of forty) would be the participant's score. After administering the test, we could then determine its split half reliability by comparing the number of correct responses for even numbered statements for each social worker with his or her number of correct answers for odd numbered statements. If the estimate of split half reliability is high and positive, this would suggest that the level of difficulty of the test items was consistent throughout the test. If it is not, the level of difficulty of items may vary too much to use them as intended.

An even better (more accurate) estimate of this indicator of reliability could be achieved using the related method that we will describe next. While mathematically much more complicated than the split half method, this is no longer a major concern now that computers are so readily available to do the work for us.

Coefficient Alpha.   If a measurement instrument can be split in half, it also can be further subdivided into as many parts as there are contained within it. A better estimate of the overall reliability of the instrument than split half reliability may be obtained by securing the correlation between every pair of its items (answers to questions about child abuse reporting laws in the previous example). Coefficient alpha is a statistic that summarizes the results of this kind of analysis. It provides an estimate of the reliability of a measurement instrument by generating the average correlation among all pairs of items. If the results of coefficient alpha analysis are a high positive correlation coefficient, responses to individual items or questions have been found to be highly correlated with each other. Most personal computers have a statistical software package that can perform this operation.

Some measurement instruments are designed to be multidimensional in nature—for example, occupational inventories or tests that measure different aspects or dimensions of personality, each with its own subscale. For these instruments, it would not be appropriate to estimate reliability by using a measure of internal consistency such as coefficient alpha or split half reliability. One would expect to get a low correlation coefficient if they were used. Some other method of reliability estimation (such as the test-retest method) might be more appropriate, or each subscale could be treated as a separate variable using coefficient alpha or split half reliability.

Interobserver Agreement.   When more than one person makes observations or reviews data such as videotapes, another method of assessing reliability can provide an estimate of the reliability of the measurement process. Interobserver agreement can estimate the degree to which two or more researchers agree in their measurements of a variable. As is true with other estimates of reliability, the higher the positive correlation between the measurements of two observers or interviewers, the greater the indication of consistency in measurement.

When is interobserver agreement considered to be important to the quality of a research study? Traditionally, it has been more important in quantitative research than in more qualitative studies. That makes sense because findings about the relationship between variables are worthless unless the variables were measured in a way that provides consistent measurements. But reliability is important for qualitative measurement as well. For example, a study using grounded theory (Chapter 8) may entail videotaping of in-depth interviews with research participants who recently experienced some event. Then two or more judges can review the tapes and record how they think each participant experienced the event. An estimate of the reliability of their measurements can be calculated (a correlation coefficient) using methods to estimate interobserver agreement.

Which indicator of reliability is most important? It depends primarily on what variable is being measured, how it is measured, and how the measurement is to be used. Test-retest reliability might be desirable in many studies (especially quantitative ones), but estimating it may not be practical. For example, it may be too costly or too big an imposition on research participants to ask that they allow the same variable to be measured twice using the same method of measurement. Demonstration of parallel forms of reliability would be important and relevant (and possible) only in research that uses equivalent forms of the same measurement instrument. Split half reliability and coefficient alpha would be important for measurement of knowledge or attitudes where internal consistency of measurement is desirable. We might expect some demonstration of either or both if a new test or measurement instrument were being used. Interobserver agreement would be relevant and important when more than one interviewer or observer is used to collect data. We would want to know whether those collecting the data were comparably sensitized to the same behaviors or phenomena and whether they were recording their observations in the same ways.

Researchers may improve the overall reliability of measurement instruments by attending to a variety of factors. They include

- *Standardizing environmental factors during measurement.* Many factors besides the measurement instrument used can negatively affect consistency of measurement of variables. When conducting cross-sectional research, data should be collected in similar settings, at similar times, and in similar ways from all participants. In longitudinal studies, all measurements of the same variable should be conducted in similar settings.
- *Conducting a pilot study of the instrument.* In addition to its other uses (discussed in Chapter 11), the process of pilot testing a measurement instrument with a few individuals who are similar to the research participants can help to make measurement more reliable. For example, if a previously developed measurement instrument is to be used, pilot testing it can either confirm or refute the researcher's belief that the instrument is reliable when used with different research participants than those on whom it was developed. If indicated, another measurement instrument can be substituted or revisions in areas that appear to be unreliable can be made. Then the instrument can be pilot-tested again to see if problems have been corrected.
- *Increasing the number of items on a test or measurement instrument.* In general, for unidimensional measures (those measuring just one variable), adding items will improve the reliability estimate. This occurs because coefficient alpha is a function

of both the average correlation among items and the number of items on a test or other instrument. Even for instruments that are not unidimensional, adding additional, clear items can sometimes help to improve the reliability of measurement of the subscales that they contain.

Validity

When evaluating measurement, *validity* refers to "the degree of fit between a construct and indicators of it." Just so we are on the same page, a definition of a construct might be useful here. A *construct* is something that is not tangible; it cannot be observed directly. It develops through a cognitive process, exists within human brains, and is defined by established theories. A construct might be an ability, a skill, an attribute, or (frequently in social work research) a problem or deficiency in one of these areas. As we shall see, it can also be a method of intervention or a social program.

The presence of reliability is required for a measurement to be valid. But, as emphasized in Box 10.1, reliability is not in itself sufficient to guarantee that a measurement is valid. For example, a measurement instrument may claim to measure assertiveness among people. It may produce consistent results (reliability). But it may, in fact, be measuring aggressiveness or anger, not assertiveness. A valid measurement is both reliable and unbiased; that is, it contains no source of systematic distortion.

A commonly used example of a measurement that is reliable (consistent) but lacking in validity is a 36-inch cloth tape measure that has gotten wet and has shrunk by 2 inches, or a wooden yardstick that has had a 2-inch section (the first 2 inches) broken off. If the researcher were to measure a 34-inch-long table, either instrument would conclude that the table is 36 inches long. If the instruments were to be used to measure the table a month, a year, or ten years later (assuming no further change in the instruments or the table had occurred), they would again suggest that the table is 36 inches long. Other researchers could measure the table with the same instruments and arrive at the same conclusion about its length. It could be measured anywhere and under a variety of conditions, but the result of measurement would be the same—the table would appear to be 36 inches long.

The fact that multiple measurements produce the same results would suggest reliability (consistency), but the measurement would lack validity. The table would be 34 inches long and not 36 inches, despite what the measurements would suggest. Systematic distortion of the measures in the form of shrinkage and breakage served to make the instruments incapable of producing a true measurement of the table's length. Only the elimination of the bias (the use of a 36-inch-long measuring instrument) would create a valid measurement.

Validity, like reliability, is not an all-or-nothing proposition. Validity often is a matter of degree. The researcher must be convinced (and be able to convince others) that a measurement possesses enough validity to produce an acceptable measurement of key variables within a given study.

Sometimes it takes a long time before it is concluded that an instrument measures what it claims to measure. For example, the SAT examination was long held to provide a valid measurement of scholastic aptitude. Critics asserted that although it provided a reliable assessment of "something" (some said scholastic achievement), it was not a scholastic aptitude measure. Not until the 1990s was the test's name changed to reflect this position.

An instrument is said to be valid for a given use when data has been compiled and presented that provides evidence for its validity. Thus, the burden of proof is on the researcher to show that an instrument may be appropriately used in a given study to measure something.

Evidence of the validity of a measuring instrument is developed in relation to its purpose. Instruments can be categorized as serving one or more of three purposes:

1. To measure achievement in a content area. Tests of knowledge (examinations) have this purpose.
2. To predict performance in regard to some criterion. Examples would be aptitude tests or tests used to screen for admission into an educational program.
3. To provide a measure of a construct to learn if it relates to some other construct. Attitude scales or diagnostic instruments would be examples of instruments used for this purpose.

As with reliability, there are certain criteria that are commonly employed to provide an estimate of validity. They are content validity, criterion validity, and construct validity. They correspond roughly to the three purposes of measurement instruments.

Content Validity.   Content validity involves an assessment of whether a measurement adequately covers all aspects or components of a particular body of content. It also involves a determination as to whether irrelevant or inappropriate content is present in the measurement. Content validity is the indicator of validity that is of special concern to the researcher when the purpose of a measuring instrument is to measure participants' learning or achievement in some content area. For example, to measure what participants learned in a workshop, seminar, or training session, tests need to be content-validated.

Tests of knowledge that are believed to possess content validity pose questions that measure what was actually covered in a course, training session, or other curriculum package. They do not ask questions that do not relate to the curriculum's content. For example, an item on a test on this chapter that tested the reader's understanding of reliability in the context of measurement probably could be assumed to possess content validity; one that asked the names of the authors of this text (an old favorite among some professors) or one that required knowledge about content in Chapter 11 or about world history would not.

Tests are generally judged to be content valid based on how they were developed. Content validity is achieved by defining a hypothetical domain (or universe) of test items. Items then are randomly selected so that they are believed to be representative of the domain. Researchers may not actually develop a hypothetical domain of test items (sometimes called a "test bank"). They simply define each content area, identify its major categories, and then write items that correspond to the various categories or facets of the content area. This process is known as constructing a blueprint of the measure. When this is done carefully, it improves the likelihood that the measure will be content valid. Researchers reporting on the content validity of a measure are expected to describe the procedures used in instrument development that support their claim of content validity.

The use of content experts is also extremely helpful in providing evidence of the content validity of an instrument. They may be used to help define the content area so that a useful blueprint will emerge. In addition, content experts might be asked to evaluate a draft of the instrument to assess the usefulness of specific test items. Or they may be used to examine the completed instrument to state how content valid the test appears to be. In truth, this assessment really does not provide hard evidence of the content validity of the test. What it provides is information about the *face validity* of the measure, that is, that the test looks valid on the face (or surface).

Criterion Validity.   Evidence of criterion validity is important when the purpose of an instrument is to predict behavior or to measure some characteristic of research participants. Evidence of criterion validity is achieved by demonstrating that scores on the measuring instrument are consistent with some other accepted indicator of the same variable. The second indicator (which may or may not be a standardized measurement instrument per se) is known as the criterion. As with reliability, evidence of criterion validity usually is presented statistically as a correlation coefficient.

There are two subcategories of criterion validity: concurrent validity and predictive validity. *Concurrent validity* is demonstrated by producing a high positive correlation between two measures—the measurement instrument and the criterion—both of which are made at approximately the same time. For example, one might correlate scores on a newly developed measurement of student test anxiety with scores on some other well accepted measure of anxiety. If the new measure has concurrent validity, statistical correlation with the older measurement instrument should be high and positive. Or, a researcher who has developed an instrument presumed to measure charisma might demonstrate its concurrent validity by pilot-testing it with two groups: people generally acknowledged to possess charisma and those who are believed to lack it. If the instrument has concurrent validity, the first group should receive high scores, whereas the latter group should receive low measurements of the variable.

Predictive validity provides evidence of the correlation between a measure and some future performance or behavior (the criterion). To develop evidence of predictive validity, follow-up data are gathered. For example, newly developed screening inventories to predict abusive behaviors might be correlated with the results of follow-up studies of research participants who completed the inventories to determine just how well the instruments were able to predict abusive behaviors.

One example of the concept of predictive validity that is well known to students is the use of standardized tests such as SATs or GREs to predict how students will perform in college or in graduate school. The measure of how students actually perform in school is the criterion. Educational researchers interested in providing evidence of criterion validity for standardized tests would attempt to demonstrate a high correlation between scores attained by students on these tests and their later performance in school (usually as measured by grade point average or some similar indicator of academic success).

Construct Validity.   As we noted earlier, validity in measurement refers to the degree of fit between a construct and indicators of it. Then, isn't construct validity what validity is all about? Yes, in fact, it is. In some ways it might be accurate to describe the other indicators of validity (content, criterion, and even face validity) as just different facets or subelements of construct validity.

Many of the variables that we seek to measure in social work research are really constructs. Psychiatric diagnostic categories are constructs. For example, anorexia nervosa, bipolar disorder, ADHD, and schizophrenia are constructs. Their presence is inferred when certain conditions exist. For example, schizophrenia is said to exist only when a certain group of symptoms or behaviors is identified as present (certain thought disorders, inappropriate affect, and so forth). So are many other problems that we seek to address, such as unemployment, codependency, substance abuse, family violence, homelessness, and so forth. In many social work research studies—especially in single-system research (Chapter 14) and in program evaluations (Chapter 13)—these problems are usually the dependent variable, the condition that we seek to alleviate or otherwise positively influence through our interventions. Some type of intervention (that is, an individual service or social program) is what we hope will alleviate or positively influence them. Thus, the presence or absence of the intervention is often the independent variable. These interventions might be, for example, community empowerment, behavior modification, feminist therapy, supportive treatment, confrontation, reality therapy, and so forth. It is important to note that each of these interventions (the independent variable) is also a construct. So are the designs of programs, which are often articulated in their logic models (Chapter 13).

Construct validity requires that all variables are measured accurately. Thus, the construct that is the independent variable in many social work research studies (the intervention or its absence) must also be understood, explained, and appropriate indicators must be used to determine the degree to which it exists or does not exist. Why is this important for producing accurate and useful research findings? Suppose that a research study attempts to learn whether a new recreational program whose outcome objective was to reduce youth gang activity in a community was successful. Obviously, we would have to find a way to accurately operationalize and measure the variable "level of youth gang activity" (the dependent variable) in the community, perhaps before and after implementation of the program. However, before we could conclude whether the proposed program was effective in achieving its objective, we would also have to use appropriate indicators to learn if the program that was implemented was really the program that was supposed to be implemented, that is, it remained true to its original design. Our measurement will lack construct validity unless we do this, and any conclusions drawn from the research will be unlikely to be valid. Suppose we did not do this (provide a valid measurement of the independent variable) and the program that was actually implemented drifted considerably from its original model (a fairly common occurrence). If youth gang activity declined following the onset of the program, we might erroneously conclude that the program (as originally conceptualized) was successful in reducing gang activity (a cause–effect relationship) and should thus be implemented in other communities. This conclusion would not be a valid one, since it was really a different program that may have produced changes in the dependent variable. What's more, our research would also lack *conclusion validity*, that is, the conclusion that the program that was designed and the level of gang activity are even related at all would be erroneous, because one of them wasn't even present.

If an instrument is to provide a valid measurement of a construct, it must measure the essential components of the construct. Thus, if a researcher designed a data collection instrument to classify participants as homeless or not homeless, the instrument should include all items that cover all indicators of the construct of homelessness. If, for example, the instrument provides no indication of whether the participant has a permanent address accessible through the Post Office, that would suggest that the instrument is probably lacking in construct validity. Similarly, if the independent variable is the use or nonuse of a specific intervention such as a new program designed to reduce homelessness, construct validity would require that the researcher ensure that the program that was evaluated is really the one described in its design.

There is no simple, direct way to assess the degree of construct validity that is present. It is assessed by accumulating a variety of evidence, usually in the form of the other indicators of validity. This involves the use of several related types of information. Construct validity demonstrates that the construct being measured exists within a theoretical framework, thereby explaining the construct itself and how it relates to other variables. In a sense, a test of construct validity becomes both a measure of the construct and a test of its underlying theory.

Concurrent validity data can help to provide evidence of the construct validity of an instrument. For example, the researcher in the previous example could determine if people who have been classified as homeless by The Salvation Army also are classified as homeless using the current measurement instrument. If the instrument shows a pattern of relationships with criterion measures (classifications that agree with the Salvation Army classification), then there is some evidence of construct validity. Face validity— for example, the fact that it is just logical to conclude that a person living in his car is probably homeless—could also help to support claims of construct validity.

What about the measurement of the independent variable? How would we demonstrate the construct validity of its measurement? Suppose the logic model for the program to address the problem of homelessness contains services such as job training or substance abuse counseling. Concurrent validity data could be used to see if the method of classifying these services by the researcher are the same as or similar to those offered in other programs that claimed to offer job training or substance abuse counseling. Face validity might be implied in the fact that a measurement instrument was used to determine if participants in the program were given instruction in how to prepare a job application form or how to dress for a job interview.

There is another way in which support for construct validity can be demonstrated using concurrent validity. If the conceptualization of a variable leads a researcher to the expectation that two groups should differ on their measurements of the construct (for example, people classified as homeless and those classified as not homeless), then this expectation of difference can be tested. If people in the two classifications are different in important ways (as we would expect), then most likely the test really measures the construct and hence demonstrates construct validity.

Sources of Measurement Error

The validity of measurement in a research study can be negatively affected in many ways. When it is affected, this is described as measurement error. In discussing reliability earlier in this chapter, we noted that virtually all methods of measurement and measurement instruments have their limits. For example, a measurement instrument may be considered reliable for measuring some variable with males, but not with females. That may be because the data used to construct it was collected from only males and it is believed that females differ in some ways that relate to the variable. Caution should always be exercised when instruments are to be used with research participants who are different in important ways from groups with whom the existing instruments were developed and "normed." Before using an existing measurement instrument, social work researchers need to be familiar with how and on which population group(s) the measurement was constructed. It should never be assumed that established norms and benchmarks on which scoring is based apply uniformly to all participants across all settings and cultural contexts. When conducting cross-cultural research (Chapter 8), efforts should be made to find instruments normed on a variety of cultural groups or nationalities, or to look for instruments developed in a variety of cultural contexts that attempt to measure the same underlying construct. Such instruments are difficult to find. A few examples of instruments designed for and/or normed on specific ethnic and racial groups are:

- The Acculturation Rating Scale for Mexican Americans (ARSMA-II) by Cuellar, Arnold, and Maldoned (1995), which measures degree of acculturation for normal and clinical populations of Mexican Americans.
- The Hispanic Stress Inventory by Cervantes, Padilla, and Salgado de Snyder (1990), which measures psychological stress in immigrants from Latin America and in Mexican Americans.
- TEMAS (Tell-Me-a-Story) by Constantino, Malgady, and Rogler (1988), which is a thematic apperception test developed for African American and Hispanic children.
- The Cultural Congruity Scale (CCS), (1996), by Gloria and Robinson-Kurpins.

Special concerns about the preservation of reliability and validity arise when instruments are translated from one language to another for use with linguistically diverse study populations. The nonequivalence of research instruments can limit the usefulness of data obtained in cross-cultural research. Many authors suggest ways to increase the likelihood that both the reliability and validity of a measurement instrument will be maintained throughout the translation process. Below are five such suggestions:

1. Attempt to understand one's own values and cultural perspectives and how they might influence the researcher's definitions of key constructs that the instrument is designed to measure.
2. Consult with members of the group of interest to determine the cultural relevance of constructs of interest within the target population and to assess the face validity of the instrument items for measuring constructs of interest in that culture.
3. Translate the instrument from the first language to the second language, using skilled, bilingually fluent translators working individually, sequentially, or as a team. (The translators should be aware of idiomatic subtleties related to geography or social class.)
4. Translate the instrument from the second language back into the first language, using skilled translators. The back-translation should then be compared to the original version to determine the accuracy of the original translation.
5. Field-test the translated instrument using bilingual participants, in order to establish equivalence through parallel forms reliability coefficients.

What we have just described is a way to avoid something called cultural bias, a form of *systematic measurement error* often seen in cross-cultural research. However, systematic measurement error can easily occur within research in one's own culture as well. When measurement lacks construct validity, it will almost certainly occur. We might, for example, believe that we are measuring a construct such as clinical depression, but if the only questions we ask relate to physical symptoms, we may really be measuring our research participants' health status instead. Or, if we asked participants how they would respond in a crisis situation such as a hurricane or flood, they might respond very differently than if we actually observed how they reacted in such a situation. If we used their response as indicators of how they would act, we would commit measurement error. Similarly, if we asked a group of social workers how they plan to vote in an upcoming election, they might be likely to say they would vote for candidates who are endorsed by NASW, yet many might do just the opposite when they got to the polls. Their responses would reflect what they think they should say (known as *social desirability bias*)—if we used them as an indicator of what they will do, we would again have systematic measurement error. Even the wording of questions (Chapter 7) can result in systematic measurement if we, for example, word a question in such a way that virtually no one (or virtually everyone) would have to answer in a certain way.

Not all measurement errors are systematic and relatively easy to detect. There is also something called *random measurement error*, error that does not occur in any identifiable pattern or direction. If data are collected in a group setting, distractions such as cell phones ringing or the fact that the session is videorecorded may affect some peoples' responses to questions, but not others. The problem is we have no way of knowing who was affected and who wasn't. Or, some people may just be tired and quit reading the items in a mailed survey after a while. They complete the survey, just putting anything down to get finished. However, we will not know when this happened or with whom.

We have mentioned just a few ways that measurement error can occur— there are many more. In advanced books on research methodology, many of them have specific labels. As the reader has probably concluded, totally reliable and valid measurement may be unattainable. However, that does not relieve us of responsibility to do the best we can to attempt to achieve it.

Summary

Chapter 10 presented the concepts basic to measurement of variables. Two early tasks of the measurement process were identified: conceptualization and operationalization. Other measurement tasks of the researcher involve deciding just how precisely a variable can or should be measured and determining the level of measurement that was produced. The four levels of measurement (nominal, ordinal, interval, and ratio) were differentiated.

The criteria used to evaluate the quality of measurement were discussed. Reliability relates to the degree to which a measurement produces consistent results. Validity refers to the degree to which a measurement is successful in actually measuring what it has claimed to measure, that is, the construct that underlies a variable. A measurement that is valid is reliable, and it is also unbiased. Methods that researchers may use to estimate the reliability and the validity of a measurement instrument were described. Their relative importance for different types of measurement and for different research objectives were identified and discussed. We emphasized the point that, if research findings

BOX 10.2   Different Uses of the Word *Validity* in Research

Type of Validity	Research Activity	Question(s) Addressed
Internal validity	Research Design	If a relationship between variables was found, is it a causal one? Can I be certain that something else did not produce the measurements of the dependent variable?
External validity	Sampling	To what extent can I generalize the research findings beyond the research sample(s) in the current study?
Construct validity	Measurement	How well did I measure the variables/constructs that I claim to have measured?
Conclusion validity	Data analysis	Were the research conclusions correct? If hypotheses were tested, was an error made in determining whether or not there was found to be support for them?

are to be accurate, the measurement of all variables (independent as well as the dependent ones) must reflect construct validity. Finally, we examined a few ways in which reliability and validity of measurement may be influenced by cultural differences and other sources of measurement error.

Some familiar words (for example, value, reliability, normal, regression, power) have a specific meaning in research and statistics, a different meaning than they have in common speech or in social work practice. Sometimes the same word even has different meanings within different research contexts. This can be especially confusing. In this chapter, we used one word, validity, which we have used before in this book. Box 10.2 should be helpful for clearing up any confusion that this may have caused.

For Discussion

1. What are some different ways that we could define operationally the following: class participation; friendliness, ageism, homophobia, intellectual curiosity, cooperation?
2. How might cultural differences influence our ability to measure accurately the constructs in question 1?
3. Suppose you wished to measure the discipline practices of research participants who are parents of young children. How could you measure the construct (discipline practices) so that the data produced is nominal level? Ordinal level? Interval level? Ratio level?
4. If a person retakes a standardized test such as the SAT or a state licensure examination, why is it that his or her scores on both tests are usually very similar? If scores on the second test are much higher or much lower than those on the first test, does this mean that the test lacks reliability? What other factors may have caused the discrepancy?
5. How would the training of researchers who will be simultaneously observing human behavior help to increase interobserver agreement? Why would a finding of low interobserver agreement suggest that training was inadequate?

6. "Reliability is a necessary but insufficient proof of validity." What does that statement mean?

7. What (besides the author of the textbook) do teachers and professors sometimes ask on tests that may suggest that the test lacks content validity? Would the questions in the For Discussion section at the end of each chapter of this book be expected to have less content validity than a test that would determine your grade? Why or why not?

8. Do you think that the personal references or autobiographical statements often required as part of an application for admission to a BSW or an MSW program would have good predictive validity? Why, or why not? How could we find out?

9. If we developed a test to measure "business instincts," how could we estimate its concurrent validity? How could we measure its predictive validity? Would one be more important than the other? If so, why?

10. If we developed a data collection instrument to measure test anxiety among social work students, why would its construct validity be important? How could we estimate it? Is the instrument likely to be more valid for measuring the construct among some students than among others?

Endnotes

1. Rubin, A., & Babbie, E. (2005). *Research methods for social work*, 5th ed. Pacific Grove, CA: Brooks Cole, 146–147.
2. Neuman, W. L. (1997). *Social research methods: Qualitative and quantitative approaches*, 3rd ed. Boston: Allyn and Bacon, 136.
3. Ibid, 141.
4. See, e.g., Hudson, W. (1988). *CAS: The clinical assessment system*. Tallahassee, FL: WALMYR.
5. See, e.g., Fischer, J., & Corcoran, K. (2007). *Measures for clinical practice and research*, 4th ed. New York: Oxford University Press. Or Miller, D., & Salkind, N. (2002). *Handbook of research design and social measurement* 5th ed. Newbury Park, CA: Sage Publications. Or Jordan, C., & Franklin, C. (2003). *Clinical assessment for social workers: Quantitative and qualitative methods*. Chicago: Lyceum Press.

11

DATA COLLECTION INSTRUMENTS

In Chapter 7 we discussed several unobtrusive methods for collecting data that can provide needed measurement. Sometimes the measurement has been completed by others, as when we rely on secondary analysis of sources such as crime records, census data or social agency records. Other times, we can use content analysis to answer our research questions or even to test hypotheses. While we still must do the measurement ourselves, we are able to use data such as minutes from meetings, audio- or videotapes of interviews, or some other form of recorded human communication completed by others. Systematic observation of people's behaviors is another unobtrusive way to conduct measurement. Still other methods of measurement are even less obtrusive, and are called *indirect measurement*, because they require no direct contact between a researcher and research participants. For example, we might get permission to check public recycling bins to attempt to learn which electronic items are considered obsolete or not worth repairing, or ride around with our car windows open to observe which people listen to which type of music.

Whether done unobtrusively, through the mail or by electronic means, or through face-to-face contact with research participants, researchers generally use some form of data collection instrument to record their measurements of variables and to organize their data into a more or less standard format. Data collection instruments vary widely in length, structure, and content.

As Box 11.1 suggests, data collection instruments usually consist of some combination of (1) individual items, each of which provides a measurement of a single variable, and/or (2) a group of items that together provide a measurement of a single variable. We will look at the less intricate of these—one item, one variable—first.

BOX 11.1   Components of Data Collection Instruments

1. One item; one variable
   A. Open-ended items
   B. Fixed-alternative items, simple indexes
2. Two or more items; one variable
   A. Composite indexes
   B. Scales,* for example, Likert, Thurstone, Guttman, semantic differential, and so forth

*A scale may contain subscales, each of which contains two or more items. Each subscale may measure a different variable or construct.

Fixed-Alternative and Open-Ended Items

When variables or constructs can be measured using only a single item or question,. the items may be classified as either fixed alternative or open ended. An example of a fixed-alternative (also called closed-ended) item would be:

Please indicate your current legal marital status by circling the letter of one response below:

a. Married
b. Single, never married
c. Separated
d. Divorced
e. Widowed

A slightly different form of fixed alternative item, a *simple composite index,* is sometimes used for collecting data that are a little less factual, that is, more of a subjective judgment on the part of the person providing the data. An example of a simple composite index is the following:

How would you rate your marriage overall? (Circle one number.)

Very Good		Good		Fair		Poor		Very Poor
1	2	3	4	5	6	7	8	9

Note that when using a fixed-alternative item the respondent is given a limited choice from which to select his or her response. In contrast, open-ended, less structured items are those for which participants provide their own responses in their own words. The following would be an open-ended item:

In your own words, please briefly describe your experience with marriage and your current attitudes toward it.

_____

_____

_____

Most frequently, fixed-alternative items are used in instruments when the range of responses to the item can be anticipated, that is, when the researcher is quite sure what the range of different responses will be. They are also sometimes used when the researcher simply wishes the participant to consider certain responses that the participant might otherwise fail to consider.

In contrast, open-ended items are more likely to be used when the range of responses is likely to be great and/or the researcher cannot possibly anticipate them all. A researcher may also select an open-ended item format to avoid suggesting possible responses to research participants. Open-ended items also allow the researcher to collect data in the form of direct quotations. Sometimes these can be very meaningful in presenting participants' attitudes or opinions.

It is not unusual for a researcher to develop the first draft of a data collection instrument using an open-ended item to measure a variable. After pilot-testing the instrument (discussed later in the chapter), it is observed that answers tend to fall within a small range of value categories. Consequently, a fixed-alternative item is substituted in the final draft of the instrument. Conversely, a pilot-testing of a data collection instrument that uses a fixed-alternative item to measure a variable may produce a larger number and range of responses than anticipated. Many of them may be in the "other" value category that is frequently offered as an alternative. Then the researcher may decide to revise the instrument to substitute an open-ended item to measure the variable.

Open-ended items provide a more in-depth understanding of a topic than do fixed-alternative items. They are especially useful when the purpose of an item is to secure qualitative data. However, this advantage may be offset by a number of potential disadvantages that must be considered.

- Participants are less likely to complete items that require them to write out their responses. Thus, the overall return rate may be low.
- The researcher cannot precode response categories for computer data entry because open-ended items do not presuppose the use of certain responses by participants.
- The researcher may experience difficulty in analyzing data that reflect wide variation and are not readily amenable to quantitative analysis. Although there are now data analysis software programs for analyzing qualitative data, they often are less readily available than those designed for use with quantitative data.

Composite Indexes and Scales

Although it is often possible to measure a variable such as age, gender, or marital status by asking a single fixed-alternative or open-ended item, many other variables that are constructs are not so easily measured. For example, attitudes, beliefs, and many behavioral patterns generally cannot be accurately measured by a response to a single question or item. They require that the researcher use multiple items in order to accurately measure them. The items constitute what is referred to as a *composite index* or a *scale*. In a composite index or scale, the response to each item contributes to the researcher's understanding of the participant in relation to the variable being measured. Ultimately, all the relevant responses (viewed as a whole) make it possible for the researcher to assign a value (a number) representing his or her measurement of the variable.

Composite indexes and scales (especially the latter) tend to be highly structured and highly refined. They can be used as independent data collection instruments or as one component of a larger instrument. Although composite indexes and scales both perform measurements of more complex variables, they do it in different ways.

Composite Indexes

A composite index consists of a number of items that are believed to be important indicators of the construct being measured. In general terms, the more items that participants indicate as applying to them, the greater the quantity of the construct they are presumed to possess. An example of a composite index to measure "clinical depression" might be the following:

> *Place a check mark in front of each feeling that you have experienced during the past week:*
>
> _____ *Sadness*
> _____ *Hopelessness*
> _____ *Powerlessness*
> _____ *Just not caring*
> _____ *Wanting to be alone*
> _____ *Anxiety*

A composite index requires a research participant to respond to each item in a dichotomous manner, often by simply checking or circling those items that apply (as in the above example) or by indicating "yes" or "no" for each. The number of check marks or yes answers then becomes his or her measurement of the variable. The measurement thus produced is, at best, ordinal level. Although measurement produced by composite indexes is sometimes adequate, often it is not. That is why researchers prefer to use scales.

Scales

A scale is constructed so that it addresses one or both of the following realities of measurement:

- Not all indicators of a variable or construct are equal in importance. Thus they should not carry the same weighting in the measurement of the variable.
- The degree or intensity of an indicator should also be considered. For example, the amount of agreement that a person feels with a statement or how frequently a behavior occurs should be a factor in his or her measurement of a variable or construct.

Linear or Summated Scales. A common form of scale, known as the linear or summated model, is similar to a composite index in that it allows the researcher to derive a measurement of the variable for each participant by adding up the responses to individual scale items. An example of a linear scale to measure clinical depression would be:

Indicate how often you experienced each of these symptoms by circling the appropriate number.

	Never				Often
1. Sad/down	0	1	2	3	4
2. Hopeless	0	1	2	3	4
3. Powerless	0	1	2	3	4
4. Apathetic	0	1	2	3	4
5. Withdrawn	0	1	2	3	4
6. Anxious	0	1	2	3	4

On the preceding scale, participants would be asked to circle a number for each item, and these numbers would then be totaled. Thus, the highest possible score that could be attained would be 24, and the lowest possible score would be 0. On this type of scale, lower scores are operationalized to mean a lower level of the variable being measured (clinical depression); relatively higher scores indicate a higher level of it.

Linear or summated scaling is very popular among social science researchers. Many variables (especially constructs) that social work researchers are interested in studying can be scaled using this model. It is appropriate whenever the researcher can construct multiple items that reflect comparable dimensions of the variable.

The best known type of summated scale is known as a *Likert scale*. In a Likert scale, a set of attitude items is supplied. Participants indicate their level of agreement with each item to indicate the intensity of their feelings. For example, a Likert scale might be used to measure client satisfaction with worker services.

Indicate your level of agreement with each of the items listed below by circling the appropriate number: 1 = strongly disagree; 2 = somewhat disagree; 3 = undecided; 4 = somewhat agree; 5 = strongly agree

	Strongly Agree				Strongly Disagree
1. My worker seemed prepared for sessions.	1	2	3	4	5
2. My worker was considerate of my schedule.	1	2	3	4	5
3. My worker seemed preoccupied.	1	2	3	4	5
4. My worker acted professionally.	1	2	3	4	5

	Strongly Agree				Strongly Disagree
5. My worker did not care about me as a person.	*1*	*2*	*3*	*4*	*5*
6. My worker tried to understand me.	*1*	*2*	*3*	*4*	*5*
7. My worker really wanted to help me.	*1*	*2*	*3*	*4*	*5*

Likert scales generally contain a mixture of items that are so-called positive and reversal items. *Positive items* are those where a high level of agreement with the item would reflect a high quantity of the variable being measured and where a low level of agreement with the item would reflect a low quantity of the variable (such as items 1, 2, 4, 6, and 7 in the preceding example).

Reversal items (such as items 3 and 5) are worded in such a way that a high level of agreement with the item reflects a low quantity of the variable being measured, and vice versa. In scoring reversal items, scoring is reversed; that is, responses of "strongly agree" are given a 1; "strongly disagree," a 5; and so forth.

Why do researchers include reversal items in a scale? They are included primarily to determine whether the participant has answered honestly. When reversal items are included, an individual completing the scale is less likely to determine what is being measured, gauge about where they fall in relation to the variable, and then simply circle the same number for all items. To further ensure honesty, the researcher would not want simply to alternate positive and reversal items, a pattern that could soon be identified by the participant. A random mixture of positive and reversal items allows a researcher to determine whether participants really read and carefully considered each item before responding to it. If they did, a consistent pattern of responses (reflecting a measurement of the variable) should be evident in both types of item.

In a Likert scale, all items contribute equally to the measurement of a variable. Although this characteristic makes scoring simple, it is also the scale's greatest weakness. Invariably, no matter how much time and effort has gone into the construction of a Likert scale, some items continue to reflect "more" of the variable than others or are a stronger indicator of it than other items. Yet this is not reflected in the scoring of the scale—the items are not "weighted" in any way. Thus, measurements are less precise than they might be. For this reason, Likert scales are generally considered to produce ordinal-level data, not interval-level. Nevertheless, it is common in research reports and professional journal articles to see measurements produced by a Likert scale that were treated as if they were interval-level for purposes of statistical analysis. This is a practice that is questionable at best. It can hurt the credibility of a researcher's findings. What's more, it is unnecessary. There are plenty of good statistical tests available that can be used to examine the relationship between variables when the measurements of one or both can be considered to be only ordinal-level.

Thurstone Scales.   Like linear or summated scales, Thurstone scales can be used to measure constructs such as attitudes or other personal attributes. Developing a Thurstone scale entails constructing a large number of potential items. Then judges (often people knowledgeable about scale construction and/or the construct being measured) are asked to indicate how favorable each item is toward the object of the attitude. They can rate each item between one and eleven, with one being "extremely unfavorable" and eleven being "extremely favorable." Some items will be eliminated because there is little consistency in their ratings. Based on the median (middle) rating for each remaining item it is assigned a *weighting,* a number reflecting its relative importance to measurement of the concept. The items are then placed randomly within the scale. Responses of agreement with some items "count" more or less than others. For example, a Thurstone scale might be constructed to measure the severity of behavioral problems reflected by preadolescent children. It might ask parents if their child had engaged in any one of ten behaviors during the past month. Based on the opinions of experts and a long, time-consuming series of tasks leading to its development, the scale would contain different weightings for different behaviors reflecting their severity. For example, "fought with other children" or "*refusing to obey your requests*" might get a low weighting, say, 3.7 or 2.1. In contrast, a behavior judged to be more symptomatic of serious difficulties such as "torturing animals" or "starting fires" might have a weighting of, say, 9.9 or 10.2.

In a Thurstone scale, items are placed randomly, not in the order of their weightings. There are both positive and reversal items. The weightings are known to the researcher and are used in computing the measurement of the variable, but are not included on the research instrument so that they are not available to the research participant. If the scale measures an attitude (as is frequently the case), participants are asked to indicate their level of agreement with each item (for example, strongly agree, agree, disagree, or strongly disagree). Less frequently, when the variable is a behavior as in our hypothetical example, frequency of the behavior or some other words representing gradation is added. A Thurstone scale for our example might look something like this:

During the past week, did your child engage in any of the following behaviors? (Please circle "yes" or "no.")

(Yes/No)   1. *Fighting with other children.*

(Yes/No)   2. *Intentionally destroying property.*

(Yes/No)   3. *Showing kindness toward others.*

(Yes/No)   4. *Refusing to obey your requests.*

(Yes/No)   5. *Starting fires.*

(Yes/No)   6. *Volunteering to help with chores.*

(Yes/No)   7. *Torturing animals.*

(Yes/No)   8. *Swearing or using vulgar words.*

(Yes/No)   9. *Throwing things at others.*

(Yes/No)   10. *Touching others inappropriately.*

If this were a real Thurstone scale (which it is not!), scoring would consist of adding the weighting for each item to which the respondent answered "yes," then adding up the total for all weighting. Items 3 and 6 would be "reverse scored," since they represent positive behaviors. If a parent circled a "yes" for either item, its weighting would be subtracted from the total score, that is, its weighting would be a negative number.

Thurstone scales are very timeconsuming to develop. Social work researchers rarely develop them, preferring instead to use the more easily constructed Likert-type scale. However, when existing ones can be located and used, Thurstone scales provide more precision of measurement than do Likert scales. Although, as we noted earlier, Likert scales are generally believed to produce only ordinal level measurement, Thurstone scales can approximate interval-level measurement.[1] This increases the number of options for statistical analysis of data (Chapter 12).

Gutman Scales.   A Gutman scale is developed in a way similar to the method used for constructing a Thurstone scale. A large number of items are developed. Then judges rate each item as yes or no, based on whether they perceive it as positive or negative toward the object of the measurement. Where there is major disagreement about ratings, items are discarded. Remaining items then may be revised and judged again and again (as necessary) until the remaining items can be rank-ordered to form a kind of continuum based upon the number of judges who viewed them as positive.

Ultimately, a Gutman scale contains certain rank-ordered statements. Gutman scales are what are known as *cumulative scales*, that is, they are designed so that if a respondent agrees with a statement in a list of statements, he or she should also agree with all of the previous ones. For example, suppose item number three is the highest numbered statement with which Karen agrees. Her score is a three. Then she should also have agreed with statements one and two. If the highest numbered statement that Jermaine agrees with is two, he should also have agreed with statement number one, but not statements three or four.

What might a Gutman scale look like? Suppose it were designed to measure prejudicial attitudes about TANF recipients. It might contain statements that reflect attitudes about them that range from neutral or slightly negative to very negative. Participants would be asked to check each statement with which they agree. Our hypothetical Gutman scale might look this:

Please place a check mark in front of each item with which you agree:

1. _____ *TANF recipients are content to be supported by others.*

2. _____ *TANF recipients really don't care if they have work.*

3. _____ *TANF recipients will only work when they are forced to.*

4. _____ *TANF recipients are just plain lazy.*

The process of construction of Gutman scales is very timeconsuming. It continues until consensus among judges is achieved. Because the statements above have not undergone the many stages of review and revision that frequently are required to produce a fully developed Gutman scale, the reader may disagree about the precise order of one or two of them. That is to be expected.

In the final rank-ordering of statements, different people would first register disagreement at different points. It could be assumed, for example, that if a person disagreed with a somewhat negative statement, he or she would also disagree with all of the more negative statements (and agree with all of the less negative ones). In a well-constructed Gutman scale, that is exactly what would happen.

A Gutman scale is generally believed to produce ordinal-level measurement. It and the other scales described, in this chapter can be described as *unidimensional*. What does that mean? It means that they measure just one variable (prejudice toward TANF recipients in the previous example) or even just one indicator of a variable, perhaps, beliefs about the motivation of TANF recipients. Because it is a cumulative scale, a Gutman scale has one additional feature. Remember that in our example we said that two people (Karen and Jermaine) had different degrees of prejudice toward TANF recipients. Karen's was greater than Jermaine's. Thus, Jermaine's responses were the same as Karen's, but only to a point; for example, both individuals would have placed a check mark in front of items 1 and 2. However, Karen would also have checked item 3. Because they are cumulative, Gutman scales have a unique quality—people with the same scores have the same response patterns, a different one from people with different scores. Thus, if we know a person's total score on a Gutman scale, we are able to predict with accuracy how he or she responded to individual items. This characteristic is known as *reproducibility*. It is present in the best Gutman scales and the type of scale we will discuss next, and is not characteristic of the other kinds of scales discussed earlier in this chapter.

Bogardus Social Distance Scales.   A Bogardus Social Distance scale is similar to Guttman scales in that they are both cumulative, and are developed using similar methods. However a Bogardus social distance scale measures one specific attribute of people— the degree to which they would be willing to interact with people who are different from themselves, such as people of a different ethnic group or people with a different sexual orientation. Participants review a group of rank-ordered statements, each of which describes a closer interaction with the other group than the previous one. They then indicate if they would be willing to tolerate each level of interaction. The researcher would note at what point each participant would "draw the line." The number of tolerable interactions would, with a single number, give a good indication of each participant's willingness to interact with others.

For example, if that group were a person recovering from crack addiction, the items might be something like this:

It would be OK if a person recovering from a crack addiction:

1. _____ *lived in my town.*
2. _____ *lived on my block.*
3. _____ *lived next door.*
4. _____ *became friends with one of my family members.*
5. _____ *became my son's or my daughter's best friend.*
6. _____ *dated my son or daughter.*
7. _____ *married my son or daughter.*

Semantic Differential Scales.   Likert, Thurstone, Guttman, and Bogardus Social Distance scales all measure a variable quite directly. That is fine, if the variable is not an especially personal or sensitive one. However, some variables of interest to social work researchers require us to measure them a little more indirectly. Simply to come out and ask straightforward questions might only produce politically correct or socially desirable responses, not a true measurement. Then a semantic differential scale might be appropriate. A scale of this type is characterized by the following:

- It is used to measure variables when direct questions might not produce honest answers.
- It provides an indirect measurement of the variable.
- It is "projective" and often seeks unconscious feelings or attitudes.
- Respondents are instructed to respond quickly, not think too long or look for the "right" answer.

A semantic differential scale provides a list of word opposites (for example, slow/fast, simple/complicated, old/new, and so forth). They may seem to have only a vague or indirect relevance to the construct being measured. The words may be placed on opposite ends of equal length lines. The research participant is instructed to place an X on each line to indicate his or her response in relation to the construct being measured. Alternately, numbers (for example, the numbers one through nine) may be placed between the two words at equal distances and the respondent be asked to circle one number per pair of words.

A semantic differential scale is a kind of word association game. The assumption underlying it is that, in completing it, the participant will somewhat unintentionally reveal something about himself or herself in the responses to the pairs of word opposites—often his or her true attitudes. For example, suppose that our research required us to measure two variables, attitudes toward corporal punishment and attitudes about old age among social work students. To be successful, we would have to avoid responses that reflect "attitudes that social workers *should* have." We might use two semantic differential scales that look something like these:

Attitudes about Corporal Punishment

Good	_____	*Evil*
Pleasant	_____	*Unpleasant*
Sour	_____	*Sweet*
Happy	_____	*Sad*
Healthy	_____	*Sick*
Love	_____	*Hate*
Fair	_____	*Unfair*

Attitudes about Old Age

Pleasant	_____	*Unpleasant*
Sour	_____	*Sweet*
Happy	_____	*Sad*
Healthy	_____	*Sick*
Love	_____	*Hate*
Fair	_____	*Unfair*

Like composite indexes and Likert scales, semantic differential scales do not provide very precise measurements. Thus, they produce what is generally regarded as ordinal-level data. Not surprisingly, semantic differential scales are most often designed by psychologists. After all, they are just a variation of the projective testing methods clinical psychologists often use for diagnostic purposes.

Of course, psychologists are not the only professionals to use various forms of composite indexes and scales in their professional practice. While we have focused on their use for measurement of certain variables in research, they have utility in our practice as well. Social workers are likely to encounter different forms of them, especially in clinical work with individuals, families, or groups.

Other Scales.   There are still other types of scales. While they are used less frequently in social work research than the ones described, each has its own specialized use. In addition, new methods of scaling are constantly being developed and refined.[2] As they gain acceptance, the scales that they produce are published and made available for others' use in books or in journals such as in the Instrument Development section of the journal, *Social Work Research.* Box 11.2 contains a listing of some reference volumes that contain and/or describe scales and other data collection instruments that might be appropriate for use in social work research.

Construction of Scales.   Scales generally are developed by researchers following rigorous rules and procedures. Many scales have been developed, tested, and repeatedly

BOX 11.2   References for Scales, Tests, and Other Types of Measurement Instruments

Beere, C. A. (1990). *Gender roles: A handbook of tests and measures.* New York: Greenwood Press.
Beere, C. A. (1990). *Women and women's issues: A handbook of tests and measures.* San Francisco: Jossey-Bass.
Buros, O. (1978). *Eighth mental measurements yearbook.* Highland Park, NJ: The Gryphon Press.
Corcoran, K., & Fischer, J. (1987). *Measures for clinical practice: A sourcebook.* New York: The Free Press.
Corcoran, K., & Fischer, J. (2007). *Measures for clinical practice,* 4th ed. New York: Oxford University Press.
Goldman, B. A. (1978–1995). *Directory of unpublished experimental measures,* vols. 1–6. New York: Human Sciences Press.
Hammill, D. (1992). *A consumer's guide to tests in print.* Austin, TX: Pro-Ed.
Holman, A. M. (1983). *Family assessment: Tools for understanding and intervention.* Newbury Park, CA: Sage Publications.
Hudson, W. W. (1982). *The clinical measurement package.* Homewood, IL: The Dorsey Press.
Miller, D., & Salkind, N. (2001). *Handbook of research design and social measurement,* 6th ed. Newbury Park, CA: Sage Publications.
Mitchell, J. (2001). *Mental measurements yearbook.* Lincoln, NE: University of Nebraska, Buros Institute.
Rauch, J. (1994). *Assessment: A sourcebook for social work practice.* Milwaukee: Families International Incorporated.
Touliatos, J., Perlmutter, B. F., & Straus, M. A. (1990). *Handbook of family measurement techniques.* Newbury Park, CA: Sage Publications.

revised and honed over decades. Up to this point, we have only generally described some of the methods employed in constructing the various types of scales mentioned in this chapter. However, scale building is an exact science. It is the focus of graduate courses in statistics and measurement. Only rarely would a social worker attempt to construct a new scale as part of a research study. But to gain an appreciation of the effort that goes into their construction, we will mention briefly the usual sequence of events in constructing a scale.

1. *The variable to be measured is operationally defined.* The definition should refer to all relevant indicators of the variable. A clear definition enables the researcher to write an *item pool,* a preliminary set of items (ideally, 80–100) that may be included in the scale. The item pool should be as exhaustive as possible, so that less relevant items later can be eliminated while leaving enough items to constitute the scale. The items are then reviewed by judges. Their role is to evaluate the items for clarity, relevance, appropriateness, and ease in responding. Then items should be revised as needed. A draft instrument is produced, and a pilot test of the instrument is conducted. Pilot test participants are asked to respond to the items and to provide a critique of them. They are encouraged to make comments about the items themselves, for example, which items are not clear, which contain words that they do not understand, and so on.

2. *Data from the pilot test are analyzed.* This is accomplished using a correlation statistical process known as *item analysis.* The process typically involves the calculation of two statistics by computer: item-to-total-scale correlations (for each item) and a reliability coefficient that provides a measure of the internal reliability of the scale (such as coefficient alpha). They are calculated to ensure that all of the items that are to comprise the scale are measuring the same construct and that the items, when taken together, represent the unidimensional measure that is sought.

    The item-to-total-scale analysis determines how responses to each item correlate with how participants responded overall to the scale. (It is similar to the item analysis that professors sometimes use on multiple-choice or true/false tests to eliminate bad test items—those that were missed by students who did well on the test overall and/or were answered correctly by students who did poorly.) A researcher would want to retain only items with the highest positive item-total correlations. Items with low or negative item-total correlations are usually deleted. The analysis required for item-total correlations is conducted using statistical software packages specifically designed for social science data. When this is done, a reliability estimate of the scale describes the statistical effect of deletion of individual items. This assists the researcher in deciding which scale items to keep and which ones to delete.

    Coefficient alpha, we will recall, reflects the degree to which individual items correlate with each other. Scales that are designed to measure a unidimensional construct should reflect a high degree of internal consistency. Scales that are multidimensional in nature (for example, the MMPI [Minnesota Multiphasic Personality Inventory]) would not be expected to reflect it, but their various subscales would.

3. *The scale is modified as needed.* Items are deleted or revised, often as a result of a statistical procedure known as factor analysis. If items are added at this stage, they

should be subjected to pilot testing and further statistical analysis. Once the scale is fully developed, data about the reliability and validity of it and of individual scale items are retained for reporting and for future analysis.

When a scale (or at least a portion of it) is published in a book of data collection instruments or in a professional journal, the process of its development is described, along with a description of the people who contributed data for its development. Conclusions about its reliability and validity (based on statistical analyses) as well as about their limitations are noted. For example, we might read that "The scale was found to have a test-retest reliability of .89 among a sample of Latinos under age sixty-five who reside in the United States and Canada for whom Spanish is a first language. However, its reliability among other Spanish-speaking people was only .45."

Using Existing Data Collection Instruments

The generic term *data collection instruments* is used to describe the document used to assist the researcher in acquiring necessary data and recording them. As we noted at the beginning of this chapter, data collection instruments vary widely in length, structure, and content. Some, for example, in many qualitative exploratory studies, may consist of little more than a group of topics to be covered in interviews in no particular order, or just a list of questions to be addressed. At the other extreme, perhaps in a quantitative study designed to discover if there is support for several research hypotheses, a long, carefully worded data collection instrument or a group of instruments may be used. They are likely to contain a mixture of fixed alternative items, open-ended items, and/or indices and scales.

When we discussed data collection methods in Chapter 8, we suggested that secondary analysis of data collected for some other purpose can be a real time- and effort-saver in some situations. Similarly, if it is possible to use a data measurement instrument or even part of one that was developed by another researcher, a great deal of time and effort can be saved. The process of developing new instruments often represents a major research project in and of itself. Thus, where appropriate, researchers should consider using instruments or portions of instruments that have already been developed.

In determining if an existing measurement instrument would be appropriate to use in a given research study, a number of issues need to be examined. First, the researcher needs to determine if the instrument can appropriately be used with the population of interest. Is it likely to provide reliable measurement with the researcher's participants? Measures are developed for specific uses with specific research populations. Are the proposed research participants similar enough to the participants with whom the instrument was developed and tested so that the instrument will yield reliable data? Cultural differences, especially the meaning of words within subcultures or within different ethnic groups, should be given special attention.

The question of validity requires a comparison of conceptual definitions. Before using an instrument developed as part of another study, we would want to be sure that what the instrument purports to measure is the same variable that we need to measure. In order to use an existing measure, a researcher has to (1) find one that was developed using the same (or similar) conceptual definition of the variable that needs to be measured or (2) adapt a current conceptual definition to that which was used in the development of the existing instrument. For example, a researcher interested in measuring parenting skills could try to find a measurement tool that was developed using a conceptual definition of parenting skills that is the same as the conceptual definition suggested by the researcher's review of the literature. If this proves to be impossible, it may still be possible to find a measurement tool that seems to measure most aspects of parenting skills of interest and then conceptually redefine the variable to be consistent with the conceptual definition of parenting skills used by the developer of the instrument. Fortunately, reference material regarding specific measures often includes the conceptual definition of the variable that was used by the author of the instrument.

Information about the instrument may also include how to contact the author of the measure or how to obtain it. If the instrument is copyrighted (most composite indexes and scales are), it may have to be purchased from the publisher or directly from the author. If it is not copyrighted, it can usually be used with the author's written permission. Of course, if the instrument is in the public domain, it may be used without permission of the author.

Revising Existing Data Collection Instruments

If the researcher is unable to locate an existing measure that is appropriate without revision for use in a given study, there may still be an existing instrument that, it appears, could be modified and used. For example, an instrument may be available that measures client satisfaction with services received from an out-patient mental health clinic. If the researcher is interested in measuring client satisfaction with services received within an in-patient mental health setting, it may be possible to modify the existing instrument for use. Several items may be borrowed from the instrument exactly as written and others reworded for use in the current study. This "new" instrument should then be pilot-tested with a sample of participants who are similar to the intended study group, to see if measurement problems may have been introduced by the revision.

If the research study is exploratory or if the instrument to be used is just a guideline for use by the researcher (for example, in a qualitative study in which data collection is conducted using unstructured interviews), modifications of existing instruments can be made with little concern about the effects of the changes. When these data collection methods are used, parts of different instruments may be freely borrowed and changed as deemed appropriate. There is little reason to be concerned about how a change in wording might affect the validity of measurement. Instead, an assessment of the quality of measurement is often based on the researcher's judgment of the degree of candor and truthfulness that participants seemed to display in response to its use.

In more quantitative studies that rely heavily on accurate measurement of variables in order to test hypotheses, rewording of existing instruments or changing them in any way should be undertaken with extreme caution. When using revised instruments, advice regarding the possible effects of the modifications in wording on quality of measurement may be obtained by contacting the original instrument's author. If large sections of a data collection instrument are borrowed from an existing instrument (especially if it is copyrighted), the researcher also must gain permission to use the instrument from the author or publisher. If only a few items are used, and if the original wording is substantially altered, permission is usually not necessary.

When borrowing items from an existing instrument, we should remember that assessments of its reliability and validity were based on the instrument as a whole. Thus, it would not be correct to borrow and alter items or add or delete others and then to assume that those assessments are necessarily still accurate. Composite indexes and scales are especially sensitive to revision. Adding or deleting items or changing even a word or two can threaten their capacity to provide valid measurement.

Constructing New Data Collection Instruments

If it is not possible to use an existing data collection instrument, then a new data collection instrument will have to be developed. In those more qualitative studies that rely on a data collection instrument to ensure that certain topics will be addressed but do not seek to standardize data collection methods, it is often simplest to create a new instrument from scratch, rather than to try to revise an existing one that is likely to have been developed to study some other question with some other group of research participants. The process of developing such an instrument may be relatively simple. It may consist primarily of thinking through and discussing with others what areas should be explored, within the context of an in-person interview, focus group, and so forth, as well as, perhaps, the best sequence in which to explore them.

In more quantitative studies that rely more on careful, standardized measurement of variables, construction of a new data collection instrument is an exacting and demanding task.[3] Whichever formats and methods are selected, the task requires careful attention if one is to derive measurements that are regarded as reliable and valid.

Issues in Development

There are a number of issues that should be considered in developing a new data collection instrument. They relate to its intent, formatting, and sequencing of questions, as well as to its length, clarity, wording, and presentation. Although they are most relevant to mailed or participant-completed instruments, most of them are equally relevant to data collection in which participant responses are recorded by the researcher.

Intent of Items.   One issue relates to the nature of what is being measured: Is an item or series of items designed to measure (1) knowledge, (2) attitudes or beliefs, or (3) behaviors of participants? The intent of the measurement determines the way in which a question or series of items is worded. Often when measuring complicated constructs, we require a composite index or a scale consisting of several items, or at least a series of questions. However, sometimes it is possible to measure knowledge, attitudes or beliefs, or behaviors:

> • *Can a friend call the hospital to learn your room number so that he or she can visit you (knowledge)?*
>
>   _____ *Yes* _____ *No*

- *How helpful was your social worker during your hospitalization (attitude or belief)?*
  _____ *Very helpful*
  _____ *Somewhat helpful*
  _____ *Not helpful*

- *During your hospitalization, how many times did you meet with your social worker(behavior)?*
  _____ *Never* _____ *Once or twice* _____ *Three times or more*

Of course, for reasons discussed earlier in this chapter, it is sometimes preferable to use an open-ended question to measure knowledge, attitudes or beliefs, or behaviors. Then the items might look more like this:

- *Please describe your understanding of the HIPAA laws and how they affect visitors to the hospital (knowledge).*
- *Do you think that your social worker was helpful to you during your hospitalization why or why not? (attitude or belief)?*
- *What were some of the questions that you asked your social worker (behavior)?*

Clarity of Items.   If items are not clearly understood by participants, their responses may not provide an accurate measurement of a variable. The best items generally are those that ask participants for a simple response, are unambiguous, and are phrased positively rather than negatively. People do not always notice a qualifying word in a question (for example, words such as *hardly, never, not,* or *barely*); therefore, they are best not used.

Use of Contingency Instructions.   When using self-administered data collection instruments, contingency instructions are sometimes appropriate. They are used to direct the participant through the instrument in an efficient manner (or, if it is administered by the researcher, to assist him or her). They also provide a way to reduce the number of items that participants are asked to respond to and to avoid asking participants to answer items that are not applicable to them. They reflect consideration on the part of the researcher and help to organize the data that are collected. An example of a contingency instruction is:

If you answered "yes" to question 2 above, please respond to questions 3 through 7; if you answered "no" to question 2, please skip down to question 8 on page 3.

Sequencing of Items.   In developing new instruments, there are two perspectives on sequencing of items. Some researchers prefer to begin with the most general (and least controversial or personal) items and then move to the more specific ones. General-to-specific sequencing may be preferable if the researcher has reason to believe that participants will be more comfortable with this sequence of item presentation. Placing demographic and/or less threatening items first may help to gain the trust and confidence of the participant. It also may be helpful to the researcher to have some understanding of the participants being studied prior to covering more specific items. The more personal or more threatening items can then be placed near the end of the instrument.

If the researcher is not concerned that some items in the instrument might be offensive to or otherwise alienate participants, the specific-to-general sequence may be preferable. Then the most important and the most specific (to the study) items are placed first. The more general data (often, demographic information) can be secured at the end. An advantage of this sequencing pattern is that if the instrument is not fully completed, some of the more important data will still be available to the researcher.

Instructions for Responding.   In securing useful data, especially if the instrument is to be self-administered, the wording of instructions is equally as important as the wording of the items themselves. Participants must understand how they are expected to respond to items. This seems self-evident; however, researchers frequently assume that the correct method to respond to items is as obvious to the participant as it is to them. Consequently, they fail to provide complete instructions for responding. If there are two or more distinct sections and/or question types used, separate instructions should be included directly above each section or question type.

Length of the Instrument.   The length issue is perhaps best addressed through use of common sense. As we suggested in Chapter 8, the longer the instrument, the less likely people are to complete it. The researcher needs to collect enough data to be able to answer his or her research questions and/or to test hypotheses. Necessary items must be included, but unnecessary ones should be omitted. Frequently, the length of an instrument can be reduced through the elimination of demographic items that are not relevant to the focus of the research. As we indicated in Chapter 5, there is no such thing as a "usual" or standard group of demographic variables that must be included within every instrument.

Presentation.   A self-administered data collection instrument should not appear crowded. Leaving adequate space for people to respond to items and not crowding questions helps participants to complete it. In addition, instruments should be error free. The goal is to make their completion a pleasant (or at least a nonstressful) experience, so that a high percentage of fully completed responses will be received.

Pilot-Testing.   Even though the researcher may think that all of the preceding issues have been addressed, newly developed data collection instruments almost always produce some surprises. Even very experienced researchers are not able to anticipate just how items on a data collection instrument will be perceived or interpreted by the participant, or how a participant might respond overall to the instrument. A panel of experts consisting of people very knowledgeable about instrument construction can provide good advice and suggestions. But what these individuals can contribute may be no substitute for the feedback provided by people like the research participants themselves. A pilot-testing of an instrument provides information on many different factors that relate to the quality of a data collection instrument. Feedback is likely to provide insights about the following:

- Clarity/misinterpretation of wording of items.
- Juxtaposition of items that may bias measurement.
- Potential offensiveness of items.
- Redundancy that may annoy participants.

- Indication that more structure is needed.
- Indication that less structure is needed.
- Time required to complete the instrument.

Some of the preceding feedback can be gleaned from the way that the pilot study participants complete the instrument. Some of it may require one or more additional broad questions that are not a part of the measurement instrument per se. For example, the researcher might add an extra question—What parts of the instrument were difficult for you to complete and why?—and leave space for pilot study participants to write in whatever they may choose. Another good question is: Do you feel that the instrument gave you an opportunity to represent yourself accurately and, if not, why not? Such questions reflect an awareness of the possibility that the newly developed instrument may somehow lead participants to answer in certain ways or that questions or items that should have been included as part of the measurement process may have been inadvertently omitted. A good pilot-test and the thoughtful revisions that it generates can result in fewer problems and better measurement when data are subsequently collected from research participants.

There is an ethical issue that often comes up when using people as participants in the pilot-testing of a data collection instrument. If no additional questions are added to the proposed instrument (that is usually a "giveaway"), participants might not be aware that they are not "real participants" unless they are told so. Should they be told why they are being asked to complete the data collection instrument or be allowed to misunderstand their role? Not to tell them seems dishonest and deceptive, but to tell them may influence the seriousness with which they approach the task. Besides, in many instances, the pilot test includes giving participants the same introduction or cover letter that will be given to other participants, in order to see how effective it is. And that is almost certain to mislead them. Sometimes the data that pilot study participants provide can be aggregated along with that of other participants, thus avoiding the issue. But in other situations, the researcher must decide the most ethical way to approach it. It may entail telling participants in general terms what their role is, stressing the importance of their unique contribution to the research effort, and asking them if they still wish to participate in it.

Use of Self-Administered Data Collection Instruments

The issues that we have discussed have related most directly to data collection instruments that are self-administered, that is, they are completed without the presence of the researcher. Self-administered data collection instruments are commonly associated with the survey (discussed earlier in Chapter 8). In surveys, the researcher generally is interested in aggregating data about the characteristics, behaviors, feelings, attitudes, or opinions of a given population. The term *questionnaire* is widely applied to self-administered instruments when they are used in surveys.

Other types of knowledge building (besides surveys) also use self-administered instruments. They are used to collect data for all levels of research. Social work practitioners also use them to secure a measurement of some aspect of client functioning in their practice. For example, a clinician may wish to get an objective measure of the level of clinical depression that clients are experiencing and may either find or develop a data collection instrument that clients can complete without any in-person instructions or supervision.

Advantages

Because they are highly structured, self-administered instruments have several advantages. They include the following:

- *Presence of the researcher is not required.* Once the instruments have been developed and distributed, the researcher is free to work on other research tasks while awaiting their return.
- *Responses and response categories can be precoded.* Analysis of the data is greatly facilitated when the researcher collects data that are presorted into computer-ready categories.
- *Data can be collected using fixed stimuli.* All participants are asked to respond to the same questions, worded in the same way. Thus, at least one aspect of data collection is standardized. This is especially important in quantitative studies.
- *There is the perception of anonymity.* Even though instruments may be precoded with identifying information, generally participants do not write their names anywhere on them. The appearance of anonymity (if not the reality of it) is thus maintained. This may increase participants' willingness to provide data. Most research that uses questionnaires for data collection reports data in aggregate form, at least enhancing confidentiality of responses. Participants can be reasonably confident that their individual responses cannot be attributed to them. This is an advantage to the researcher, both for securing truthful information and for increasing the likelihood of a larger percentage of completed questionnaires.

Supervised Administration

A major reason for supervising data collection either individually or in a group situation is a high rate of completion. If the researcher is present and distributes and collects the data collection instrument from participants, more fully completed instruments will be received than if the instrument were mailed out.

There are sometimes other reasons researchers wish to be present during data collection, for example, to clarify the intention of items or to observe whether the instruments were completed conscientiously or in a haphazard way. This latter determination would be impossible if a mailed questionnaire were used.

Supervised individual completion of instruments (perhaps in the research participant's home, office, or some neutral site—whatever is most convenient) can produce a high completion rate. But if comparisons of participants and their responses or hypothesis testing is part of the research design (as in most quantitative research), individualized data arrangements may not be desirable. Then the same setting should be used for data collection with all research participants. This ensures that the setting of data collection will not be a potentially confounding variable.

A useful alternative to the one-on-one, supervised method of data collection is instrument completion in a group setting. For example, the researcher might supervise the completion of an instrument by all members of a focus group or by all participants in a social program. Or a group consisting of the research sample might be constituted specifically for the purpose of data collection. When group supervision of data collection is used, instruments are distributed, participants complete them at their own pace or within a prescribed time limit, and they are collected. The researcher is available for clarification and to address questions related to the data collection instrument.

The major benefit of this kind of administration is efficiency—a large amount of data can be collected in a relatively short amount of time. Its relatively low cost and high rate of return are advantages that the researcher should consider when selecting a data-gathering method. However, like individually supervised completion of data collection instruments, the researcher's presence can have the potential to influence the data received. In addition, responses may be influenced by the reactions (for example, anger, embarrassment, boredom) of others in the room.

Summary

In this chapter, we looked at data collection instruments as tools for use in data collection. Some variables and constructs can be measured with a single item or question. It can be either a fixed-alternative or open-ended item, depending on the specific data needs of the researcher. We discussed the use of other instruments that require many items to measure complex variables: composite indexes and scales. An overview of the most common types of scales was presented. Construction of scales was described as a highly complex process; it generally is beyond the scope of a social work research study.

The pros and cons of the use of existing data collection instruments or of modifying those of others were discussed. We examined many of the issues that are addressed in constructing new instruments. Finally, the option of individual or group-supervised completion of data collection instruments (as opposed to self-administered ones) was discussed. Group administration is more cost-efficient than individual supervised data collection, but when using either method, the researcher's presence can have the effect of biasing data that are collected.

For Discussion

1. What are the advantages and disadvantages of using a fixed-alternative item to measure a variable such as "reason for choosing a career in social work"? Do you think an open-ended item would be better?
2. What is the greatest weakness of composite indexes? Why are they more likely to be used to measure behaviors than attitudes?

3. What would be the advantages and disadvantages of having an even number of response possibilities (for example, strongly agree, agree, disagree, strongly disagree) as opposed to an odd number (for example, strongly agree, agree, not sure, disagree, strongly disagree) in a linear scale?

4. Why do you think social workers so frequently use Likert scales in their research?

5. Why do you think Thurstone scales are generally believed to produce more accurate measurements of variables than the other types of scales described in this chapter?

6. Construct some statements that reflect attitudes toward people who are HIVpositive. If we were constructing a Guttman scale, what might be the proper rank-ordering of them?

7. How could a Bogardus Social Distance scale be used to better understand homophobia or ageism among social work students?

8. Would a semantic differential scale be better than a Bogardus Social Distance scale for measuring homophobia or ageism among social work students? Why or why not?

9. Suppose we find a good scale that has been developed to measure attitudes about people who have committed rape. Can we simply substitute the word "date rape" for "rape" every time that it occurs in the scale and use it in our study of date rape? Why or why not?

10. Suppose we wanted to use a "panel of experts" to pilot-test a new data collection instrument to be given to high school students. It is designed to learn the prevalence of "wannarexia," the phenomenon in which healthy adolescents envy people with anorexia and deliberately engage in the same behaviors to attempt to lose weight. Who might we choose for our pilot test?

Endnotes

1. Miller, D. (1991). *Handbook of research and social measurement.* Newbury Park: Sage Publications, 176.

2. See, for example, Hodge, D., & Gillespie, D. (2003). Phrase completions: An alternative to Likert scales. *Social Work Research 27,* (1), 45–55.

3. See, for example, Nunnally, J., & Bernstein, I. (1994). *Psychometric theory.* New York: McGraw-Hill.

12

ANALYZING DATA
AND DISSEMINATING
RESEARCH FINDINGS

Data can take many forms. For example, in more qualitative studies they may take the form of audiotapes or videotapes of interviews, or field notes of interaction with participants. In secondary analysis, they may be completed data collection schedules compiled from case records or some other source. In meta-analysis, they may be the reports of many studies that examined a similar problem or question. Or, when a mailed survey method of data collection was used, they may consist of a stack of completed questionnaires.

No matter what form data assume, they must be organized, summarized, and analyzed, often with the help of computer-assisted statistical analysis. Generally, we associate statistical analysis of data with more quantitative research methods. However, methods for statistical analysis of qualitative findings have also been developed. A number of software packages are now available to assist researchers in the tasks of classifying, ordering, and analyzing qualitative data.[1]

The Data in Perspective

In order to begin to make sense of the data collected, it helps to first understand their source by asking certain questions. The answers to these questions and other related ones help to put any research findings in perspective. For example, if original data were collected from research participants,

- Who were they?
- Under what conditions did they provide data?
- What assurances about anonymity or confidentiality were given?
- What understanding did they have about how data would be used?
- What prior relationship, if any, did they have with the researcher?

259

- As a research sample, do they appear to be representative of the sampling frame or accessible population from which they were drawn?
- Was the sample biased in some way?
- How might any possible bias affect the quality of the data?
- Given the size of the sample, how much might sampling error have affected the quality of the data?

When appropriate, a good place to start is to calculate the percentage of completed responses, also called *response rate*. This is done by dividing the actual number of cases for which there are reasonably complete data by the potential number of cases (all cases that the researcher sought to include in the sample). Whereas a high percentage of completed responses are more likely to produce a representative sample than a low response rate, even a high percentage of usable responses do not guarantee representativeness. For example, a researcher could post a notice in shopping malls or run an advertisement in a newspaper asking for volunteers to compete a questionnaire about some personal problem they might have. Over time, he or she might acquire quite a few volunteers and would probably get an impressively high response rate (perhaps 90 percent or more) of complete, usable questionnaires among those who volunteered. However, we could think of several reasons why the usable responses would not be representative of any group other than the volunteers in the study, and perhaps not even of them!

Generally, it is also helpful to try to identify patterns of response that may suggest the presence of sampling bias. Certain questions can be helpful in this regard. For example,

- From among potential cases within the sample, which ones contain complete data and which do not?
- Do they differ in any meaningful way?
- If so, should this be reported and discussed, or is the difference one that is probably unrelated to any research findings?

Most researchers summarize the most relevant characteristics of their data sources in a separate section of their reports. The summary helps both researchers and the readers of their reports to attempt to estimate whether their data sources were typical of the sample selected or the accessible population or sampling frame from which they were drawn. If research participants provided the data, a description of them often is presented in group form, that is, as a broad demographic profile of who they were. Sometimes, a profile of a typical participant is provided.

A demographic profile of research participants can help the researcher put the findings of a research study into perspective. It can suggest the degree of their external validity. For readers of a research report to be able to assess the relevance of the research findings to their own specific practice situations, a clear picture of those who provided data is necessary. For example, a report of a study based on a sample of low-income mothers needing assistance in developing parenting skills might include a demographic summary of the research participants in relation to the variables age, income, presence of a father or father figure, number of children, and degree of support from extended family. Readers of such a report can assess how closely the participants resembled their own clients and thus can help them determine whether the findings would be likely to apply to their own clients.

In more qualitative research, data are less likely to be aggregated. Instead, the demographic characteristics of each individual research participant may be included as the introduction to a narrative description of the researcher's interaction with him or her. For example, we might see something like this:

> *Lucretia W. is a 62-year-old Caucasian woman with three adult children, all of whom live out of state. Her husband (who was ten years older) passed away six months ago from advanced stage Alzheimer's disease. She has a high school education and worked as a cook in various restaurants until she decided to quit work about one year ago to care for her husband. She is an active church member and states that "my faith got me through it all." Her first explanation for her husband's illness was "it was God trying to make me stronger," but the longer that she and I talked over coffee in her kitchen, I began to detect that . . .*

In both quantitative and qualitative studies, researchers generally describe the setting in which the research was conducted. It allows readers of their reports (1) to judge to what degree the setting in which data were collected might have influenced findings, and (2) in the case of organization-based research, to assess whether the nature of the organization in which the research took place (and its services) is similar enough to their own that the findings of the research may be helpful in informing their own practice decision making in some way. For example, readers of a report who work in an outpatient clinic, where managed care limits reimbursement for services to only four treatment sessions, may quickly conclude that a research finding that individual treatment is more effective than group treatment is of little relevance to them. They would base this conclusion on the researcher's description, which states that the research was conducted in a private, inpatient psychiatric setting that offers primarily long-term intensive psychotherapy.

Preparing for Data Analysis

Prior to conducting data analysis and attempting to draw conclusions and findings from them, it is helpful to review the purpose of the study. It suggests the general type of analysis that would be appropriate. For example, was the research designed to assess the relative effectiveness of various treatment interventions for addressing a problem that clients were experiencing? Or was it designed merely to describe the effects that the problem has on specific client groups? In the first instance, the researcher would be expected to conduct and report on statistical analysis that would provide evidence of the relative effectiveness of the various intervention methods. In the second, only analysis that provides a clear description of the range of effects of the problems observed and some indication of their distribution within the research sample might be required.

The presence of still other research purposes would suggest other approaches to analysis of the data. For example, if the purpose of a study was to describe group performance before and after exposure to some independent variable, or to compare two or more groups in relation to some behavior or attitude, data analysis that is especially well suited to accomplishing these tasks would need to be used. If the study's purpose was to determine to what degree several variables, viewed together, may explain or predict some problem or phenomenon, then a very different form of analysis would be appropriate. Or if the purpose was to assess how effective an individual's or a program's intervention was, still other methods of analysis might be used.

A review of how research questions and/or hypotheses were stated can help in selecting the most appropriate method of data analysis. For example, sometimes questions are posed in such a way that it is clear that differences between or among groups are being sought; other times, it is clear that the degree of association or correlation between or among variables is the primary focus of the research.

There are other interrelated issues associated with the choice of methods used to answer research questions and/or to seek statistical support for hypotheses. They require the researcher to recall and review many aspects of the research design that produced the research data. Once again, certain questions can be helpful. For example:

- Were the research methods used and the kind of data that they produced primarily quantitative or qualitative?
- What general category of sampling was used (probability or nonprobability)?
- How many samples or subsamples were used?
- How large was each sample?
- How (specifically) was each selected?
- Are the variables of interest believed to be normally distributed (they would approximate a "normal curve") within the population, or is their distribution badly skewed?
- What levels of measurement were generated for each variable that will be used in statistical analysis?

Data Analysis: An Overview

An in-depth discussion of methods of data analysis is beyond the scope of this book. However, we will examine the conceptual underpinnings that are critical to understanding how statistical analysis is conducted and how it assists the researcher in drawing conclusions based on research data.

Qualitative Analysis

If the research employed primarily qualitative research methods, the data are also primarily qualitative in nature, perhaps in the form of summaries of in-depth interviews, participant observations, videotapes, or something similar. Data analysis then tends to be less traditional than that used in more quantitative designs. While it may rely on some widely practiced methods, it also may be highly creative and even unique to a given research study.

Qualitative data analysis seeks to "make sense" out of the data—to learn what actually occurred during the data collection process and what it might all mean. Even qualitative data such as words can have meaningful numbers or categories (values or value categories) assigned to them. The assignment process may be a little more subjective and a little less precise than when quantitative data are present from the outset but, once assignment is finished, the numbers and categories can be manipulated and sometimes even analyzed using statistical analysis. However, when statistical tests are used, the design of most qualitative studies (for example, use of nonprobability samples, lack of control groups, reliance on interviewing or observation for data collection, lack of emphasis on measurement of variables) seriously limits the number of available choices.

Assignment of numbers or categories often entails a certain amount of counting (quantification) of behaviors, use of certain words, or emotional responses—content analysis. It can be performed with the assistance of software packages that have recently been developed for this purpose. Or, it may entail more "human" methods such as the use of two or more "judges," all independently examining the same data and drawing their own conclusions as to what they saw in them. Afterward, the judges may meet to attempt to arrive at some consensus as to what they observed, or the researcher may attempt himself or herself to reconcile any differences in their observations. Sometimes a "majority rules" method is used. For example, if two out of three judges perceived that in a videotape a person seemed very anxious but a third judge did not, it would be concluded that the research participant was indeed anxious. Alternately, the decision may be made beforehand that an emotion or behavior will not be reported as a research finding unless all judges reported it—it must be a unanimous observation.

Quantitative Analysis

In research studies that are more quantitative in nature, statistical analysis continues to play an important part in answering research questions and in concluding whether there is adequate support for research hypotheses. It is often the final step in the process of elimination used to determine whether a relationship between variables within a research sample is likely to be a real one that exists beyond the sample.

If the amount of data (the data set) being analyzed is small and the type of statistical analysis that is to be performed is relatively simple, researchers sometimes choose not to use a computer to assist in data analysis. However, because of the many user-friendly statistical software packages now available for use with personal computers,[2] and other hand-held electronic devices, statistical analysis by hand is rarely necessary.

Complex statistical computations are performed flawlessly when electronic methods are used for data analysis, assuming that the data have been entered accurately and the appropriate method of statistical analysis has been selected. Probably the most time-consuming step in statistical analysis has always been data entry. However, even this tedious operation may soon be eliminated as technology allows us merely to scan the data into a computer for analysis. Once data are entered into the computer, a wide variety of statistical analyses can be performed, each in just a matter of seconds.

The ease with which statistical analysis can be performed by a computer represents both a bonanza and a danger for the researcher. Statistical tests that would have been outside the mathematical competence of many researchers just a few years ago are now possible for anyone with even average data-processing skills. However, because hundreds of different statistical analyses can be performed very easily and quickly, there is a real danger that either (1) findings will not be interpreted correctly by researchers or (2) they will be misleading to readers of research reports. Unfortunately, computer programs cannot always determine if a given statistical analysis has been used appropriately. They also cannot know whether a researcher has even a beginning understanding of how the results of statistical analysis should be interpreted in light of a research question or hypothesis. They cannot know how the nature of the sample that provided the data and how it was acquired may have affected results. They also cannot alert the reader of a research report that the researcher stumbled on a spurious (that is, not real) relationship between variables simply by trying an almost infinite number of combinations—something that is now quite easy to do because of the ease with which computer analysis of data can be performed.

There are a few basic understandings that are central to the successful use of statistical analyses by the researcher. We will present an overview of them in this text and suggest that they be studied in greater depth elsewhere.

Uses of Statistical Analysis

Statistical analyses are versatile. They can be used at several points in the research process to assist in decision making. In quantitative studies, they play an important role (1) in the design of research, (2) in summarizing the distribution of variables within research data, (3) in estimating the characteristics of the population from which a sample was drawn, and (4) in drawing conclusions and interpretations about answers to research questions and the presence or absence of support for hypotheses. In this chapter, we will mention only briefly the first and third of these uses, focusing most of our discussion on the second and fourth.

Designing Research.   Some statistical methods are very helpful to the researcher for making decisions related to the design of research. For example, statistical analyses can tell us when a simple random sample is sufficiently large that the impact of sampling error is acceptably low, or they can tell us the mathematical probability that a sample is sufficiently representative of a known population in relation to some variable.[3] As we noted in Chapter 11, statistical analyses also are used to help design and refine data collection instruments such as scales and indexes. They perform operations such as coefficient alpha to help assess the overall reliability of a data collection instrument. They also can be used to identify items in the instrument that appear to measure the same component of a variable, items that may be redundant or unnecessary, or that can be used to construct parallel forms of the instrument.

Summarizing the Distribution of Variables.   A second type of statistical analysis, descriptive statistical analysis, is used to provide a concise summary of data accumulated about and from those persons or cases that were studied. We use descriptive statistical analyses (sometimes referred to as *data reduction*) simply to try to reduce large amounts of data to a manageable size, so that the researcher (or the reader of a research report) will be able to visualize the major characteristics of the participants and the data that they provided.

Descriptive statistical analyses may involve the construction of frequency distributions or graphs. A frequency distribution is a table displaying how many participants or cases fell in each value category or value (measurement) of a variable. The frequencies are displayed alongside the various value categories or values of the variable. Also, if the variable is at least ordinal level, frequency distributions may include additional columns for cumulative frequencies (how many cases had a measurement larger or smaller than a given value). Another column may reflect percentages of all cases represented by the cases in a given value category or what percentage of all cases had a measurement above or below a given value (cumulative percentages). Sometimes values are grouped, that is, ranges of values are used instead of individual values, in order to make a frequency distribution table smaller. When this is done, the researcher seeks to make the table simpler to understand without giving up too much detail.

Graphs also are frequently used to describe the distribution of variables within a sample or population of cases studied. They can be very simple or very complex. The simplest forms just portray the same data that are contained in frequency distributions, that is, the distribution of values of a variable. Some commonly used examples are bar charts, line diagrams, histograms, and pie charts. Bar charts and line diagrams use bars or lines of lengths that are proportional to the number of cases that possess a given measurement of a variable. Thus, for the variable number of children, if twice as many research participants had two children as had four children, the bar or line for the value 4 (children) would be half as long as the bar or line for the value 2 (children).

Histograms are graphs that portray the shape of the distribution of a variable. They can be created simply by connecting the tops of the lines or bars in a line diagram or bar chart to form a shape (a polygon). Then the overall distribution can be described in summary form. For example, if the shape thus created is essentially bell shaped, the variable is regarded as normally distributed within the sample or population that provided the data.

Pie charts use areas of a circle or some other figure to correspond to the percentage of all cases that were found to have a given measurement of a variable. If 20 percent of participants in a study had four children, a pie chart for the variable number of children could be constructed in which a slice that is 20 percent or 72 degrees (360 degrees × .20 = 72 degrees) of the "pie" would be labeled with the value 4. If 40 percent of participants had two children, the slice containing the value 2 would be twice as large—it would occupy 40 percent or 144 degrees of the pie (a circle), and so forth.

Another commonly used graph is the scattergram that we referred to in Chapter 5. Unlike the other graphs that we have described, it portrays the distribution of two variables simultaneously. Each dot on the graph represents a case and its measurement for each of two variables. The overall pattern of dots can be used to suggest whether measurements of the two variables may be correlated and, somewhat crudely, how strong a linear correlation they possess.

Another way of describing the distribution of a variable within a data set is to report what was found to be a typical value category or value among its measurements. Several different options are available for this purpose. They are collectively referred to as *measures of central tendency.* One or more measures of central tendency for variables of interest are computed and included in the research report. The most commonly used ones include the following:

- The *mode* = The value category or value that had the largest frequency (occurred most often) within the data.
- The *median* = The midpoint in a rank-ordered distribution of an ordinal, interval, or ratio level variable.
- The *arithmetic mean* = The average of the values of all cases for an interval or ratio level variable.

In describing the distribution of a data set, it is also helpful to describe to what degree cases were homogeneous (similar) in relationship to a variable and to what degree their value categories or values reflected heterogeneity (difference). Descriptive statistics (or parameters) that do this are collectively referred to as *measures of dispersion* (or measures of variability). When reported along with one or more measures of central tendency, they offer a fairly complete summary description of the distribution of a variable among cases in a research sample or population. Some of the more commonly used measures of dispersion are the range, interquartile range, variance, and standard deviation. Statistics books provide the formula for their computation, describe how they differ, and provide criteria for determining when each should be used.

Although descriptive statistics such as measures of central tendency and measures of dispersion can be ends in themselves (for example, they are used to describe the number of times that research participants engage in a certain behavior or the variations in scores on a standardized attitude measurement scale), they are also much more. They are important tools in each of the other three uses of statistical analyses. They provide the numbers that make it possible to do the mathematical calculations that each requires.

Estimating the Characteristics of a Population.   In studies (primarily quantitative) in which random samples have been drawn, it can be useful to estimate (within a certain range) what the likely (true) measurement of a variable would have been if the researcher had studied the entire population. For example, if a random sample of clients of a given size were drawn, and their mean (average) level of satisfaction with services received were calculated with some standardized instrument, statistical analysis could tell us with different degrees of confidence where the true mean satisfaction level of all clients would lie. This is known as constructing *confidence intervals*. Reporting a confidence interval in a research report can help the reader of the report to get a better understanding of the likely accuracy of the measurement of a variable.

Answering Questions and Testing Hypotheses.   In research designs, such as descriptive research that seeks to learn if there is support for an association or correlation between variables, and, of course, in explanatory research, the researcher generally wishes to do more than simply describe the characteristics of the participants. The existence of a relationship between variables often has been predicted and stated as a hypothesis. A sample of research participants has been selected using methods designed to maximize the likelihood that they represent members of the population, and they have been studied with the goal of determining if there is support for the hypothesized relationship.

Perhaps, on first blush, there is an apparent relationship between variables—it can be seen within the data collected from the research sample. Is that sufficient proof of the relationship? No, before we can conclude that a relationship is a real one that probably exists within the population from which the sample was drawn, we must be reasonably certain that something else did not cause the apparent relationship.

Consider a rather typical scenario in which there appears to be support for a researcher's hypothesis that an experimental treatment is more effective than a traditional one. Within the data collected from a sample of clients, the experimental intervention method seems to have produced better results than the traditional one. For example, researchers might have observed that one group of ten randomly selected clients with a diagnosis of alcoholism receiving an experimental counseling method reflected a 60 percent rate of treatment success (operationally defined as alcohol abstinence for one month), as compared with members of a control group who received the usual treatment and who reflected only a 40 percent success rate.

Suppose that the research was carefully designed (using a classical experimental design) and implemented. The researchers are reasonably confident that their design has good internal validity, that is, they are reasonably certain that something else besides different treatments (the independent variable) did not cause the different results (measurements of the dependent variable). Another way of saying the same thing would be to say that "All threats to internal validity were adequately controlled." Does that mean that the relationship between the variables is a real one that exists beyond the sample? Not necessarily. What about sampling error? Wouldn't we expect to have some difference in success rates with any two relatively small groups of clients selected randomly, even if the two treatment methods were really equally effective? Yes. Remember, only sampling bias, not sampling error, was controlled by random selection and random assignment to the two treatments.

The question is: Is the difference in the success rates of the two groups of research participants (the experimental and control groups) large enough that it can safely be assumed that it is not simply the work of sampling error? Statistical analysis can determine how safe it would be to make generalizations about the relative effectiveness of the two treatments that would go beyond the participants in the current research. This third use of statistical analysis employs methods that are broadly referred to as *inferential statistical analysis.*

Using a theoretical concept called a *sampling distribution,* inferential statistical tests can tell the researcher the mathematical probability that the apparent relationship between or among variables that can be seen in the research data is the work of sampling error. They are based on the laws of probability. They can tell us the mathematical probability that the difference between a 60 percent success rate and a 40 percent success rate using two groups of only ten participants each could exist because of sampling error. Thus, inferential statistical analysis can be used to help us draw conclusions about the relative effectiveness of the treatment methods used in our hypothetical research example. Any one of several tests (there is usually one that is most appropriate) could be used to determine the exact probability that a 20 percent difference in success rate would occur with two subsamples of ten cases drawn at random just because of sampling error. If statistical analysis can successfully discredit it as a likely explanation for the apparent relationship between the treatment and success rate among our research participants, we would be able to conclude that the relationship might be a real one.

Most of the time, being more than 95 percent certain that an apparent relationship within a research sample is not the work of sampling error is good enough for researchers to claim support for a relationship between variables. (As we noted in Chapter 1, all scientific knowledge is tentative anyway.) Of course, as in our example, researchers also must be reasonably certain that threats to internal validity have been adequately controlled by the research design.

When inferential statistical analysis demonstrates that the probability of sampling error's having produced an apparent relationship between variables is less than one time in twenty (referred to as $p < .05$), researchers customarily describe the relationship between variables as *statistically significant* (see Box 12.1). Of course, the researcher may

BOX 12.1   Statistical Significance: What It Is and What It Is Not

It is mathematical evidence, based on the laws of probability, that the relationship between or among
variables within a sample is very unlikely to be the work of sampling error (chance).
It is not 100 percent proof that the relationship within the sample was not the work of sampling error.
It is not 100 percent proof that the variables are related.
It is not proof that something else (some threat to internal validity) did not cause the relationship.
It is not proof that the relationship is necessarily a strong one.
It is not proof that the relationship is necessarily a meaningful one.

(with justification) set the level of statistical significance at some other level (referred to
as a *rejection level* or *alpha level*), such as .025, .01, or even .001. If so, statistical significance would require demonstration that the likelihood of sampling error having produced the apparent relationship between variables is less than the rejection level selected.

It is possible to imply whether a statistically significant relationship was found to exist
without actually using the words *statistically significant.* For example, in a report, a
researcher might summarize the findings of a study simply by stating, "Among low-
income women without extended family support, women who used casework services
were more likely to possess a higher level of awareness of the medical needs of infants
than those who did not use casework services. However, clients who used casework services were no more likely to use outpatient medical facilities for their babies' treatment
than those participants who did not receive casework services."

It is important that we not make too much of a finding of statistical significance. First
of all, as we have suggested, a finding of statistical significance, like all of the findings of
scientific inquiry, is only a tentative conclusion based on reasonable certainty. It says only
that sampling error is a very unlikely explanation of the apparent relationship between or
among variables that occurred among cases that were studied. It never totally rules it out.

As we also suggested, even if there is a statistically significant relationship between
variables, a true relationship between them or an important one still may not exist. A
finding of statistical significance says nothing about the other possible causes of the
apparent relationship within the research sample (besides a true relationship) that might
make the dependent and independent variables appear to be related. For example, some
other variable or variables or a badly biased sample may have produced it.

Sometimes, statistically significant relationships between or among variables that are
not the work of sampling bias or any of the threats to internal validity are real. But they
still are not terribly valuable! They reflect real relationships, but they are relationships
between or among variables that are virtually worthless because they are not very strong.[4]
This is especially likely to happen if the researcher is using relatively large research samples. Statistical significance is achieved quite frequently and easily if very large samples
are used. But statistical significance thus achieved may be of limited or no practical value
to the social work practitioner. Researchers can minimize the likelihood of achieving
significance when the relationship between variables is so weak as to be meaningless if
they use a sample that does not exceed the size recommended for a given type of statistical analysis. The choice of statistical analysis to be used relates to the issue of practical
application. A good question to ask is: If a relationship between variables is found, how

strong would the relationship have to be, to be considered meaningful? While a statistically significant relationship says that the two variables probably are related beyond the sample, it says nothing about the strength of the relationship. Fortunately, there are types of statistical analyses that produce something called *measures of association* that are indicators of the strength of the relationship. They can be helpful in putting a finding of statistical significance in perspective.

Finally, meaningless statistical significance also is sometimes achieved even when the recommended sample size is used and the analysis is performed correctly. The problem is the research finding is nothing new or unexpected! This occurs fairly frequently when statistical tests are used to determine if a correlation between two variables is probably a real one. Some correlations are valuable; but many others are not, even if they are real. For example, among a group of human service organization clients, we could almost certainly demonstrate a statistically significant positive correlation between income and the amount of money spent on groceries. But would such a finding be valuable? It is highly predictable, because one generally has to have money (or at least good credit) to spend it. Besides, would the finding help us to be more effective in our intervention with human service organization clients? Probably not.

All statistical tests have assumptions that underlie their use. However, there also are certain situations in which it is acceptable to ignore one or more of the usual assumptions for the use of a statistical test—the results will still be quite accurate. Even the selection of a frequency distribution, graph, or other descriptive statistic to report central tendency or dispersion is not always simple. Statistical analysis requires that the researcher be knowledgeable about rules and conditions that must be met. It also requires an ethical commitment to portray the distribution of variables as accurately as possible. As we all know, it is very easy to lie with statistics by selecting a type of analysis that portrays the data the way we want them to look.

Fortunately, even the process of identifying the correct statistical analyses is becoming easier thanks to advances in computer technology. Software packages and Internet websites are now available that use a series of questions to help the researcher narrow the list of analyses that might be appropriate. However, they still require a good basic understanding of research design. For example, to use them correctly, we have to understand factors specific to our research study, such as the sampling methods that were used, the level of measurement that was produced, and how certain variables tend to be distributed.

Interpreting and Reporting the Results

Once data have been analyzed and, where appropriate, statistical analyses have been performed, the results still must be interpreted. Any limitations of the methods of data analysis used should be identified and interpreted as to their possible effects.

The results are first examined in relation to the focus of the research. What do the results suggest about the answer to the research question or questions? What do they indicate about any hypotheses? Were they supported? If so, what does that mean? If not, how could the researcher's prediction have been wrong? How can the results of data analyses be used to better understand the research problem or even to suggest effective prevention or intervention methods for alleviating it? What are the implications for the social practitioners who are seeking to provide better social work services? How will any findings make them better evidence-based practitioners?

The data analysis generates many different findings. Often they can be interpreted in a variety of ways. The specific meaning of each individual finding must be determined. Often, individual findings may need to be reinterpreted in light of other findings from the current research study or from the studies of others. This often requires researchers to make use of their practice experience. It also often requires them to look again at the relevant literature in an attempt to reconcile their findings with those of other researchers. Eventually, they must use their best judgment, knowing that they can always be wrong in their interpretations.

When research participants provide data, it is often a good idea to build into the research design a strategy for early feedback of study results to participants and their communities. It is often possible to share major study findings with study participants and their communities (in nontechnical language) and enlist their help in interpretation. This should occur before publication of the results in formal reports or scholarly journals. There are several advantages to doing this, especially in cross-cultural research (Chapter 8). First, people who know the community well offer a unique perspective on a study's findings. They often can suggest differences in interpretation that might never occur to the researcher. They can also help to determine how best to use the study findings to address community concerns and problems. Finally, sharing the data prior to dissemination to the professional community reinforces the notion of partnership in the research enterprise and communicates respect for study participants and the communities they represent.

Interpreting research findings is not easy. For example, how do we interpret the descriptive finding that adolescents have such widely differing attitudes toward the use of contraception to prevent unwanted pregnancies? Or, that the staff perceives a program to be highly successful while community leaders express resentment about it? Or that a software program that is used to perform content analysis of transcribed conversations with college students shows that anti-Semitic attitudes still persist among them? Or that a test of statistical significance supports a hypothesis that two groups of research participants really are different in relation to some variable? Or that another statistical finding that one variable really is associated with another in some consistent pattern? Does it suggest that one variable really is contributing to variations in the other variable? Or is it the other way around? Is the strength of the correlation really all that strong?

Because of the difficulty of drawing definitive conclusions from research data, researchers sometimes simply report findings, suggest several possible interpretations, and let the readers of their report draw their own conclusions. When inferential statistical analysis has been used, both findings of statistically significant relationships between variables and findings of nonsignificance can be equally valuable to readers. All research findings from soundly designed and implemented research are potentially valuable to others. For example, even the finding that "No support was found for a relationship between type of treatment and treatment effectiveness" can help other researchers to avoid the mistake of believing and acting on an erroneous belief that one treatment method is superior to another. It can help practitioners to avoid believing what logically ought to be true, but is not. Thus, it can help them to make better decisions.

Disseminating Research Findings

A major reason for conducting research is to contribute to the social work knowledge base. In order for this to occur, research findings must be interpreted and communicated to interested audiences. As we have emphasized throughout this text, the researcher has an obligation to the research and practice communities to communicate the results of research to those individuals who can use it to improve their work.

There are many vehicles that can be used to share research findings. We will mention some of the more commonly used ones.

Reports and Monographs

If research is sponsored (funded) by some organization or if it is designed to meet a graduate degree requirement, it is expected that it will be written using a fairly standardized format and bound. The written report generally is quite lengthy. In the case of funded research, the report may be distributed to interested parties as a research monograph (Chapter 4). If the research was a degree requirement, it may be called a *thesis* (master's degree) or a *dissertation* (doctorate). The report is placed in the library of the university where the student completed the degree. It is also made available to others through interlibrary loan systems in either hard copy or via electronic communication. Whatever its distribution and no matter what it may be called, a complete research report provides a detailed description of the entire research process, including the methods used. Sufficient information is offered so that readers can either replicate the research and/or evaluate whether the researcher's conclusions and recommendations appear to be justified and appropriate for implementation in their own practice.

Reports of Quantitative Studies.   Usually, there are eight sections to a full research report. Sometimes two or more are combined, but the researcher is expected to provide sufficient detail about each of the eight areas. They tend to follow the same general sequence as the content in earlier chapters.

1. *Introduction.* The historical background of the study is described, and the origin of the researcher's interest in the topic may be noted. The research problem is specified and a description of its scope and its significance is stated and documented. The broad research question that was the focus of the study is stated.
2. *Review of the literature.* A summary and synthesis of literature relevant to the research question is presented (see Chapter 4). The literature assembled is used to summarize what is already known about the research question and to identify how the current research study promised to build on and extend knowledge previously available. It provides the rationale for research hypotheses and/or more specific research questions, and for the design of the research.
3. *Statement of research questions and hypotheses.* Related to the purpose of the study and following logically from the review of the literature, a specific set of research questions and/or hypotheses that were examined are stated. Operational definitions of key terms (also derived from the review of literature) may be included here, or they may appear early in the next section.

4. *Methodology.* A detailed description of the research design is presented. It includes the methods of selection of research participants or objects that were studied and, frequently, the rationale for that method. Methods for conducting measurements of key variables are described, including a discussion of the selection and/or development of any data collection instruments that were used. The methodology section reports in detail what was done, to whom or what, and by what method(s). The rationale for all major methodological decisions is presented (sampling, measurement, data collection methods, and choice of methods for statistical analysis). The section enables the reader of the report both to assess the credibility of the researcher and the research findings and to replicate the research, if desired.

5. *Results.* The principal findings derived from the research are presented. Outcomes of statistical analysis are summarized and interpreted. The findings section generally contains tables, graphs, or other methods of summarizing the results of analyses to help the reader to visualize what was found.

6. *Discussion, conclusions, and implications.* The findings are discussed in relation to the research questions and/or hypotheses. Answers to questions are proposed, and, if applicable, evidence of support or nonsupport for hypotheses is presented. Findings are also discussed in relation to the literature. Findings that corroborate those of other researchers and theoreticians are identified, and findings that conflict with what has been reported elsewhere in the literature are discussed and, where appropriate, reconciled. The implications of the findings for social work practice are an especially important component of this section of the research report.

7. *Limitations.* The researcher lists and discusses methodological shortcomings of which he or she is aware. No research is perfect—all research tends to be limited somewhat by one or more inherent design constraints or by obstacles encountered in attempting to implement the design. For example, an explanatory design may contain inherent problems because of the ethical impossibility of using a true control group or because of the researcher's need to draw a sample from an available sampling frame rather than from the accessible population. Limitations also can result as a function of other methodological difficulties, such as the need to use a data collection instrument that had not yet been demonstrated to be reliable with the participants used in the research or because of constraints on the kinds of data that were allowed to be collected. There are many issues in research that prevent studies from being designed and/or executed flawlessly. The reader requires an honest description of these limitations to know how to interpret and evaluate findings. A useful format for the discussion of each major limitation consists of (1) a specific description of the nature and scope of the limitation; (2) an explanation of why the limitation was unavoidable; (3) the researcher's speculation on how the limitation may have negatively affected the research and its findings; (4) a description of what, if anything, was done to minimize the potential negative effects of the limitation on the research; and (5) an assessment of how successful the effort was.

8. *Conclusions and recommendations.* A description of how the study is believed to have advanced knowledge in the problem area is presented. The researcher also identifies needs for further research and suggests ways in which it might be designed and implemented both to build on the achievements of the current research and to avoid its shortcomings. Generally, the researcher also makes specific suggestions as to

how the findings might be implemented to improve the delivery of services to social work clients, that is, what changes in intervention methods appear to be indicated based on the findings of the study.

9. *Appendices.* Data collection instruments are sometimes included along with other materials that may be of interest to just a few readers of the report such as agency-written program descriptions or the details of statistical analyses. They are referred to in the body of the report.

Reports of Qualitative Studies. If the research was primarily qualitative, the same general format may be used. However, there are likely to be several important differences in the report. For example:

• The introduction section is likely to be briefer and contain fewer facts and numbers, since less is generally known about the problem than in more quantitative studies.

• The review of literature section is shorter, reflecting that (1) there often is relatively little known about the problem, and (2) the literature was reviewed less thoroughly prior to data collection than in more quantitative studies.

• There are research questions but, very rarely, research hypotheses.

• The methodology section is likely to be shorter than in a report of a quantitative study. Such tasks as sampling and measurement tend to be less rigorous. Since replication of a qualitative study is not very likely to occur, there is generally less need to describe the research design in as great a detail as in quantitative research reports. A notable exception might be if the design employed grounded theory (Chapter 8) in which certain tasks and a specific sequence of events are prescribed. The reader may want to know whether they were adhered to in order to evaluate the credibility of the research findings.

• The findings section may be quite long, often containing case vignettes or extended narrative descriptions with verbatim quotations from research participants. It may contain some descriptive statistics, but the results of inferential statistical testing would be rare.

• The discussion, conclusions, and implications section may be quite long and contain numerous references to the literature as the researcher attempts to relate his or her observations and conclusions to what was previously known about the problem. It may contain one or more story lines, theories or hypotheses that have evolved from the research and are now proposed for testing by other researchers.

• The limitations section may be shorter than in the report of a quantitative study, or even nonexistent. Since there are usually no claims to objectivity or to, for example, sample representativeness or control of confounding variables in most qualitative studies, there is no need to speculate on their likely effects. Design rigor is simply less important when not testing research hypotheses.

• While there are conclusions and recommendations, they may be more tentative and cautious than in reports of quantitative studies.

Whether a report describes a quantitative study or a more qualitative one, the reader should receive a clear picture of what the research was designed to accomplish, how it was conducted, and what was learned from it. A research report reveals both the communication skills of its author and his or her knowledge of research methods.

The technical aspects of research report writing such as footnoting style, use of certain terminology, whether or not to include data collection instruments in the Appendices, and so forth are beyond the scope of this book. However, there are entire books devoted to them,[5] along with the actual reports that usually can be found in most all human service agencies and can answer any questions the author might have.

Internal Correspondence and In-Service Training

There are many reasons why one may choose to disseminate research findings through internal correspondence or in-service training sessions. For example, research studies with limited external validity, research on unique client populations, or unreplicated evaluation studies all may be appropriately disseminated through mechanisms internal to the organization. Many organizations, particularly larger ones, have monthly or semiannual newsletters. Their editors are looking for materials to include. As vehicles to disseminate research findings, these outlets have several advantages for researchers. When they submit a summary of their research (emphasizing its findings) to the editor of such a publication, it is almost certain to be published, especially if an inquiry to see what form it should take has been made in advance. If published, the summary is very likely to be read because staff members generally like to read about what is going on in their work setting. In addition, the findings will be read and put to use with only minimal time lag following completion of the research.

If the researcher's organization also has a program of regular in-service training or staff development, such a forum can also be a good place to disseminate the results of research. Some organizations prefer to do this informally, for example a voluntary attendance, brown bag lunch program where staff members take turns leading discussions about various work-related issues. This type of program attracts those who have a genuine interest in a researcher's findings and increases the likelihood that findings will be disseminated quickly and put to use.

Major Conferences

Research findings of a more general interest can be disseminated through presentations at professional conferences and symposia. As we observed in Chapter 4, many national and international social work organizations—for example, NASW, SSWR, American Public Welfare Association, Child Welfare League of America, CSWE, The International Federation of Social Workers, and the Group for Human Services Technology Applications (HUSITA)—hold conferences at various locations throughout the United States and (in some instances) the world. Some of them sponsor conferences that may be more geographically limited or more narrowly focused, such as conferences relating specifically to services to people with HIV, family support and preservation programs, long-term care, family violence, homelessness, or some other specialization within social work. In addition, there are still more (hundreds) of other major conferences in related fields, such as psychology, sociology, public health, public administration, or education, that are held regularly or sporadically and that generally include presentations that are of multidisciplinary interest.

The largest and most prestigious conferences usually solicit proposals and abstracts for presentations about a wide range of topics that are loosely related to a theme. A "call for abstracts" or "call for proposals" and a deadline for their receipt is published in professional journals or newsletters, or mailed to the organization's members along with advertisements for the conference. Typically, a prospective presenter is asked to write a brief overview and/or abstract of what is to be presented and to indicate in which area of the program it would best fit. Many major conferences now have a separate grouping for proposals for presentations that are empirically based and another for those that are more conceptual or theoretical in nature. Proposals for presentations of research generally are expected to follow an outline that is provided—usually a miniversion of a traditional research report—plus descriptions of the methods for presentation. The author may be asked to indicate those individuals who would be most likely to benefit from and be interested in the presentation. The presentation overview or abstract itself generally does not include any identifying information, allowing it to be reviewed anonymously. A separate or detachable cover page usually is required. It includes the proposed presenter's name and affiliation, phone number, e-mail address, and other identifying information.

Generally, the major conference planning committees receive many more proposals for presentations than there are places for them on the program. It is not unusual for a major conference to accept only 10 or 20 percent of all proposals received. The review process takes time. Often there is a lag time of about six months between the proposal's receipt (acknowledged through e-mail or on a postage-paid card supplied by the proposer) and notification of a decision by the planning committee.

The major conferences tend to use a large number of volunteer reviewers. A proposal may be read anonymously by two or three professional peers who provide a numerical rating on a scale devised by the conference planning committee. The system is likely to give points for such criteria as the proposal's relevance to the conference theme, the potential interest of conference participants in the topic, the quality of the research described, or how well the proposal is written or conforms to guidelines. The review criteria to be used usually are listed in the call for abstracts.

All people who submit proposals are notified at the same time of the decision of the planning committee. Those who are invited to present are asked to respond in writing whether or not they can commit to attend. Audiovisual equipment can be requested, if needed, usually at some cost to the presenter, or what is needed sometimes can be brought from home.

Presentations can take a number of different forms. A researcher may be asked to write and present a formal paper, leaving time for discussion and questions from those in attendance. Although it is possible to simply read the paper, this is not very enjoyable for anyone involved and is now rarely done. The single-paper presentation is less popular today than it once was. Now it is more common to group two or three related papers in one session where each individual has an allotted period of time to present. A moderator introduces the presenters, monitors the time, and generally makes sure that all presenters are treated equitably. Presenters offer a brief overview of their work, usually in an informal manner. Especially in international conferences, presenters tend to use slides or, most frequently, PowerPoint. If these aids are not used, handouts summarizing major findings for those in attendance usually are expected.

Another format is the poster session. It is similar to how high school students showcase their research in science fairs (only without the seedlings, household products, or batteries!). The presenter is located in a large hall with many others who are also there to present and discuss their work. Typically, they are provided with a mobile display board to exhibit visually and a table with chairs at which they can discuss informally their research methods and findings. Interested conference attendees come by to sit and talk with them about their research.

No matter which type of presentation method is used, presenters generally are expected to pay for travel expenses and accommodations, or to get their employers to pay for them. Only invited speakers and those who give keynote addresses usually are reimbursed for expenses by the conference sponsor. Some conferences provide a reduced registration fee for those who are presenting; some do not even offer that.

Presentations at major conferences, particularly those that report on research, can be good public relations for organizations and universities. Thus, professional travel assistance from one's employer may be forthcoming, depending on available funds and policies. If the research was funded by some outside source, there may be money in the budget for presenting its findings at conferences.

Even if presenting at a major conference costs the researcher some of his or her own money, the expenditure may be justified and productive. It can be intellectually stimulating to discuss your research with colleagues, some of whom invariably challenge some aspect of the research design and/or question the findings and recommendations. Those individuals who choose to attend a researcher's presentation generally have shared interests and may even be doing research in the same problem area. Opportunities to share findings and even to collaborate in some future research project can develop. In addition, a researcher learns a great deal about research from attending others' presentations.

The presentation of research at a prestigious conference can enhance a social work career. This is especially true for academicians or for those who work for research-oriented organizations such as teaching hospitals. In addition, continuing education units (CEUs) can be obtained and applied to help meet state licensure requirements. Because major conferences also tend to be held in interesting places, there are also opportunities for sightseeing and recreation. Attending them can be just plain enjoyable.

Many conferences also help with the dissemination of research knowledge in another way. Presentations or a summary of them often are put together in electronic or monograph form and are sold (or sometimes distributed at no charge) to members who either attended the conference or were unable to attend. If the sponsoring organization has its own professional journal or journals, presenters may be asked to submit (for publication consideration) a paper based on their presentation.

Other Professional Gatherings

There are many other smaller conferences—for example, local and regional meetings—where researchers also can disseminate the results of their research. Getting on the program of, for example, a state NASW symposium or regional conference may be a less prestigious achievement than presenting at a major national or international conference. However, especially if the findings are primarily of local interest, a local or regional conference may be the best vehicle to share newly acquired knowledge.

Local and regional meetings have certain advantages. They generally are less expensive to attend than the major national ones. Costs associated with presentation (travel, registration fees, lodging, and so forth) tend to be lower at smaller conferences that have fewer attendees and that are held in less exotic locales. Opportunities to meet and network with fellow professionals may be better in some respects. At local and regional conferences, researchers can interact with those individuals whose help may be valuable for meeting daily job responsibilities or for acquiring needed support for future research projects. In addition, most of the other benefits available at major conferences are also available at local or regional ones.

Publication in Professional Journals

The most traditional and potentially the most effective way to disseminate research knowledge is through the publication of an article in a professional journal. On the surface, we might think that a published article will ensure that one's findings will be widely disseminated and used. Not necessarily. A few such journals have very wide circulations, but most do not. Besides, there is no way to know if, just because an article is published, it will be read.

Professional journals are purchased by libraries, where they are available to students, scholars, and researchers to use in the development of their research literature reviews and thus in their own research on a problem. Increasingly, they are also available on the Internet. They remain available for use indefinitely, long after a conference presentation has been forgotten.

A potential journal article should be sent to only one journal at a time. Anything else is considered unethical. Most journals use volunteer, unpaid reviewers who give of their time as a service to their profession. It would be a major imposition for an author to send an article to several different journals simultaneously, perhaps getting it accepted by two or more. Because only one ultimately can publish it, the reviewers from the other journals would have wasted their time reviewing and critiquing it. However, once one journal indicates that an article has been denied publication, it is ethical to send it elsewhere. It is not unusual for an article to be rejected by several journals until finally accepted by one.

Getting an article published in a professional journal can be a very tedious, time-consuming, and sometimes frustrating experience. Among the most prestigious journals, many more prospective articles are submitted than are accepted for publication. Many people want to publish in them; academicians want and sometimes even need to be published in them to maintain or advance their careers. While the best known journals publish only a small percentage of articles submitted for publication, in contrast, some of the more narrowly focused and less well known may accept up to 50 percent of articles submitted, even more.

There are reference books available to help prospective authors find the journals most likely to publish a report of their work.[6] Colleagues who have been published (especially academicians) often are another good resource. Many journals have printed pamphlets or flyers that explain the procedure for submission of an article for publication; others describe the procedure in each issue of the journal or on their websites. The procedures are more alike than dissimilar.

Those journals that use a "blind review procedure" use a group of consulting editors (usually relatively accomplished academicians and other professionals who serve limited terms). They have agreed to read anonymously those articles in an area of research or practice that appear to have some publication potential or, in some cases, all articles submitted.

Two or three reviewers, selected by the editor based on their expertise or interest in the topic of an article, read and critique the article and recommend what should be done with it. The final decision, however, generally remains with the editor, a small committee, or an editorial board.

What can happen when an article is submitted to a professional journal? Usually, the author can expect one of three possible responses:

- *The article is accepted for publication without revision.* This happens rarely, especially among the best-known, most prestigious journals.
- *The article is rejected by the journal.* This can happen one of three ways. Depending upon the journal, the length of time between submission and rejection may suggest which one occurred.
  1. The editor, in a cursory reading, may have concluded that the article is either simply not publishable at all or not appropriate for the journal. Thus, the decision was made not to send it out to reviewers. If the author gets a rejection letter in a very short time, say, just a few weeks, this is most likely what happened.
  2. If rejection takes longer, the editor may have decided that the article might have publication potential and sent it out to reviewers, but a majority of them decided that the article should not be published.
  3. If an even longer period between submission and rejection occurs, the initial reviewers may have read the article but disagreed as to whether it should be published. It was then sent to another reviewer who cast the deciding vote not to publish it.
- *The article is not accepted in its present form but the author is provided with suggestions for revisions.* He or she is encouraged to make the requested revisions and then to resubmit it. The author can then choose to (1) seek publication elsewhere, or (2) inform the editor that he or she will make all or most of the required revisions. As a general rule, the latter alternative is the better choice. While not a guarantee of publication, if the author is conscientious in responding to suggestions by either making revisions as suggested, or (occasionally) explaining why they should not be made, the article usually will be accepted for publication. The research findings will be disseminated sooner than if the article were to be submitted to some other journal where the review process would begin anew. However, if the author believes that the suggestions for revision are incorrect or otherwise unacceptable, it makes more sense to seek publication elsewhere than to refuse to make many of them and then resubmit the article to the same journal. This stonewalling generally just results in rejection.

Even in instances in which an article is rejected outright, it has become common practice to provide the author with limited feedback and, sometimes, suggestions for other methods for dissemination. This is both a professional courtesy and a useful service. It acknowledges that (1) a considerable amount of work went into preparing an article for possible publication, and (2) it may still be possible to find some other venue (such as those we have discussed) where at least some of the author's efforts will be rewarded. For example, it may be tactfully suggested that, while the findings may not be publishable, they might make an excellent poster presentation at a conference.

Although the quality of the article and of the research methods employed are major considerations in whether an article is accepted for publication, luck and timing also play roles. For example, assuming that the article is a good one or has the potential to be, its acceptance may depend in part on when it is submitted to a journal. Its chances are enhanced if it arrives when the journal needs another article to complete an upcoming issue. If the journal already has accepted but not published some other article on a similar topic or issue, that could be fortuitous, or it could work against the researcher. The journal may decide to accept the article along with the previously accepted one, to complement it or even to make the topic the focus of a special issue including still other articles related to the same problem area. But the other, already accepted article on the issue or topic may also work to the researcher's detriment. The editor may decide that the article that the researcher submitted, although otherwise publishable, is simply not needed.

There are intangible rewards for having an article published in a professional journal. There is something very gratifying about seeing it in print and perhaps cited in someone else's work, and to at least be able to hope that it is being read, appreciated, and used by others. But journals do not pay authors for their articles when they publish them; in fact, publishing an article can be expensive (the costs of postage—some journals will not accept submission by fax or e-mail attachments—word processing, and so forth). Unfortunately, publication in journals also does not result in rapid dissemination of research findings. Getting an article accepted can take a year or more. Once accepted, it may not be published for another year or two. Despite these disadvantages, publication of one's research methods and findings in a professional journal probably remains the most generally accepted acknowledgment that a researcher has met an obligation to the scientific community.

Summary

Chapter 12 described the general processes involved in analyzing research findings and disseminating them so that they can be used to inform practice. Some of the more commonly used methods of data reduction (frequency distributions and graphs, measures of central tendency and dispersion) were described. It was emphasized that the researcher has an obligation to describe accurately the research sample or population from which data were collected. Results of descriptive statistical analysis usually are reported to portray participants' relevant demographic characteristics.

If hypothesis testing is undertaken (as is the case in most quantitative studies), inferential statistical analysis of data is undertaken to determine the likelihood that sampling error may have produced a relationship between variables within a research sample. An overview of both the theoretical underpinnings and the limitations of statistical testing were presented. The limited meaning of statistical significance was discussed. It was explained how, in some situations, a finding of a statistically significant relationship between variables may be of little practical value.

All statistical tests of significance have assumptions—conditions relating to sampling methods, level of measurement, and so forth that are requirements for their use. They are described in books on statistics and are also addressed in the many Internet sites and "help" menus of statistical software packages that are now available to assist the researcher in selecting the appropriate test.

The eight sections of a typical research report were described along with how the report may vary if the research was primarily qualitative. The research report or monograph was proposed as just one vehicle that researchers use to communicate research findings to interested audiences. Other alternatives for research dissemination that were discussed are internal correspondence and in-service training, major conference presentations, other professional gatherings, and publication in professional journals.

For Discussion

1. How does the task of data analysis in a qualitative study differ from that in a quantitative one? If research participants were people who lost a son or daughter in a war in the Middle East, what additional description of research participants (beyond demographics) might be included?
2. What are the advantages of presenting frequencies using graphs? Why would we not always use graphs to present frequencies?
3. Why would reporting only the average age of research participants not communicate a very accurate picture of their ages? What else would the reader of a research report need to know?
4. Do you think the term "statistically significant" is misleading to many people? What might have been a better term for it?
5. In a research study, statistical analysis reveals that the relationship between child-rearing practices and delinquency is very likely to have been the work of sampling error. If the two variables really are related, what are some ways that this could have happened?
6. How did coming up with an answer to the previous question rely on both (a) your knowledge of research design, and (b) your knowledge of human behavior?
7. Do you think that a report of a predominantly qualitative research study should be required to use the standard research report format that was designed for more quantitative studies? Why or why not?
8. What are some criteria that might be used in evaluating the overall quality of the knowledge that is disseminated at national or international conferences?
9. What is the relative importance of circulation, methods for review of submissions, and acceptance rates in evaluating the quality of a professional journal? How would each of these factors enter into your decision about whether to submit a report of your research to a given journal? What else would you consider?
10. Do there seem to be more reports of quantitative studies in social work journals than of qualitative ones? Do you think the mix is about right, or does it reflect a bias on the report of reviewers?

Endnotes

1. See, for example, Patton, M. (2001). *Qualitative research and evaluation methods.* Thousand Oaks, CA: Sage Publications. Or Fielding, N., & Lee, R. (1998). *Computer analysis and qualitative research.* Thousand Oaks, CA: Sage Publications.

2. See, for example, Norusis, M. (2003). *SPSS 12.0 Statistical procedures companion.* Englewood Cliffs, NJ: Prentice Hall. Or Bordens, K., & Abbott, B. (1995). *Labstat statistical software for research design and methods: A process of approach.* New York: McGraw-Hill.

3. Sudham, S. (1976). *Applied sampling.* New York: Academic Press.

4. See, for example, Weinbach, R., & Grinnell, R. Jr. (2007). *Statistics for social workers.* Boston: Allyn and Bacon, 96–98.

5. See, for example, Pyrczak, F., & Bruce, R. (2007). *Writing research reports.* Glendale, CA: Pyrczak Publishing.

6. See, for example, Beebe, L. (1999). *Professional writing for the human services.* Washington, D.C.: NASW Press. Or NASW Press Staff (1997). *An author's guide to social work journals.* Washington, D.C.: NASW Press.

PART IV

EVALUATION RESEARCH

13

EVALUATING PROGRAMS

Evidence-based practice is possible today because of the work of researchers. While basic research has provided the knowledge of human behavior that has made it possible for us to understand human problems and their origins, it has been the findings of applied research that have allowed us to make practice decisions and offer interventions that we have reason to believe will be effective. The bulk of this applied research has taken one of three forms in recent years:

1. Meta-analysis (discussed in Chapter 8) has informed us about which type of intervention has proven effective (or ineffective) with certain types of problems. It has been used to evaluate theories of intervention.
2. Program evaluation (the topic of this chapter) has evaluated specific social programs at various stages of their development.
3. The services of individual social work practitioners have been evaluated in systematic ways to provide feedback to them about their effectiveness in working with some problem of a specific client or client system. (Chapter 14).

Many of the examples that we have used in the previous chapters referred to real and hypothetical program evaluations. We chose them because they provide both clear examples of many of the methodological issues that were discussed and good illustrations of how research can inform practice and help us to make better decisions. However, program evaluation is such an important part of social work research activities today that we also believe it merits a whole chapter devoted exclusively to it.

Program evaluation is an important research enterprise. There are individuals who specialize in it, and there are many whole books and articles that focus on it.[1] They go into great detail about the specific methods for conducting it. In this text, we will focus on developing a good general understanding of what program evaluation is, what different focuses it can assume, and how it relates to our discussion of social work research in earlier chapters.

What Is Program Evaluation?

Program evaluation encompasses a wide range of activities and attempts to answer many different questions about programs. In the broadest sense, program evaluation can be thought of as "the application of both quantitative and qualitative research methods to evaluate the merit, worth or value of a program."[2] The focus of a program evaluation may be an old well established program, a relatively new one, or one that is just being considered.

Programs are subunits of organizations, constructed in a unique way to address some social problem. They are more or less self-contained and autonomous. What they hope to accomplish should be consistent with the organization's mission and its vision statement. However, programs generally have their own goals, objectives, policies, rules, procedures, strategies, services, staff, budget, space, and so forth, which may differ from those found elsewhere in the organization.

For social workers, the pressure to evaluate the effectiveness of programs is increasing. Many of these pressures come from a program's stakeholders. A *stakeholder* is anyone who "has a stake" (an investment) in a program and its success. The most obvious stakeholders might be donors—voluntary donors and those who "donate" through their taxes or health insurance premiums. Other donors might be funding organizations such as The United Way or private foundations that provide financial support to programs. However, there are still other stakeholders. They might include board members who are responsible for an organization's operation, government regulatory organizations, and the staff members who invest their time and talents to work in a program. Of course, we cannot forget clients—they have a very big investment in a program that they enter with the expectation that it will be of help with some problem they have.

Use of Logic Models

We referred to logic models back in Chapter 8. A program's logic model displays what the program is all about, what it hopes to accomplish, how it hopes to accomplish it, and how it will determine if it has been accomplished. It is both a description of a program and a management tool. It describes a program in concise form and, if well articulated, can result in a well integrated, efficient program. There is no single template for a logic model, but logic models generally consist of a description of the program's following components:

1. *Inputs.* Inputs are all of the resources that are available to the program, both monetary and nonmonetary. Common inputs would be reflected in the program budget but would also include other resources that the program has, such as the services of volunteers or donations in kind.
2. *Activities.* Activities are how the program's inputs are used. Services to clients are generally a very important activity, but so are other actions that support services or make them possible, such as the work of program managers. For example, fundraising, marketing of the program, or development of referral sources would be important activities within a program.

3. *Outputs.* Outputs are what the program produced, generally, what it accomplished in quantifiable terms. Examples of outputs might be number of clients served, number of workshops offered, or number of new cases opened.

4. *Outcomes.* Outcomes are the degree to which the program accomplished what it intended to accomplish, generally the elimination or reduction of the problem that the program sought to address. They are the degree to which clients or client systems benefited from the program—how much of a difference it made. Outcomes are often described as short term, intermediate term, and long term. A *short-term outcome* might be how clients who complete the program are different from how they were when they entered it. Or, it might relate to other objectives such as serving a specific targeted population or demonstrating a certain level of program efficiency. *Intermediate-term outcomes* often relate to objectives of continued client growth and progress following their completion of a program such as the continued career advancement of clients who complete a job training program. *Long-term outcomes* (sometimes called impacts) often reflect a wide range of changes that may result from the program, such as reduction of the problem within society, effect on the need for other programs, or the long-term impact on clients. Evaluating the degree of achievement of intermediate-term and long-term outcomes often requires follow-up of former clients and/or a longitudinal component in a program evaluation design.

5. *Indicators.* Indicators are the methods used to evaluate the degree to which outcomes have been achieved. They are how program success is measured.

Box 13.1 reflects the contents of a relatively simple logic model. Note how its various components fit together. A program manager would articulate the logic model for his or her program by describing the various forms that each component would take. Indicators would be attached to each outcome objective. If a more complex logic model is used, it may also contain content on other factors that describe the program and the likelihood of its success. Two common ones are constraints and mandates. *Constraints* are limitations that affect the program. For example, there may be certain conditions imposed on it by the organization in which it is housed, by legal restrictions such as confidentiality requirements, or ethical limitations that will not allow it to function as it might in a

BOX 13.1   The Contents of a Typical Logic Model

Inputs	Activities	Outputs	Outcomes		
			Short-term	Intermediate	Long-term
Resources (human and material) allocated to the program	What takes place within the program; how inputs are used to attempt to produce outcomes	Products of a program's activities; what the program produced	How the problem was reduced by the program; how its clients benefited	Continued effects of the program over time	Ultimate effects of the program on its clients and others

less-restricted world. A *mandate* restricts the program in a related but somewhat different way. It is a requirement (often a legal one or one required for licensure or accreditation) that something must be in place or must happen in a certain way. For example, a program may be mandated to offer certain services or to offer them in some prescribed way.

A good logic model can help a program to stay "on track" and thus increase its likelihood of success. It can also help an evaluator to understand what a program hopes to accomplish and how it is designed to function. However, even the best logic model cannot guarantee success and should not be used as the primary indicator of a program's merit, worth, or value. Unless an evaluator is careful, he or she can slip into the trap of being overly impressed by a complete, well written logic model or thinking less of a program because it lacks one. However, it should be remembered that some programs (by the nature of what they do and how they go about accomplishing it) have an easy time "fitting into" a logic model. Others, for some of the same reasons, are more likely to struggle with it. In either case, it might be unfair to reward or penalize the program based on the quality of its logic model.

Why We Conduct Program Evaluations

Program evaluation seeks to improve the quality of social programs. The programs may be involved in social action, prevention, treatment, or any other form of intervention that improves human conditions. The primary task of program evaluation is to test the theoretical models that underlie a social program. Most programs "sound good"—they seem like they ought to get underway easily and accomplish their objectives. But a program that sounds good "in theory" may not work or be what is actually needed in the real world.

As we have already described, program evaluation occurs at all stages of program development. It occurs when programs are in the planning or formulation stage. Then the goal of the research is to describe accurately the need for a program and, if it is found to be needed, to tailor the program to meet that need. Once programs are underway, other forms of program evaluation look at how well a program has been implemented. Still other forms of program evaluation look at accountability issues such as, did the program achieve its objectives? The results of these evaluations are used for making a wide range of decisions about whether a program should be offered, continued, modified, or terminated.

Although program evaluations can and are planned to be undertaken at any time in the life cycle of a program, certain events sometimes precipitate them. For example, a politically prominent critic of the program may have questioned the need for the program, professionals or clients may have expressed doubt about its effectiveness, or a funding organization may have determined that extended funding will not be offered until it has demonstrated its ongoing accountability.

Historical Background

Program evaluation as it is currently employed is a relatively new form of research, first receiving widespread attention during the Great Depression and during and after World War II. The need for it became especially great in the 1970s and 1980s, when conservative government leaders carried through on election promises to take a careful (some would say hypercritical) look at social programs that were accused of having failed to solve problems like poverty, unemployment, delinquency, and substance abuse. Other constituencies also began to voice demands for accountability at about the same time. Members of the general public wanted to know how their taxes were being spent, and they sought documentation of the success of social programs that they were supporting. The consumer movement that surfaced in the 1960s and 1970s also produced another group of people—clients—who wanted proof that programs were accomplishing their objectives. Helping professionals themselves began to recognize the importance of evaluating the success of programs. Faced with threatened and real funding cutbacks, they sought methods to help them to use limited resources in the most economical and productive ways. In the late twentieth century, rising costs of health care and related programs and the threats of privatization of what have historically been social work programs only increased the emphasis on program efficiency. It was now not enough to demonstrate that a program accomplished some good things. We also had to be able to show that it did this at the least amount of cost or, frequently, more cheaply than some other program.

Of course, program evaluation of some form has always been around. What are relatively new are the comprehensive focus of today's program evaluations and the use of comprehensive research designs for answering key questions. In the past, methods for evaluating existing programs were often narrowly focused, focusing on some aspect of a program that one or more stakeholders deemed especially important to program success. For example:

- *Budget reviews* determined if a program stayed within budget and whether expenditures in any area were excessive or extravagant.
- *Social accounting* examined program records to look for problems such as missing or incomplete client records, ambiguous categories of services, and the overall accuracy of record-keeping and recording.
- *Audits* were conducted by outside auditors to search for financial irregularities such as double billing of third parties for services or misuse of funds for the personal benefit of staff members.
- *Administrative audits* examined the degree to which a program was well managed. They determined whether managers performed the tasks of planning, staffing, organizing, controlling, and leading well. For example, they might look to see if employees received timely performance evaluations or whether there was an up-to-date manual outlining a program's rules, policies, and procedures.
- *Time and motion studies* examined how staff used their time. They sought to identify nonproductive activities or other areas of inefficiency such as inconvenient placement of office equipment that might reduce productivity or otherwise interfere with a program's functioning.
- *Functional evaluations* attempted to learn whether the program was run "properly," often operationalized as the degree to which clients were treated professionally.
- *Structural evaluations* focused on such factors as the academic credentials and diversity of staff, the esthetics and healthiness of facilities, and the presence of state-of-the art technology. An accreditation review is often a form of structural evaluation.
- *Cost-benefit analysis* was used to compute a cost-benefit ratio when both costs and benefits could be measured in monetary terms. It was designed to determine the

degree to which a program was able to produce a net overall saving for its stakeholders through its presence.

- *Cost-effectiveness analysis* was used to compute the cost of an individual program "success" by dividing the number of successes by the overall cost of the program. Then these costs could be compared with the cost effectiveness of other programs that might be attempting to accomplish the same objectives.

These methods of evaluating some component of a program are still around. Each has its merit. However, when they are used in today's program evaluations they are generally just one piece of the evaluation design. They contribute to an assessment of the overall value, worth or merit, of a program, but they certainly are not a sufficient indicator of it in themselves.

At the time when demand for more comprehensive program evaluations first began to occur, social workers were fearful that it would result in a loss of many valuable programs. Although some programs were lost, the fears proved to be mostly unfounded. By now we have become quite comfortable with program evaluations as a part of responsible practice. We recognize both their necessity and their value. We understand that many programs within human service organizations receive funding through grants and contracts with government organizations and private charitable organizations, and we acknowledge that these organizations have a right to know if the money that they provide is being used productively. We are no longer surprised that almost all such agreements now require that the recipient provide a rigorous evaluation of the way that monies are spent and some documentation of a program's success. Besides, if a program is not effective, we would like to know it anyway, so that we can revise it or drop it and spend our time and energy on some other program with greater success potential.

Types of Program Evaluations

There are two types of programs: time limited and permanent. Time-limited programs are often grant funded and have a specified duration, for example, three or five years. They may or may not be funded for one or more additional "cycles," often depending on the results of program evaluations. Permanent programs may be mandated by law or may have begun as time-limited programs but are now a relatively permanent component of an agency or organization. Unless there is evidence to the contrary, they are assumed to be needed and will continue indefinitely. There are also three general categories of program evaluation. In time-limited programs they correspond roughly to the stage of development of the program. In permanent programs the parallel is less direct. The three categories are: (1) needs assessments, (2) formative evaluations, and (3) outcome (sometimes called summative) evaluations.

Needs Assessments

In the broadest sense, the purpose of a needs assessment for a proposed program is to describe the need for such a program and, if it is found to be needed, to propose a program to best respond to that need. Typically, a needs assessment also defines the problem of concern, (actual conditions and how they differ from what is desirable), identifies unmet needs, and describes obstacles that might prevent a program from being effective in meeting them.

What type of questions does a researcher try to answer in determining if there is a need for a program? The most basic one is: Does the problem that we believe to exist really exist? Answering it often entails a documentation of the existence of the problem, who it affects, its magnitude, the forms that it takes, and the costs that result from it.

Almost always, the need for a program can be documented. After all, a program is often considered because we have already observed a need such as the absence of services that our clients require. However, just because the need for a program has been verified, that does not mean that we will offer the program as initially envisioned or even that we will offer it at all. That is why a needs assessment must address many other questions. Here are just some of them:

- What appear to be the causes of the problem in this community?
- How severe or widespread is it? Who appears to suffer most from it?
- Are we the best organization to address the problem?
- How adequate are existing programs for addressing it?
- What additional services appear needed?
- Do other organizations or programs have plans for offering them?
- Are there existing program models that could be successfully implemented here?
- What would be reasonable objectives for a program that would address the problem?
- What would be the budgetary and staffing requirements of such a program?
- Is there potential for outside funding for such a program? Where?
- Would the program have the potential to be self-supporting at some point?
- What organizations and individuals would welcome the proposed program? Who might oppose it?
- How might the program's existence affect other programs both inside and outside the organization?
- If offered, what potential clients should it target?
- How likely are targeted clients to use the program?
- What are potential referral sources for the program?
- How should the program be marketed in order to make it attractive to potential clients?
- What logistical obstacles to client participation exist? How could they be overcome?
- What would be a realistic timeframe for implementing the program?
- What tasks would have to be completed before the program would be operational?
- How, when, and by whom should the program be evaluated?

Accurate answers to these and other related questions are absolutely essential if the findings of a needs assessment are to have value. A needs assessment can be a valuable planning tool, or if it contains major design flaws, it can be a real liability to the achievement of the objectives of a program. A poor needs assessment is worse than none at all. It can mislead an administrator into making decisions based on an inaccurate reading of the requirements of a program. Poor decisions will occur. Valuable resources will be misdirected and wasted.

One way to increase the likelihood of accurate answers to questions in any program evaluation is to obtain several different perspectives, a process that researchers sometimes describe as *convergent analysis*. It means, essentially, collecting data from three (or more) sources, each having different perspectives on an issue. It usually can be assumed that no one group, influenced by its own concerns, priorities, experiences, and vested interests, can provide a totally accurate assessment of any situation. In convergent analysis, the different sources help to verify or to refute each other. Although any one source may be misleading, when data from all sources are examined together, the truth will emerge.

How might convergent analysis or triangulation work in a needs assessment? Suppose that a needs assessment is being conducted in preparation for the development of an HIV prevention program within a community judged to be at risk for high incidence of the disease. Politicians, medical professionals, public educators, clergy, elders, and potential recipients of services who might be surveyed or interviewed might all be knowledgeable about the problem and its solution to some extent, but also might provide very different answers to the same questions. Collectively, these people might be described as key informants. Still other answers might be suggested through an analysis of organization records, community demographics, and other sources of both qualitative and quantitative data collected for a variety of specialized uses.

Somewhere within all of the (often conflicting) data collected, there will be found the knowledge needed to create and implement a successful program. The researcher or research team conducting the needs assessment has the difficult job of finding it and conveying it accurately in a research report.

When they are comprehensive enough to construct one, an effective way to synthesize all of the data collected in a needs assessment is to provide a clearly articulated logic model in the report that describes the "ideal program." This allows administrators and others responsible for implementing the program to compare their personnel and financial resources with the model's requirements to assess the feasibility of such a program. They may conclude that the program is feasible, or they may conclude that, while such a program would be desirable, the organization lacks the capacity to offer the program at the current time. If it is the latter, they may still decide that even a scaled-down program would still be "better than nothing," or they may decide to wait until they have the resources to "do it right."

Although needs assessments are most often associated with programs that are in the planning stage, they also are conducted in more permanent programs. They can be used (1) to answer the basic question: Is this program still needed? *Or*, (2) to determine what changes in the program are necessary for it to retain its relevance. Conditions that create a need for a program change over time. A program that was once needed and made a valuable contribution to a community may now have its usefulness questioned, thus suggesting the appropriateness of a needs assessment.

What clues may suggest that a needs assessment of an existing program should be designed and implemented? Certain client groups may have stopped participating in the program, or the nature of the community (its economic well-being, age or ethnic mix, and so forth) may have changed. Perhaps other organizations may have begun similar programs that now compete with the program, or technological changes may have occurred that now make the program appear old fashioned or even obsolete. These and other changing conditions may suggest that it is time to conduct research that can be used either to justify continuing a program, to modify it, or to phase it out completely in a way that is least destructive to its clients and staff members. Data from needs assessment also can be used to convince others of the continued need for a program, or to budget for either an expanded or scaled-down program. They can also help in marketing a program if it is concluded that it is still needed, and for planning for future changes designed to keep the program viable and relevant.

Formative Evaluations

Once a program is underway, program evaluation involves securing data about the degree to which the program is operational as planned and, if it is, what changes might be desirable for increasing the likelihood of it achieving its objectives. This form of program evaluation is referred to as a *formative evaluation.* In formative evaluations, the evaluation is designed to determine if the program is on schedule and doing what it was intended to do. It seeks to generate suggestions for overcoming obstacles to program implementation and to recommend ways to improve the program. Evaluating program implementation generally yields three kinds of data: (1) documentation that the program is really in operation as planned; (2) data designed to help program planners know how well program activities are being managed; and (3) data about program design defects or undesirable unintended consequences of the program. Emphasis is upon the support system for services and on the services themselves as perceived by clients and staff members.

In many formative evaluations, the researcher's role is very close to that of consultant. Feedback to the sponsor of the research is likely to be regular and ongoing. Interim reports may be provided, in addition to a final written report of the evaluation. As problems are identified, changes are made and their success is then evaluated.

Formative evaluations often require the researcher to collect new data from a variety of sources. They might include many of the same sources that are used in conducting needs assessments, such as telephone surveys, mailed questionnaires, focus groups, interviews with key informants, structured and unstructured firsthand observation, and other methods that were described elsewhere. However, secondary data analysis is often part of a formative evaluation, too. For example, daily attendance sheets might provide the evaluator with data about how well a program is recruiting and retaining clients, or personnel data might suggest whether staff turnover is a problem.

A formative evaluation is designed to provide feedback (more accurately, "feedforward") to program administrators. The researcher who conducts a formative evaluation hopes to identify strengths and weaknesses of a program in its early stages and to recommend needed changes while the program is still in its earlier stages of development. In a formative evaluation, the evaluator asks many of the same questions that a conscientious program manager asks on a regular basis. This function of managers is called *program monitoring*; the ongoing tracking of a program to be ensured that it is functioning as planned. However, the evaluator in a formative evaluation can offer an outsider's perspective. He or she has no vested interest in the program's success and thus is more likely to provide constructive criticisms of the program (even its management) than is the manager of a program who is immersed in its day-to-day operation.

When a similar evaluation is conducted later in the life cycle of a program, sometimes even when the program is nearing completion, a different term, *process evaluation,* is more appropriate. A process evaluation also relies on a mixture of qualitative and quantitative data to gain insight into the functioning of a program. It is much like a systems analysis. However, whereas a formative evaluation might try to learn what is working and what is not working, a process evaluation would be more of a post mortem. It would try to learn why an objective apparently will not be achieved or why one component of a program has been successful whereas another was not, so that desirable changes can be made if the program is offered again or other programs can learn from the current program's mistakes.

Outcome Evaluations

Outcome evaluations remain the best known form of evaluative research. Because their findings have the potential to threaten the existence of programs and the careers of people who work in them, they are sometimes also the most feared form of program evaluation. However, there are many benefits to outcome evaluations. They are beneficial to future clients by increasing the likelihood that they will receive services that work and will not receive services that are ineffective. The findings of outcome evaluations also are more likely to have utility for people not directly related to the program than the other types of program evaluation that we have discussed thus far. Why? When the results of an outcome evaluation are disseminated to others not involved in the program but working in the same area of practice, they are likely to learn something that is potentially useful to them in their work. If a program is found to be successful, they may then wish to try the same type of intervention or adapt it to meet the needs of their own client population.

If a program is found to be unsuccessful in achieving its objectives, other professionals can still learn from its failings in important ways. For example, they might learn that the program was not well conceptualized in the first place. Or the program, though theoretically good, might have failed to successfully address the problem for a variety of logistical reasons or because cultural issues were inadequately addressed. Another possibility is that the program was unsuccessful because the problem was not what it is generally believed to be. When this occurs, not only is something learned about the possible solution to a problem, but our understanding of the problem itself can be enhanced. Learning about why a program was unsuccessful can be very useful to other professionals seeking to address the same problem—it can keep them from making some of the same mistakes.

In the past, the success of programs was often evaluated based on their outputs. For example, the conclusion that "This program offered services to 140 hospice patients and their families during the past year, an increase of more than 22 percent over the previous year" was adequate evidence that a program had been successful. However, accountability pressures now require that documentation of how many people were served, and similar outputs are no longer adequate evidence of a program's success. Now a major emphasis is on outcomes, that is, the degree to which a program has been successful in achieving its objectives at a reasonable cost. Thus, this kind of evaluation often involves a dual-focused emphasis on program effectiveness (achievement of objectives) and program efficiency (the relationship of outcome to expenditure of efforts and resources), often using yardsticks of cost-benefit analysis or cost-effectiveness. Comparisons between two related programs often are helpful in this regard. They might reveal that one program may be achieving its objectives, but at an extremely high cost, whereas another program may be achieving the same objectives, but at a much lower cost. Thus, both are effective, but they get very different marks in efficiency. We will use an example to show how this could occur and how it is often difficult to determine which one is the better program.

Suppose that program A and program B are both job training programs. Program A carefully selected three clients and offered each client room, board, full tuition, and expenses to attend a junior college for two years, as well as free weekly counseling. At the end of two years, all three clients have found jobs (a success rate of 100 percent). The total cost of program A was $150,000, or $50,000 per client.

The total cost of program B was only $45,000, much lower than program A's. It was able to keep down costs by designing and offering its own intensive job training course. But program B also had a much lower success rate; only three of twelve (25 percent) of its graduates found good jobs. However, program B could claim that it had been successful in placing three clients (the same number as program A) and at a cost of only $15,000 per client!

It could be argued that program B was more efficient than program A, because the cost of each success in program B was less than one-third the cost of each success in program A. It could also be argued that program A was more effective because of its higher success rate. Or it could be argued that it was equally as effective as program B (but less efficient), because both programs successfully helped three clients to find good jobs. So, which was the more successful program? It is hard to say. We probably would be concerned about the per capita cost of helping people find employment under program A. But we also could not help being concerned about the low success rate of program B. What about the human costs related to those nine clients who completed the program, hopeful of getting good jobs, who were not successful in finding employment?

Still other factors might further complicate a comparison of the two programs. Perhaps program B offered its clients more career choices. However, program A's clients were hired for better paying jobs or higher level jobs. The interaction between success (and failure) and their costs is never a simple one. Weighing the relative merits of effectiveness and efficiency objectively is one of the most difficult tasks faced by the evaluator. Studying program outcomes typically requires the evaluator to assess client gains and losses, the side effects and unintended consequences of the program, and the costs (including economic, social, and psychological) of operating it. As we have found with other forms of research, good outcome evaluation studies must rely heavily on the knowledge, skills, and professional values of the social worker.

In time-limited programs, outcome evaluations are conducted at or near the completion of the program's funding cycle. They focus on the achievement of short-term outcomes, but the program design may also include additional follow-up in order to learn whether longer term objectives were achieved. In permanent programs or programs that are intended to be permanent, an outcome evaluation is generally conducted for the first time at the point where it would be fair to expect that the program should have demonstrated success. Then subsequent outcome evaluations may occur at periodic intervals, perhaps, every five years, to determine if the program is continuing to be successful and valuable.

Determining the Appropriate Design

There are many different ideas about what constitutes a fair yet rigorous evaluation design for a social program. It is probably safe to say that a design developed for any one program is ill suited for another. That is why no two are alike. In order to design an appropriate evaluation, one must first identify the stage of program development of the program.

Is it in the planning stages, laying the groundwork for future services? Is it offering some services but still seeking to expand through outreach and publicity? Or are most activities devoted to services that are in place, well known, and relatively stable? The stage of development of a program is determined by such factors as the activities of staff and how they spend most of their time, funding priorities within the program, and the kind of data (records) collected and used by it. It is not synonymous with how long the program has been in existence. A program could be decades old but still actively seeking community sanction and client acceptance. Conversely, a program that is only a year or two old may devote most of its energies to the delivery of needed and legitimized services.

The pressure for accountability of social programs in recent years has produced a wide variety of different evaluation designs and strategies. Many have been borrowed from basic research methods and modified to a greater or lesser degree to adapt them to social programs. Some have come into fashion quickly and fallen out of fashion about as quickly. We will not attempt to examine individual evaluation models (presented in many books and government documents, and a topic for advanced study). However, we will offer some general principles relating to the design of evaluation studies in each of the three categories that we have discussed.

All program evaluations now typically combine elements of both quantitative and qualitative research methods. In needs assessments, the methods employed are generally a combination of exploratory and descriptive. For example, the open-ended question—Do you think there is a need for an HIV infection prevention program in our community?—might be asked of people representing a wide variety of backgrounds and perspectives in either one-on-one interviews or in a focus group. Or the same question (along with others) could be part of a mailed survey sent to community leaders. Much of the data required in needs assessments also can be found through secondary analysis of social indicators, census data, and other sources of data collected for some other purpose.

Formative (or process) evaluations tend to be primarily descriptive. For example, the evaluator may wish to gather a wide array of descriptive data (including personal observations) to evaluate how well a program seems to have gotten off the ground and to make recommendations for needed changes. Descriptive designs also may be used to answer other questions about program implementation, for example: Are the clients who were targeted for services actually being served? Confidential, in-depth interviews with clients and staff may be conducted and the content of interviews examined using content analysis.

Outcome evaluations strive to be explanatory. Thus, when possible, they often employ the same basic explanatory designs that we described in Chapter 6 (experimental and quasiexperimental) to attempt to learn not only whether or not a program achieved its objectives but also whether or not the program can "take credit" for any achievements. They test the null hypotheses about program effectiveness by using inferential statistical analyses to learn the probability that the relationship between the program and some indicator of success was a real one, and not just a function of sampling error. By using designs that rely on random assignment of clients to programs (and to control groups), it is also possible to conclude that it was the program, and not something else, that produced any successes (the issue of internal validity). Of course, for ethical and logistical reasons, it is not always possible to use explanatory designs. Then designs that are more descriptive are used. They contain a mixture of qualitative and quantitative methods.

Researchers conducting outcome evaluations attempt to rely on measurement that is as quantitative as possible. However, even when explanatory designs can be used and quantitative measurements of the achievement of program objectives can be undertaken, qualitative methods are still likely to be used to gather some data, Sometimes they are used to attempt to confirm impressions obtained using more quantitative measures. For example, confidential follow-up interviews might be used to try to better understand the high number of responses in a survey of staff members that seem to suggest that the program is not favorable to cultural diversity. Qualitative research methods may also be used to assess other indicators of the merit of a program. For example, interviews might be conducted with key informants to attempt to learn the reputation of the program in the community or how well its staff members are perceived as collaborating with staff members from other programs that address the same problem. Interviews with the program manager or grant writer might be used to learn how much progress is being made in moving toward financial independence. Or, a focus group of staff members might help in evaluating the quality of materials developed by program staff (for example, training manuals or computer software), to attempt to learn if they represent a valuable side benefit of the program.

If experimental or quasiexperimental designs are ethically feasible and if program outcomes have been well stated and quantified (for example, "Following completion of the program, clients who completed the program will have a lower rate of re-hospitalization that those who did not participate in the program"), the determination of whether or not the program achieved its objective is a relatively simple, statistical one. However, if the objectives of the program were never well articulated or the program was not implemented as articulated in its logic model, then any conclusions relating to the value, worth, or merit of such a program become much more difficult. When this happens, someone (often another evaluator) may first have to examine the program's activities and, based on them, use an inductive process to identify and specify the program's mission, goals, and objectives. This is known as *evaluability assessment*. It makes outcome evaluation more possible.

In an outcome evaluation, the evaluator must have a clear understanding of the anticipated outcomes and be very careful in the selection of appropriate outcome measures (indicators). If judgments are to be made on the basis of its outcomes, then rigorous but fair outcome measures are needed. Often they are already available in the form of standardized indexes or scales. But it may be that, in the interest of fairness, original evaluation instruments will need to be developed for the evaluation. If this is necessary, then the researcher must use instrument development procedures that will ensure that measures will be valid (see Chapter 10).

One notable trend has been evident in recent years. Increasingly, evaluations of existing programs are being required, by outside funding sources, to include input from consumers of services (clients). This trend generally has met with little resistance from social workers since, when asked (or, perhaps, because they are asked) clients generally report a high level of satisfaction with programs and services. Besides, it just seems right that we should ask our clients about their impressions of our programs. However, the validity of any findings from client satisfaction surveys are highly suspect for several reasons, the most obvious being that client satisfaction is not a valid indicator of program effectiveness. Clients can be satisfied or dissatisfied with a program for any number of reasons that do not relate to the quality of the program. In some fields of practice (for example, protective services or the juvenile justice system) where clients are "involuntary," some social workers have argued especially vehemently that consumer satisfaction is an unfair yardstick for measuring program success.

Most outcome evaluation designs focus on short-range success (outcome). However, there has been concern that they do not adequately address two issues: (1) the program's success may not hold up over time and (2) they give inadequate attention to the impact of the program on other programs and services—the unintended consequences of the program. In response to these concerns, some evaluation models have attempted to address them. They determine whether programs have resulted in permanent desirable changes. For example, they might ask whether street crime rates and unemployment rates stayed low or declined even more following the completion of athletic and recreational programs for youth.

Program evaluations that look at the long-term impacts of a program also look beyond a program itself to examine how the program's presence may have affected other programs or phenomena. They are recognition (consistent with systems theory) that almost any change or innovation within a system is likely to produce both anticipated and unanticipated changes within other system components. For example, if this type of evaluation were used to evaluate a hospital's new bereavement program for caregivers of terminally ill patients who have recently died, many questions that would go beyond whether the program itself was effective would be asked. They might include, for example,

- How has the program changed the daily activities of social workers in the hospital's existing hospice program?
- How has the morale of the hospice social workers been affected?
- How has the new program's presence changed the informal power structure of the social work department?
- How has reallocation of funding affected the work of other staff?
- Are former caregivers more likely to serve as volunteers (after the required waiting period) than they were prior to the existence of the program?

Evaluating program impact requires the evaluator to extrapolate from the data collected in program outcome studies and to creatively use current social indicators. A problem with studies that include an assessment of a program's impact is the presence of a multitude of other variables that may have produced apparent impacts, especially because these studies generally employ a longer time framework for conducting an evaluation. So many different events and circumstances can intervene that it becomes very difficult to attribute any apparent impact directly to the effects of a program. In our previous example, it would be very hard to attribute changes within the hospice social work program directly to the presence of the new bereavement program rather than to other events or phenomena. For example, staff turnover, the lack of pay raises in more than three years, or burnout might have been the real reasons for any changes. Perhaps no changes were produced by the program at all. Or they might have been even more dramatic if the bereavement program had not been implemented!

The difficulty of isolating the longer term impact of a program and of determining how other (confounding) variables may relate to any apparent program impact is certainly not unique to social work program evaluations. For example, impact studies in the 1980s were used to examine the relationship between lower speed limits and rate of traffic fatalities. But how can people say (as many do) that fewer fatal accidents in the 1970s and the early 1980s were the result of federally imposed 55-mile-per-hour speed limits or that an increase in fatalities in the late 1990s occurred because speed limits were relaxed? One would need to control for many other possibly intervening variables, such as gasoline prices, number of miles driven, the work of Mothers Against Drunk Drivers (MADD), inconsistent punishments for driving while under the influence of alcohol or drugs, changes in automobile safety equipment, changes in size and design of automobiles, the advent of cellular phones, and literally hundreds of other variables that may contribute to traffic fatality rates. Similarly, it would be very difficult to learn whether a program to reduce teen smoking has been successful in achieving its objectives when, during its operation, smoking was made illegal in restaurants, the sales tax on cigarettes was increased, the dangers of second-hand smoke were verified, and public hostility toward smokers was on the increase.

Ultimately, since an outcome evaluation is designed to learn whether a program reduced or alleviated a problem (a cause–effect relationship between two variables was demonstrated), the value of an outcome evaluation design and the findings that it produced come down to questions of validity. The four types of validity are those summarized in Chapter 10; however, they have a specific meaning in outcome evaluations:

1. *Construct validity.* Was the intended program implemented as planned, and were intended outcomes measured using appropriate indicators?
2. *Conclusion validity.* Do the evaluator's conclusions about the program appear to be sufficiently justified?
3. *Internal validity.* Were desirable changes in the problem *caused by* the program?
4. *External validity.* To what extent would other programs benefit from the findings of the evaluation?

Who Conducts Program Evaluations?

In a general sense every social work professional is involved in program evaluation to a greater or lesser extent. It is a requirement for social workers in the twenty-first century, one that is consistent with the goal of evidence-based practice. At the very least, as employees of social programs or as professionals familiar with them, social workers are a potential data source for program evaluations. They possess a valuable perspective on them. At some point they will be called upon to share that perspective as research participants. Other social workers will more actively assist others conducting program evaluations, perhaps by providing help in conducting research interviews or assisting in data tabulation and analysis. Others, those who have a little more expertise and a special interest in evaluation research, may participate in both the design and implementation of program evaluations.

College and university faculty members may design and conduct program evaluations from time to time as part of their research agenda or as a service to their community or profession. Still other individuals who we might describe as social work program evaluation specialists spend most or all of their professional time designing and conducting program evaluations. Some are employees of large human service organizations. One of their major responsibilities is to conduct evaluations of its programs. Other evaluation specialists are employed within institutes or centers associated with universities or in the private, for-profit sector. Their program evaluation services can be purchased through contract.

From the perspective of the the program, the issue of who is the best person to design and conduct a program evaluation often centers around one question: Is it better for the evaluator to be in house or external to the organization and its programs? In making this determination, three factors may be considered: (1) requirements, (2) convention, and (3) advantages and disadvantages.

If major funding for the program was provided by some foundation or similar organization that awarded a grant to support all or part of the program, it may be stipulated in the agreement signed by all parties involved that an outside evaluator be used. The evaluator may be an employee of the funding organization or an outside evaluation expert with whom they regularly contract. Or, a list of approved evaluators may be provided to the program manager. Then he or she may select an individual to hire with funds designated for evaluation within the grant's budget. An external evaluator is most likely to be required for an outcome evaluation, but sometimes it is a requirement for a formative evaluation as well. Less frequently, it is a requirement for a needs assessment unless one is mandated as part of a grant application.

Even if there is no requirement for an outside evaluator, convention suggests when an in-house evaluator or an external one is more appropriate. Needs assessments generally are conducted by agency employees, often as a cost-saving measure. However, if funds are available, they may be contracted out in order to get what is likely to be a more objective assessment. Formative evaluations may be conducted in house, but they are more often conducted by external evaluators with no personal or professional investment in the program. When this is the case, the evaluator still receives considerable assistance from program staff, especially managers and/or quality control personnel, who should already have been collecting data and interpreting it as part of their own program monitoring. While outcome evaluations are sometimes conducted in house, they are most often designed and conducted by outside evaluators. Since so much (jobs, funding, and so forth) is at stake in an outcome evaluation, employees of the program cannot be expected to be totally objective. If an outcome evaluation is conducted in house (as sometimes occurs when the program receives no outside funding), the credibility of the research findings can easily be questioned.

Assuming there is a choice in the matter, another issue to be considered is the relative advantages and disadvantages of using in-house evaluators or external ones. One advantage to using in-house evaluators is that they are already familiar with the organization's functions, policies, programs, people, and politics. There is little need to acquaint in-house evaluators with any of these aspects of an organization; they can hit the ground running. Because they are in-house, they also should have sensitivity to the client populations served and some sense of the organization's purpose and direction. This knowledge should help them in selecting or developing appropriate and sensitive methods of measuring key variables. Assuming that in-house evaluators also have expertise in data analysis and interpretation or have access to resources for these purposes, the evaluation study can proceed smoothly and at minimal cost to the organization. Because they are already on the payroll of an organization, no additional expenses are incurred. However, there still is a cost. In-house evaluators must be given release time from their usual duties. Other staff may need to be hired to cover for them while they conduct their program evaluations.

Of course, there also are disadvantages to using an in-house evaluator. One relates to a given evaluator's experience and expertise in program evaluation. Many individuals claim to be knowledgeable in the areas of research and statistics, and some are. But program evaluation has important differences from most other forms of research, and few persons who are employed within organizations perform program evaluations on a regular basis. Unless the person is competent to perform all necessary research tasks, the quality of the evaluation may suffer. Of course, outside consultants may be hired to help perform specialized tasks; this may be necessary to successfully implement an evaluation that uses an in-house evaluator.

A second disadvantage, one that was suggested earlier, involves the extent to which in-house evaluators can be objective about the findings of a program evaluation in the organization where they are employed. Evaluation involves making judgments about programs; these judgments should be based on the data collected and on nothing else. In-house evaluators may have difficulty being objective (an understandable difficulty if the evaluator has had even minimal involvement with the program or has acquaintances or friends who have). Or, as an employee of the organization, the evaluator might feel pressured to present findings in a way consistent with the wishes of administrators—an ethical dilemma that a nonemployee would be less likely to face. If, for whatever reason, the evaluator's objectivity is compromised, the quality and value of the research will be severely damaged.

A third disadvantage involves the way that other staff may perceive the in-house evaluator. Suddenly the evaluator may appear to have been elevated in status (perhaps with justification). The evaluator may have the power to influence the functions and even the job status of coworkers. This may result in staff resentment and resistance (more than if an outside evaluator were to be used), and it may prompt staff to be uncooperative or even to sabotage the evaluator's work. After completing the evaluation, the in-house evaluator may find relationships with coworkers to be negatively affected or even irreparably damaged. This can be costly to the organization as well as to the individuals involved.

Expertise and objectivity are two major advantages to using outside evaluators. Unfortunately, there are also distinct disadvantages to using them. Hiring an outside evaluator often requires an organization to find the money to pay someone to design and conduct a program evaluation. Given the austere budgets that often characterize human service organizations, the cost of hiring outside evaluators may be prohibitive. Outside evaluators generally are paid well for their time and expertise, and they may require more time to conduct an evaluation than would an in-house evaluator. Before they can even begin to design and implement an evaluation, an external evaluator first needs to learn about the organization and its programs. If this is not done, an evaluation design that is inappropriate and unfair may result. The amount of time needed to educate an outside evaluator varies with the complexity of the organization and its programs. But it is always necessary for an outside evaluator to spend time trying to understand what a program is trying to accomplish (its goals and objectives), the ways in which it goes about trying to accomplish them, and the stage of development of the program.

A fourth potential disadvantage concerns the extent to which external evaluators (particularly those who are not social workers working in a related practice setting) are likely to be insensitive to certain realities within which a program must operate. They may have difficulty understanding the many sources of resistance that confront clients seeking to change some aspect of their lives or the hostile task environment that exists for many unpopular programs that social workers offer. For example, they may not understand that programs designed to protect children from abuse or to prevent the spread of sexually transmitted diseases are often resented by community members who may create obstacles to their success. An outside evaluator also may have difficulty developing appropriate evaluation instruments and standards to assess the success level of such programs. Can an outside evaluator understand that a 30 percent success rate for a program to train people who are chronically unemployed may constitute an acceptable level of success? Or that historically, treatment programs for people who are chronic sex offenders have had a very low rate of success? Of course, if the program has clearly articulated realistic objectives from the outset and if the program is evaluated based on them, this problem can be greatly reduced.

The advantages of external and in-house evaluators can be maximized while minimizing the disadvantages of both. *Empowerment evaluation* is an approach to program evaluation that combines the use of in-house and external evaluators in a unique way. It has the expressed purpose of helping program staff evaluate themselves and their programs in order to improve practice and foster self-determination.[3] Like other forms of program evaluation, it employs both qualitative and quantitative methodologies. Program staff members conduct their own evaluations using a form of self-evaluation and reflection; it is very process oriented. An outside evaluator acts as a coach or facilitator depending on the capabilities of program participants and staff.

Empowerment evaluation is consistent with social work professional values. It is being used in a variety of human service organizations in many different countries, particularly with those that serve more powerless and historically disenfranchised populations. Zimmerman[4] describes the empowerment process as one in which attempts to gain control, obtain needed resources, and critically understand one's social environment are fundamental. Through this type of evaluation, people develop skills to become independent problem solvers and decision makers. Because all of the program staff (and, to a lesser degree, clients) are involved with the evaluation from its inception and form a team with the external evaluator, some of the power dynamics and areas of distrust typically associated with external evaluations are minimized.

The assessment of a program's value is not the end point of empowerment evaluation, but part of an ongoing process of service and quality improvement. The goal is to have program staff internalize and institutionalize self-evaluation practices. It allows them to practice ongoing program evaluation and improvement in the face of population shifts, changing knowledge about practice, and evolving external political forces that affect the social welfare environment. Fetterman identifies several facets of empowerment evaluation: training, facilitation, advocacy, illumination, and liberation.[5]

Training. Skilled evaluators teach program staff how to conduct their own evaluations with a focus on mastery and internalization of evaluation principles and practices as an integral part of program planning.

Facilitation. Skilled evaluators serve as coaches to help program staff conduct their own self-evaluations. Tasks include goal setting, specifying of performance indicators, establishing baselines, developing rating scales, and monitoring goal attainment.

Advocacy. Program staff members are helped to use the findings of the evaluation to gain more leverage over resources and to participate in the political process. Advocate evaluators use findings to try to change public opinion and influence the policy decision-making process.

Illumination. Program staff members are helped to gain new insights and understanding about program dynamics and roles of various stakeholders.

Liberation. Liberation is the ultimate outcome of empowerment evaluation. It is a process through which program staff members are freed from preexisting roles and constraints as they learn more about what works and what does not work. They are helped to discover new opportunities, to use existing resources in innovative ways, and to redefine the roles they play in continuous program improvement.

Participating in Program Evaluations: Concerns and Issues

When social workers and other professional staff are asked to be involved in the implementation phase of a program evaluation, they may be involved in data-gathering activities, such as submitting work documents to the evaluation team, completing questionnaires or interviews, or asking their clients to provide evaluative data. Both professional and nonprofessional staff members may express concern and skepticism when they are asked to supply data that will be used for evaluating a program. They may be fearful both for the future of the program and for their own welfare.

One possible recommendation of an outcome evaluation is that a planned or existing program should be terminated or significantly modified. Even if the decisions that are to be made about a program and its future aren't of the "continue" versus "terminate" type, staff are aware that the process of evaluating always entails making a judgment (either directly or implicitly) about the value of a given program. They also know that good outcome measures are sometimes difficult to develop and that the real, lasting achievements of a program and its overall merit, worth, or value may not be evident for many years. Thus, they fear that what they perceive to be a valuable program may show up in a bad light.

There also may be concern that an individual staff member's work performance will be assessed by the evaluator using data provided, and then shared with administrators or supervisors. The study design may, in fact, require that individual workers submit time sheets, activity logs, and other process documents. However, a goal of program evaluation studies typically is not to evaluate individual work performance (although they almost always reflect on the performance of a program's top administrator). Individual employee performance evaluations are generally conducted at regularly scheduled intervals (often, annually) by the worker's supervisor and are separate and unrelated to program evaluation studies. The evaluator is likely to receive better cooperation from staff if they are reminded of this.

A program evaluation also should be viewed as part of a greater political process for two major, related reasons. The first has to do with the purpose of the study, and the second concerns the use and potential misuse of evaluation data. As we have noted, program evaluation studies sometimes are conducted at the request or mandate of organizations that have provided funding for a program. They are conducted to address accountability concerns or to assist in answering some question, for example: Should the program be funded for another year or cycle?

In addition, program evaluations can legitimately be requested by boards of directors and funding organizations at any time. Unfortunately, such a request may not always be based on a desire for constructive feedback or other evaluation data designed to improve the program being evaluated; there may be other hidden agenda. Sometimes evaluations are requested because boards of directors simply wish to secure damaging evidence about an unpopular program or its administrator. For example, an evaluator may be hired because the board is seeking documentation to justify the firing of a program's director. Or, if a program provides desirable employment for friends or relatives, the board may be seeking justification to continue it, despite the fact that it is believed to be ineffective. As we suggested earlier, an external evaluator is likely to have more credibility and is assumed to be more objective than an employee of the organization where a program is based. However, even an external evaluator is vulnerable to being "used" unless (1) they are politically astute, and (2) they adhere to ethical standards and insist on reporting their findings in a way that presents a complete and accurate picture of a program.

Hidden agenda are a fact of life in many program evaluations and often are the impetus for them. When an evaluator from outside (or even within) an organization is asked to conduct a program evaluation, he or she should be aware that there may be motives besides a desire to improve the program. Skilled evaluators attempt to determine if they exist before agreeing to conduct program evaluations. They ask questions about the purpose of proposed evaluations and explore what possible uses may be made of the data. If it appears after some inquiry that something other than an honest evaluation is being sought, and that the evaluation will simply be used to support a decision that has already been made an ethical evaluator may refuse to participate in it. However, if the decision is not irreversible and assurances are made that the findings of the evaluation will be considered with an "open mind," the evaluator may agree to conduct it.

Other Ethical Issues

There are ethical issues in any type of research. We discussed some of the more general ones in Chapter 2. They apply to program evaluations as well as to research that is designed to build general knowledge for our profession. For example, confidentiality, anonymity, and informed consent issues must be addressed, because people who provide data for program evaluations often are vulnerable to retaliation if they are critical of a program and the source of their comments is revealed to administrators. When conducting program evaluations, however, there are also some very specific ethical dilemmas that must be confronted. Because the evaluator usually has a considerable amount of latitude in making certain critical decisions about how the research will be conducted, it is quite easy for unethical evaluators to influence the results of an evaluation.

Suppose that you have been asked to conduct an outcome evaluation of a program that was established to provide assistance to couples and individuals seeking to adopt children from Korea and China. The program is a new one to the agency, which had not previously offered international adoption services. If you were unethical, could you "stack" the evaluation so that the program would look highly successful and so that your friend who works in the program can remain employed? Yes. Or, conversely, could you design the research to make the program appear ineffective? Yes.

Evaluators make a number of important design decisions, sometimes with the "help" of powerful people like administrators, but often unilaterally. Most likely, the program has several objectives, some of which have been achieved and some of which have not been achieved. By choosing to focus on those where you know the program has been successful (for example, in expediting paperwork) and either not addressing or deemphasizing those where it has not been successful, it is possible to make a program look better than it really is. Conversely, a focus on the program's shortcomings (for example, its failure to attract single parents) could make it appear worse than it really is.

Similarly, the decision of who will provide data (sampling bias issues) can distort results. Interviewing parents of newly adopted children (as opposed to those who dropped out before the adoption was completed) can make the program look good. Interviewing staff from agencies that compete with the program for clients can make it look bad. Or, knowing what we do about different methods of data collection (for example, that in-person interviews have very high completion rates but mailed questionnaires have lower, often biased completion rates), it would be possible to get whatever results are sought. Statistical analysis and interpretation of findings also would provide opportunities to deliberately misrepresent the results of the evaluation.

In contrast, an ethical researcher would strive to produce an evaluation that is feasible given budgetary constraints and given the need not to disrupt client services, but also one that is fair and accurate. Fairness would entail getting a wide array of perspectives on the program and reporting them in a way that no group feels that their input was ignored. Accuracy would relate to the reliability and validity of the data, as well as to the correct use and interpretation of statistical analyses.

Reports of Program Evaluations

As we have repeatedly emphasized, the purpose of a program evaluation is a little different from that of other kinds of social work research. Although (like other research) it seeks to acquire needed knowledge, the knowledge sought is specific in nature. The readers of the report are likely to be those most directly related to the program, some of its stakeholders; few others (including clients) may ever see it. Consequently, research findings are also reported somewhat differently.

There are some special characteristics of reports of program evaluations that relate to the nature of evaluative research.[6] Because program evaluation is applied research which is typically conducted for the purpose of making one or more decisions about the future of a program, the report of a program evaluation is written to reflect the kind of decisions that the evaluator is attempting to facilitate. There is no standard format for all program evaluation reports. They tend to vary, dependent largely on the type of evaluation that was conducted. However, some variation of the following is frequently used.

1. *Executive summary.* The executive summary presents the essential elements of the total report, including why the evaluation was conducted. It highlights the major findings and recommendations, is brief (typically about one page), and usually is written after the rest of the report has already been prepared. In some respects, it may be the most important part of the report of a program evaluation. Like the abstract of a journal article, it may be the only part of the report that is read by all concerned. The executive summary should be written with great care, so that it captures the

main points of the report and serves as a kind of teaser to the reader to examine the rest of the report in greater detail.

2. *Program description.* The program description includes data about the development of the program, its goals and objectives, data about the client population the program is intended to serve, and (for existing programs) an account of what happens to clients after they first enter the program (the flow of activity). Data about program staffing is also included. After reviewing this section of the report, the reader should have an understanding of why the program was considered or already exists, what it intends to accomplish, and how it would achieve or already is attempting to achieve its goals. The program description section of the report can be quite long, but the author of the report usually tailors this section of the report to the intended audience. Readers who already are very familiar with the proposed or existing program will require less data in each area than, for example, a board of directors consisting of several new members who may be only marginally knowledgeable about it. The program's logic model may be included in this section of the report (if it is relatively short) or it may be referred to and included as an appendix.

3. *Program evaluation design.* The third section of the report restates the specific purpose for which the study was conducted, along with the type of evaluation design used (for example, needs assessment, formative, or outcome evaluation). Any data collection instruments that were used are described, and the reader is referred to the appendix of the report, where they are included. Any available data regarding their reliability and validity are provided. The methods of data collection are described in detail. Any limitations inherent in the evaluation design (for example, time constraints or limited access to needed data) are specified and discussed, much as they are in any other research report.

4. *Results.* In the fourth section of the report, the evaluator generally addresses each of the evaluation questions in sequence, through a discussion of relevant data. Descriptive data are presented in tabular or graphic form. Results of the use of statistical analyses generally are presented in as straightforward a manner as possible, with numbers and statistical notations kept to a minimum. If administrators or others ask the evaluator to give an oral report of the results of an evaluation study to select groups such as the board of directors, it is this section that forms the basis for such a report. But the evaluator generally adapts the way findings are presented to the anticipated interest area of the group (but not the findings themselves).

5. *Discussion.* The overall results of the study are discussed in the report's fifth section. If the evaluation was a needs assessment, efforts are made to reconcile conflicting data sources. If a need for a program has been found, a description of what such a program should look like may appear here or later in the recommendations section. If it was a formative evaluation, then the discussion of results would be more likely to address the apparent success of development or implementation of the program to date. If it was an outcome evaluation, then there is a discussion of whether the program seems to have had the desired effect or impact on program participants, as well as its apparent overall merit. The researcher is careful also to note those areas of evaluation where, because of lack of data or other methodological limitations, no definitive conclusions could be drawn.

6. *Recommendations.* In a recommendations section, the evaluator proposes a course of action as suggested by the data. If it has been made clear that specific recommendations are sought, recommendations are made in descending order of importance. Direct and persuasive language is appropriate.

When data have been conflicting or otherwise inconclusive, recommendations for additional evaluation may be appropriate. In those rare evaluation studies in which the evaluator has determined that specific recommendations are not being sought by the person or group that commissioned the evaluation (because they wish to formulate their own recommendations), this section is deleted and the evaluator's report concludes with the discussion section (part 5).

Summary

This chapter was an overview of program evaluation research, the use of both qualitative and quantitative research methods to evaluate the merit, worth, or value of proposed or existing programs. It is, in part, a response to demands for accountability by the stakeholders of programs.

In a general sense, program evaluation can be understood as a critical component in an ongoing process of planning for, fine-tuning, and passing judgment on programs. There are three major types of evaluation studies: needs assessments, formative evaluations, and outcome or summative evaluations. We described the purpose of and the research questions addressed by each in some detail. All program evaluations employ unique research designs, a variety of data sources, and data-gathering techniques.

When the option is available, the decision as to use an in-house or an outside evaluator to conduct program evaluations is a complex one. Both alternatives have advantages and disadvantages. An alternative that uses both in-house and outside evaluators—empowerment evaluation—was presented as a compromise that often combines the best features of both.

Program evaluations are action-oriented and decision-oriented research; decisions about programs and their continuation are likely to be made as a result of them. This fact and others were discussed in the context of political and ethical factors that can affect the researcher's capacity to design and conduct program evaluations.

Finally, the unique purposes and characteristics of reports of program evaluations were noted. They provide knowledge and recommendations that are specific to a given program. Some evaluations (especially those that examine program outcome) also can contribute to our professional body of knowledge.

For Discussion

1. Why do researchers rely heavily on qualitative data such as findings from confidential interviews, personal observations, and focus groups in conducting needs assessments and formative evaluations? What are some examples of quantitative data that would also be informative?

2. Why would the findings of some outcome evaluations be more likely to have a higher degree of external validity than the findings of the other types of program evaluations?

3. In a Meals on Wheels program, is the number of meals delivered an input, a service, an output, or an outcome? Should it be considered an indicator of success regardless of the category where it fits best?

4. What might be some indicators of program success in a hospice program? Why might some of the usual indicators be inappropriate?

5. Why is it not a good idea to evaluate a program based on how well its logic model is articulated? What is the best use of a program's logic model in conducting an outcome evaluation?

6. How can a cost-benefit analysis or a cost-effectiveness analysis be helpful in an outcome evaluation of the overall merit, worth, or value of a program? How could it be misleading?

7. Why is it not a good idea to rely on a single data source in answering research questions in a needs assessment? Why is triangulation or convergent analysis desirable in all types of program evaluation? Is it more important in program evaluations than in basic research?

8. Why are program staff members generally less fearful of formative evaluations than of outcome evaluations? Why are they generally not conducted by people who are employed by the program being evaluated?

9. Would it be better to use an in-house evaluator or an external evaluator to conduct a process evaluation of a federally mandated child protection program? When would empowerment evaluation work?

10. Why is it more difficult to use a "one size fits all" outline for a report of a program evaluation than for a report of basic research? How would we expect a report of a formative evaluation to differ from a report of an outcome evaluation?

Endnotes

1. See, for example, Weinbach, R., (2005). *Evaluating social work services and programs.* Boston: Allyn and Bacon. Or Royse, D. et al. (2001). *Program evaluation: An introduction.* Chicago: Nelson-Hall Publishers. Or Nugent, W., Sieppert, J., & Hudson, W. (2001). *Practice evaluation for the 21st century.* Belmont, CA: Brooks Cole. Or Unrau, Y., Gabor, P., & Grinnell, R. Jr. (2001). *Evaluation in the human services.* Itasca, IL: F. E. Peacock. Or Rossip, Lipsey, M. and Freeman, H. (2004). *Evaluation: A systematic approach.* Thosuand Oaks, CA: Sage Publications.

2. Weinbach, R., op.cit, 30.

3. Fetterman, D. M., Kaftarian, S. J., & Wandersman, A. (Eds.) (1996). *Empowerment evaluation.* Thousand Oaks, CA: Sage Publications.

4. Zimmerman, M., Israel, B., Schulz, A., & Checkoway, B. (1992). Further explorations in empowerment theory: An empirical analysis of psychological empowerment. *American Journal of Community Psychology, 20*(6), 707–727.

5. Fetterman, D. M., Kaftarian, S. J., & Wandersman, A. (Eds.) (1996). *Empowerment evaluation.* Thousands Oaks, CA: Sage Publications.

6. Morris, L., Fitz-Gibbon, C. T., & Freeman, M. F. (1987). *How to communicate evaluation findings.* Newbury Park, CA: Sage Publications.

14

EVALUATING INDIVIDUAL PRACTICE EFFECTIVENESS

In the previous chapter, we saw how many of the research concepts and methods that we discussed in earlier chapters are also useful for evaluating social programs. However, social work practitioners also need to know how well they are doing in their individual practice interventions; that is, in the services they offer to clients and client groups. We require regular feedback if we are to be evidence-based practitioners. In this chapter, we will look at how research methods can be used to provide it.

Before Single-System Research

As we have suggested repeatedly throughout this book, there are many potential sources of research data. The data that social workers need to assess their effectiveness also can come from a variety of sources. We will mention a few of them briefly and then shift our focus to what we believe to be an especially good way to evaluate individual practice effectiveness.

Supervisor Feedback

A potential source of data for feedback on one's practice effectiveness is the social worker's supervisor. In supervisory conferences, social workers are encouraged to evaluate objectively their progress with individual clients or larger client systems. Along with the supervisor (often a very experienced, accomplished practitioner), achievements are identified and applauded, and shortcomings are analyzed. The supervisor suggests better ways to accomplish the goals of intervention. At least, that is the way it is supposed to work. Unfortunately, supervisory conferences have other agenda that may get in the way of useful feedback. One problem is that supervisors are also asked to perform annual performance evaluations of their subordinates, often with little knowledge of their work other than what they learn during supervisory conferences. Thus, while trying to be helpful, they are also evaluating. Not surprisingly, supervisees are not always totally candid when discussing their interventions. They sometimes are unwilling to jeopardize salary increases or promotions by describing those interventions that appear to be less than effective. Thus, they are deprived of much of the feedback that might have helped them to become more effective practitioners.

In recent years, trends within our profession have made supervision an even less likely source of useful feedback. Cost-cutting measures in many settings, such as hospitals and psychiatric facilities, have eliminated many supervisory positions. If a social worker has a supervisor at all, it is likely to be someone who is seen only rarely, is unfamiliar with the supervisee's work, and may belong to another professional discipline. In other settings, alternative models of supervision (for example, group supervision, peer supervision, or even supervision via e-mail) have replaced the former supervisor–supervisee relationship.

Even annual performance evaluations that supervisors or others conduct have limited value as indicators of practice effectiveness. If data collection instruments are used at all, they rarely have undergone validation using scientific methods. Often, written evaluations consist of subjective judgments based on occasional firsthand observations, data provided by the individual being evaluated, and impressions shared gratuitously by other staff members. Some analysis of case records also may be used. Thus, they are not very good indicators of a social worker's practice effectiveness.

Consumer Feedback

If feedback from supervisors is of little value, why not get it directly from those consumers who are supposed to benefit from our interventions? Aren't they in the best position to tell us if we are helping or making a difference in their lives? Yes, but unfortunately, our clients often fail to provide honest answers.

Suppose, for example, that a social worker decided to draw a random sample of past and/or active clients and to construct and mail out a brief questionnaire asking them to evaluate the services received. Would this provide an accurate assessment of the social worker's effectiveness? Probably not. First, those clients most likely to return the data collection instrument would be those most satisfied with services and, perhaps, a smaller number who were least satisfied with them—an uneven, biased response rate. Others who might really be less than totally satisfied might still report that they were satisfied, simply because they were impressed that the social worker cared enough to ask. For a variety of reasons, the presence of a past or present helping relationship with individual clients and client groups tends to influence the results of a client satisfaction survey. We alluded to this problem in the previous chapter when we referred to client satisfaction surveys as a component of program evaluations. We also noted that satisfaction is not synonymous with successful intervention. Thus, if social workers use client satisfaction as an indicator of their effectiveness in their individual practice, they may learn a considerable amount about how satisfied their clients are, but little about how effective their interventions are. A client might be satisfied with intervention because it was convenient or inexpensive, because the social worker seemed to really "care," or for any number of other reasons, even though no progress on a problem was made. Conversely, dissatisfaction may have occurred because the social worker offered some needed but unpleasant form of intervention (for example, confrontation) that ultimately proved effective, because they were court-ordered to seek help, or because of some negative transference relationship. Even if clients are surveyed in such a way that questions focus on client progress rather than on satisfaction, it is almost impossible for satisfaction issues not to influence the results. (This same phenomenon often occurs when students are asked to evaluate the teaching effectiveness of their instructors.)

Despite their problems, client surveys sometimes can provide some useful feedback of individual practice effectiveness. They are most likely to yield useful data when carefully developed data collection instruments are used that contain open-ended questions (for example: What help were you expecting to receive?), along with fixed-alternative items or scales.

Goal Attainment Scaling

Another method of evaluating the success of an individual social worker's intervention methods, goal attainment scaling (GAS), also frequently must rely on consumers (clients) to provide data. However, the data reported are the behaviors of clients or client systems, rather than their satisfaction with services. Thus, it is believed to be less vulnerable to bias.

GAS has a relatively long history of use by social workers; it was first used back in the 1960s among therapists working with psychiatric patients. Since then, it has been used in a wide variety of settings where social workers are employed. When using it, a social worker identifies (along with the client or client system) a small number (usually, three to five) of specific behavioral problems. They should be problems of importance to the client and ones for which it is reasonable to expect that social work intervention might produce some positive changes. Although GAS is used most frequently to evaluate the success of interventions with individual clients, it is also applicable when working with problems within groups, families, institutions or communities, as long as the problem and its incidence can be easily quantified. For example, a social worker employed in a community agency might use it to assess her effectiveness in increasing the percentage of the local population who register to vote in an upcoming presidential election.

Once having identified and specified a small number of problems and the goals of intervention associated with them, a range of five levels of goal attainment are specified and listed in rank order. They are assigned a number between –2 and +2. Zero is assigned to what will be the expected outcome if intervention is successful. Plus scores are assigned to goal attainment that is greater than expected and minus scores to goal attainment levels that are less than expected. To return to our previous example—the social worker attempting to increase voter registration prior to a presidential election in a community where current registration is only 20 percent might use the following scale:

Most unfavorable outcome (–2)	20% or less
Less than expected outcome (–1)	21–25%
Expected outcome (0)	26–30%
More than expected outcome (+1)	31–35%
Most favorable outcome (+2)	over 35%

The decision as to which percentage of registration would represent expected outcome (0) and which percentage would be appropriate for the other four levels would be based on an assessment of what was realistic, given the time available for the intervention, and what past experience has taught the social worker about the likely impact of the intervention. Setting them at the appropriate levels requires a good understanding of both the client group and the likely impact of the intervention method being used.

The results of goal attainment in addressing different problems (perhaps, in our example, participation at community meetings or attendance at PTA meetings) can be combined mathematically to suggest, overall, how effective a social worker has been in working with a client or client system. The different problems can also be weighted to reflect their relative importance. Methods are even available to convert results to a scale with scores ranging between 1 and 100.

GAS is designed for use with well motivated clients who will work to set realistic goals and honestly report their behaviors, as well as with larger client systems where valid measurement of behaviors is possible. It also is designed for social workers who want honest feedback about their effectiveness, not social workers who just want to appear successful. If, either unintentionally or deliberately, the different levels of success are scaled too high or too low or if the measurement of success is inappropriate for some other reason, the results of GAS will be of little value as feedback to the social worker. For example, if both the social worker and an adolescent with a problem of severe shyness in social situations set an expected goal of two Internet chat-room conversations per week (+2 = four; –2 equals none), a 0 level or even a +2 level might be accomplished. It would make the social worker appear successful, but would this really represent successful intervention for the client's shyness? Probably not, because the goal levels were set so low that they could easily be achieved. In addition, the goals may have been inappropriate, because there is little reason to believe that increased Internet conversations might help the problem of shyness in social situations.

Single-System Research

The development of GAS was an effort to quantify success in treatment intervention, to make evaluation of our own practice less subjective. Single-system research relies even further on the methods characteristic of quantitative research, for example, careful measurement of variables and statistical analysis of findings.

Single-system research (also referred to as $n = 1$, single-case time-series, single-subject research, and idiographic research) refers to a collection of research designs that are both similar to and different from the traditional group research designs that we examined in earlier chapters. Unlike many of the other types of research that we have discussed in earlier chapters, the primary goal of single-system research is not building knowledge about some phenomenon or experience or uncovering relationships between variables that may be of use to many other people. In that sense, it is more similar to program evaluation—its findings have little or no external validity. Single-system research simply seeks answers to the question: Does what I am doing with this client or with this client system seem to have made a difference in the problem?

As in all other research, social workers conducting single-system research collect, record, and analyze data, and interpret it. Their research has some (mostly superficial) resemblances to some of the specific designs that we have discussed. Like program evaluation, it seeks to evaluate practice effectiveness. It is longitudinal research; it entails the repeated measurement of the same variable over time. It even introduces an independent variable and uses a variation of a control group. Because of these latter characteristics, some writers have even gone so far as to describe some certain single-system research designs as experimental. However, many people (including the authors of this book) believe that this is "stretching it a bit," since "samples" are not constructed using random selection or random assignment. Much of the terminology used in single-system research is common to all forms of research. However, in single-system research, many terms have different, specific meanings. Still other research terms are not often used, but they are implicit in the designs of single-system research studies. This can be confusing, so we have grouped some of the more important research terms together in Box 14.1 along with how they are understood to exist in single-system research. The reader may wish to refer back to them in the discussion that follows.

There also are many other differences between single-system research and the other forms of research that we have examined. Other research is often conducted by research specialists who do little else but conduct research studies. When practitioners conduct other types of research (especially quantitative studies), they tend to leave their role as practitioner behind and assume the role of researcher. In contrast, single-system research is conducted by practitioners for their own use (feedback). Often the research is integrated with the practice intervention. However, in terms of priorities (and when ethical issues arise), a social worker is a practitioner first and a researcher second.

BOX 14.1   Research Terms and Their Equivalents in Single-System Research

Design The number and sequence of alternating A (baseline) and B (treatment) phases

   Exploratory design A design with no A phase (baseline), e.g., BC or BCD.

   Descriptive design A design with a true baseline and one or more interventions, e.g., AB or ABC.

   "Explanatory" design A design that uses repetition or withdrawal of the intervention to observe whether a pattern of the dependent variable reoccurs, e.g., BCBC, ABA.

Independent variable The intervention or its absence (or, less frequently, the magnitude of the intervention). It is almost always a nominal-level variable.

Dependent variable The severity of the target problem or its incidence as measured through all phases of the research. It can be any level of measurement.

"Case" A single measurement of the dependent variable in either an A phase or a B phase.

"Sample" The total number of measurements of the dependent variable in a single A phase or B phase

"Control Group" The measurements of the dependent variable in an A phase.

"Experimental Group" The measurements of dependent variable in the B phase that follows an A phase.

Sampling error The normal fluctuation of the dependent variable; a possible reason why measurements in an A phase may differ from those in a subsequent B phase.

Sampling bias The tendency of a sample of measurements of the dependent variable (especially in a true baseline) to be atypical for the client or client system.

When Is Single-System Research Appropriate?

The focus in single-system research, the research participant, can be any person or system that is normally the target for social work treatment or intervention, that is, any client system. Although it can be (and most frequently is) an individual client, it also can be a couple, a family, a group, an organization, or a community.

Single-system research is best suited to those situations in which (1) a primary treatment goal is change in some client behavior, attitude, perception, or other characteristic; and (2) whatever the social worker is seeking to change (the target of the intervention) can be easily and accurately measured. Because easy, accurate measurement is required and behavior is relatively easy to measure, most single-system research has focused on changes in client behavior. When something other than behavior is the target for change, self-administered indexes and scales are often used to measure it.

To use single-system research, the target problem must exhibit an identifiable pattern, for example, stable, increasing, or decreasing. The problem may be some undesirable or dysfunctional behavior or attitude of the client or client system that the social worker hopes to reduce or eliminate through some specific type of intervention. Or, it can be a desirable behavior or attitude that the social worker is attempting to increase, enhance, or foster.

Whenever possible, it is preferable to define the goal of intervention in a positive way. This is consistent with practice values that stress our building on client strengths (the "strengths perspective"). For example, it would be preferable to define our goal as "increasing the number of self-esteem–enhancing comments made by Ms. X to her son" rather than "decreasing the number of deprecating comments made by Ms. X to her son."

Single-system research is not designed to test theories or types of interventions; that is best accomplished through meta-analysis. It is also not appropriate for evaluating the effectiveness of all or even most practice interventions. Some of the most common of these are listed in Box 14.2. In order to use it, the researcher/practitioner must be able to specify exactly what change is sought and how it will be measured, as well as the specific method that will be used repeatedly over some time interval or intervals to attain it. If progress toward attainment of a goal cannot be easily measured, or if the intervention method cannot be easily specified, single-system research is not appropriate. For example, a social worker providing marital counseling could attempt to reduce verbally abusive behavior by a spouse by raising her hand each time he engages in it in a counseling session. She could use single-system research to evaluate her practice effectiveness while using this technique with her client. But the same social worker would not be able to use single-system research to evaluate her practice effectiveness with another client where she is using something as general and broadly defined as providing advice and support to the client to encourage him to leave an abusive relationship. However, it might still be possible to use it with just one component of her treatment, such as a specific intervention to influence just one of his problem behaviors that is contributing to his inability to leave.

The target for change should be something that the social worker can directly influence through work with the client or client system. A social worker might, for example, use some repeated form of intervention to attempt to get her client, a mother who she is counseling, to spend more time helping her son with his homework. What she would be attempting to influence (the amount of time the client spent) would be the dependent variable in her single-system study. It would not be the son's grades, whether or not he completes his homework, and so forth. She also could not use single-system research to

BOX 14.2   Some Situations Where Single System Research Is Not Appropriate

- When target problem or problems cannot be easily and accurately measured.
- When multiple measurements of target problems over time are not logistically possible, as is often the case with short-term or crisis interventions.
- When the intervention is a complex one or otherwise cannot be clearly specified.
- When the intervention is "one shot," as in making a referral or in conducting discharge planning.
- When the intervention is "indirect," as is the case in working with teachers around how to better manage classroom behaviors or in working with community members to help them to reduce gang violence.

evaluate the effectiveness of an intervention such as a referral to her client's son's guidance counselor. There are two reasons for this: (1) how successful the referral is in helping her client will be more of an indicator of the effectiveness of the guidance counselor's practice effectiveness than her own, and (2) a one-shot intervention like a referral is never an appropriate intervention for evaluation using single-system research. In single-system research the same intervention is repeatedly offered over some period of time. Research that entails only two measurements (for example, a pretest-posttest design) is not single-system research.

In single-system research, the target for change need not be the central problem or the major focus of the social worker's treatment plan. It can be just one symptom of the problem (it often is) or even something that may be only tangentially related to the central problem but is contributing to the client's or client system's problem in some way. For example, a social worker might use some method of intervention repeatedly over time to attempt to influence how frequently his client, a woman with a diagnosis of schizophrenia, talks to herself in public places.

Over the past few decades, researchers and theoreticians have greatly expanded the number of practice situations where single-system research can be used. Progress has come from at least three sources. First, social work researchers have created and refined scales for the measurement of such hard-to-measure variables as marital adjustment and family relations.[1] These scales have been shown to possess both reliability and validity when used repeatedly with the same clients or client groups. Second, other scholars have designed highly sophisticated single-system research designs. There is now a design that is suitable for nearly every practice situation.[2] Third, still other scholars have developed computer software to make the recording and analysis of data nearly effortless for the practitioner.[3]

Underlying Assumptions and Terminology

The basic assumption underlying single-system research designs is that, if an intervention makes a difference, a client or client system will show a response to it (change). With most designs, we are expecting (hoping?) that the target of the intervention will change when the intervention is introduced. The stronger the pattern of agreement between the presence or absence of intervention and changes in its target, the greater the evidence that the intervention makes a difference. For example, if one pattern is evident during the presence of the intervention and another pattern can be seen both before the intervention is introduced and when it is removed, the evidence that the intervention makes a difference is especially strong. Such consistent patterns would constitute an unlikely coincidence, one that would defy the laws of probability. They would suggest that the intervention and changes in its target are related. Of course, we would hope to demonstrate that intervention is accompanied by a desirable change in the target, one that is consistent with intervention goals. But the observation that the presence of intervention is accompanied by undesirable change or even that it makes no difference would still be valuable feedback to the practitioner. Either would suggest that the intervention was not successful, at least not with that particular client or client system.

There are a few terms that are central to understanding how single-system research works. An *A phase* is a block of time in which the effects of the intervention whose effects are being evaluated is not present, but measurement of whatever the social worker will be attempting to influence still occurs. Other forms of assistance to the client (the usual treatment) may continue during an A phase.

If an A phase occurs before the intervention is first introduced, it is known as a *true baseline* or sometimes just a baseline. It is used to represent the usual pattern of the behavior or other target of the intervention, the starting point for the intervention. Once the intervention has been introduced, any subsequent A phase is no longer indicative of the usual pattern of the target—the intervention may continue to influence it.

There is no consensus as to what constitutes an adequate baseline. Ideally, it should contain a large number of measurements of the target of the intervention so that the effects of sampling error (normal fluctuation) are minimized. However, because of time constraints and other logistical problems, this is not always possible. So, can just five or ten regular measurements of the problem constitute a baseline? Or, are more needed? The answer is, it depends. Theoretically, a good baseline can be established using relatively few measurements if they accurately reflect the usual pattern of the target of the intervention. But more generally is better. Often, the adequacy of a baseline comes down to a social worker's subjective judgment, his or her answer to the question, Have I captured the usual pattern prior to offering my intervention?

Fortunately, a baseline containing a large number of measurements sometimes can be created retroactively. If good records have been kept (for example, school attendance records) or observations and accurate measurement already have been made and are available, the usual pattern of the problem can be determined. However, this entails secondary data analysis, which, as we have discussed, can have serious limitations. Among other things, it is dependent on the ways in which the problem was conceptualized and operationalized, and how conscientiously it was measured, often by someone else.

A period of time (of predetermined length) in which the intervention is present and repeatedly offered is called an *intervention phase* or *B phase*. It is identical to an A phase except for the presence of the intervention whose effect is being studied. The behavior or other phenomenon that the social worker is seeking to influence is referred to generically as the *target problem* and is regarded as the dependent variable for research purposes. The presence (B phase) or absence (A phase) of the specific treatment or intervention that is used serves as the independent variable.

A phases are supposed to serve the same general function as control groups do in experimental research designs. They provide a source of comparison by indicating what occurs with the target problem when the intervention either (1) has not yet been introduced, or (2) is withdrawn following a B phase. It has been suggested that in single-system research a case thus serves as its own control (during an A phase).

The B phases are regarded as being the rough equivalent of the experimental groups in an experiment. However, the lack of a true control group creates a need for some other way to control for threats to internal validity, that is, to know that it was the intervention and not something else that produced any changes in the target problem.

As we shall see, different single-system designs are also used to compare the relative effectiveness of different interventions (always introduced one at a time), to attempt to learn which sequence of interventions worked best, and even to examine whether a given intervention seemed to work more effectively with one target problem than with another. In the latter situation, only one problem at a time receives the intervention. This is a cardinal rule of single-system research—during any B phase, there is only one intervention and one target problem. If this were not the case, it would be almost impossible to know which intervention was associated with change, in which target problem.

When using single-system research designs, regular measurements of the target problem are made over the entire course of the research. Ideally, this involves using more than one observer or some other method to ensure that they are reliable and valid. Measurements are recorded as they are made, usually using standard graph paper or a computer software package designed to produce the graphs that are characteristic of single-system research. The presence or absence of intervention at the time of each measurement is clearly indicated on the graph by labeling time intervals either as A (for an A phase) or B (for a B phase). If measurements of the target problem are interval or ratio level, they are often displayed using a scattergram (Chapter 12) with measurements of the variable displayed along the vertical axis and units of time displayed along the horizontal axis. Thus, each dot on the graph reflects a measurement of the target problem and the point in time when the measurement took place. If the target problem is a dichotomous variable (for example, attended/did not attend group treatment, complied/did not comply with medication, or completed/did not complete all homework), a horizontal line is placed on the graph with one value category above it and one below it on the vertical axis. Then an X or a dot is placed either above or below the line each time that the target problem is measured to reflect its measurement.

Target problems that are likely to occur frequently are usually measured using small time intervals, such as days, hours, or even minutes. For example, certain speech mannerisms or involuntary behaviors, such as repeated throat clearing, may occur so frequently that the entire research study might be completed in an hour or even less time. If the target problem occurs less frequently, larger units of time are used, for example, a period of weeks, months, or even years. Figure 14.1 displays the planned efforts of a social worker to get a legislator to consult with the social worker about pending social legislation. The intervention consisted of regular mailed reminders of the social worker's availability for consultation. Note that the effects of the intervention appear to be rather minimal over the 27 months in which the single-system research occurred. There was relatively little change in the legislator's behavior when the intervention was introduced (B phase).

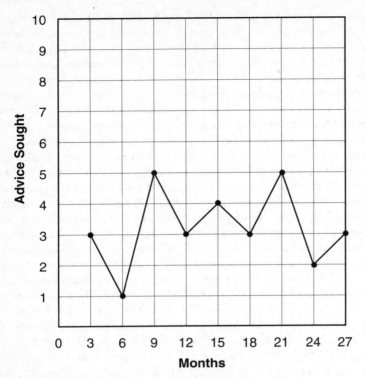

**FIGURE 14.1 Number of Times Advice Was Sought
on Pending Social Legislation**

What Is Measured?

Like any other variable, there are many different ways in which a target problem can be measured. Some common ways used in single-system research are:

1. *Frequency.* For example, we might measure the number of times that an inpatient psychiatric patient attends recreational therapy each week.
2. *Duration.* For example, we might measure the length of time that family members spend eating their evening meal together over a two-month period.
3. *Interval.* For example, we might measure the length of time between incidents of racial conflict within a community over a period of five years.
4. *Magnitude.* For example, we might measure the amount of research grant money coming into a human service organization over a ten-year period.
5. *Presence or absence.* For example, we might record whether or not an adolescent attends school each weekday.

There are still other possible ways to measure a problem. For example, we might be interested in influencing when or where a behavior occurs, who sees it, or even how accepting of it our client or client system is. Which type of measurement of the target problem is most appropriate for a given research study? The answer to this question relates in part to research issues and in part to treatment ones. The availability of valid measurement instruments for one or the other type of measurement may be an important consideration, especially if the target problem is one that is not easily measured, for example, an attitude or belief. It may also be more feasible to conduct one type of measurement than another. For example, the frequency of certain behaviors, such as substance abuse, may be difficult to measure with precision or may not be particularly relevant to intervention goals. But its presence or absence each day or the interval between occurrences may be both.

The goal of intervention is an especially important consideration in determining how the dependent variable will be measured. For example, a practitioner may conclude that increasing the number of times that two parents discuss child-rearing practices or decreasing the interval between discussions is not consistent with intervention goals. This might be the case if, in the past, such discussions have always been superficial and brief. A more appropriate treatment goal might be to increase the duration of discussions of child rearing instead. Thus, it would be their duration (rather than their frequency or the interval between them) that would be measured and recorded.

As we discussed in Chapter 10, good measurement is both reliable and valid. However, in single-system studies, other issues must be considered. Measurement of a variable should be sensitive enough that it will record meaningful changes, yet not so sensitive that it will record changes that are meaningless in relationship to the goals of the intervention. It also should be as unobtrusive as possible, so that it does not interfere with the intervention itself.

Measurement also must be acceptable to the client or client system. This is in part an ethical issue. Because a power differential exists and because they may fear displeasing the social worker, clients might agree to provide data that they would prefer not to provide or to permit measurement in a way that they might otherwise resist. Thus, it is the social worker's responsibility to ensure that both the measurement itself and its method of collection are acceptable to the client or client system.

Use of Statistical Analysis

If measurements of the target problem in an A phase constitute what is believed to be a good baseline, simply "eyeballing" the data on a graph can provide a pretty good idea of how much change occurred and whether it is in the predicted direction. But it is possible to do even more. In descriptive studies where there is a baseline A phase followed by a B phase, statistical analyses of the data can be used to determine the mathematical probability that any differences in the dependent variable between the A and B phases represent nothing more than normal fluctuation. There are several easily computed tests (beyond the scope of this book) that can tell us if the difference between the measurements in the A phase and the subsequent B phase is statistically significant, that is, it is large enough that the probability of its representing just normal fluctuation over time is quite small. They are based on the following assumptions:

- The A (baseline) phase is an accurate representation of the dependent variable and its variability (it is a representative sample).

- The same pattern of its variability would continue following the A phase if the intervention were not introduced.
- Any difference between the pattern of the dependent variable in the A and subsequent B phases *may* be attributable to the presence of the intervention during the B phase.

Steps Involved in Conducting Single-System Research

We have presented an overview of what single-system research is and some of the issues that are considered in designing it. There is a general sequence of steps that are followed. They are presented in Box 14.3.

Notice that seven of the eleven steps in Box 14.3 are conducted before the research data are collected. As we have emphasized in other types of research, careful planning is critical to research success. With single-system research, steps 2 and 4 take on special importance if we are to learn about our practice effectiveness. We need to know exactly what our intervention is and what it is that we hope it is influencing. Otherwise, any findings are of little practical value. The importance of the other steps in Box 14.3 will become more evident in our next discussion.

BOX 14.3   The Usual Steps for Conducting Single-System Research

1. Describe the client's problem (or at least its symptoms).
2. Specify the target problem—the behavior, attitude, and so on (the dependent variable) and how you propose to measure it.
3. Identify the pattern of the target problem believed to exist (stable, rising, falling, and so forth).
4. Identify professional literature that describes the problem or something similar and suggests the interventions that may be effective.
5. Briefly specify the precise treatment or intervention to be used and how it will relate to other, ongoing services to the client.
6. Select from among the various single-subject designs the one that you will use. Justify why it is best, given such factors as time, ethical constraints, need to control for other variables, treatment goals, and so forth.
7. Determine which pattern of the target problem would indicate that your intervention may be related to a desired effect, that is, the treatment goal. Also determine which pattern(s) would suggest the possibility that your intervention may have promoted unhealthy dependency or some other unintended consequence.
8. Conduct the research, carefully graphing measurements of the target problem over time.
9. Carefully analyze the results of the research relative to step 7.
10. If the intervention appears to have been associated with success, consider replicating the research with other similar clients or client groups who might also benefit from it.
11. Disseminate the results of the research to colleagues who might benefit from knowing them.

A slightly different version of this box appeared in Compton, B., Galaway, B., & Cournoyer, B. (2005). *Social work processes*, 7th ed. Pacific Grove, CA: Brooks Cole; and Weinbach, R. (2005). *Evaluating social work services and programs*. Boston: Allyn and Bacon.

Some Popular Designs

Just like the research designs that we discussed in earlier chapters, different single-system designs have been created to answer different questions. Some are exploratory. They lack an A phase and seek simply to answer the question: Do changes occur with the presence of an intervention? Others are descriptive. They contain a baseline A phase and are used to answer the question: How *much* change occurs when an intervention is introduced? Still others are (at least loosely) described as explanatory. They contain a series of alternating A and B phases, and attempt to answer the question: Did the intervention actually cause changes in the dependent variable? Explanatory designs tend to be the most complex because they must attempt to control for threats to internal validity. We will look at examples of all three types, paying special attention to their specialized uses.

B. The most basic of exploratory designs is the B design. It consists of the introduction and continuation of the intervention and then the monitoring of any changes that occur in the target problem during a predetermined period. It is exactly what most responsible practitioners already do to some degree. However, if the monitoring were conducted as single-system research, (1) careful measurement (quantification) of the target problem would take place; (2) the research would end at the predetermined time (which may precede the termination of treatment); and (3) the measurements would be graphed and carefully interpreted. Other exploratory designs are BC or BCD, in which different interventions are tried in a predetermined sequence.

AB. An AB design is just slightly more complicated than B and is considered descriptive. It consists of just two phases—a beginning baseline phase during which the intervention whose effectiveness is being evaluated is not offered, followed by an intervention phase when intervention is present (Figure 14.2). It cannot answer two important questions: (1) How do I know that it was the intervention and not something else that occurred at the same time that caused any changes (or lack of change) in the target problem? and (2) What would happen if I were to discontinue the intervention?

When using an AB design, the intervention being evaluated is not offered until a true baseline phase of measurement takes place or is constructed from available data. Thus, a social worker might have an ethical objection to using an AB design with a client or client system that is in imminent danger because the target problem is life threatening or otherwise destructive. For example, we might not want to use an AB design to see if a promising intervention is effective in reducing the number of times that a new client who is at high risk for contracting an HIV infection engages in unsafe sexual practices. We could not ethically justify waiting to offer the intervention just because we preferred to use an AB design. However, if we already have or can acquire valid measurements of the client's usual sexual practices prior to seeking assistance, we might be able to use them as our baseline.

AB is often the design of choice when permanent learning or nonreversible behavior or attitudes are a likely consequence (and a goal) of the intervention. Some behaviors, once learned, are not likely to spontaneously revert if intervention were to be withdrawn. Perhaps the behavior is even self-reinforcing. Then an AB may be appropriate. For example, a social worker may select a specific intervention to increase the frequency of assertive behaviors in a client. The intervention may be accompanied by an increase in

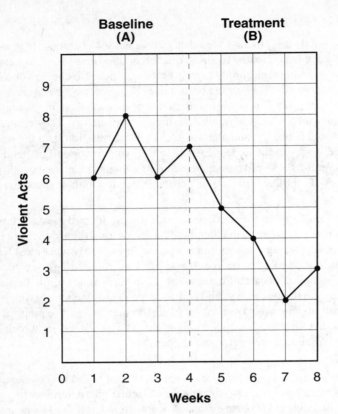

FIGURE 14.2 AB Design: Patient Violence toward Staff

these behaviors, as reflected in the B phase of the design. The AB design may be all that is needed to know that the intervention worked. The literature and our experience would tell us that the client is likely to continue assertive behaviors when appropriate, because they promote desired responses from others.

In all single-system research designs, the dependent variable (target problem) must be measured accurately. But it should not be measured so narrowly that another similar behavior can simply be substituted for it. In the example portrayed in Figure 14.2, where intervention was used to attempt to reduce or eliminate physical attacks on staff within an inpatient psychiatric setting, we would not have wanted to use the variable "attacks on nurses" as the target problem, even if that is exactly what the target behavior was. A dramatic decline in the dependent variable during the intervention phase might have suggested successful intervention. However, during the time that the patient stopped attacking nurses, increased attacks on social work staff may have occurred. This phenomenon is referred to as *symptom substitution.* In the example (Figure 14.2), we might still question whether the possibility of symptom substitution has been fully eliminated. The patient's decline in violent behavior toward staff conceivably could still have been redirected toward other patients. This undesirable behavior would not be measured in the social worker's research because of the way the target problem was conceptualized and operationalized. It might have been even better to define the target problem as "physical attacks on other people," thus including other patients and even visitors.

When using descriptive designs such as AB (or ABC or ABCD), a social worker does not control for other variables (besides the intervention) that might produce change in the target problem. In the research portrayed in Figure 14.2, for example, the decrease in attacks on staff during the B phase may have been the effect of the intervention, but it is impossible to know for sure. It may also have been the result of changes in the patient's diet or medication, help offered by other staff, visits from the patient's relatives, pressure from other patients, the passage of time, and any of hundreds of other factors working alone or in concert.

Perhaps the A phase (baseline) was just an atypical time for the patient (sampling error) and the B phase is simply more typical of the patient's behavior or the difference between the A and B phases just represents normal fluctuation for the client. Then the B phase did not really reflect change at all. Descriptive single-system designs can only answer the question: How much change occurred? This is possible only if they have good baseline measurement which describes accurately the normal pattern of the target problem prior to the introduction of the intervention.

ABA. If a second phase of observation and measurement is used following an A phase and then the introduction of an intervention, we have an ABA design. This example of an "explanatory" design is an effort to address potential threats to internal validity. If the target problem shows improvement during the B phase and then it seems to get worse again during the second A phase, this may provide some evidence that the intervention (and not something else) may have caused the problem to diminish. However, it is not necessarily an indication of the effectiveness of the intervention. It can suggest what may be an undesirable dependency on the intervention, because the problem only seemed to get better during the time when it was offered.

What if, for example, the intervention goal was to reduce marijuana usage? This occurs during the B phase, but usage increases again during the second A phase, as illustrated in Figure 14.3. The amount of marijuana usage and the presence or absence of the intervention seem to be related in a desirable direction. However, does that mean that the intervention was successful? Some treatment methods (for example, those used by Alcoholics Anonymous) actually promote dependency or, perhaps more accurately, seek to substitute one form of dependency for a more desirable one. However, they are rare. Unless, in our example, this was a goal of the intervention (which is unlikely), we might conclude that the intervention was at best a partial success. It had the desired effect, but the problem did not continue to improve or even remain at the same level after the intervention was discontinued, a phenomenon known as *treatment carryover*. The results of research that uses an ABA design (as well as those of many other designs) must be interpreted with special attention to the issue of the desirability of client dependency on the continued presence of an intervention.

The second A phase of the ABA design (and of other designs that use more than one A phase) can be characterized by either withdrawal of the intervention or reversal, a deliberate attempt to reverse the pattern of the target behavior within the prior B phase. Withdrawal generally is the method used in second and subsequent A phases in single-system research. Not surprisingly, many social workers object to the use of reversal methods during later A phases. Could a social worker ethically attempt to increase marijuana

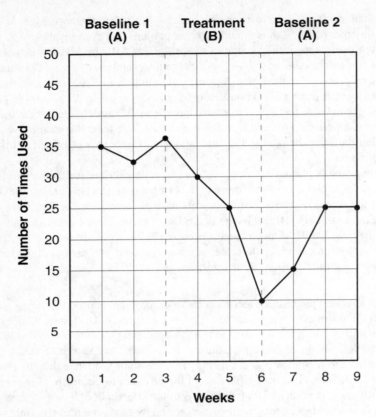

FIGURE 14.3 ABA Design: Marijuana Usage

usage or some other behavior that, in treatment planning or contracting with the client, was identified as a problem? Or, ethically, should a social worker attempt to decrease the frequency of a client behavior that is judged to be in the client's best interests, just to attempt to find further evidence of the effect of a treatment intervention on it? For ethical as well as logistical reasons, ABA and other designs that use reversal are generally not used in social work single-system research.

Although an ABA design can tell the researcher what happens to a behavior after the intervention stops (which an AB design cannot do), it is not a favorite among some social workers. This is probably because it both begins and ends with an A phase in which the intervention believed to be effective is not given. Unless good data are already available about the prior pattern of the target problem, it requires the social worker to wait a period of time before offering a promising form of intervention. Later, the research is completed in a second A phase, during which the intervention is again not offered. This may make some social workers uncomfortable because it does not parallel the natural course of treatment in many social work practice settings. For example, patients hospitalized with acute medical and psychiatric problems often are in the greatest need of intervention from social workers just after entering and just before leaving the hospital.

There are two common misunderstandings that probably contribute to a reluctance to use ABA and other designs that begin and end in an A phase. First, some people mistakenly think that all assistance or services to the client or client system are denied during an A phase. This is not correct. During A phases, only the specific intervention that is the independent variable within the research (often an adjunct to the usual services) is withheld. Usual services continue to be offered. Second, there is no reason why the course of a single-system design has to coincide with the course of social work treatment. The research does not have to start at the time that treatment is begun; it can begin later. Nor does it have to end at the time of treatment termination; it can end (and often does) while the client is still being offered services. Thus, a treatment that appears to have been successful based on an evaluation using an ABA design can be reintroduced and continued indefinitely after the second A phase has been completed and the research has ended. A social worker would be very likely to do just that if the research seemed to indicate that the intervention was beneficial to the client.

ABAB. The addition of one or more alternating A and B phases helps to provide additional evidence for a possible cause–effect relationship between the intervention and the target problem. Figure 14.4 is the graph of an ABAB design, another example of an

FIGURE 14.4 ABAB Design: Independent Decisions Made by Client

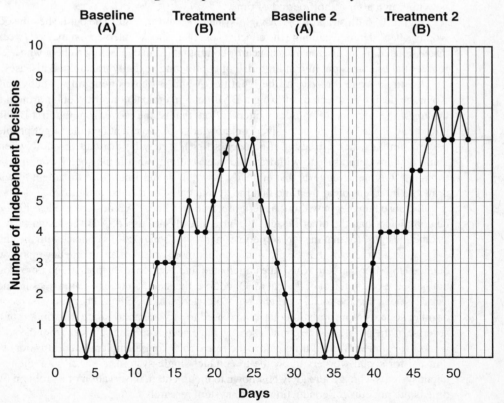

explanatory design that a social worker used with a client whose problem was an inability to make decisions. The social worker sought to increase the frequency of the client's independent decision making through an intervention method that had been devised. As Figure 14.4 suggests, the intervention appears to have produced more independent decision making, but the frequency of the dependent variable declined when the intervention was withdrawn during the second A phase, then increased again during the second B phase. The client's desirable behavior seemed to be very much dependent on the presence of the intervention by the social worker. Can this finding really be interpreted as an indication of success in treating a client whose problem was one of excessive dependency to begin with? Very likely no, for reasons noted in the previous example. Carryover into the second A phase would be more indicative of success.

Unlike the ABA design, the ABAB ends in an intervention (B) phase. This is considered a plus by those social work researcher/practitioners who, justifiably or not, have misgivings about using those designs that end in an A phase.

BAB. BAB designs are quite popular among social work practitioners. They begin and end in an intervention (B) phase, characteristics that appear to be consistent with social work practice values and ethics. They are especially well suited to crisis situations where the social worker believes that conducting a baseline measurement prior to offering the intervention would be unethical, but where it is believed that the intervention can safely be withdrawn after a short period of time.

Figure 14.5 illustrates a BAB single-system research design. The public health social worker selected it for examining the effectiveness of a "shock" intervention method (weekly discussions of rising disease rates in nearby communities) in counseling a client whose current sexual practices put him at high risk of contracting sexually transmitted diseases.

In single-system research, the length of A and B phases generally is determined when the design is selected. In using a BAB design, ethical concerns center around the timing of the decision to withdraw intervention, that is, the move from the first B phase into the A phase. Without extensive foreknowledge of the client and the target problem pattern (unlike when a true baseline occurs first), it may be difficult to know when it could be considered safe to withdraw the intervention. What if the social worker's professional judgment suggests that ethically it would be detrimental to the client to withdraw the intervention at the time that the design calls for it to be withdrawn?

Because they begin without benefit of a true baseline, BAB designs are less likely to be completed than the other designs we have already discussed. A BAB design (as well as other designs, for that matter) sometimes has to be "scrapped" as contact with the client or client system reveals that the problem is either more or less of an emergency than it was believed to be, or that removal of the anticipated intervention at the prescribed time would not be in the best interest of the client. Of course, the lack of a true baseline does not necessarily mean that the social worker has no knowledge of the client. There may be records or other sources of information that can be used to provide an accurate description of the severity of the problem. The client also may have been receiving services from the social worker for some period of time before the research design is implemented. It is not at all unusual for social workers to decide to conduct single-system research with clients or client systems who are already well known to them. Often, observation of a problem over time is the impetus for conducting single-system research.

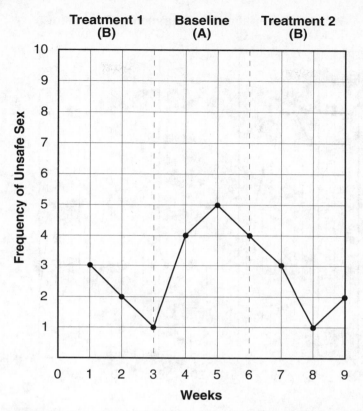

FIGURE 14.5 BAB Design: Client Practice of Unsafe Sex

ABCD. Sometimes, as practitioners, we know of several different interventions that may be effective, but none of them is clearly indicated to be the most effective. We seek some general guidance as to which may be best or, to be more precise, which one or series of them seems to work best with a given client or client system. The ABCD design examines several different interventions, each introduced one at a time. It thus is used to examine the relationship among several interventions and a single dependent variable (a target problem). An ABCD design can provide a beginning indication of the relative effectiveness of several different interventions.

Figure 14.6 illustrates the efforts of a public health social worker to evaluate the relative effectiveness of several interventions with a client in a smoking-cessation program. That is not always the case with ABCD designs. However, if different-length intervention phases had been used, the different lengths allotted for interventions might constitute a confounding variable.

Note that in the research (Figure 14.6) three different consecutive interventions were introduced (B, C, and D). If there had been four, the design would have been ABCDE; if there were five interventions, it would have been ABCDEF, and so forth.

Figure 14.6 also has no nonintervention (A) phases between interventions. If they had been present, we would have had still another design (ABACAD). Such a design would

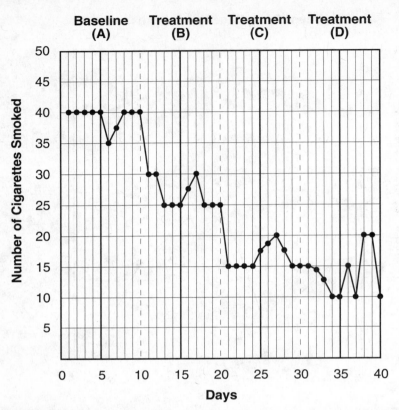

FIGURE 14.6 ABCD Design: Client Effort to Reduce Cigarette Smoking

give us a clearer indication of the relative effectiveness of the three treatments. But, its downside would be that the cumulative effect of, for example, treatments B, C, and D would not be as easy to determine because of the presence of A phases between them. When using an ABCD design, the potential for treatment carryover from one phase into subsequent ones can make it difficult to determine just which intervention produced the most change in the dependent variable (target problem). For example, the continuation of a desired behavior at approximately the same level following the shift from one intervention to another, as in the D phase in Figure 14.6, may mean that interventions C and D are equally effective. It may also mean that the effects of intervention C continued on through the D phase. If so, it may be this carryover and not intervention D that produced the level of the desired behavior in the D phase. Another interpretation may be that intervention D may simply be ineffective or may even promote smoking. If this is true, the social worker would have even further support for the effectiveness of intervention C. But how can we know this is what happened? The possibility of treatment carryover can severely limit any conclusions about the relative effectiveness of different interventions when ABCD designs are used. If this is what the social worker hoped to learn, an ABA-CAD design would have been preferable.

ABCD designs like the one illustrated in Figure 14.6 can still provide some useful information about the sequence of interventions that is associated with the best results. The researcher who conducted the smoking-cessation research could use the same participant again (or another one with a similar problem), again use an ABCD type design, but reverse the order of interventions. This time, the researcher could begin in an A phase but then introduce interventions C, B, and D in sequence. Then the sequence might be interventions D, C, and B, and so forth. It might be possible to use the same participant over and over again in our example, given what we know about smoking recidivism ("Quitting smoking is easy, I've done it at least a hundred times"). Eventually, the best sequence of two or more treatments might be identified, especially if the research were to be replicated many other times with similar participants. Obviously, this use of ABCD designs would not be possible with many types of target problems; it would not be suitable where a problem or behavior does not tend to reoccur. But unfortunately, problem recidivism does occur in our work. When addressing problems where it is common (for example, family violence, substance abuse, truancy, delinquency), the repeated use of the ABCD design can be quite enlightening.

Ethical concerns related to use of ABCD designs are not as great as with some other designs. One issue sometimes voiced relates to withdrawing an apparently successful intervention in order to substitute one that may not be found to work as well. But this is not as problematic as it might seem at first, because most often the withdrawal of an apparently successful intervention is immediately followed by another promising intervention, not by an A phase.

Multiple Baseline. Sometimes the social worker may use an intervention method that may be suited to influencing two or more (usually related) target problems. There is a need to verify its overall effectiveness, but also to find out if it seems to influence one target problem more effectively than the other. In this situation, the social worker has one independent variable (the intervention method and its presence or absence) and more than one dependent variable (target problems). Then a multiple-baseline, single-system design may be the design of choice.

When using a multiple-baseline design, an A phase precedes the introduction of the intervention. During that phase, baseline measurements of the two or more dependent variables are taken. Then the intervention is introduced to attempt to influence one of them. Generally, it is applied first to the target problem that has reflected the clearest pattern of occurrence during the initial baseline measurement (A) phase. As the intervention is offered (the first B phase), baseline measurement of the other target problem(s) continues, thus creating an extended A phase for it. Following efforts to influence the first target problem with the intervention (the first B phase), a second B phase occurs. During it, intervention shifts to the second target problem, while a second A phase occurs for the first target problem—the intervention is no longer applied to it. If there are more than two dependent variables, the intervention then shifts to the third variable, while the first remains in an extended second A phase and the second enters a second A phase, and so forth.

Figure 14.7 illustrates an application of a multiple-baseline design that had only two target problems. The researcher, a social worker assigned to a home health program, was trying to get her patient, a 64-year-old woman who was recovering from a stroke, to be

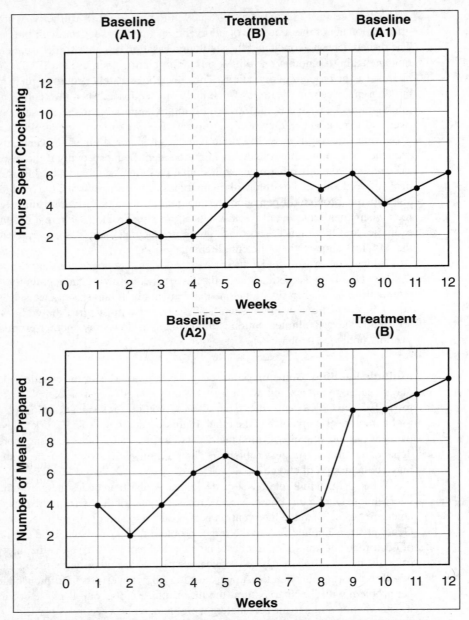

FIGURE 14.7 Multiple-Baseline Design: Crocheting and Meal Preparation

more involved in the activities that she had enjoyed prior to her illness. It was believed that renewed participation in them would be physically therapeutic and would also help the patient to feel more self-confident and thus improve her overall attitude toward life. The patient identified two such activities: crocheting and meal preparation (the dependent variables). The intervention (the independent variable) consisted of bringing along magazines and other written materials on one and then the other activity to weekly home visits and spending fifteen minutes each visit discussing them with the patient. The patient kept a record of her involvement in both activities for the duration of the research and shared it with the social worker at each weekly visit. The social worker graphed both activities as in Figure 14.7. During the first four weeks, only the usual counseling took place. It formed the baseline phase (A) for the first target problem (crocheting) and the first half of an extended baseline phase (A) for the second target problem (meal preparation). During weeks 5 through 8, materials on crocheting were brought and discussed (intervention). However, no similar discussion of meal preparation took place. Discussion of meal preparation materials (recipes, cooking magazines) provided by the social worker did not take place until weeks 9 through 12. During that time, no crocheting literature was provided or discussed. Thus, a second baseline phase (A) was established for crocheting during weeks 9 through 12, because efforts to influence crocheting activities had been withdrawn.

How might we interpret the data displayed in Figure 14.7? At first blush, it appears that the intervention was accompanied by more success when applied to meal preparation than to crocheting. But if we examine the graph a little more carefully and apply our knowledge of social work practice, many other possible interpretations might be proposed. Some of them relate to possible interaction between the two dependent variables. For example, notice that during weeks 2 through 5, meal preparation was already on the increase, even though the intervention had not yet been applied to it. We might speculate that the decline in meal preparation during weeks 5 through 7 was related to the patient's increased involvement in crocheting during that time. Perhaps the crocheting actually made it more difficult for the patient to prepare her meals, a logical conclusion. We might also question whether the dramatic increase in meal preparation during weeks 9 through 12 was not just a resumption of the trend that had been evident during weeks 2 through 5. Perhaps it was not the intervention that produced it, but just the patient adjusting to the increase in her crocheting activity. Or perhaps the increased amount of time spent in meal preparation during weeks 9 through 12 may have been the result of the intervention. It also may have limited any further increase in time spent crocheting. Still other interpretations of changes in both target problems are possible.

Interpreting findings from any single-system research requires a heavy dose of logic and an awareness of treatment goals. It also entails an understanding of the client or client system's limitations and wishes. We know that, during the time the patient in our example was crocheting, she could not be preparing meals, and vice versa. There also was a limit to how many meals the patient might reasonably have been expected to prepare in a week (probably twenty-one, if she had no physical limitations). There was a less obvious limit to the amount of time we might have expected her to spend crocheting. Was it six hours a week? Ten? What was reasonable, and what would have been therapeutic for her? What was her pattern of behavior before she had the stroke? What was she capable of and desirous of doing at the time of the research? At what point would she have been spending too much time crocheting or cooking meals? What would have been the optimal amount of time spent in either activity, given her limitations and her need for other activities such as physical therapy or just resting or socializing?

Regardless of which activity may have been influenced more by the intervention, one interpretation of the research might be that the social worker may have demonstrated at least some degree of overall success in helping the patient become more active. Of course, there is no way to know even this for certain. The patient's greater activity during the latter weeks of the research may have been more attributable to improved health, a relative's cajoling or threats, or some other event or events rather than to the social worker's intervention.

Multiple-baseline designs are well suited to situations where two or more related target problems can be measured and where a single intervention shows promise for influencing either or both of them. Primarily because of the fact that this combination occurs so frequently in social work practice settings, they have been widely advocated for evaluating individual social work practice. Unlike some of the other designs that we have discussed, multiple-baseline designs in this example do not present as many ethical issues related to withdrawing an intervention that may have been accompanied by some success. Once an intervention is introduced, it is continued in a related form. Of course, because it shifts from one target problem to another, there is the potential for treatment carryover. This produces some of the problems that we encounter in attempting to interpret findings. One way to reduce the likelihood of treatment carryover is to add an A phase between each introduction of the independent variable, where it is not applied to any target problem. Of course, doing this produces a different and even more complicated design.

There are many different ways in which multiple-baseline designs can be used; we have mentioned just one of them. In addition to situations in which there is one intervention and two target problems, they can also be used when there is one intervention and two or more similar settings. For example, we could use a multiple baseline to attempt to answer the question: Was the intervention more effective in an in-patient or an out-patient setting, or was it more effective in a rural community or an urban one? We could also use the same design (with the same graphing methods) if we have one intervention but two or more similar clients whose problem is the same, perhaps, a male and a female. Then we could use it to answer the question: With which client did the intervention work best?

Reports of Single-System Research Studies

Since single-system research studies are designed for use by the individual social workers who conduct them, a write-up or report may never be written. When it is (as when the social worker attempts to have the results published or shared with coworkers in a staff meeting), it generally has a different format than that used in other types of research including program evaluations (Chapter 13). For example, the literature review is shorter and more narrowly focused. Box 14.4 contains a suggested outline for a report of a single-system study.

Strengths and Weaknesses

Single-system research is not new. It has been discussed in the social work literature for more than thirty years. During the 1980s, it was rediscovered and touted as a logical bridge between research and practice, two activities that, as we suggested in Chapter 1, all too often had occurred independently of each other.

BOX 14.4   An Outline for a Report of a Single-System Research Study

Description of the client or client system and the problem.
Review of relevant literature with a focus on:
   the problem.
   methods of intervention with the problem.
Methodology (including limitations).
Findings.
Discussion and implications.
Conclusions and recommendations:
   for future intervention.
   for future research.
Appendices (graphs).

An objective assessment of the place of single-system research would probably conclude that it falls somewhere between those of its most vocal advocates and critics, recognizing that it has both strengths and some very definite weaknesses. On the positive side of the ledger, single-system research designs are inexpensive to implement. They cost very little in time and other resources, something that generally cannot be said of many of the other forms of research that we have described. They are easily comprehended; a short workshop or staff development program is all that is needed to get staff started in using them to evaluate their practice. They offer almost instantaneous feedback regarding a social worker's practice effectiveness. There is no need to wait months or even years to acquire and disseminate research findings—a phenomenon that is more typical of many other forms of research. In single-system research, data are collected and are interpreted on an ongoing basis while practice intervention continues. Application of findings is thus easily and quickly accomplished.

Findings from single-system research are never obscure or esoteric; they are in a form that is amenable to utilization. They can provide useful early feedback about new or experimental intervention methods. The methods can be quickly evaluated and either discarded or, if they seem to be promising, evaluated more thoroughly using other types of research.

Single-system research provides good feedback for evaluating the effectiveness of our practice intervention methods, especially those that are primarily task centered or problem solving in nature. Sometimes a series of studies using the same intervention and the same target problem, the same designs, and participants with the same behaviors or problems can begin to suggest knowledge that transcends any one case. This method (replication) is the only way that single-system research can make any claim to generalized knowledge building or to producing findings with external validity. However, any such claim is a tenuous one at best, given what we know about the uniqueness of all people and their situations.

There are a number of inherent design weaknesses in single-system research. It often must depend on a client's own measurement and self-report of target problems or the reports of others such as friends or relatives (especially when used anywhere other than in institutional settings). The accuracy of this method of measurement can easily be questioned. (This potential problem is no stranger to the social worker. Almost all intervention must rely heavily on the belief that what others tell us is truthful and accurate.)

As we showed in Box 14.1, in single-system research a "research sample" is a group of measurements of the target problem. In most designs, there are two or more such samples of measurements (taken during A or B phases). Ideally, as in true experiments, we would like these to be fairly large samples that were randomly selected from some population and then randomly assigned to A phases (the "control groups") and the B phases ("experimental groups"). Of course, this cannot occur. Of necessity, the samples of measurements may be quite small. There is also nothing random about the samples. They are not even compiled at the same time or under the same conditions. Thus, the two samples of measurements (1) are likely to be prone to sampling error, and (2) cannot be considered comparable in all respects except the presence or absence of the intervention. The fact that the measurements in, say, a baseline and the subsequent B phase are not random samples also calls into question the validity of the findings of any statistical tests of inference that rely on sampling distributions in determining the mathematical probability that sampling error might have produced any differences between the measurements in an A phase and those in a B phase.

Another problem related to single-system research is that it cannot be used productively unless work environments support its use. Even though the research requires relatively little time and effort on the part of the practitioner, problems can occur unless administrators and supervisors are convinced of its value. A supervisor who fails to share a commitment to it and who does not understand it may view it with suspicion and even perceive a supervisee to be wasting time conducting it. No one will want to conduct single-system research if a supervisor demands to know why the social worker is "fooling around with those graphs when you should be seeing clients or keeping your records up to date."

Single-system research is vulnerable to misuse. If it is not understood and valued by administrators and supervisors, a problem can occur. A supervisor may attempt to use the research findings (including graphs) as evidence of the supervisee's competence (or lack of it). They may be used for annual performance evaluations or to support personnel actions. This practice can be tempting for supervisors seeking "objective" criteria to justify their actions. But it is a gross misuse of single-system research. The research is not intended as a vehicle to assist the supervisor in evaluating the researcher; it is intended as feedback for the researcher/practitioner. Any other use will quickly discourage a social worker from conducting it. However, on occasions when a supervisor has understood and appreciated the purpose of single-system research, some supervisees have been able to discuss their findings safely and productively in case supervision conferences designed to help them use their research findings to become more effective practitioners.

Single-system research has also proven vulnerable to misuse in another way. Ironically, this misuse has occurred because of the increased popularity of and need for program evaluations. As evaluators and program managers have sought ways to demonstrate the effectiveness of services, they have sometimes turned to reports of single-system studies (conducted by social workers for their own use) as evidence of successful or unsuccessful programs. They have increasingly been used as indicators of outcome achievement. This does not appear to be a good trend. Like use of them to evaluate individual professional competence, it is likely to cause social workers to distort findings to look more favorable and thus to defeat the purpose of why they were conducted in the first place—to receive honest, objective feedback about their practice effectiveness.

Despite the fact that it has been taught about and practiced in schools of social work for over two decades, single-system research is still not used by many social work practitioners on a regular basis. Time constraints are often mentioned as an excuse, along with the other problems that we have cited. There are also many critics of single-system research who are skeptical about its value, and many of their criticisms are justified. Alternatives have been proposed for situations when it is not appropriate[4] but to date, none of them has gained widespread acceptance. We all agree that we want to become evidence-based practitioners and to rely more on research to guide us in evaluating our practice interventions. In the future, single-system research may gain in popularity, or it may go out of favor altogether if better methods to accomplish this are devised. Only time will tell.

Ethical Issues

We have alluded to a number of ethical concerns that have been voiced regarding the use of single-system research. However, most of them, when examined carefully, are really nonissues. For example, as we noted, contrary to some misconceptions, A phases need not be time periods when no services are offered; only the intervention that is being evaluated is withheld. Similarly, a design that ends in an A phase does not mean that a client cannot later receive an intervention method that was associated with a desirable change in the target problem. Duration of treatment can be longer (on both ends) than the duration of the research.

Even the strongest advocates of single-system research would never suggest that the research should take precedence over the welfare of those we are committed to help. Suppose that a single-system design requires a change, for example, the removal of an apparently successful intervention or the introduction of one that, based on new knowledge of the client, may prove injurious. If so, the research may simply have to be terminated or the design altered, despite the fact that either decision may result in less valuable feedback to the social worker. Or, if the design calls for no change to occur and the current A or B phase appears to not be in the client's best interest, the research design also may have to be discarded. Practice values should always take precedence over the researcher's need for knowledge. This same principle applies in all forms of research. However, when single-system designs are used, the cost of ending the research prematurely or changing the design for ethical reasons is rarely great. In contrast, in many types of basic research, it can be very expensive.

There are a few ethical issues that have yet to be resolved. They relate to what we discussed back in Chapter 2. Some people claim that conducting research with one's clients comes dangerously close to a dual relationship and may therefore be unethical. Others suggest that the only way to avoid this conflict is to have clients sign consent forms, thus ensuring that the principle of voluntary informed consent has not been violated. Still others content that single-system research is just part of good practice; it is not research per se. Thus, a signed consent form is not necessary. They see nothing unethical about using a method to systematically monitor and evaluate one's practice in order to ensure that the best possible interventions are offered. In fact, they suggest, it would be irresponsible for a professional not to do so.

Different agencies have different rules and policies on the use of consent forms and the necessity of review of single-system proposals by institutional review boards (IRBs). Administrators in some settings (for example, teaching hospitals) contend that a client receiving services has already agreed to participate in research and that no additional requirements must be met. Other settings may require one or both for their legal protection. Even universities have different policies on the issues. The university where one of the authors of this book once worked requires professors of students conducting single-system research to submit a summary of all proposed studies to an IRB for approval and that students request their research participants (clients) to sign an informed voluntary consent form. At the university where the other author now teaches, there are no such requirements, because single-system research is seen more as a part of social work practice than as research.

Because there is a lack of consensus on a number of ethical issues related to single-system research, a social worker must be careful to check out what rules and policies are in force in the agency or other institution under whose auspices the research will be conducted. Generally, any rules or policies in effect are not very prohibitive and should not discourage anyone from conducting it.

Summary

In this chapter, we examined several alternatives for practitioners who wish to receive feedback about their practice effectiveness. The one that relies most on the research methods discussed in this book, single-system research, involves a careful monitoring of changes in certain behaviors, attitudes, perceptions, or other characteristics of clients or client systems. Design variations are employed to attempt to answer different questions, to attempt to control for the effect of other variables, and to be able to conduct research in a way that is not in conflict with professional values and practice ethics. We discussed only a few of the simpler designs that can be used, stressing their specialized usage and individual strengths and shortcomings. We demonstrated the importance (and the complexity) of interpreting research findings.

Single-system designs are intended for the use of the individual practitioner. They are not appropriate for evaluating some types of social work intervention. They also are of very limited use in contributing to our generalized body of knowledge.

For Discussion

1. How was goal attainment scaling an improvement over the other, traditional ways of evaluating practice effectiveness? What is required for it to be informative?
2. Why is a measurement of a target problem before intervention and one after it (a pretest-posttest design) not considered single-system research? What is missing?
3. In single-system research, the target problem is often just a symptom of an underlying problem. Does examining changes in it following the introduction of an intervention provide a valid indicator of a social worker's practice effectiveness? Why or why not?

4. How does a design with multiple phases, such as ABABAB, do a better job of controlling for threats to internal validity than a design such as AB?

5. When single-system research suggests that treatment carryover may have occurred, does that suggest that the intervention was successful?

6. What factors might affect the degree to which the measurements in a baseline phase constitute a representative sample?

7. Some books describe different single-system designs as exploratory, descriptive, or explanatory. Would it be more accurate to describe them all as "exploratory-descriptive"?

8. Does single-system research interfere with good practice or promote it?

9. Do you think that the recent popularity of qualitative research methods has prevented single-system research from being more widely used? How would a social worker use more qualitative methods to determine if his or her intervention has been effective?

10. If a client has voluntarily sought help for a problem, should that be sufficient evidence that he or she has given "voluntary informed consent" to participate in single-system research? Why or why not? What about involuntary clients, such as those court ordered to receive treatment—should they be required to sign a voluntary informed consent form?

Endnotes

1. Hudson, W. (1982). *The clinical measurement package: A field manual.* Homewood, IL: The Dorsey Press.

2. See, for example, Berlin, S., & Marsh, J. (1993). *Informing practice decisions.* New York: Macmillan. Or Tripodi, T. (1994). *A primer on single subject design.* Washington, D.C.: NASW Press. Or Weinbach, R. (2005). *Evaluating social work services and programs.* Boston: Allyn and Bacon, 53–103. Or Bloom, M., Fischer, J., & Orme, J. (1999). *Evaluating practice: Guidelines for the accountable professional.* Boston: Allyn and Bacon.

3. Bloom, Fischer, and Orme (1999).

4. Staudt, M., et al. (2004). Practice evaluation: Moving beyond single-system designs. *Arete XXVII* (2) 71–78.

POSTSCRIPT

We began our discussion of research methods for social workers by noting the gap that once existed between research and social work practice. We ended it with a discussion of research methods whose findings have immediate practical use for the social work practitioner. This was not unintentional. We wanted to end this book by reminding the reader that the gap between research and practice no longer exists, or at least there is no reason for it to exist. Research now informs practice and practice now informs research.

A lot has happened since 1991, when the first edition of this book was published. Both the production of and utilization of social work research studies have increased dramatically. The acceptance of the importance of qualitative research methods has caused many social workers who might previously have regarded research as "someone else's thing" to feel a new appreciation for research and a new sense of ownership toward it.

Progress toward evidence-based practice has been especially noteworthy during the last decade. There has been a growing commitment to the use of the findings of research studies in our practice, along with the increased recognition that research and practice have much to offer each other.

This is an exciting time for those of us who have taught and written about research for many years. The future of social work research appears bright.

Index

339